SMARTER
NEW YORK
CITY

SMARTER
NEW YORK CITY

How City Agencies Innovate

EDITED BY
ANDRÉ CORRÊA
D'ALMEIDA

Columbia University Press
New York

Columbia University Press
Publishers Since 1893
New York   Chichester, West Sussex
cup.columbia.edu

Library of Congress Cataloging-in-Publication Data
Names: Corrêa d'Almeida, André editor.
Title: Smarter New York City : how city agencies innovate / edited by
    André Corrêa d'Almeida.
Description: New York : Columbia University Press, [2018] | Includes
    bibliographical references and index.
Identifiers: LCCN 2018003484 (print) | LCCN 2018005726 (ebook) |
    ISBN 9780231545112 (ebook) | ISBN 9780231183741 (cloth : alk. paper) |
    ISBN 9780231183758 (pbk.: alk. paper)
Subjects: LCSH: Municipal government—Technological innovations—
    New York (State)—New York. | Public administration—Technological
    innovations—New York (State)—New York. | Administrative agencies—
    Technological innovations—New York (State)—New York. | New York (N.Y.)—
    Politics and government—21st century.
Classification: LCC JS1234.A1 (ebook) | LCC JS1234.A1 S73 2018 (print) |
    DDC 352.3/67216097471—dc23
LC record available at https://lccn.loc.gov/2018003484

Columbia University Press books are printed on permanent
and durable acid-free paper.
Printed in the United States of America

Cover design: Catherine Casalino
Cover photograph: © Francois Roux/Alamy

For all New Yorkers and you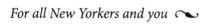

CONTENTS

FOREWORD

STEPHEN K. BENJAMIN, *mayor of Columbia, SC,*
and president of the U.S. Conference of Mayors

As a student of cities, I've watched Columbia, South Carolina, develop over the last three decades into an incredible microcosm of global society. Citizens from two hundred countries who speak ninety different languages, all engaged in the natural process of building a community, call Columbia home.

I have had an opportunity to serve on numerous boards for nonprofit organizations such as Columbia Urban League, Benedict College, and the Greater Columbia Chamber of Commerce among others, and I have realized that directing our efforts toward serving our communities is a building block of city development.

The city has always been regarded as an almost living, breathing organism that has responded to natural developments, societal innovation, and industrial shifts over centuries. The city as a society develops and changes over time—it is not a perfectly carved rectangular box drawn by cartographers negotiating political disputes, nor is it gerrymandered for political purposes by rival factions every decade or so. Cities are alive, and they must become smarter to survive.

In the study of the development of our society, it is important to recognize two consequential truths. The first truth is that development is never just a goal; it is also a continuous process, one in which a "fully developed society" is paradoxical and impossible in nature. The second truth is that the fuel need to break the status quo and move toward a "more developed" state is innovation.

Ironically, innovation is commonly perceived as simply the creative process of discovering something that was previously unknown, and as hinging on breakthroughs in technology and science. However, viewed more accurately, innovation is a broader concept that includes not only new findings but also new processes that drive us to those findings to discover better results, products, and services.

Cities will prosper not only through smart technologies but also through smarter ways of integrating that technology into existing functional systems. This book shows us how to expand the responsibility and role of technology and innovation in smart cities through case studies from some of the brightest minds in this field.

Imagine these concepts of development and innovation not as abstract ideas but as integral details of our everyday lives. The past decade has brought unprecedented changes in the ways we live our daily lives and in the ways we aspire to shape our future. Technological shifts are accelerating, and their reach is deepening in our societies. Some of these changes are visible and easy to recognize, such as a dramatic shift in the way we shop. Others are not so visible but equally present. For instance, congestion pricing as a traffic-management tool changes the preferences of commuters. This change isn't self-prompted; nevertheless, it impacts commuter behavior steadily and surely. Amazon has changed the way that much of the world shops, and the advent of the tech and app-enabled sharing economy has upended the taxicab livery business and disrupted the hospitality industry in most major cities.

It is impossible to miss that over the past few years, cities have swiftly taken center stage in discussions of sustainable development by becoming independent centers of power, position, progress, and thought leadership. Cities have overcome traditional institutional hierarchies of local, state, and federal government to address issues previously believed to be priorities of higher levels of government. In order to understand the heightened role of cities in urban sustainable development and their ongoing transformation from at times disorganized urban sprawls to structured smart cities, we must acknowledge the following.

Cities as Public Favorites

The United Nations projects that by 2050, about 70% of the world's population will live in urban areas: by 2020, half of Asia will inhabit urban areas and by 2035, the urbanization rate in Africa will reach 50%—the fastest ever in the shortest time period. Cities offer economic opportunities, upward mobility, entrepreneurial climates, and scope for innovation and growth. They are burgeoning not only in size and population but also in what they have to offer. Interestingly, 60% of urban land is not developed yet, which opens infinite possibilities for infrastructure developers and impact investors. In that sense, the future—quite literally—is the cities. Rural to urban migration is growing exponentially and cities, for all the right reasons, are becoming the public favorites.

Cities as Networks

Global directives (such as Sustainable Development Goals, Agenda 2030, and the New Urban Agenda) inform better practices and efforts with clear goals and objectives. While these directives are rather generic and global in scale, there are countless initiatives, conferences, and events targeted toward development of cities and innumerous avenues to discuss the specific challenges that cities face, as well as their potential solutions. Participants range from business leaders to academics, from political leaders to artists. The importance of multistakeholder collaboration is fundamental to and a backbone of sustainable development. Mayors are fostering efforts to bring coherence to bottom-up and top-down approaches by increasing public engagement in decision-making processes. These global collaborations are allowing cities to operate as networks.

Cities have shown exemplary leadership in advancing the agenda of climate change, sustainable development, and energy efficiency among other pressing challenges by adhering to their commitment for a more futuristic approach in dealing with these issues. As a result, we see the development of municipally owned solar farms, net-zero water utilities, and urban forests. I have had the pleasure of cochairing in partnership with the Sierra Club a bipartisan effort to achieve a 100% clean energy commitment in American cities. Cities can now be reimagined as networks of change, no longer bound by their political and geographic boundaries. Cities are incubators of innovation, platforms of thought experiments. More importantly, the divide between citizen and authority is collapsing, allowing citizens to become change makers themselves. Never before has there been such an opportunity for cities and their citizens to exchange ideas, innovations, and best practices and to learn from each other through collaboration. The private sector has shown a rapidly growing interest in purpose-driven businesses. Public–private partnerships (PPPs) led by companies, nongovernmental organizations, and foundations are making several interventions achievable in cities across the globe.

Cities as Neo-Political Entities

Cities are politically less bureaucratic than federal agencies, which allows for more room to implement new projects and policies. The stark difference in the attitudes of the current federal administration of the United States and cities of all stripes across multiple states affirms this point. On June 1, 2017, after President Donald Trump announced the withdrawal of the United States from the Paris Climate Deal, we witnessed a remarkable display of commitment when hundreds of cities across the nation—including major metropolises like Atlanta, Boston, Los Angeles, and New York City—voiced their support for the climate deal and strengthened their plans to further the objectives of the agreement. Support came not only from the mayors but also from individuals and corporations, and perhaps moved states to also uphold the agreement independent of the federal government. By this act of solidarity, we saw a profound shift in political power, authority, and influence. Some now even view cities as neo-political entities.

* * *

Now, with a more nuanced understanding of the key roles cities play in development, it becomes important to drive the conversation toward the scope of innovation in cities. As I mentioned previously, innovation drives development, but then we need to ask what drives innovation. This book identifies overarching drivers of innovation across social, institutional, and technological spheres. This book also expertly elucidates that these drivers are interconnected in their collective impact on the end result and in their influence on one another.

Traditionally, government agencies have not enjoyed the reputation of being change makers. However, it is important to remember that they have greater responsibility and accountability toward a broad and diverse expanse of citizen stakeholders, the people they serve, as opposed to the private sector, which too has its obligations but as fiduciaries to shareholders rather than to large swathes of society.

In the effort to become a more sustainable society, city agencies are becoming more flexible, more willing to change, and more open to allowing symbiotic and mutually beneficial relationships with the private sector. City agencies alone are inadequate to bring about necessary changes and commercialize groundbreaking technologies. However, with purpose-driven partnerships, cities are now addressing issues of race, gentrification, gender, crime, education, and health through groundbreaking interventions in transportation systems, public health, public schools, natural resource management, food production, open space management, and green infrastructure. As complex as development efforts are due to interdisciplinary forces, the results often have ripple effects across multiple sectors.

City agencies can benefit from the efficiency and resources of the private sector while the private sector can benefit from city systems and the ability to test scalable ideas directly with our citizens. Public-private partnerships are becoming more common, and purpose-driven and data-centric projects are making their way into city strategies and policy packages. People are getting more avenues to voice their opinions, concerns, ideas, and feedback. It is a golden time for cities to determine the direction of their respective sustainability efforts. Cities are expanding through special agencies dedicated to the futuristic shifts in technology and the way we live in the nexus of sociopolitical and climate change realities. This book showcases the groundbreaking interventions New York City has adopted and through these cases, it subtly hints at the power and importance of city agencies in implementing and scaling these projects.

In our effort to integrate advanced technologies and practices to make our cities sustainable and cutting-edge, we must not lose sight of the ultimate goal, which is to serve all people in healthy, inclusive communities that reflect the prosperity of our cities. Though all of our efforts directed toward creating smart cities, it is important to keep in mind that social behavior is the backbone of any pathbreaking development. Social development includes fairness, gender equality, decent work opportunities, and adaptability to cope with inevitable future changes. In 2014, I introduced the "Justice for All" initiative, which implemented new training, competitive pay, diverse representation, and community engagement to strengthen the trust and accountability that exists between our communities and local law enforcement agencies. Initiatives like this help to shape residents' perception of their government, build trust, and facilitate development for all. It is through changing people's perceptions that we can shape an urban future. In that sense, innovation is more intangible in its long-term impacts as it creates a system that influences people's behavior. For example, one can create highly energy-efficient light bulbs but it is still crucial to infuse the knowledge into people that when not needed, the light needs to be turned off. As simple as it sounds, we must understand that the smart city is not only about technological adequacy but also about social resilience that stems from within our social consciousness.

In my role as president of the U.S. Conference of Mayors, I foster ties between U.S. cities and their mayors as someone who is himself a city representative. I deeply understand the vast range of issues and unique sociopolitical challenges that each city faces, which drives home the fact that there is no one right approach to deal with these issues. In that context, I am delighted that this book, through the examples of innovative developments in multiple sectors in New York City, essentially presents us with a path of innovation from within our own city structure. Every city is different; each city has its own unique challenges. But even so, there are many common objective components and tenets, including the importance of good data, technological integration, purpose-driven businesses, stakeholder collaboration, and community engagement. The book elaborates on these crucial areas, making it a powerful guide for all cities to find their own respective paths to building a better future for its people.

PREFACE

ANDRÉ CORRÊA D'ALMEIDA

A Very Personal Vision

I moved from Denver to New York City in September 2007. For almost four years, between 2010 and 2013, I was a visiting professor at Pratt Institute while at Columbia University as well. At Columbia, my office was, and still is, located on W. 118th Street, in Upper Manhattan. At Pratt, my classroom was located on W. Fourteenth Street, in Lower Manhattan. It was during this time, with a regular six-mile commute between Upper and Lower Manhattan, that the idea of this book began to take shape.

The first time I talked about it was with my friend and colleague Mary McBride, who leads Pratt Institute's Creative Enterprise Leadership initiative and is a contributor to this book. This regular up and down across 104 streets helped me understand how interconnected New Yorkers' lives are with the city systems that shape our aspirations. We share more than just the public space, some social ties, and the air we breathe. In a city that brings together over 27,000 people per square mile, we all intensively share physical systems, social norms, and institutions as well. While setting most of the rules of our daily lives, these features of our "urban gorgeous mosaic," as my colleague and former mayor David Dinkins likes to call it, are also facilitators of personal growth and happiness. In Edward Glaeser's (2011, 249) words, "cities magnify humanity's strengths." Otherwise, why would we want to live most of our lives in cities?

City-management systems bind our behavior and options and can be designed, or reengineered, to become smarter, more efficient, inclusive, and responsive and, in the end, to empower people. If we look at these systems not as undifferentiated boxes provided by some higher authority but as malleable and interconnected parts, at least two possibilities emerge. First, we can open these systems up and let information about organizations' and citizens' needs, aspirations, wants, dreams, and desires pollinate them. Second, with that information, we can surgically intervene to improve these systems incrementally and, as a result, enhance our own experience in the city. Simply put, as Richard Schragger (2016) has suggested, we can democratize these urban systems and make them sources of strength for all, equally.

My relationship with these two institutions—located at opposite sides of Manhattan—also made me wonder how much our city could benefit if, instead of (mostly) competing with each other, universities from all around the city came together to work on improving the city systems we share. If cities empower humanity, the collectively shared knowledge produced by universities citywide has the potential to empower the city as a whole in return. Back in 2013, however, I did not yet know what my contribution would be to better understand an already very sophisticated and complex life in the city.

The Idea for the Book

In November 2013, serendipity helped define the contours of my idea a little further. In Doha, Qatar, Jerry Hultin, founding partner and chair of Global Futures Group and president emeritus of Polytechnic Institute of New York University, and I sat at the same table in the same workshop at the World Innovation Summit for Education. We had never met before. The topic of discussion in that particular session was innovation and the future of cities. Guess what! Our ideas and thoughts connected as quickly as the sense of immediate belonging on a first trip to New York City. Once back in New York, Jerry—also a contributor to this book—and I started working on a series of ideas to help advance innovation and creativity in the city. The persisting critical development gaps that New York City faces, in areas like Brownsville, Brooklyn, where more than half of the population receive some sort of government assistance, were the center of our attention. We worked to show the role information and communication technologies (ICTs) can play in advancing creativity, innovation, and access—all critical to fighting socioeconomic inequality and fostering development. For example, in Hunts Point, Bronx, Startup Box is transforming the neighborhood into a new hub for computer-software testing; or consider the work the Broadband Technology Opportunity Program (BTOP) has been doing to develop technical skills and computer literacy in local Hunts Point schools. We advocated for the creation of new collaborative platforms capable of addressing the city's gap in tech and creative talent. The recently created NYC Tech Talent Pipeline is an example of how much there is to be done to connect New Yorkers with New York's businesses. In the context of these personal reflections, experiences, and dialogues, the *Smarter NYC*itywide Research Group was created, and this book emerged.

In 2014, while working with Jerry Hultin, Anthony Townsend, and Michael Salvato on a Smart City strategic plan for New York, I met Minerva Tantoco, the first New York City chief technology officer (CTO), and Jeff Merritt, director of innovation for the City of New York, Mayor's Office of Technology and Innovation (MOTI). Both Minerva and Jeff welcomed my idea to place Christopher Lewis (one of my graduate students at Columbia University) in a professional field placement at MOTI in the summer of 2015. Over three months, under my supervision, Chris identified and documented a wide range of high-potential "smart city" initiatives developed across city agencies. MOTI then used this portfolio of initiatives to plan New York City's first participation in the Smart City Expo World Congress in Barcelona in November of that same year.[1] Chris's work served as the basis for New York City's first attempt to identify and classify, in a systematic way, the ecology of smart initiatives sprawling across city agencies. One thing was immediately clear to me when I met with MOTI's team and Chris to evaluate his professional summer field placement: we must understand much better how city agencies are incubating innovation from within—not only what the city is doing but also how, who, when, and why. The idea of this book was born!

The *Smarter NYC*itywide Research Group

To move from the idea and the vision that started to emerge back in 2010 to the book you are reading now, I created a citywide research group of thirty scholars from twenty-two different research institutions and ten universities, including Columbia University, Harvard University, Cornell Tech, New York University, Pratt Institute, City University of New York, State University of New York, The New School, The Cooper Union, Mount Sinai, and the Sustainable Development Solutions Network. For three years, this new *Smarter NYC*itywide Research Group worked together under a unifying methodology that included a common framework of analysis and structure for all cases (nearly 120 interviews and fifteen participatory roundtables were held in three New York City boroughs with field experts, scientists, city officials, technology and data companies, and civic organizations). In total, nearly three hundred people, thirty city agencies, and twenty private companies were directly involved in the research for our case studies.

The majority of the participants in these interviews and roundtables were city officials—true government entrepreneurs who have the responsibility to design, implement, and administer the innovations studied. These interviews and discussions featured those who need to translate policy goals into programs as they operate on the ground every day. They are authentic guardians of the systems—free from electoral cycles—who have been working on the same problems for years and sometimes their entire careers. However, contrary to the multiple networking and knowledge-sharing opportunities developed around the world for cities' top leadership, there is a tremendous lack of opportunities for practitioners and intermediary hierarchies to exchange ideas and practices at national and international events. At such events, these practitioners can learn with their peers from other cities, potential private sector partners, and the civil society about how to better integrate innovation into their ongoing operations—how to make their cities smarter. Focused, practical, problem-solving dialogues would also allow, for example, private firms to engage with these government practitioners in early stages of product and service development and learn about city planning, major strategic and operational challenges faced, legislation affecting technical specifications and deployment, and ways to collaborate. These government entrepreneurs have shown clear signs of being highly motivated to get more involved. Particularly relevant for this book, and indeed inspiring, are the words of many of these city officials and entrepreneurs acknowledging the rare opportunities that the preparation of these cases provided to connect with and learn from colleagues from other agencies working on the same city programs or interconnected problems. You might imagine that these opportunities would abound for colleagues working on the same programs or similar problems. It is certainly not a critique per se that they do not; it is simply the realization that the dialogues the *Smarter NYCitywide* Research Group started are bridging a gap, generating value already for multiple stakeholders, and identifying new ways and opportunities to make our city smarter. The methodology and roadmaps offered in this book can also make your city smarter!

Note

1. For a sample of New York City innovations featured in Barcelona, see http://www1.nyc .gov/assets/forward/documents/NYC-Smart-Equitable-City-Final.pdf.

References

Glaeser, Edward. 2011. *Triumph of the City: How Our Greatest Invention Makes Us Richer, Smarter, Greener, Healthier, and Happier.* New York: Penguin.
Schragger, Richard. 2016. *City Power: Urban Governance in a Global Age.* New York: Oxford University Press.

ACKNOWLEDGMENTS

The first word of gratitude must go to Hon. Jerry MacArthur Hultin, founder and chair of Global Futures Group, president emeritus of Polytechnic Institute of New York University, former Under Secretary of the Navy and member of the Defense Business Board with degrees from Yale Law School and Ohio State. Jerry not only helped trigger my imagination for this book, as described in the preface, but also played a very important role in its organization and the scientific discussions that helped shape its content. He has been a true believer in this book and an inspirational personal adviser.

Thanks to my former Columbia University student, Christopher Lewis, we were able to initiate in 2015 the fieldwork necessary to get this book project off the ground. Thank you to Minerva Tantoco, the city's first Chief Technology Officer, and Jeff Merritt, New York City Director of Innovation, at that time, for accepting the idea of hosting Chris at the Mayor's Office of Technology and Innovation (MOTI) for his summer fieldwork and supporting my idea that stories of innovation from within city agencies need to be documented, better understood, and disseminated. For nine years, my colleague Glenn Denning, the founding director of Columbia University's Master of Public Administration in Development Practice (MPA-DP), has been creating just the right environment for intellectual stimuli and professional innovation at the School of International and Public Affairs.

At Columbia University, other colleagues offered different types of important support at different stages of our research project: former mayor Michael

Nutter, Rohit Aggarwala, Paul Lagunes, Doru Cojoc, Robert Scott, Lynda Hamilton, Maria Barcellos-Raible, Nancy Cieri, and Judy Jamal. I am thankful for my university community.

Jonathan Woetzel, director of the McKinsey Global Institute and senior partner at McKinsey & Company, provided very important advice in the early stages of designing the research agenda that produced this book. Katherine Oliver, principal at Bloomberg Associates, played a very similar advising role in the design phase of this project. In spite of her incredibly demanding global agenda, Katherine was always very gracious and generous during the conversations we had concerning the challenges faced by city administrations around the world. I was very fortunate to meet Janet Balis, partner and Global Advisory Leader for Media and Entertainment at Ernst & Young (EY), toward the end of the book project. Janet helped sharpen the final versions of my chapters and connect my ideas with a broader audience.

While also part of the network of contributors to this book, whom I will thank collectively in a little bit, Arnaud Sahuguet of Cornell Tech deserves a special word of gratitude. Arnaud was the first non–Columbia University scholar to join the *Smarter NYC*itywide Research Group I was creating back in 2015. His understanding of my vision was particularly relevant when I was still testing my ideas and the approach for a citywide collaborative research project. His "yes" helped confirm my hypothesis that there were both a collaboration and a knowledge gap that needed to be addressed. Before joining the group of contributors to this book, Kendal Stewart, an MPA-DP alumna, helped me develop the management structure of this project. She brought order to the project.

Thank you also to my former students Jeremy Lakin, Arishaa Khan, and Manasi Nanavati for helping with the coordination of a research group of thirty scholars—not an everyday task! This publication would not have been possible without Bridget Flannery-McCoy, Columbia University Press editor, who shared the vision that we need to understand, at a much more practical and integrated level, how urban systems operate and evolve. Thank you for your guidance and patience with the successive revisions of my chapters. Thank you, Christian Winting, as well, for your detailed revisions of my texts.

Without the graphic designer Giselle Carr, my former Pratt student, I would not have been able to translate into infographics some of the most important lessons included in the book. This book also benefited from the energy and ideas of my friend and entrepreneur Barbara Paley, whose commitment to New York City communities is an incredible source of inspiration.

They are not New Yorkers, but they have been a professional and intellectual inspiration throughout my adult life. Luís Valadares Tavares, author and professor at Lisbon's Instituto Superior Técnico, initiated me into the field of urban systems and innovation back in 2000—long before "smart cities" became a hot topic. Together we led a major "Sintra: Digital City" initiative in Portugal. In my early days in the United States, Peter deLeon, author and professor at the School of Public Affairs, University of Colorado Denver, provided remarkable academic mentorship with incredible dedication and patience. He will always be a paramount reference of academic rigor and sharp humor. With Roberto Carneiro, former Portuguese Minister of Education, author and professor at Catholic University of Portugal, we are adapting my "Smarter Cities" applied research program to a cluster of four neighboring cities—Lisboa, Cascais, Sintra, and Oeiras—in my home country, Portugal.

A vision cannot be materialized without a group effort and collective action. Without each one of the contributors to this book, we would not be able to understand the way we now do how New York City agencies, as a system, innovate from within. This seems an obvious and trivial statement. What is less obvious is that a group of thirty scholars from twenty-two research institutions and ten universities agreed to participate in a research project and stuck together for nearly three years in an ongoing collaborative and creative process. It is thanks to their experience, academic rigor, generosity, and love for New York that we now understand better how we can further improve life in the city. Needless to say, our work would not have been possible without the collaboration, insights, feedback, and precious time of dozens of city leaders, city officials, heads of agencies, managers, and practitioners. Key informants in our project include several local community organizations and private firms involved in the innovations described in this book.

The last word of gratitude and admiration goes to David Fenyo and Helena Albuquerque, the first New Yorkers I met when in 2005 I crossed the Atlantic Ocean to start a new phase of my life in the United States. They have since then been a guiding light, a source of support, hope, self-awareness, sense of belonging, professional inspiration, and endless laughter. Together with my life partner and incredibly supportive wife Sara, they are my family in New York City.

André Corrêa d'Almeida

SMARTER
NEW YORK
CITY

INTRODUCTION

ANDRÉ CORRÊA D'ALMEIDA, *Columbia University*

There were two central doctrines of the Enlightenment: the first was the belief that change was possible, and the second was the belief that through rational and scientific enquiry we can learn, and what we learn can be used to improve wellbeing.

—Stiglitz 2016, 8

This book is about how innovation within city administration makes urban systems smarter and shapes life in New York City. It is also a practical roadmap about how the lessons learned in New York City can be replicated in other cities. Heather McGowan and Chris Shipley, world-renowned education consultants and business strategists, leave no room for hesitations: "The future of work is learning" (2017, 1).

Practical Limitations of "Smart"

Over the last few decades, city development strategies have come to see idealized futures, driven mostly by information and communication technology, as the goal. The origins of this technocentric perspective of development can be traced back to the 1990s, when certain categories of professionals—such as scientists and engineers—started using the Internet and other networked activities to try to solve industry-specific problems. In 1997, the International Center for Communications coined this new form of community organization as "smart communities." In the same year, IBM's computer Deep Blue beat world chess champion Garry Kasparov and Microsoft released Internet Explorer 4 to integrate the Web with the Windows user interface. The last decade of the twentieth century showed the potential of artificial intelligence to enhance human-made systems and dramatically increased the possibilities for commercialization of products and services based on new information and communication technologies. The first scientific publications connecting cities with the idea of "smart" appeared in the 1990s as well (Gibson, Kozmetsky, and Smilor 1992). Since then, the number of publications on smart cities published each year increased from sixteen in 1992 to more than nine thousand in 2015 (Mora, Bolici, and Deakin 2017).

Within the last ten years especially, research on smart cities has become a popular and fast-growing new area of scientific enquiry. The "smart cities" trend is worldwide, as evidenced by numerous forums, expos, and contests hosted by governments, multilateral banks, private companies, and nonprofit institutions. The India Smart Cities Challenge, launched by the Government of India, offers financial and technical assistance from Bloomberg Philanthropies; Bloomberg Philanthropies also partnered with Harvard University to launch the Bloomberg Harvard City Leadership Initiative, which seeks to advance public-sector management and innovation. Other events include the Rockefeller Foundation's 100 Resilient Cities; the Smart Cities Council, which organizes a major Smart Cities Week in Washington, D.C., every year; and the Smart Cities Initiative, announced by the White House in 2015, which seeks to accelerate community development efforts through multisector collaborations and advancements in science and technology. In 2017, the City of New York hosted Smart Cities NYC '17. In Europe, there is the Smart Cities Expo World Congress (Barcelona) and the Smart Cities and Communities: Connecting Citizens (London), among many others. There are countless important examples of entities encouraging smarter cities, including groups like NewCities Foundation and the Knight Foundation, technological corporations like IBM and Cisco, and consulting firms like Deloitte and McKinsey.

Despite this excitement, there is little consensus about what the term "smart city" actually means. Adjectives to describe smart cities abound: resilient, happy, democratic, data-centric, intelligent, futuristic, empowering, empowered, collaborative, tech, connected, fixable, crowd-sourced, creative, responsive, utopian, diverse, sustainable, low-carbon, livable, green, digital, and others (Mora, Bolici, and Deakin 2017). Sam Musa (2016, 1) offers the most concise definition of "smart city" I have found: "a city that engages its citizens and connects its infrastructure electronically."

The lack of clarity around the definition of a smart city, and the idea that a "smart city" denotes an idealized modern (and tech-centered) future, can hinder the actual implementation of innovation, for two interconnected reasons.

First, the path to the future is best understood as a process of innovation and not a dichotomy of "smart" versus "not smart." While representing phenomena in dichotomous terms—on/off, yes/no, black/white—is a distinctive trait in the human psyche, Anthony Townsend (2013, 279), an internationally recognized technology consultant and systems thinker, reminds us that "even in Singapore, with its long proven tradition of technocratic planning, smart infrastructure projects move at a snail's pace." It is crucial to remember this lesson: city innovations are incremental in nature. While the world convenes frequently on the topic of disruption and dramatic overnight shifts in industries, the reality of innovation in the urban context is that even disruptive concepts are deployed at a somewhat thoughtful pace, building on prior models.

Second, an idealized "smart" future is, at any given point in time, untenable by definition because of the continual technological advances that constantly push the future forward. The goal line of what it means to be "smart" moves continuously. People do not deal well with the prospect of unattainable goals; they spark fear and discourage innovation. Michael Batty (2017, 9), a British urban planner and professor at University College London, agrees that the promise of idealized futures poses serious limitations on current possibilities and argues that "cities have been considered to be in equilibrium and their improvement has been largely phrased in terms of idealized plans without any realistic time horizons for implementation." "Smart" planning that idealizes holistic, "fully smart," or "all-encompassing" policy interventions is not practical policy design or realistic implementation. Such an approach fails to consider development priorities, local conditions, what is feasible and equitable, and existing incentive systems, as well as available resources.

At the 2017 Smart Cities Week in Silicon Valley, California, a city representative told me in a somewhat embarrassed tone, "We are not smart yet!" Surprised by his candid statement and sense of unworthiness, I replied, "Of course you are! What you want is to become smarter." This exchange illustrates well why "smart," when it points to an idealized modern future, is problematic for practical urban policy and innovation.[1]

"Smarter" Is Better Than "Smart"

The emphasis in this book, thus, is not on "smart," but rather on "smarter." Here we take a cue from Nam and Pardo (2011, 1), who see "a smart city not as a status of how smart a city is but as a city's effort to make itself smart." It is this effort to become smarter that is the focus in this book, looking at the historical, institutional, and organizational factors driving innovation processes in New York City's agencies. The focus shifts away from an idealized, technocentric perspective of urban innovation and toward a more holistic, multidisciplinary, nuts-and-bolts understanding.

This book asks, what is making New York City's systems smarter? What is driving innovation? How are city agencies adapting to and adopting innovation in practice? Who are the players involved, and what are their roles? How are data and technology employed? What is the role of organizational structure, leadership, and regulation in these innovation processes? How relevant are networks and interagency collaboration? What new ways of doing, seeing, analyzing, deciding, and assessing are necessary in order to improve, advance, evolve, or optimize a city?

This book seeks to expand the concept of "smart" to look at data and technology, both critical drivers of innovation, within the broader city-administration ecosystem and in parallel with other equally critical internal and external innovation forces (see figure 0.1). Each of the case studies in this book includes a data and technology component, not to suggest that data and tech are necessary conditions to make an urban system smarter, but to expand the number of cases and lessons about how tech and data can be "urbanized," to use Saskia Sassen's terminology (2016). Sassen, an acclaimed Dutch American sociologist and author of the seminal book *The Global City*, raises serious concerns about the "deurbanizing" impact of technology as a driver of urban innovation. She calls for a redefinition of "urban intelligence"—one in which technological innovations take into consideration the particular social and cultural fabric in which they are to be implemented. The ultimate goal is to "urbanize" technology—to put it at the service of the citizen, not the other way around.

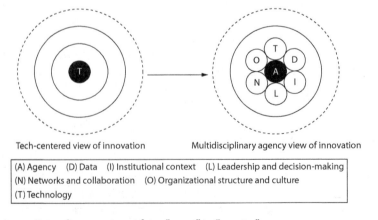

Tech-centered view of innovation   Multidisciplinary agency view of innovation

(A) Agency   (D) Data   (I) Institutional context   (L) Leadership and decision-making
(N) Networks and collaboration   (O) Organizational structure and culture
(T) Technology

FIGURE 0.1 Expanding smartness: from "smart" to "smarter".

To ensure the lessons are practical and offer actionable insights for cities in the United States and around the world, the innovation processes in each case is described through three phases:

- Problem formulation/definition: how are problems appraised or innovation opportunities identified?
- Design/pilot: how are solutions or new opportunities designed and tested?
- Implementation/evaluation: how are solutions or opportunities implemented and assessed?

Christopher Blattman (2017), now at the University of Chicago, argues that "the best research changes the intellectual conversation." This book will change your understanding of how New York City's public agencies adapt to and adopt innovation, and help you advance conversations on how local government can make your own city smarter. This work will show how cities innovate from within, what forces drive or constrain innovation, what types of problems cities try to address, and what goals they set. With this book you will learn, in practical ways, what "smarter" means to the City of New York, and how this concept can help make your city smarter as well.

The Practical Meaning of Smarter: Learning and Replicability

Cities have always been smart. Ever since the Neolithic Revolution, when human societies transitioned from hunting and gathering to farming, people have gravitated toward cities. An increase in food production led to a significant growth in population and the rise of cities, a phenomenon that continues to this day all around the world 12,000 years later. From Eridu (7,500 BCE) to Babylon (2,000 BCE) to Athens (500 BCE) to Florence (fourteenth century) to Paris (nineteenth century) to New York (twenty-first century), cities have always been the center of human activity. Edward Glaeser's (2011) *Triumph of the City: How Our Greatest Invention Makes Us Richer, Smarter, Greener, Healthier, and Happier* points exactly to this supremacy of cities as living spaces; for him, that cities themselves are "smart" is not a question. If cities have always been smart, then the more interesting question is: what does it mean for a city to become smarter?

Tech and data industries created the idea of "smart cities." Now academia is challenged with discovering its practical meaning. Urban strategists Cohen and Muñoz (2016) seem to agree with this evolutionary perspective that cities are becoming smarter. They write of an evolving smart-cities movement, primarily initiated by multinational technology companies who sold the vision of highly efficient, technology-driven cities. These authors argue that forward-thinking mayors and city administrators then began to take the lead in collaboration with the private sector and that, most recently, "citizen co-creation" has emerged in which city residents actively participate in the process of innovation.

It matters more now than ever that cities become smarter. Henry Ford (1922a, 156–57) once declared: "The ultimate solution will be the abolition of the City, its abandonment as a blunder . . . We shall solve the City Problem by leaving the City." Contrary to his prediction, the world's population living in cities grew from 13% in 1900 to 50% around 2007 and will continue to grow to 70% by 2050. In Townsend's words (2013, 1), "cities accelerate time by compressing space, and let us do more with less of both. They are where jobs, wealth, and ideas are created." The ways in which cities are designed and managed have a direct impact on our daily lives—how we live them and how we end them. Cities are where we "live, work and play," says David Gann (2013, 3), the chairman of the Smart London Board and Vice President for Innovation at Imperial College London. For Charles Montgomery (2013), an award-winning journalist and urban-engagement specialist, cities are where we pursue happiness. Cities also concentrate our environmental footprint and therefore will dictate the future of the planet and the likelihood of global sustainable development.

Cities need to become smarter because "the demand for efficiencies and enhanced performance is continual, as governments attempt to man- age demands for expenditure to improve the quality of life that exceed their incomes" (Dodgson and Gann 2010, 15). By 2050, the total world population will have grown from the current 7.5 to 9 billion inhabitants, and 6.3 billion of us will be living in cities (United Nations 2015). The demand for public services and the pressure on urban systems have already reached unprecedented levels, and this pressure will only grow.

The problem, however, as Batty (2017, 8) alerts us, is that "what exists so far in terms of the smart city is largely ad hoc, more intention than actual implementation, more heat than light." Our idea of "smarter" asks us to pri- oritize the mind-set and responsibility of an operator, instead of a theorist, to substantively think about how to design and implement new ideas. For the practitioner perspective to thrive, the approach must consider not only data and technology availability, but also local cultural, institutional, and organi- zational drivers. While the focus of our work is on New York City's practical means of achieving efficiencies and enhanced performance, each case shared in this book also points the reader to the broader, longer-term implications of each innovation concept.

This book looks at innovation from both bottom-up and top-down per- spectives. On the one hand, "smarter" is being driven by citizens' demands and aspirations for inclusive and participatory decision-making, as well as a greater desire for transparency. On the other, there is a strategic degree of networked administrative planning necessary to fund, design, scale up, organize, coordinate, and deliver new urban improvements being demanded. These transformations require a purposeful focus to materialize. The OneNYC case (chapter 1), which shows how the city embraced a large community and stakeholder consultation to develop and implement a local version of a global plan—the Sustainable Development Goals (SDGs) adopted by 193 countries at the United Nations in 2015—illustrates this top-down/bottom-up duality.

This book seeks to answer several critical questions. What can city officials learn from how New York City's agencies make decisions, collaborate, and integrate new data and technology to improve life in the city? How are city agencies working to make their public-service systems more inclusive and responsive to decision-making and citizens? How can central governments develop domestic intergovernmental (central/local) coordination? How can educational programs incorporate lessons learned from the New York City experience into their curricula and research to help students reimagine government innovation and urban development? How can enhanced mutual understanding between public and private stakeholders help business developers and local governments improve public/private partnerships (PPP) and accelerate innovation?

The case studies in this book are designed to be relevant at the policy, operational, educational, and research levels. They offer roadmaps on how to develop and improve specific urban systems; they offer lessons on how to define a problem and identify intervention opportunities; and they detail what it takes to design and implement a new program. They also offer an integrated perspective of how different dimensions of life in the city intersect in a complex system. For example, the Midtown in Motion case (chapter 12) explains how the seemingly intractable problem of traffic congestion in Manhattan is addressed through a combination of leadership, collaboration, and advanced data-processing and technology.

This book also seeks to augment prevailing knowledge about public innovation. The general lack of awareness that innovation resides and sometimes even thrives in local public administration is somewhat surprising, given that the current public-sector paradigm of New Public Management puts a lot of emphasis on innovation (Andrews and Van de Walle 2013). It is even more problematic when this perceptual gap, from both a practical and a conceptual perspective, is manifested among local government practitioners and city officials, because it further reinforces within city administration the view that the public sector is noninnovative (Nählinder 2013).

Geoff Mulgan (2014, 4) offers a list of reasons why innovation is not favored in public administration, such as a "discouraging reward and incentive systems," "lack of mature risk management methods and experimentation," and "lack of dedicated budgets, teams, processes and skills." However, what is critical for the research in this book is that too much attention is dedicated to describing what does not work—flaws, limitations, and inefficiencies. Instead, more attention should be dedicated to explaining how public systems emerge and develop; what their particular features are; how they vary across cultures; what they do; how they do it; and under what set of conditions, interdependencies, dynamics, and feedback loops. To fully capture Goldsmith and Crawford's (2014) promise of a "Responsive City"—a city where smarter systems integrate new tech and data with other innovation drivers to transform local government, improve public service, and engage citizens—a clearer explication must be formed of how drivers and impediments to program innovation in local government actually work.

Fear and Innovation from Within

Schumpeter's ([1942] 1994, 83) concept of "creative destruction"—"the process of industrial mutation that incessantly revolutionizes the economic structure from within, incessantly destroying the old one, incessantly creating a new one"—has been around since the 1950s. Furthermore, Acemoglu and Robinson (2012, 84) assert that the "fear of creative destruction is often at the root of the opposition to inclusive economic and political institutions." This fear comes from innovation's potential to shift the status quo to a new equilibrium point by redistributing power and resources, disrupting contracts and relationships, modifying preferences and beliefs, and redefining who wins and loses.

The goal of this book is to produce the type of knowledge prescribed in Everett Rogers's (2003) stages of the innovation adoption process, which facilitates practical learning and mitigates the fear of creative destruction. The procurement strategy implemented by the city to build the world's largest free super-fast public broadband Wi-Fi network was extremely complex and risky from a social, political, operational, and financial standpoint. The LinkNYC case (chapter 3) lays out a practical roadmap of how a participatory and revenue-generating model helped the city manage and mitigate the risk of repurposing existing infrastructure. As Dodgson and Gann (2010, 128) put it, "greater appreciation of the contributions and difficulties of innovation will help address the very high aversion to risk in the public service."

To the extent that these case studies document and explain how New York City adapts to and adopts innovation, this book also reduces the uncertainty of new adopters in other cities and further mitigates the fear of and aversion to creative destruction. Because they encourage organizational change and innovation, these case studies have the potential to similarly empower New York City agencies that were not covered by this research. Take the Mayor's Office of Data Analytics (chapter 2), originally created to coordinate the city's response to the 2008 financial crisis. The office was reinvented five years later to provide advanced analytics services to other city agencies, facilitate data-sharing across agencies, and administer the city's Open Data program. A few of these cases also demonstrate how the city has implemented technological solutions created outside of New York City, such as Vision Zero (chapter 11), which originated in Sweden in 1994, and ShotSpotter (chapter 10), which originated in California in 1996. This book is as much about what others can learn from New York City as it is about what New York City has learned from others. In this sense, the book also helps other New York City agencies learn how to innovate from within and modify programs for their own purposes. As McGowan and Shipley (2017, 1) put it, "In the past, we learned in order to work; now and into the future, we must work to learn."

Cities in the United States and around the world can use these case studies to inspire dialogue, design plans, pilot programs, and harness innovation to address similar problems. By understanding how New York City innovates, other cities can initiate locally contextualized dialogues about issues affecting their communities and also innovate from within. In this sense, this book rejects the rhetoric that city agencies are for the most part unmovable and ineffectual bureaucracies. Ultimately, the task of innovation "demands that we listen to the parts of ourselves that are more inclined toward curiosity, trust, and cooperation" (Montgomery 2013, 316). The notion that intellectual curiosity is resident and thriving within city agencies may seem counterintuitive, but the facts point to a critical inspiration point for innovation models to be applied far beyond the city administrative context.

While it is true that many scholars and organizations are rallying around city innovation, there is a resistance—methodological and conceptual—to studying those internal mechanisms of city agencies that drive innovation. Studies conducted by the business media and management, obsessed over the accomplishments of private organizations around innovation, change management, leadership, entrepreneurship, and business development, proliferated in the last hundred years. The equivalent passion for understanding the impact of local government innovation remains insufficient.

There are correlations and connections drawn between modern concepts like design thinking or innovation and activities in the public sector, but the literature consistently underplays the level of creativity and entrepreneurial thinking present within city agencies. To be clear, local government is profusely mentioned in both academic literature and media. However, the literature generally takes public programs and platforms as given, as exogenous factors to the analysis (The Economist 2016). In other cases, the literature focuses on how design methods can be applied to address public challenges, but looks at innovation as a novelty imported into city agencies (Clare and McConnell 2017).

Carol Stimmel (2015) proposes a general model for future smart-city projects also based on human-centered design. However, she focuses on a macro perspective of how tech, data, and human needs should inform program design and not so much on the operational and management details of program implementation. Stimmel's encouragement of city planners to shift their thinking from outcomes to process is relevant for this work.

When the literature focuses specifically on government programs, it typically lacks practical insights (Anthopoulos 2017); projects idealized futures with more attention paid to empowering citizens than to learning how local public administration operates (Newsom and Dickey 2014); or does not conceive local government as a driver of innovation from within (Araya 2015). Tim Campbell's (2012) focus on learning, networks, and innovation is particularly relevant for our work, but it does not get at the program-specific level as our case studies do.

Geoff Mulgan (2014) discusses several innovations originated from within the public sector, such as the Internet, World Wide Web, and new ways of combating AIDS. The limitation of the perspective offered in this type of literature, however, is twofold. First, programs are described in terms of goals, lacking an understanding of the historical and institutional context in which they are designed and implemented. Second, these accounts are anecdotal and/or dispersed from across multiple cities for the sake of international comparison, not studied in parallel with other cases from the same city. This does not allow for any type of general and practical understanding of how a city actually innovates, of how local innovation patterns emerge, or of how a network of city agencies can be viewed as a cluster for innovation. In *The Creative Destruction of Manhattan, 1900–1940*, Max Page (1999) also utilized case studies. However, he approached the subject from an architecture and urbanism perspective only.

Since city governments continue not to be viewed as innovators or change agents, partnerships with those agencies are often not sought after—despite the current interest in urban innovation and smart cities. Typically, city governments are viewed as adversarial in nature, with more attention paid to their bureaucracy and lack of agility. Sometimes these views focus on the regulatory and oversight role cities exercise. For example, procurement laws and data privacy protection are often viewed as barriers to business development. Other times, these negative views result from conflicting positions regarding bureaucratic inefficiency and a potential for lawsuits.

Even when city administrations are viewed more positively, innovation is rarely viewed as an integral element of government operation. In these cases, local administration is seen as a place in which innovation can be enabled, but not as the impetus or driver for innovation. Intellectual property laws, subcontracting R&D, antitrust laws, and procurement push are examples of government's enabling but not necessarily creating innovation. City leaders are known to talk about big-picture innovation, but the details about the positive and practical role city agencies play in innovation are publicized much more rarely.

The reason the role of city agencies in innovation is so poorly understood is that they are not envisioned as innovators, unlike, for example, other types of private small or large organizations that are seen as cradles of innovation. City agencies have a reputation as a kind of black box, and their organizational dynamic and interdependent operations are often left unstudied. Furthermore, the level of talent at all levels within the public sector is often underestimated; it is assumed that the private sector and academia are the only magnets for top thinkers. It is time to correct these intellectual biases and embrace the possibility that city agencies innovate from within—and, as this book aims to do so, explore exactly how they do so. At the end of this discovery and learning journey about New York City's experience with innovation, this book will offer a definition of what it means for New York City to become "smarter."

Case Studies and a Common Framework of Analysis

To achieve the goals described thus far, this book documents and maps part of the ecosystem of innovation in New York City through a series of twelve case studies based on current innovations that were identified across city agencies. These cases cover more than thirty agencies and units distributed across all levels of the city administration.

In addition to specific innovations investigated in 2015 via the Mayor's Office of Technology and Innovation, as explained in the preface, other programs are included in this book thanks to the inputs and collaboration of field experts and scholars from across the city. The twelve case studies were selected with the goal of imprinting on this book project a multidisciplinary and integrated approach that includes economists, engineers, computer scientists, sociologists, business managers, educators, designers, advertisers, lawyers, environmentalists, health scientists, public officials, technologists, planners, design thinkers, and private consultants.

In total, the portfolio of innovations spans the last three New York City administrations: Rudy Giuliani (1994–2001), Michael Bloomberg (2002–2013), and Bill de Blasio (2014–present). Each innovation is studied using a common framework of analysis, which follows three main principles (see figure 0.2). These principles—innovation process, innovation drivers, and analytical tools— are the three building blocks of the practical innovation roadmap each one of the cases offers.

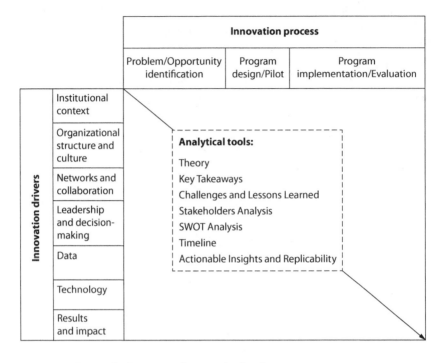

FIGURE 0.2 Case studies' common framework of analysis.

First, the case studies examine innovation—"ideas successfully applied" (Dodgson and Gann 2010, 13)—as a process. From problem formulation and theorization to program design, piloting, and implementation, each case study adopts Rogers's (2003, 5) idea that diffusion and adoption is "the process in which an innovation is communicated through certain channels over time among the members of a social system." Time, institutional space, actors, information, and interactions between actors are five key components for the adoption of and adaptation to innovation.

Second, the framework departs from previous research in this field, which evidences a technological and data bias resulting in a narrow analysis (Mora, Bolici, and Deakin 2017) that misses other critical innovation drivers. More specifically, this book looks at five additional innovation drivers cutting across all cases:

1. Institutional context and legislation: laws, protocols, norms, beliefs, incentives, reward mechanisms
2. Organizational structure and culture: organizational behavior, agility and resilience, practices, processes, size, talent, teamwork, autonomy, hierarchical structure, feedback loops

3. Networks and collaboration: interagency connectivity, coordination across agencies, public/private partnerships, stakeholder engagement, civic engagement, peer-to-peer learning, communication
4. Leadership and decision-making: entrepreneurship, inclusiveness, responsiveness, delegation/control, behavior, individual attributes, decision styles, knowledge, skills, roles, responsibilities, ethics
5. Results and impact: metrics, changes in systems, changes in services delivered, changes in perceptions and/or behavior, improvements, outcomes, externalities

Rudolf Giffinger and his colleagues (2007) were perhaps the first authors to move the "smart cities" concept away from an excessively technocentric perspective and offer the type of multidisciplinary understanding of urban innovation that this book adopts. However, these authors focus on cities in terms of broad areas for regional planning and development and not so much in terms of the specifics of program innovation. After them, several other authors have been expanding the concept of "smart" to include the types of innovation drivers the cases in this book now integrate (Windrum and Koch 2008; Nam and Pardo 2011; Batty 2013; Mayor of London 2016; Parmar et al. 2014; Mulas and Aranguez 2016).

From an epistemological standpoint, three well-established scientific fields support the decision to include those seven innovation drivers in our framework. From the business-management literature, we borrow Dodgson and Gann's (2010) six typologies of innovation risks to establish a parallel with the public arena:

1. Demand risk—e.g., the risk associated with citizens' satisfaction with and support for new public services and improvements
2. Business risk—e.g., the administrative and operational risk of a new innovation and/or its costs and benefits
3. Technology risk—e.g., the risk associated with the reliability, scalability, and durability of new technology and data chosen
4. Organization risk—e.g., risk of creative destruction, barriers to change, retention of talent, and motivation
5. Network risk—e.g., risk of bureaucratic competition, lack of ownership by key stakeholders, disruption of old ties, collaboration, and trust
6. Contextual risk—e.g., political risk, internal compliance, unions, jurisprudence

In political economy, the decades of work by the 2009 Nobel Laureate Elinor Ostrom (1990, 2005) focusing on the institutional analysis of economic governance, especially the commons, were formative for this book. Ostrom talks about "action arenas" in which actors, with their individual attributes, roles, and status, are faced with a set of potential actions/decisions that jointly produce outcomes—i.e., city agencies and stakeholders interacting to address common problems with innovation in our case studies. She sees these action arenas as dependent on three types of exogenous variables:

- Biophysical/material conditions, such as data, technology, infrastructure, and funding
- Attributes of community, such as culture, values, trust, reputation, networks, leadership, and organizational structure
- Rules, such as formal institutions, legislation, written agreements, incentives, and rewards

A central aspect of Ostrom's institutional innovation framework is the role of evaluation criteria to assess different scenarios, trade-offs, satisfaction, and results. This is the information stakeholders use to assess costs and benefits, which serve as incentives and deterrents, assigned to decision and outcomes.

In the public administration literature, Walker (2006) and Nam and Pardo (2011) discuss innovation types and diffusion in local government as well as the factors driving adoption of innovation. Walker classifies the drivers into two categories: environmental determinants, such as the social, political, and economic context (similar to Ostrom); and organizational determinants, such as size, structure, leadership, management, learning, and politics. Nam and Pardo's framework includes the same dimensions as Walker's, but organized in four categories. Technology (as a tool for innovation) and policy (as an enabler of innovation environment) are elevated to key-category level.

A practical and smarter understanding of innovation within city agencies requires the consideration of all seven drivers of innovation included in our framework of analysis, with no exceptions.

Third, the framework applies a series of analytical tools, such as a timeline, SWOT, and stakeholder analysis, to explain the complexity, nonlinearity, challenges, limitations, and lessons learned from each innovation and program studied. Each case study discusses key takeaways, replicability, and actionable insights regarding the drivers of different innovation pathways found in New York City.

This book showcases New York City as an incubator and test bed for innovative urban initiatives and explains each model's replicability beyond the five boroughs of the city. This integrated collection of case studies will also help cities reimagine new bottom-up possibilities for innovation from within city agencies, which—given current predominant national and international top-down "smart cities" frameworks as well as a lack of mutual understanding between city governments, private-sector groups, civil society, and academia—have not been considered and studied sufficiently. The case studies reveal different aspects of the innovations' dynamics, such as empathy, ideation, prototyping, testing, development, implementation, and evaluation—all concepts widely embraced in the private sector as core processes for innovation. In parallel, these case studies also seek to highlight how innovation can occur at different levels and functions of a city administration, such as management, leadership, procurement and contracting, operations, service delivery, and civic engagement. Understanding how the innovation occurred increases the significance and widens the applicability of these cases to potential innovators across New York City's agencies, cities around the world, private developers, and academia in general.

Each contributor to this book is an expert in the topic covered in their respective case study—a crucial element to the book's design. Contributors fall into four broad categories:

- Theorists or lab researchers: academic experts in their fields of work with limited professional ties with the city's administration
- Applied researchers: academic experts in their fields of work with ongoing research ties with the city's administration
- Entrepreneurs: expert businesspersons paired with scholars to foster academia/private sector dialogues and enhance cases' accuracy and practical relevance for new business development and education
- Former or current city officials: expert administrators paired with scholars to foster academic/practitioner dialogues and enhance cases' accuracy and practical relevance for policymaking, implementation, and education

Why Is New York City So Relevant?

The case of New York City is worth studying and disseminating for several important reasons. First, in 2015, under Bill de Blasio's administration, New York City was named number one in the world for technology, innovation, and entrepreneurship in a joint study from Accenture, Nesta, and Future Cities Catapult. One year later, New York City was named the "2016 Best Smart City" by the Smart City Expo World Congress. Since at least 2002, when Michael Bloomberg became the 108th mayor of the City of New York, the city has consistently introduced major technology and data innovations in its administration—change that can be traced and studied. For example, in 2010, in the midst of the post-financial-crisis recovery, Mayor Bloomberg and the newly appointed commissioner Katherine Oliver launched NYC Digital—a new unit for citywide digital strategy to make "the city government more efficient and citizen-centric" (Mulas and Aranguez 2016, 19)—to make it smarter. In the following year, the city appointed Rachel Haot as its first Chief Digital Officer (CDO), and in the same year New York City launched the "Road Map for the Digital City." In 2014, the city appointed Minerva Tantoco as its first Chief Technology Officer (CTO). Within just two years, to address the historical lack of both homegrown tech talent and engineering and science offerings at the university level, the City of New York announced three important applied sciences and research partnerships with top universities: the Cornell Tech Campus (2011), the Institute for Data Science and Engineering at Columbia University, and the NYU Center for Urban Science and Progress (both in 2012).

Second, as the largest U.S. city and one of the largest in the world, New York City offers an excellent example of what other expanding cities will be facing in the near future—not only in size but also in density and diversity.

Third, New York City is one of the top ten most income-disparate cities in the United States, which means that change can be studied vis-à-vis critical development challenges. These case studies cover a multitude of development issues also faced by other cities, in both developed and developing countries, such as sustainable development (chapter 1), government capacity (chapter 2), universal affordable broadband access (chapter 3), business development (chapter 4), energy consumption and sustainability (chapter 5), water management and climate change (chapter 6), urban waste and environmental justice (chapter 7), public health (chapter 8), neighborhoods and civic participation (chapter 9), criminality and gun violence (chapter 10), traffic deaths and injuries (chapter 11), and traffic congestion and air quality (chapter 12).

Fourth, in comparison to Europe, the North American literature on smart cities and innovation in urban systems—to a large extent produced by the business community, such as IBM and Forrester Research—remains disproportionately technocentric.[2] The result of this tech bias in the North American literature is the lack of attention paid to leadership attributes, organizational intelligence, social nuances, cultural implications, and the institutional features needed for a more comprehensive and integrated understanding of what smarter means in urban innovation. Our "system of systems" (Palmisano 2009) approach to the New York City case can help bridge this research gap (Hollands 2015).

What This Book Is Not About

A word on what this book is not about. First, because most of the cases studied are relatively recent innovations, by editorial choice, it is too early for a comprehensive evaluation. While all cases include empirical data to discuss some results and impacts, they are not meant to provide assessments of programs developed by the City of New York. They do address issues of performance, but they do so to offer an indication of the preliminary results obtained with the innovation efforts. Even if, in the mid to long run, some programs prove less successful than envisioned, what is central for this book are the dynamics and processes of innovation sprawling across the city—the ways in which trial and error unfolds within city agencies.

Even if the data available are limited, incomplete, preliminary, or just covering the pilot phase of the program or innovation, all cases use what is available to discuss how initial results compare to the original expectations. Since the focus of our work is on historical, institutional, social, organizational, management, and technological aspects of innovation processes, the results of each innovation, though important, are not as critical for this book. As stated, even if innovations and programs end up falling short of what was expected, decision-makers, practitioners, and students will still be left with a series of roadmaps on how New York City's agencies embrace trial and error to innovate.

Unpredictable events occur, and as Townsend (2013, 315) puts it, "even if [smart cities] fail to deliver efficiency, security, sociability, resilience, and transparency—the ambitions of all those stakeholders this book has covered—they will undoubtedly be incredible laboratories for studying how cities grow, adapt, and decline." In the words of Henry Ford (1922b, 19–20), "Failure is only the opportunity more intelligently to begin again." In this way, this book looks at innovation from an evolutionary theory perspective, in which individual local agencies search for, select, test, and implement new solutions whose outcomes are not necessarily known or expected when they are launched. In evaluating the cases, embracing adaptability as a core mind-set enables the lessons to be applied more readily. In this "age of accelerations," as Thomas Friedman (2017) calls it, "the new killer skill set is an agile mind-set that values learning over knowing" (McGowan and Shipley 2017).

The innovation processes discussed in this book allow for the identification of emergent features of innovation (e.g., leadership style, skills, organizational structure, regulations, civic engagement, processes, technology) even if the outcomes of the different innovation pathways are uncertain or even fail to match initial expectations. After all, as Batty (2017, 2) states, "cities are examples par excellence of complexity in the raw involving systems whose forms and functions emerge from the great diversity of activity that characterizes them at their most elemental and individual level."

Second, this book does not pretend to offer a complete perspective of all the innovation occurring across city agencies. Several important topics, such as food, nutrition, and education, are not directly covered by these twelve cases. Initiatives that are taking place in New York City in these sectors include the Farmers Market program, the Eating Healthy Initiative, the NYC Tech Talent Pipeline, and Computer Science for All.

Third, this book is not about innovation in the city at large. For example, New York City has recently become the second largest tech-startup ecosystem in the United States, and one may argue that smarter public/private partnerships may benefit from these expanding opportunities. However, the focus of the book is not on the broader technology and entrepreneurial expansion outside of city agencies, but about the innovation drivers that enable city agencies to innovate from within.

Finally, this book does not presume that other cities should simply copy-and-paste the New York City experience. Even where the problems are similar, the design and implementation of solutions need to be locally contextualized. This book does offer a practical roadmap for the development and adaptation of innovation based on the three pillars described in figure 0.2, but it requires local intelligence and experience to customize concepts to each set of local circumstances. Rather than looking solely at the data and technology involved in these programs, we have focused on the whole process and the drivers needed to implement innovation. While technology and new data systems are often a crucial component of the solution, the focus here is not just on the technology but on the whole process needed to successfully integrate it into city life. Data and technology are often perceived to be the most complex challenge, when in fact, the issues around people, process, and change are far more daunting.

Book Structure and the Sequence of Cases

The book is organized into four main parts. The first three parts present the twelve case studies; they focus on the city's agencies and program innovation. Part IV consists of a Conclusion and an Epilogue. The Conclusion offers a meta-analysis and summary of the major themes embodied in the definition of "smarter" as experienced by New York City; it focuses on city administration as an innovation cluster and presents the Becoming Smarter Framework (BSF), which can be applied to all cities around the world. Finally, the Epilogue offers an analysis of what the New York City experience means for the future of cities around the world; the focus here is international and global.

Part I of the book (chapters 1–3) focuses on the data architecture, organizational structure, and technological infrastructure of a smarter city.

Chapter 1. OneNYC and the SDGs: *A City Strategy with Global Relevance*

The book opens with a case that shows how a local strategy, developed in alignment with global ideals and with the UN Agenda 2030, can help cities and metropolitan areas drive progress toward local and global productive and inclusive sustainable development goals. This case teaches how a large community and stakeholder consultation with the support of a robust data and metrics-oriented information system allows the city to evaluate progress and report it in an annual public update. The key lesson here is that coordination, consultation, measurement, and a broad definition of "sustainable development" are all critical elements of an innovative and comprehensive sustainability and resilience plan.

- Problem: City long-term sustainability
- Solution: Adapt to city-level scale a global plan for sustainable development (SDGs)
- Focal agency: Office of Sustainability
- Other key agencies involved: More than seventy-one New York City public agencies brought together in eight cross-departmental working groups

Chapter 2. The Mayor's Office of Data Analytics: *Institutionalizing Analytical Excellence*

This case examines the Mayor's Office of Data Analytics as an example of an institutional innovation that sits at the center of several recent trends in public administration, including an increased understanding of the capacity of data science, a growing appetite for organizational innovation, and more sophisticated knowledge-management strategies in relation to government data. This case teaches how the organizational structure of a city was adjusted to create an in-house consultancy that uses data to provide advanced analytics services to other city agencies, improve the delivery of their operations, facilitate data-sharing across agencies, and administer the city's Open Data program.

- Problem: Open Data for all
- Solution: Organizational redesign to equip the city with an agency capable of developing and implementing a consistent strategy for citywide data analytics
- Focal agency: Mayor's Office of Data Analytics
- Other key agencies involved: Mayor's Office of Operations, Department of Information Technology and Telecommunication, Mayor's Office of Technology and Innovation, Financial Crimes Task Force

Chapter 3. LinkNYC: *Redesigning Telecommunication to Activate the Twenty-First-Century Creative City*

This case study focuses on the criticality of communications infrastructure for civic engagement, inclusiveness, equality, and progress. It shows the feasibility of building a profitable public broadband high-speed network in New York City without taxpayer support. This case offers a roadmap on how to set up a public/private partnership to enable an information highway for all at unprecedented scale within a reasonable time frame. The real innovation of LinkNYC is that its design enables it to use technology intentionally to shape attitudes and values making up the city fabric, as it engages, enlivens, and harnesses the creative economy for better citizen services, urban growth, and cultural enrichment.

- Problem: Repurpose existing infrastructure (old payphones, street conduits, etc.) to build a twenty-first-century citywide communications infrastructure
- Solution: Build the world's largest free super-fast public broadband Wi-Fi network
- Focal agency: Department of Information Technology and Telecommunications
- Other key agencies involved: Mayor's Office, Department of Transportation, Department of City Planning, Public Design Commission.

* * *

Part II of the book (chapters 4–9) focuses on different services or domains of life in the city: economy, energy, water, waste, air, and health.

Chapter 4. The New York City Business Atlas: *Leveling the Playing Field for Small Businesses with Open Data*

This case study shows how New York City is using open data to foster economic development. With a focus on entrepreneurship and small-business development, the Business Atlas empowers entrepreneurs with neighborhood-specific social, economic, and environmental information, typically accessible only to large firms with the resources to produce or purchase that strategic information. This case teaches how organizational flexibility and strong leadership allowed the city to completely shift the focus from top-down data provision, which was not reaching the targeted audience, to users and their problems. "If you build it, they will come" is not an optimal strategy for open data initiatives. The Business Atlas's pivot toward a clearer problem definition and more targeted engagement with partners placed it on a stronger path toward meaningful positive impact on small businesses.

- Problem: Economic development and the information gap small-business owners face compared to larger companies with more resources
- Solution: Drive small business growth with analytics

- Focal agency: Mayor's Office of Data Analytics
- Other key agencies involved: Department of Small Business Services, Department of Consumer Affairs, Department of Finance, Department of Health and Mental Hygiene, Business Integrity Commission, Department of Environmental Protection, Department of City Planning, Department of Housing, Department of Buildings, Fire Department of New York

Chapter 5. Demand Response: *Incentives for Smarter Energy Management*

This case study teaches how a city can generate revenues for its agencies by simultaneously reducing energy consumption needed to power its systems and raising awareness across its workforce regarding efficiency energy and sustainability. This case illustrates how the historical understanding of patterns of energy consumption across city agencies allowed the city to design and implement an incentive system capable of enrolling dozens of agencies and hundreds of city buildings with a smarter energy-management system.

- Problem: Energy management and resiliency
- Solution: Utilize a range of innovative technology—including real-time electricity metering equipment and a web-based monitoring system—to curtail building electricity use at peak times, helping to prevent failures in the city's power grid
- Focal agency: Department of Citywide Administrative Services
- Other key agencies involved: New York Independent System Operator, New York Power Authority, Con Edison, plus twenty-three other partnering agencies and organizations

Chapter 6. Green Infrastructure Plan: *Opportunities for Innovation in Climate-Change Resilience*

This case study explains how national and local regulations, natural ecosystem processes, new technology (such as automated water metering and 311 data), and community engagement are integrated to enhance operations of the city's sewer system. Special attention is dedicated to how enhanced stormwater management can improve water quality and mitigate urban flooding. Lessons from this case are even more relevant when considering the city's density, age, and physiography. These lessons are particularly useful for climate-change resilience planning.

- Problem: Water management in an ultra-urban setting

- Solution: A Green Infrastructure Plan engineered to mimic natural water-cycling processes to improve stormwater management
- Focal agency: Department of Environmental Protection
- Other key agencies involved: Department of Design and Construction, Department of Buildings, School Construction Authority, New York City Housing Authority, Department of Parks and Recreation, Mayor's Office of Operations (NYC311)

Chapter 7. Residential Curbside Organic-Waste Collection Program: *Innovation for Sustainability*

This case study shows how the world's largest sanitation agency is using organics diversion to fulfill a vision of sustainability that encompasses economic, environmental, and equity goals. This case demonstrates that large, complex sanitation systems can adapt their infrastructure and human assets to be innovative drivers of sustainability in cities. The key lesson here is how to leverage ambitious policies, key private-sector partnerships, and a phased piloting approach to implement the country's largest organics-diversion program.

- Problem: Economic equity, environmental protection, and environmental justice
- Solution: Implement and scale up organics diversion
- Focal agency: Department of Sanitation
- Other key agencies involved: Mayor's Office of Long-Term Planning and Sustainability

Chapter 8. Syndromic Surveillance System: *The Science and Art of Using Big Data to Monitor the Health of New York City*

This case study explores the technological infrastructure, operational protocols, and analytical techniques required to collect and analyze massive amounts of primary raw data to monitor disease patterns in near real-time. A key lesson here is that even seemingly simple routine administrative data can generate powerful insights in the hands of knowledgeable, talented, and, above all, curious professionals.

- Problem: Unanticipated changes in morbidity (diseases) and mortality (deaths) across a number of high-priority syndromes (a group of symptoms associated with a particular illness)

- Solution: Set up an early warning and response system to improve public health locally and globally by reducing the burden of communicable diseases
- Focal agency: Department of Health and Mental Hygiene
- Other key agencies involved: Mayor's Office, Emergency Management Office, New York Fire Department, Centers for Disease Control and Prevention

Chapter 9. Solving City Challenges Through Neighborhood Innovation Labs: *Moving from Smart Cities to Informed Communities*

Part II of the book closes with a case that describes how to build a new integrative multisector collaboration model involving city agencies, industry, academic institutions, and local communities with the goal of making urban innovation processes more inclusive and responsive to the needs of city residents. Neighborhoods are built in different ways, with specific complex iterations and environments that affect individual and social well-being. This case teaches how new technologies and data analysis are used in selected neighborhoods to test and pilot scalable future city solutions.

- Problem: Making urban innovation processes more inclusive and responsive to the needs of city residents
- Solution: Develop a network of innovation centers throughout the boroughs to test and pilot scalable future city solutions
- Focal agency: Mayor's Office of Technology and Innovation, Economic Development Corporation
- Other key agencies involved: New York City Housing Authority, Department of Environmental Protection, Small Business Service, Department of Parks and Recreation.

Part III of the book (chapters 10–12) focuses specifically on two increasingly critical challenges cities face: safety and mobility (people and vehicles).

Chapter 10. NYPD ShotSpotter: *The Policy Shift to "Precision-Based" Policing*

This case study documents how the city is innovating to improve security for all, everywhere, and in real time. The capability to identify the sound of a gunshot in real time triggers a series of top-down and bottom-up reactions with smarter results. Mayor de Blasio promised to shift the NYPD from "stop-and-frisk" to "precision-based" policing. This case teaches how data decentralization and new technologies in the hands of street patrol officers help boost motivation across police precincts around this new policy shift.

- Problem: Gun violence and gunfire response for public safety
- Solution: Implement a wide-range gunshot detection system that can detect, locate, and alert law enforcement agencies of gunfire incidents in real time
- Focal agency: New York Police Department
- Other key agencies involved: None

Chapter 11. Vision Zero NYC: *Toward Ending Fatalities on the Road*

The Vision Zero program was launched in January 2014, the same month Bill de Blasio was sworn in as New York City mayor. This case study shows how traffic casualties can be avoided, and that the approach can be replicated—effectively and affordably—in other urban environments. The key lesson here is that street casualties that kill or severely injure 4,000 people in New York City every year can be prevented and must be looked at and handled as a public health issue. This case details how a "zero street casualty" vision, enabled by data, top-down leadership, collaboration, and a broad civic coalition, was translated into a city's official road policy.

- Problem: Traffic deaths and injuries on the streets
- Solution: Set up a data-driven, collaborative, and participatory system to avoid casualties
- Focal agency: Department of Transportation
- Other key agencies involved: Mayor's Office, New York Police Department, Taxi and Limousine Commission, Office of Management and Budget, Department of Education, Department of Citywide Administrative Services, Department of Motor Vehicles

Chapter 12. Midtown in Motion: *Real-Time Solutions to Traffic Congestion*

The closing case study offers a multisystem perspective on how the city employs state-of-the-art traffic sensors, advanced communications networks, and complex computer algorithms to improve vehicular flow in a specific section of the city and, in the process, to develop and build communities. NYCDOT developed and implemented a large-scale traffic management system to detect and respond to changing traffic conditions, thus improving traffic operations in the central business district. The primary lesson here is that public-sector leadership and commitment to innovation, in partnership with experts from the private sector, can provide the building blocks necessary to quickly implement a successful state-of-the art traffic management system.

- Problem: Traffic congestion in Manhattan
- Solution: Set up a "system of systems" to improve vehicular flow
- Focal agency: Department of Transportation
- Other key agencies involved: New York City Department of Information Technology and Telecommunications

* * *

Overall, we hope that you will find this book to be inspiring, as it identifies important problems and features smarter solutions; descriptive, as it documents why, how, when, who, and happy and sad endings; evidence-driven, as it explores both qualitative and quantitative impact; and actionable, as it offers a roadmap of what is feasible, what is needed, and how to proceed.

At the dawn of the age of sustainable development, it is time to look at local government with fresh eyes. John F. Kennedy (1963) once said that "by defining our goal more clearly, by making it seem more manageable and less remote, we can help all people to see it, to draw hope from it, and to move irresistibly towards it." By providing roadmaps on how twelve urban management problems were formulated and addressed using new tech and data innovations, this book aims precisely to offer a contribution to cities around the world on how to move purposefully toward smarter ways of conceiving and running their urban systems. With these case studies we hope to shed light on how change can be planned, achievable, less fearfully embraced, and accelerated. We also hope to offer a contribution toward advancing the use of case studies as a research and teaching method; the teaching notes that follow provide some ideas for how these case studies can be used in the classroom. Each one of these cases offers a framework of problem appraisal, program design, implementation, and evaluation that helps reduce the uncertainty and risk of change.

Teaching Notes: The Use of Case Studies as Teaching Materials

There are many ways to incorporate case studies in the classroom and use them to engage students in problem-solving, hands-on, and practical activities. For twenty years, I have been using them in courses I teach or taught in the United States, China, Jordan, and Portugal. For example, the Vision Zero case study (chapter 11) has already been used successfully in a workshop that Arnaud Sahuguet and I offered at Smart Cities NYC '17. Bernice Rosenzweig is using her Green Infrastructure case (chapter 6) at the City University of New York with exciting results as well. Other cases are also being used in various teaching and professional settings, both in the United States and abroad. Students' reactions to these materials are fascinating!

There are at least three general pedagogical and teaching strategies I choose from when using case studies in my classes, depending on the learning goals set for each (see Table 0.1).

Multiscenario and Decision-Making

The first strategy focuses on alternative program interventions and emphasizes policy/program priorities and outcomes. In this teaching strategy, students are asked to discuss alternative future scenarios, strategies, courses of actions, or decisions vis-à-vis the problem presented in the case. Each alternative has a different cost/benefit profile associated, which may relate to different stakeholders and their interests, preferences, and agendas; different policy or programs goals; different contextual variables; or other factors/variables associated with the program moving forward.

The discussion in this strategy is about trade-offs based on the information provided as well as the uncertainty of future scenarios. Since all cases offer an historical account of how innovations evolved and the main challenges faced at the time of writing this book, instructors can look for updates (online or other sources) to build class activities around the topics and issues suggested above.

For example, the centralized Midtown in Motion program (chapter 12) faces important challenges with the advent of decentralized artificial intelligence. What options could the Department of Transportation (DOT) consider moving forward regarding vehicular flow in Midtown Manhattan? The class can be broken down into groups, each playing the role of a consultancy firm responsible to advise DOT on how to move forward. One group of students can be assigned to play the role of the client—DOT—who will have to assess the merits and flaws of the different proposals presented during the discussion in the second half of the activity.

Vision Zero (chapter 11) allows the city to collect massive amounts of data about citizens' and vehicles' mobility. How should the City of New York deal with the ethical tension between sharing data for business opportunities and protecting individual rights and privacy?

The syndromic surveillance system (chapter 8) has been developed since the late 1990s by an entrepreneurial epidemiologist. How can the Department of Health and Mental Hygiene develop internal institutional memory mechanisms, a knowledge base, and an incentive system to avoid organizational disruption once Dr. Don Weiss retires?

The LinkNYC case (chapter 3) can be used to break down the class into three groups—civil rights advocates, private developers, city officials—and develop

TABLE 0.1 Strategies for Using Case Studies as Teaching Materials

Teaching strategy	Case setting or plot	Classroom implementation	Learning goals and skills (examples)
Multiscenario formulation and decision-forcing model	Situation (or critical problem) + context + alternative solutions/ approaches	Activities about the decision/solution adopted or to be adopted	Cost-benefit analysis Scenario building Decision models
Retrospective decision-points (or decision-making) narrative model	Situation (or critical problem) + context + chronology of decision-points and associated alternatives + decisions made	Activities about the decision process and analysis of trade-offs and cost/ benefit	Historical analysis Critical thinking Networks and complexity Strategic management
Role-play model	Situation (or critical problem) + context + actors + alternatives + trade-offs	Negotiation simulations by groups + debriefing	Stakeholder and institutional analyses Negotiation and conflict resolution Empathy and public speaking Leadership

role-play discussions around the potential use of data collected by the city for local economic development.

Retrospective Critical Decision Points

In contrast to the previous strategy, the second strategy focuses on the past decision process surrounding program design and implementation. This strategy emphasizes management practices skills. Throughout program rollout, and at each decision point, those in charge of making decisions considered several possibilities, analyzed trade-offs, assessed consequences, etc., before a decision was made. Each decision had an impact on the program and led to a subsequent decision point, and a new decision tree was formed. Management practices can be discussed retrospectively vis-à-vis the complete sequence of decision trees, individual critical decision points, or decisions not taken (i.e., branches of the decision trees not followed). This type of teaching strategy can use the case studies to explore "what-if" analyses and the short- versus long-term effects of decisions.

Since each case offers a timeline of how innovations evolved, instructors can select critical junctures and use the SWOT analysis, in combination with the drivers of innovation identified, to organize discussions around the merits of alternative decision scenarios and their hypothetical consequences. For example, the future of MODA (chapter 2) was far from obvious when Bill de Blasio took office in January 2014. Extinction was considered. MODA ended up redesigned to become an in-house consultancy for city agencies to improve the delivery of their operations. But what other strategic and operational decisions regarding the future of MODA could have been made in 2013/2014 (if any), considering the development priorities and the needs of New Yorkers?

While the New York Police Department (NYPD) continues to believe in the value-add of ShotSpotter (chapter 10), the cost/benefit of this program faces multiple challenges. How could modern monitoring and evaluation methodologies have been set up to better inform the city's decision to invest in this program?

The current version of the organics collection programs (chapter 7) builds upon decades of successive new legislation that allowed the Department of Sanitation of scale up the program. Looking back, what were the most critical pieces of legislation to motivate private firms and households to join efforts toward environmental protection and environmental justice.

The Business Atlas case (chapter 4) can be used to trigger a series of role-play activities and/or discussions around the role internal coordination within MODA and interagency collaboration across the city could have played in the design and implementation of a program that faced the risk of being closed down.

Role Play

The third strategy focuses on negotiation and conflict-resolution skills. This teaching strategy can be applied to either past decision points or future scenarios. In this teaching strategy, each student plays the role of a specific stakeholder featured in the case and, in groups of different stakeholders assembled by the instructor, engages in negotiations with other students/stakeholders about a specific situation of the case, such as a conflict, an uncertainty, or a future decision.

This type of teaching strategy works better with case studies that provide more information about stakeholders' preferences, attitudes, possible reactions, and sensitiveness to program/innovation or decision alternatives. The preparation for the negotiation may require each student/stakeholder to collect updated information about each stakeholder involved in the negotiation, because there will be a time lag between the time the case was finalized and the time the student reads it. The focus of this strategy is on knowledge, skills, and competencies that favor trust-building, collaboration, and coordinated action toward some desired outcome, such as a certain technology adoption, a public/private partnership, or some public service improvement.

Cases featuring a wider range of stakeholders can be used in complement with new information, as suggested in the first strategy, to develop negotiation and conflict-resolution activities. Have students adopt the case study as baseline information accessible to all in the class. Then, assign students to play the role of selected stakeholders and ask them to find updated information online or in other sources about the innovation picked for the activity. Ask students (i.e., stakeholders in each negotiation group) to agree on a plan for how to move forward. Use the different agreements reached (depending on how many students the class has and how many parallel groups were created) to compare students'/stakeholders' relative performance (i.e., final overall agreements, who got what, who conceded what).

Each of the activities suggested above assumes that, before or after, there is a discussion about the concepts, tools, skills, and knowledge students are expected to learn and apply to their class activities. For example, the OneNYC case (chapter 1) can be used to develop classroom activities and discussion around stakeholders' engagement and coordination across cities to advance the SDGs at the local level.

The energy case (chapter 5) can be used to have students play the role of agencies not yet involved in smarter energy management and come up with new incentive systems for participation. Perhaps the Department of Citywide Administrative Services (DCAS), in charge of this program, would even be willing to consider internships, capstones, or independent research opportunities for graduate students or research scholars.

The Neighborhood Innovation Labs case (chapter 9) can be used to develop role-play activities with students representing different actors, such as a local association, a research institute, a private firm, a city agency, and marginalized groups, with the goal of making city innovation more inclusive and responsive to the needs of residents.

The green infrastructure case (chapter 6) can be used to break down the classroom into different groups, each playing the role of a city agency mentioned in the case. The classroom activity would aim at having students understand the problem of water management from within the city administration perspective as well as come up with new interagency incentive mechanisms to expand green infrastructure in the city.

Overall, these cases are compelling evidence-based stories that can make classroom discussions more lively, real, practical, and engaging. They are detailed in such a way as to offer instructors enough room to determine what type of discussion best fits the learning goals for each class. Case studies are great tools to help flip the class and make the students—not the instructor— the center of the learning experience. Because these case studies explain how innovation drivers operate in local government, they have the potential to encourage research on innovation in local governments and administrations; trigger dialogues around PPPs; stimulate the imagination of young and aspiring entrepreneurs regarding the huge opportunities for innovation in government processes and services; increase interest in internships and educational opportunities in governmental agencies, and public service in general; change perceptions about the functioning of the local public sector; and encourage systems thinking and multidisciplinary approaches in scientific fields such as urban development, technology, and SDGs while developing related skills, talent, and competencies. Departments and schools can use these case studies for student competitions and case challengers as well.

Notes

1. Another example of the problematic influence of language and meaning on behavior and practice: In a study on how local government practitioners understand the concept of innovation, Nählinder (2013, 321) tells of a government official commenting that "the word [innovation] is paralyzing, it limits the thought. The word in itself implies new, new, new. The word innovation is difficult—it has to be so revolutionary to be an innovation."
2. Between 1992 and 2012, authors from academic institutions produced 68% of the European literature on smart cities (and 72% of the citations). In North America, IBM and Forrester Research alone were responsible for nearly 70% of the literature produced, and 50% of the citations (Mora, Bolici, and Deakin 2017).

References

Acemoglu, Daron, and James A. Robinson. 2012. *Why Nations Fail: The Origins of Power, Prosperity, and Poverty.* New York: Crown Business.

Andrews, Rhys, and Steven Van de Walle. 2013. "New Public Management and Citizens' Perceptions of Local Service Efficiency, Responsiveness, Equity and Effectiveness." *Public Management Review* 15, no. 5: 762–83.

Anthopoulos, Leonidas G. 2017. *Understanding Smart Cities: A Tool for Smart Government or an Industrial Trick?* Cham, Switzerland: Springer.

Araya, Daniel, ed. 2015. *Smart Cities as Democratic Ecologies.* New York: Palgrave Macmillan.

Batty, Michael. 2013. *The New Science of Cities.* Cambridge, MA: MIT Press.

——. 2017. "The Age of the Smart City." *Spatial Complexity Working Paper.* Accessed August 30, 2017. http://www.spatialcomplexity.info/files/2017/06/BATTY-Working-Paper-The-Age -of-the-Smart-City.pdf.

Blattman, Christopher. 2017. Twitter post, July 6, 9:46 a.m. http://twitter.com/cblatts.

Campbell, Tim. 2012. *Beyond Smart Cities: How Cities Network, Learn and Innovate.* New York: Earthscan.

Clare, Michael, and Paul McConnell. 2017. *Designing for Cities.* Sebastopol, CA: O'Reilly.

Cohen, Boyd, and Pablo Muñoz. 2016. *The Emergence of the Urban Entrepreneur: How the Growth of Cities and the Sharing Economy Are Driving a New Breed of Innovators.* Santa Barbara, CA: Praeger.

Dodgson, Mark, and David Gann. 2010. *Innovation: A Very Short Introduction.* New York: Oxford University Press.

Ford, Henry. 1922a. "The Modern City: A Pestiferous Growth." In *Ford Ideals: Being a Selection from "Mr. Ford's Page" in the Dearborn Independent,* 154–58. Dearborn, MI: Dearborn Publishing Company.

——. 1922b. *My Life and Work.* Garden City, NY: Garden City Publishing Company.

Friedman, Thomas L. 2017. "Folks, We're Home Alone." *New York Times,* September 27, 2017. https://www.nytimes.com/2017/09/27/opinion/globalization-trump-american-progress .html.

Gann, David. 2013. "Chair's Foreword." In *Smart London Plan: Using the Creative Power of New Technologies to Serve London and Improve Londoners' Lives.* Smart London Board. https://smartnet.niua.org/sites/default/files/resources/smart_london_plan.pdf.

Gibson, David V., George Kozmetsky, and Raymond W. Smilor, eds. 1992. *The Technopolis Phenomenon: Smart Cities, Fast Systems, Global Networks.* Lanham, MD: Rowman & Littlefield.

Giffinger, Rudolf, Christian Fertner, Hans Kramar, Robert Kalasek, Nataša Pichler-Milanović, and Evert Meijers. 2007. "Smart Cities: Ranking of European Medium-Sized Cities." *Centre of Regional Science, Vienna University of Technology.* Accessed June 1, 2017. http:// www.smart-cities.eu/download/smart_cities_final_report.pdf.

Glaeser, Edward. 2011. *Triumph of the City: How Our Greatest Invention Makes Us Richer, Smarter, Greener, Healthier, and Happier.* New York: Penguin.

Goldsmith, Stephen, and Susan Crawford. 2014. *The Responsive City: Engaging Communities Through Data-Smart Governance.* San Francisco: Jossey-Bass.

Hollands, Robert G. 2015. "Critical Interventions into the Corporate Smart City." *Cambridge Journal of Regions, Economy and Society* 8, no. 1: 61–77.

Kennedy, John F. 1963. American University Commencement Address, June 10.

Mayor of London. 2016. "The Future of Smart: Harnessing Digital Innovation to Make London the Best City in the World." London: Greater London Authority.

McGowan, Heather, and Chris Shipley. 2017. "Work to Learn: The Future of Work Is Learning." Accessed October 7, 2017. http://www.futureislearning.com/.

Montgomery, Charles. 2013. *Happy City: Transforming Our Lives Through Urban Design*. New York: Farrar, Straus and Giroux.

Mora, Luca, Roberto Bolici, and Mark Deakin. 2017. "The First Two Decades of Smart-City Research: A Bibliometric Analysis." *Journal of Urban Technology* 24, no. 1: 3–27.

Mulas, Victor, and Mikel Gastelu Iturri Aranguez. 2016. *New York City: Transforming a City into a Tech Innovation Leader*. Washington, DC: World Bank.

Mulgan, Geoff. 2014. *Innovation in the Public Sector: How Can Public Organisations Better Create, Improve and Adapt?* London: Nesta. Accessed July 15, 2017. http://www.nesta.org .uk/sites/default/files/innovation_in_the_public_sector-_how_can_public_organisations _better_create_improve_and_adapt_0.pdf.

Musa, Sam. 2016. "Smart Cities—A Roadmap for Development." *Journal of Telecommunications System & Management* 5, no. 3: 1–3.

Nählinder, Johanna. 2013. "Understanding Innovation in a Municipal Context: A Conceptual Discussion." *Innovation: Management, Policy & Practice* 15, no. 3: 315–25.

Nam, Taewoo, and Theresa A. Pardo. 2011. "Smart City as Urban Innovation: Focusing on Management, Policy, and Context." Presentation at the Annual International Conference on Theory and Practice of Electronic Governance (ICEGOV), Tallinn, Estonia, September 26–28.

Newsom, Gavin, and Lisa Dickey. 2014. *Citizenville: How to Take the Town Square Digital and Reinvent Government*. New York: Penguin.

Ostrom, Elinor. 1990. *Governing the Commons: The Evolution of Institutions for Collective Action*. New York: Cambridge University Press.

——. 2005. *Understanding Institutional Diversity*. Princeton, NJ: Princeton University Press.

Page, Max. 1999. *The Creative Destruction of Manhattan, 1900–1940*. Chicago: University of Chicago Press.

Palmisano, Sam. 2009. "Smart Cities as Systems of Systems." *Irving Wladawsky-Berger blog*, July 6. Accessed September 3, 2017. http://blog.irvingwb.com/blog/2009/07/smart -cities-as-systems-of-systems.html.

Parmar, Rashik, Ian Mackenzie, David Cohn, and David Gann. 2014. "The New Patterns of Innovation: How to Use Data to Drive Growth." *Harvard Business Review*, January–February.

Rogers, Everett M. 2003. *Diffusion of Innovations*. 5th ed. New York: Free Press.

Sassen, Saskia. 2016. "Redefining Notions of Urban Intelligence." *Live Mint*, June 29. Accessed February 10, 2017. http://www.livemint.com/Specials/m21w1rzMM8KpbE9KO1iFVK /Redefining-notions-of-urban-intelligence.html.

Schumpeter, Joseph A. [1942] 1994. *Capitalism, Socialism and Democracy*. London: Routledge.

Stiglitz, Joseph E. 2016. *The State, the Market, and Development*. United Nations University-WIDER Working Paper 2016/1. Accessed August 24, 2017. https://www8.gsb.columbia .edu/faculty/jstiglitz/sites/jstiglitz/files/WIDER%20The%20state.pdf.

Stimmel, Carol L. 2015. *Building Smart Cities: Analytics, ICT, and Design Thinking*. Boca Raton, FL: CRC Press.

The Economist. 2016. *Empowering Cities: The Real Story of How Citizens and Businesses Are Driving Smart Cities*. Intelligence Unit. Accessed July 30, 2017. http://empoweringcities .eiu.com/wp-content/uploads/sites/26/2016/09/Empowering-Cities.pdf.

Townsend, Anthony. 2013. *Smart Cities: Big Data, Civic Hackers, and the Quest for a New Utopia*. New York: Norton.

United Nations. 2015. "World Urbanization Prospects: The 2014 Revision—Final Report." Department of Economic and Social Affairs. Accessed June 30, 2017. http://esa.un.org/unpd/wup/.

Walker, Richard M. 2006. "Innovation Type and Diffusion: An Empirical Analysis of Local Government." *Public Administration* 84, no. 2: 311–35.

Windrum, Paul, and Per M. Koch, eds. 2008. *Innovation in Public Sector Services: Entrepreneurship, Creativity and Management*. Cheltenham, UK: Edward Elgar.

PART I

DATA, ORGANIZATION, AND TECHNOLOGY

CHAPTER 1

OneNYC AND THE SDGs

A City Strategy with Global Relevance

JESSICA ESPEY, *Sustainable Development Solutions Network*
NILDA MESA, *Columbia University*

WITH

SANDRA M. RUCKSTUHL AND MIHIR PRAKASH,
Sustainable Development Solutions Network

Executive Summary

In 2015, two new frameworks for sustainable development were launched in New York: New York City's local long-term sustainability plan and the UN's Agenda for Sustainable Development. The city's plan, One New York: A Plan for a Strong and Just City ("OneNYC"), covered New York's unique environmental, resilience, economic, and social challenges, tailoring the then-draft global vision to a city-level scale for a more sustainable future. At the same time, information gained during the development of the city's plan provided useful insights for the finalization of the seventeen Sustainable Development Goals ("SDGs"), agreed to by 193 heads of state and government as part of the global Agenda for Sustainable Development. OneNYC built on previous city plans—notably PlaNYC—in striving to make New York greener and more resilient, while adding an explicit focus on equity and inclusive economic growth. OneNYC provided a vision for the city's future that acknowledged the interconnectedness of residents, the local economy, the built infrastructure, and the natural environment.

OneNYC is a groundbreaking approach to long-term city sustainability planning for five key reasons:

1. The OneNYC strategy integrates access to key public assets, environmental security, and economic growth, as well as social and economic inclusion and mobility.

2. The plan harmonizes with global efforts, providing input on best practices and metrics to inform implementation of the global development agenda.

3. The plan takes a long-term perspective, charging specific lead agencies with coordinated budget planning and monitoring to ensure funding and accountability.

4. The core design process involved nearly every city agency plus consultations with city elected officials, an advisory board, private sector representatives, and residents.

5. OneNYC is data- and metrics-oriented, using specific indicators to evaluate progress toward the city's goals and reporting on this progress in an annual public update.

This chapter considers the innovative design of OneNYC. Although it is too early to assess the programmatic impact of the approach, we consider other cities' attempts to replicate this kind of planning process, and tease out replicable lessons. Our intention is to show how a local strategy, developed in alignment with global ideals, can help cities and metropolitan areas drive progress toward sustainable development goals.

Key Takeaways

- OneNYC was the first city development strategy developed in concert with the SDGs, along with other then-nascent frameworks such as the Rockefeller Foundation's 100 Resilient Cities.[1] As the largest city in the United States, New York wanted to lead the way in supporting these initiatives, while also providing a concrete model that other cities could replicate.

- OneNYC is an integrated, holistic plan that, like the SDGs, considers economic, social, and environmental concerns at once. Operationalizing such a broad framework can be challenging. OneNYC overcomes this challenge by using a vertical-tiered system, beginning with four broad value-based visions that branch into their own goals and initiatives. At the same time, it uses these visions as lenses to assess the sensitivity of other goals and initiatives and so promotes horizontal, cross-sectoral collaboration.

- OneNYC has a strong focus on both growth and the poorest and most vulnerable, aligning with Mayor Bill de Blasio's priorities, as well as the global 2030 Agenda's "leave no one behind" principle. At the same time, the plan is largely anchored in physical infrastructure such as buildings, transportation, and the equitable neighborhood distribution of investments, rather than broad qualitative measures such as curriculum development.

- OneNYC was devised using an inclusive design process, unique in its depth and breadth, echoing the global process for devising the SDGs.

The cross-departmental and interdisciplinary working groups from more than seventy agencies helped break down silos and spur innovation.

- OneNYC takes a medium- to long-term perspective, and uses long-term modeling exercises, to come up with ambitious, forward-thinking goals for the city (even when these goals require the cooperation of state, federal, and nongovernment actors). It has created a clear narrative for city residents and policymakers, serving as a unifying document as programs are disaggregated to the agency level.

- Both OneNYC and the global SDG agenda focus on data and monitoring. OneNYC includes a detailed set of indicators to monitor progress. Where baseline data did not exist, programs were developed using the best available data and analysis, to minimize delay. The challenges associated with gathering these data suggested new approaches to data collection, consolidation, and integration to support implementation.

- OneNYC, and its alignment with the SDGs, is resonating with many cities across the United States (e.g., San Jose and Baltimore) and around the world (e.g., Bogota, Colombia) now seeking to learn from the process and to follow the blueprint.

Theoretical Background, Contextual Environment, and Problem Definition

In January 2014, Bill de Blasio took office as the mayor of New York City. The city was working to implement the ambitious resiliency plans outlined in *A Stronger, More Resilient New York* under PlaNYC,[2] released after Hurricane Sandy, but residents were also clamoring for a spotlight on inequality. As Mayor de Blasio described on the campaign trail, New York was a "Tale of Two Cities," with enormous wealth alongside increasing poverty and inequality. The question of how to foster inclusive economic growth while also maintain housing affordability was therefore paramount to his campaign, alongside an environmental focus on climate, energy, and recycling (de Blasio 2014).

Up the road from City Hall, 193 member states, including the United States of America, were locked in fierce UN negotiations over a new global development agenda. The eight Millennium Development Goals agreed upon in 2002 were coming to a close in 2015, and there was strong support for a new, holistic framework that would consider global social needs alongside economic and environmental imperatives as well as rising inequalities.

In 2015, the world's governments were set to establish the United Nations Sustainable Development Goals for 2015–2030, focusing not only on ending extreme poverty and hunger but also on the challenges of ensuring more equitable economic growth and environmental sustainability. OneNYC follows the same path, recognizing the critical link between sustainable and inclusive growth moving forward, not only for our city, but for the world.

The parallels were clear. Both globally and locally, discussions focused on how to chart a developmental course that encourages economic growth, while ensuring no one is left behind, environmental resources are judiciously managed for equal benefit, and all segments of the population are prepared for the environmental shocks and stresses that are expected to affect coastal cities with greater frequency in the years to come.

Under New York City's charter, the city is required to develop a long-term sustainability plan every four years, to include at a minimum consideration of housing, open space, brownfields, transportation, water quality, infrastructure (see chapter 6), air quality, energy, climate change, and population growth. The next report was due in time for Earth Day 2015, or April 22. Mayor de Blasio and his team at City Hall identified this as an opportunity to prepare a broader, more integrative strategy for the city that would consider economic and environmental challenges, but also social inclusion and equity; the effort was titled "OneNYC."

In 2025, New York City will be celebrating its four hundredth anniversary. The OneNYC design process asked what the city would need over the next ten years and beyond to thrive and grow, to promote inclusivity and equity for its residents, to be sustainable environmentally, and to be resilient against future crises. It mirrored the long-term perspective in the global discussions, with questions such as where the world wants to be by 2030, and how 193 countries can pull in the same direction toward common goals and priorities. As the OneNYC and SDG processes unfolded, it became apparent that there was much to be gained by attempting to align their goals.

Designing and Operationalizing a Comprehensive Sustainable Development Strategy for New York

Establishing the Planning Process

A new team at City Hall began developing a strategy, updating the economic and population trends and current conditions, reporting on the ongoing PlaNYC efforts, and broadening the original sustainability definitions so as to reflect the new mayor's priorities on fostering equity. The team was to solicit the input of residents and to consider regional perspectives, making it an extremely complex and broad undertaking. The group's members were set to task in December 2014 and had to deliver the strategy by April 2015, giving them a mere four and a half months (figure 1.1).

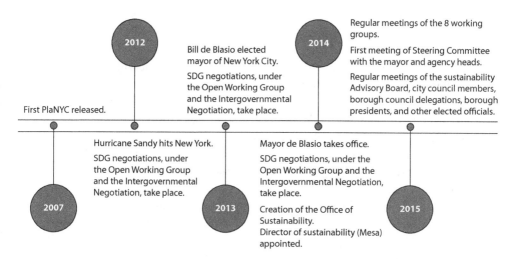

FIGURE 1.1 OneNYC timeline.

In order to proceed, the mayor fused two mayoral departments (the Office of Environmental Coordination and the Office of Long-Term Planning and Sustainability) into a new Office of Sustainability ("NYMOS"), while separating the resilience functions into another office. The first deputy mayor chaired a steering committee of deputy mayors, the chief of operations, representatives from the budget office, the city planning head, the resiliency director, and the sustainability director. The sustainability director led the overall project.

Eight cross-agency thematic working groups were established to identify unmet needs and develop initial proposals. Senior agency officials chaired the working groups with input from City Hall. A core team of city staff and steering committee designees supported the intensive process of reconciling information and proposed initiatives from the city agencies in order to formulate the contents of the plan. In addition, a Sustainability Advisory Board, with members from the private, nonprofit, and public sectors, advised the steering committee. Mayor de Blasio designated three co-chairs: Professor Jeffrey Sachs, Special Adviser to the UN Secretary-General and leading developmental economist; Larisa Ortiz of the City Planning Commission; and then-chair of the New York City Council's Environment Committee, Council Member Donovan Richards. At the time of his appointment, Professor Sachs was deeply immersed in the global negotiations on the new sustainable development agenda and was eager to share information on that process to inspire the city-level discussions.

According to representatives from the Mayor's Office of Sustainability, there were three concurrent prongs to the planning process: (1) deep research, modeling, and analysis of the current population, economic, social, and environmental conditions in the city, along with a review of existing and proposed infrastructure; (2) broad stakeholder and community consultations; and (3) widespread commissioner and senior-level staff engagement with draft policy designs, with further development by interdepartmental technical teams of subject matter experts and consultants. The latter two methods were a break with the traditional way of designing city strategies, enabling broader nonexpert and cross-departmental engagement with program design.

Particularly important to in-depth technical program design were the integrated working groups. More than seventy-one New York City public agencies joined in eight thematic cross-departmental working groups, organized around consensus values of the de Blasio administration, to identify gaps and analyze trends, develop priorities, and gain the benefit of multiple expert perspectives from a wide range of agencies. Two senior agency executives co-chaired each working group, facilitated by external consultants, ensuring these groups were neutral spaces for frank discussion in the design phase. The process was a bottom-up approach to a top-down requirement (see table 1.1).

A human-centered design approach launched the process. Agency heads were given recent data for a number of subject areas, ranging from crime to health to environment, so everyone had the same foundational information about the city, the boroughs, and the region as a whole. They rotated through set thematic stations in three-minute fixed time increments, armed with sticky notes, and were asked to jot down big, small, and creative ideas on how to deal with the challenges featured. The notes left behind were anonymous, and there were hundreds of them from the best policy minds working in city government. They were a rich trove from which to mine the beginnings of the policy solutions and goals that would turn into OneNYC. These became the raw material that the thematic working groups received and formed into goals and initiatives through their process.[3]

The working groups were tasked with envisioning how the physical city should be shaped to address a range of social, economic, and environmental challenges on the municipal and regional scale. This exercise required deeper consideration of the relationship between physical and human capital and an acknowledgment that the built environment has manifest implications not just for economic growth and development but also for public health and the delivery of essential services. This process helped break down agency "silos" and resulted in an ambitious set of visions, realized through supporting goals and initiatives, that crossed the traditional boundaries of city agencies and their focus areas of activity.

Once the working groups had identified priority issues and started to tease out ideas for initiatives, they assessed feasibility, ambition, scalability, funding, and external dependencies. A particularly important consideration

TABLE 1.1 Key Stakeholder Table

Stakeholder name	Role played	Interest in the program	Positive/negative effect on the program	Incentives needed to engage
NYMOS	Directed the OneNYC process, including design, development, coordination, and management of agencies, stakeholder organization, advisory board liaison, interface with City Council, resolution of conflicting goals and budgets, coordination with steering committee, devising metrics and accountability with other team members, writing and editing the final report and website.	Responsible for the city's long-term sustainability plan	*Positive:* provided vision and focus to the plan; managed input and complex priorities among more than seventy agencies and City Hall, as well as other elected officials and external stakeholders; set the tone for public engagement, produced final plan	NYC Charter mandates MOS to produce a long-term sustainability plan every four years, with annual updates; director appointed by the mayor
Consultants	Technical analysis, modeling, coordination of meetings, research verification outside expertise, synthesis of input	Business, local government experience, access to city information	*Positive:* acted as partners; were able to perform rapid complex data analysis and synthesize quantities of information	Opportunity to build expertise and extend skills for other similar city efforts

(continued)

TABLE 1.1 **Key Stakeholder Table** (*Continued*)

Stakeholder name	Role played	Interest in the program	Positive/negative effect on the program	Incentives needed to engage
NYC residents and businesses	Provided input on priorities and challenges to growth and city livability	Quality of life and economic and environmental health of NYC	*Positive*: provided needed on-the-ground information and preferences	Ease of providing input to city; user-friendly website; polling; community meetings
Agencies	Programmatic development and financial support for implementation, operations, metrics, and tracking implementation, final implementation	Responsible for funding and managing initiatives and projects and encouraging cross-agency collaboration to advance citywide sustainability objectives	*Positive*: subject matter expertise was invaluable; collaborations during planning process extended to implementation	Inclusion in the planning process so as to promote functioning of key agency programs and objectives
Sustainability Advisory Board	Sounding board for NYMOS and OneNYC team, providing valuable feedback in early, middle, and late stages; provided information and research	Promoting sustainability in NYC	*Positive*: input improved initiatives and programs; flagged unintended consequences; helped with public engagement; linked to global SDG process	Assurances that their input and advice would be timely, valuable, and incorporated as much as possible
City Council	Needed to enact necessary implementing legislation	Key members served on Sustainability Advisory Board, others provided input and information on their neighborhoods	*Positive*: facilitated mechanisms needed for implementation, including the budget and oversight process	Members wanted to ensure their districts' concerns were represented

Communications, digital, and community engagement offices	Developed strategy and mechanisms to engage public	Worked with OneNYC team and agencies to conduct polling and outreach as well as design interactive website; media relations	*Positive:* visually engaging and user-friendly website made it easy for residents to view the plan and provide input	Role in promoting transparency and engagement for NYC
Steering committee	Provided senior administration leadership, guidance, and policy resolution, set budget priorities, agency management	Implementing administration priorities, long-term planning	*Positive:* mobilized resources, including agency personnel, information and deep knowledge of city history, systems and infrastructure	Mayoral priority given to long-term planning process, leadership of first deputy mayor
SDG team, made up of representatives from the UN Sustainable Development Solutions Network, experts from Columbia University	Under the direction of Jeffrey Sachs (co-chair of the SAB and Special Adviser to the UN Secretary-General), a team of SDG experts provided relevant information on the global SDG processes, helped identify common targets, aligned metrics, and promoted OneNYC among UN member states	Encouraging widespread adoption of the SDGs	*Positive:* helped ensure consistency and alignment with the global discussions on sustainable development; made NYC the first global city to align with the new SDG framework	Invited in by Sustainability Advisory Board and NYMOS; provided space to present SDGs to board and city officials

was whether something could be funded. Proposals were vetted by the agencies that would be accountable for them and went through the simultaneous ongoing budget process, undergoing review and costing by the Office of Management and Budget. Ongoing programs such as Vision Zero (see chapter 11) were integrated into the overall picture. Goals and initiatives that addressed regional issues and were dependent on other non-city partners were identified as such. Finally, the planning was coordinated with the ten-year capital planning cycle, the annual budget, and the annual poverty report, all of which had somewhat different timelines. This system grounded the sustainability planning process in practical considerations such as feasibility and longevity.

In addition to internal structural and operational decisions, a number of important design principles and external processes informed OneNYC planning. These included synthesizing with the global SDG agenda, coordinating with 100 Resilient Cities and the Regional Plan Association, and undertaking private sector, elected official, and community consultations.

Aligning the OneNYC and SDG Processes

In early 2015, the OneNYC effort was well underway, with widespread consultations. These consultations included discussion of the status of the emerging global development agenda. A consensus eventually emerged that the new NYC plan could become a "local vision of the SDGs" (Abeywardena and Mesa 2016). It would use the "lenses of growth, sustainability and resiliency that were in previous citywide strategic plans, but add new emphasis on equity inspired by the Global Goals [the SDGs]."

At the UN, thematic and regional consultations and a member state–led design process (known as the Open Working Group) had culminated. A proposed draft was now under the noses of member states, who were locked in a line-by-line negotiation. It was at this point that the members of the OneNYC steering committee and the Mayor's Office of Sustainability engaged with representatives from the UN, including Professor Sachs, to foster alignment between OneNYC and the SDGs. The value of aligning the processes was threefold:

1. Greater alignment would sense-check local-level priorities against national and international concerns and ensure New York City was pulling in the same direction as the global sustainability movement.
2. New York would be a test-bed for the global SDGs, to see how these broad global goals resonated with local communities.
3. Aligning the plans would give New York a platform to showcase its new planning approach and encourage other cities to follow suit.

To achieve this alignment, Professor Sachs and other representatives from the UN made presentations to representatives from city government on the SDG process and its goals and targets, while New York City staff presented their planning process and explained how they had turned broad sweeping visions and goals into practical, workable strategies. At a series of roundtable discussions led by the Mayor's Office of Sustainability, working group co-chairs and members presented to stakeholders and advisory board members the specific research on city conditions and trends, OneNYC draft targets, and early-stage policy proposals. The ensuing discussion focused on prioritization, accuracy, whether the proposals would address the underlying issues identified, ambition, and alignment with the SDGs. The poverty goal was an example: OneNYC aims to lift 800,000 people out of poverty or near-poverty by 2025. While the figure specified is tailored to New York City, this ambition clearly contributes toward the global goal (SDG 1, target 2) to "reduce at least by half the proportion of men, women and children of all ages living in poverty in all its dimensions according to national definitions" (United Nations 2015).

New York's experiences also fed into the global debate about the feasibility of implementing and monitoring goals at the local level. An ongoing challenge for many cities worldwide is the global indicator set. An Inter-Agency and Expert Group (IAEG) under the UN Statistical Commission devised SDG indicators (United Nations 2016), but they are tailored to national governments and lack the local specificity relevant for cities. The OneNYC indicators are quite different from the global indicator set, as is true of other city sustainability and carbon reduction plans. It is unclear how city methodologies and reporting will be reconciled at this time so as to avoid gaps and double-counting at the national and global SDG scale, but OneNYC provides a useful model of how the global indicators can be tailored to speak to local priorities (Sustainable Development Solutions Network 2016; Biron 2017).

Cross-sectoral Visions

Overarching principles or visions can also serve as lenses to apply to all policies, plans, and initiatives to promote co-benefits and maximize efficient operations. The OneNYC process sought to avoid past agency isolation and stovepipe approaches to city sustainability planning, whereby one agency developed and implemented programs without input from or knowledge of other agencies' programs. Agencies would not necessarily know how their initiatives intersected, leading to avoidable complications, duplication, or missed opportunities for synergistic operations. From the original eight working groups, the OneNYC steering committee distilled four visions that would also serve as lenses for all initiatives and programs. These double-duty visions were growth, equity, sustainability, and resiliency. For example, on parks and open space, applying the equity lens led the city to promote operational support for parks in disadvantaged neighborhoods. On growth, policymakers looked at transportation access to jobs and job growth across sectors and boroughs to find gaps in links between transportation, housing, and jobs, which also integrated with equity and sustainability goals. The working groups designed the plan's draft initiatives collectively, with a lead agency designated to oversee implementation.

At the global level, the interconnectedness of goals, their spillovers and dependencies, was a subject of extensive debate. Member states discussed the need to use cross-ministerial task forces and teams to help ensure ministries did not pursue the goals in isolation. They also discussed the necessity to use the three pillars of sustainability—economic, social, and environmental—as lenses through which to assess interdependencies. OneNYC and its four visions provided an example of how this could be achieved in practice.

A Spotlight on the Equity Vision

OneNYC's strong spotlight on equity provides another good example of how to localize the principles enshrined in the global 2030 Agenda at the local level. The new administration's sustainability plan wove equity considerations across all city operations with growth, environment, and resiliency. According to OneNYC, equity was at "the forefront as a guiding principle." The plan envisioned that everyone across the city would have "a fair shot at success." An integrated approach to economic, social, and environmental planning also intended to make the plan more effective: "We know that a drive for a sustainable environment leads to innovations that create whole new businesses, while driving out poverty leads to healthier people, and safe neighborhoods spur businesses to grow. They all grow together" (City of New York 2015a, 11–12).

Looking at job growth highlights the value of an integrated and equity-driven approach. While the Manhattan-based finance, insurance, and real-estate ("FIRE") sectors are still the financial engines of New York City's economy, recent job growth spikes are concentrated in the other boroughs and in sectors such as health care, technology, media and film, and higher education (NYC Planning 2016). The city's economic strategies are thus focused on expanding those business districts and preparing workers with low educational attainment for jobs in emerging sectors. Research demonstrated a strong connection between transportation and social mobility, so it was imperative that OneNYC focus on improving public-transit access to jobs. OneNYC working groups discussed this phenomenon and considered multimodal transportation solutions, such as expanded bus and ferry services and the expansion of protected bike lanes.

Including Community Voices

Input from residents was facilitated by means of an online survey (nyc.gov/ideas), telephone surveys, and resident outreach exercises, between January and April 2015. More than 10,000 residents were able to submit their views via these mechanisms, with many more represented by their constituency leaders, city council members, and borough presidents, as well as local advocates. Respondents provided feedback in seven languages, showing the diversity of residents across the city. The overwhelming majority of respondents emphasized the importance of access to quality education and housing, while others talked about jobs, safety, health, and infrastructure (City of New York 2015a, 18). For example, a number of residents highlighted the pollution and transportation problems facing the Bronx River Corridor. According to Dave S. from Youth Ministries for Peace and Justice, "our community has long been known as the 'Toxic Triangle' between the Sheridan, Bruckner and Cross Bronx Expressways. We see a direct correlation between health issues and access to open space and we're trying to bring recreation opportunities to the area" (City of New York 2015a,16). OneNYC therefore includes a set of distinct initiatives seeking to reduce congestion, improve access to open space, and improve job opportunities in the Bronx River Corridor area.

NYC staff also reached out to all fifty-nine community boards throughout the five boroughs, presenting the outline of the plan and collecting direct feedback from residents around the city. Tight timelines meant much of the consultation was conducted while concurrently drawing up the plan, which meant it was both a verification exercise (testing draft priorities) and a gathering of new ideas for agencies to advance beyond the plan. Some civil society representatives on the Sustainability Advisory Board suggested more time for resident input, but given the necessity to deliver a plan by Earth Day (per the City Charter), the breadth of the consultation exercise was unprecedented. More consultation occurred after the plan was released and continues as it is being implemented. Community boards and other fora are engaged with each progress report.

It is important to note that OneNYC was designed with two different platforms in mind: the physical book and a website. The website was seen as the most likely place for residents and interested parties to look at OneNYC. The style guide for both platforms required that it be written so as to be accessible to a wide audience, as free as possible from jargon and technicalities. The website was dynamic, drawing in readers with attention-grabbing colors and graphic design, and a portal for comments. Readers could quickly find the overall framework and easily dive into the sections that most concerned them. This step was crucial to ensure citizens could engage with the plan and monitor and provide feedback on implementation, to be documented in the annual progress report.

Businesses were another key constituency engaged during the consultation period. The OneNYC team organized roundtables with business leaders based in New York City, asking them what the city could do to facilitate their growth and what obstacles they regularly encountered. For example, representatives highlighted that bandwidth is slower in New York than other cities, which was hampering their ability to grow.

Other stakeholders engaged in the consultation process were elected officials, including members of City Council and the borough presidents. They provided feedback grounded in their constituents' concerns. Examples included senior and disabled access, Hurricane Sandy recovery, and park investments. Council members also helped to ensure that key OneNYC legislation would be passed. According to Daniel Zarrilli, director of the Office of Recovery and Resiliency at the time of the process, "consultation was central to OneNYC" and, having asked for residents to invest time in designing the strategy, there was a clear duty to deliver; "it is also important to avoid consultation fatigue and to respect the fact that some stakeholders (e.g., lower income households) may have limited time and resources to participate."[4]

The global SDG process similarly included broad consultation. In 2012, UN Secretary-General Ban Ki-moon tasked the United Nations to launch a program of consultations, surveys, and workshops around the world to solicit views on the new global development agenda. The scale of engagement was unprecedented for a UN process; more than 9.7 million people provided input through the MyWorld Survey,[5] with many more participating in eleven thematic and eighty-three national consultations. The consultative processes employed in both cases were not new—consultation and community engagement have long been heralded as effective means of ensuring understanding and local buy-in (Cuthill 2001; Halseth and Booth 2003)—but their scale was unprecedented at both local and global levels. The consultations helped to ensure a high level of ambition and to ground goals in local concerns, and served to promote accountability to ensure that local and national governments would fulfill their commitments. According to David Donoghue, co-facilitator of the Intergovernmental Negotiation on the SDGs,

> It [the consultative process] was never far from negotiators' minds over the two or three years of this combined process [of negotiation]; member States frequently invoked findings which had been made by the MyWorld survey and emphasized the weight of public hopes and expectations around the world which that survey had revealed. (Donoghue 2016)

Long-Term Modeling

OneNYC takes a medium- to long-term perspective. It projects the city ten years hence, as well as discussing the city's potential one hundred years into the future. According to Mayor de Blasio, "it is a blueprint for the New York City we want our children to inherit" (City of New York 2015a, 3).

Projecting so far into the future helped lay out bold visions and strategies, such as a commitment to develop well-paying jobs and opportunities for all New Yorkers, with a quantitative objective of 4.896 million jobs across the city by 2040. Other specific initiatives that can help drive radical change are programs to promote eligibility for minority/women-owned business enterprises to qualify for contract awards.

The cross-agency working groups assessed the feasibility of each initiative and its goals. These discussions attempted to "backcast" what it would take to reach the goal within the allotted time frame. Backcasting is an approach recommended to support implementing the global SDG agenda. It means "generating a desirable future, and then looking backwards from that future to the present in order to strategize and to plan how it could be achieved" (Vergragt and Quist 2011). In the context of the SDGs, backcasting is a problem-solving framework that envisions how development should progress, with intermediate actions based on long-term quantitative targets. Unlike forecasting, which estimates the probabilities of various outcomes based on expected trends, backcasting begins with a projection of the desired outcome(s) and works backward to understand what is needed for their realization. The core is a long-term plan that maps out targets, milestones, and steps to achieve the desired endpoint by the desired date, including financing needs. The milestones are then translated into a quantified strategy—typically including an investment plan and financing strategy—that can be used within ministries and released to the public for broader consultation. The Sustainable Development Solutions Network (SDSN) utilized this approach, with great effect, to map out how countries might diversify their energy systems to meet the Paris Climate Agreement, capping carbon dioxide emissions to ensure a maximum temperature change of 2 degrees centigrade (Sustainable Development Solutions Network 2014).

In the case of OneNYC, the plan lays out how the initiatives, targets, and indicators would achieve the goals and visions. As with the previous PlaNYC, it does not explicitly claim that every initiative alone will achieve the goals. This is a strength, insofar as it allows city departments authority to develop more detailed, aligned plans and to hang them off the OneNYC framework. Indeed, *New York City's Roadmap to 80 x 50*,[6] which lays out the city's strategy to achieve an 80% reduction in carbon emissions by 2050 (and an interim target to reduce GHG emissions by 40% by 2030), specifically presents itself as a roadmap to achieve the climate goals set out in OneNYC. Agencies are then charged with developing short- to medium-term programmatic details to achieve the goals, the milestones (in conjunction with the OneNYC team) for implementation, and reporting monthly to City Hall oversight. Moving forward, these tracking measures will be important to sustain momentum and ensure the effectiveness of the plan.

A Robust Monitoring System

One of the most innovative things agreed in the global negotiations on the SDGs was a strong focus on data and metrics. Paragraph 48 of Agenda 2030 clearly says "quality, accessible, timely and reliable disaggregated data will be needed to help with the measurement of progress and to ensure that no one is left behind. Such data is key to decision making" (United Nations 2015). The framework is therefore underpinned by a series of quantifiable targets and indicators, a call for all governments to invest in building their statistical capacity, and an annual review process via the High Level Political Forum and the UN Statistics Commission.

OneNYC mirrors this emphasis, providing a clear set of measureable indicators at the vision level and for twenty-one of its twenty-seven overarching goals. The remaining six goals are tracked through their components, at the granular "initiative" level (City of New York 2015a, 262). With some exceptions, indicators are predominantly quantitative and are accompanied by a specific target and achievement date—for example, "Ensure there are 4.896 million jobs in the city by 2040" (263). The achievement dates for the targets range from 2020 to 2040. The indicators are reported on in the annual Progress Report, which is mandated under the same section of the City Charter that requires a long-term plan every four years (City of New York 2004). The first OneNYC Progress Report, released in 2016, includes available data on fifty-seven of the seventy OneNYC indicators; with a few exceptions and additions, these have been updated in the 2017 Progress Report. For thirteen indicators, new data were not available. Past PlaNYC initiatives are also tracked in OneNYC until the programs are completed.

Collating the data required to track NYC's progress toward the twenty-seven ambitious goals outlined in the plan is a challenge. The 2016 and 2017 Progress Reports highlight the difficulty of collecting annual data for a number of important measures, such as transit capacity, the number of mental health disorders, and the number of residents benefiting from coastal defenses. Interviews with city officials revealed problems of data sharing between departments, an insufficient budget for robust monitoring, and challenges utilizing third-party data because of privacy and robustness concerns. However, in some instances these may be offset by reporting and data collection in complementary city reports, such as the Mayor's Management Report, which also tracks OneNYC progress.

In addition, New York has a series of citywide data initiatives underway, such as the Social Indicators Report and the new City Planning neighborhood portal. In 2012, New York passed Local Law 11, or the Open Data Law, which encourages city departments to share data that are created by government openly with citizens. A primary objective of the law is to ensure residents have easy access to timely local information and are empowered to partici- pate in local governance and decision-making. To deepen the commitments in Local Law 11, in 2015 the city published an Open Data Plan, which calls for each city agency to identify and ultimately publish all of its digital public data for citywide aggregation and publication by 2015 (City of New York 2015b). The city has also established an Open Data Portal (https://nycopendata .socrata.com/) through a partnership between the Mayor's Office of Data Analytics (MODA) and the Department of Information Technology and Telecommunications (DoITT). The Open Data Portal houses more than 1,700 data sets that are available for public use, with more data sets being added regularly (see chapter 2). According to Jeff Merritt, Director of Inno- vation at the Mayor's Office of Technology and Innovation,[7] the city is also looking to generate data from new sources such as retrofitted phone booths, which will provide more real-time information such as data on the environ- ment and traffic conditions (see chapter 3).

Impacts and Results

Although it is too early to assess the full programmatic impact of OneNYC, there is initial evidence of its success as a planning framework that is helping to unify efforts across the city government, as a tool to devise more integrated programs and budget capacity, and as a model for other cities looking to imple- ment the global sustainable development agenda.

A Broad but Unifying Operational Framework

Like its PlaNYC predecessor, OneNYC retains a strong focus on the economy and environment. However, it has expanded with an explicit focus on equity and resilience, linking the components together, and in doing so it tackles the three pillars of sustainable development: economy, environment, and equity.

With so many themes under consideration, it can be hard to prioritize programs and to identify specific accountabilities. However, two years into the implementation process (and with emerging results featured in two Progress Reports[8]), it is clear that the breadth of the plan has been an asset rather than a challenge. OneNYC's holistic visions have provided a unifying tent for the activities of all of the city's departments, while the interagency planning process has helped to foster connections between departments, now jointly implementing programs and initiatives. The success of such a broad planning process has been noted and is now being mirrored by other U.S. cities, such as San Jose, California, which commissioned a new Sustainability Plan to use a similar planning frame. More specifically, San Jose has specified that this new Sustainability Plan must utilize the SDGs as its guiding framework.

Integrated Program Design

OneNYC features four visions that are not only guiding principles for the plan, but are an operational tool. These visions are growth, equity, sustainability, and resilience. Under each vision is a set of programs and initiatives related to economy, equity, sustainability, and resilience. The visions are also lenses through which to assess the relevance and efficacy of programs and initiatives in other areas. The equity lens, in particular, was used by the working groups, the steering committee, and the technical design group to assess the impact of any given program or initiative on the city's residents, taking into account neighborhood variables such as infrastructure and income. This mandatory stress test of programs and initiatives encouraged different city departments to work together to design more holistic programs, with multiple overlapping outcomes in mind.

A good example of OneNYC encouraging cross-sectoral and cross-departmental programming is provided by Hunts Point. A flagship economic and environmental initiative in OneNYC is the redevelopment of a food distribution center in Hunts Point, in the Bronx, to respond to food shortages and disruptions caused by extreme weather events. But the redevelopment also presents a unique opportunity to upgrade the quality of the distribution center and its environs for local residents. OneNYC includes a plan to work with the New York State Department of Transportation (NYSDOT) to make efforts to reconfigure the Bruckner-Sheridan Interchange and Sheridan Expressway to improve vehicle access. Not only would this enhance truck and employee vehicle access to the distribution center, but it would also reduce truck traffic on local streets and decrease overall congestion, increasing pedestrian and bicyclist safety, improving air quality, and better connecting local residents to new parks and the South Bronx waterfront.

Inspiring Other Global and American Cities

The primary focus of Agenda 2030 and the SDG agreement is national govern-ments and national-level action. However, rapid urbanization and the acute challenges facing cities and human settlements mean that local government leadership will be pivotal to the success of the 2030 Agenda. As Agenda 2030 does not speak to local governments explicitly, models are required to help cities and local governments "localize" the agenda. OneNYC provides the first example of a city aligning with the SDG process. In particular, OneNYC's inte-grative approach, consultation, and measurement plans all illustrate methods for contextualizing the SDGs in the city space. This approach is having global resonance with many cities across America (e.g., San Jose and Baltimore) and around the world (Bogota and Durban) now seeking to learn from the process and to follow its blueprint. Baltimore and San Jose have specifically sought to learn more about the OneNYC process, borrowing from New York's approach while incorporating their own methods for localizing the SDGs. In the case of San Jose, emphasis has been placed on the alignment of ongoing planning efforts; in Baltimore, the SDGs have been used to structure community consul-tations and to identify appropriate, meaningful indicators that could be incor-porated into the planning and budgeting processes.

Challenges and Lessons Learned

As global population continues to boom, urbanization accelerates, and the effects of climate change become more acute, city government and stakehold-ers will need to work together to identify the best development strategies. The OneNYC process demonstrates how a large, global city is responding to the knotty challenges associated with sustainable development, while also being sensitive to local residents' views and aspirations. Though many aspects of the plan will be relevant for other cities, there are five general transferable lessons that other global cities and human settlements may look to, to set them on a path toward inclusive economic and social development and environmental resiliency. Where possible, we have illustrated these lessons with reference to two other U.S. cities now attempting to localize and implement the SDGs: Bal-timore (MD) and San Jose (CA).[9]

1. *The SDGs allow cities to broaden the definition they utilize for "sustainable development" and to ensure "no one is left behind."* OneNYC, like the SDG process, recognizes that sustainability is no longer just about environmental sustainability. With population growth and widening disparities between the

Strengths	Weaknesses
"No one left behind" approach	Consultations were constrained by time and resourcing
Comprehensive and inclusive sustainable development strategy	The nonalignment of legislative budget and reporting deadlines with the OneNYC deadline forced potential programs to be cut
Comprehensive data and monitoring initiative	
Close consultation with legislative body	
Strong advisory board	Difficulty developing comprehensive measurable indicators, in part due to the lack of existing data as a benchmark
Inclusive cross-agency design process	
Good database to build off and design initiatives with	
Expert agency staff participated directly in the analysis and program development	

Opportunities	Threats
Adoption and localization of the SDGs and the global development agenda	Competing budget prioritization and cycles
Long-term visioning and planning	Accessibility of data
Increased participation from residents from enhanced citizen data portals	Complexity of developing quantitative long-term plans
Better monitoring and tracking can improve future designs	Maintaining political interest
	Nonalignment with state and federal policy priorities and funding
	Uncertainty with the state legislature's support for programs

FIGURE 1.2 OneNYC SWOT analysis.

haves and the have-nots, economic and social equity is of paramount concern, not least because it has direct implications for how we plan for environmental sustainability and multiply its beneficial effects. It can be hard to operationalize principles related to social justice within an instrumental plan, though, particularly one that covers economy, infrastructure, and resilience. New York City made the equity principle an operational part of its plan by sense-checking every strategy and initiative to see how it served vulnerable populations.

2. *There is no single approach for aligning with the SDGs.* OneNYC aligned with the SDGs by being goal-based, being equally focused on economic, social, and economic objectives, and paying special attention to the poorest and most vulnerable, thereby aligning with the SDG's objective to "leave no one behind." Baltimore took an entirely different approach to SDG alignment, from the bottom up. Community consultations on the city's sustainability strategy were oriented around the SDG frame and found great resonance, as social equity and justice are a key priority for the city. It became evident

in these consultations that citizens, nongovernmental organizations, foundations, academics, and government affiliates were involved in a wide range of SDG-aligned social-justice-oriented initiatives. The SDG frame brought a sense of coherence to these initiatives and helped structure coordination among them. The frame and resultant structure are now being incorporated into the new city Sustainability Plan that is under development. This initiative has received the endorsement of the mayor of Baltimore, Catherine Pugh.

3. *A common vision should be developed through consultation.* Consultation efforts in New York aimed to help create common priorities. This serves as an inspiration for other cities, but New York's consultations were also resource and time intensive. Baltimore recognized the importance of consultation for a common vision, but the parties leading early discussions on a comprehensive, SDG-aligned city sustainability strategy felt it important to find creative ways to effectively involve all stakeholders—including the city's low-income residents and their advocates. As several community engagement activities were already going on in the city, it was determined that the most efficient way to document those concerns was to conduct a "listening-to-the-listening" exercise. Members of the SDG team (including city representatives, council members, and academics) attended these meetings, recorded what they heard, shared their findings via traditional communications and social media, and brought these into their own meetings to discuss. The findings were then used in broad stakeholder discussions to set targets and measurement indicators for the city of Baltimore.

4. *If it cannot be measured, it cannot be done: the importance of comprehensive performance indicators.* OneNYC illustrates the importance of quantitative metrics, to help set clear targets, allocate resources, and monitor outcomes. Quantitative targets also enable cities to develop clear "backcasted" strategies that map out how the plan's goals will be achieved in the medium to long term, modeling different scenarios and policy decisions—a good example being New York's 80 by 50 plan to reduce carbon emissions. San Jose and Baltimore have taken on these data and monitoring issues with equal fervor, drawing heavily from the SDG indicator guidance of the UN's Inter-Agency and Expert Group on SDG Indicators. San Jose has conducted a data assessment, using the SDG indicators as a framework, in order to inform the development of a dashboard for its Environmental Sustainability Plan. Baltimore used the list of SDG indicators to assess existing city-level metrics, to identify data that were readily available to track achievement, and to identify missing—yet valuable—measurement indicators that warrant investment.

5. *If it cannot be funded, it cannot be done: aligning with the budget process.* To ensure OneNYC would be an operational plan, it was critical to identify funding sources for the initiatives and cement those sources before the plan was released. However, one of the difficulties was that the budget processes

and the OneNYC timetables were not entirely in sync, which meant that when the OneNYC initiatives were announced, the budgets assigned to the initiatives could not be announced because the official city budget was not due to be released until later in the month. Aligning the schedules in the City Charter would have made it much easier to see in real time that the OneNYC initiatives were funded, thus avoiding initial unfounded skepticism about the feasibility of the initiatives. Where the city could align other processes, it did—for example, the Mayor's Management Report and the Center for Economic Opportunity Report. These public-facing documents now track the initiatives in OneNYC along with overall city performance. Other cities would do well to align these crucial processes.

Conclusion

OneNYC fuses the strength of its 8.5 million residents, more than seventy-one public agencies, and a legacy of data collection, sustainability, and resiliency plans into a diverse portfolio of short-, medium-, and long-term plans and programs under four broad value-based visions and goals that, collectively, are consistent with many of the standards that the SDGs strive to achieve. It is a unique planning process, combining a number of innovative approaches while concurrently aligning with global commitments to sustainable development. It is still very early to assess the impact of OneNYC, but it is having profound ripple effects on other cities in the United States. In this chapter we have discussed San Jose and Baltimore, but other U.S. cities engaging with the SDG agenda include Portland, New Orleans, Minneapolis, Boston, and many others. Globally, Durban (South Africa), Istanbul (Turkey), Accra (Ghana), Manchester (UK), Bangalore (India), and Rio de Janiero (Brazil) are also taking steps to align their local planning with the SDG process and can look to New York as an example.[10] Challenges abound when implementing such a broad agenda—including budgetary prioritization, the accessibility of data, the complexity of developing quantitative long-term plans, and the importance of maintaining political commitment—but the global endorsement of the SDG agenda and the drive to achieve the SDGs by 2030 with strong city commitment can help to give longevity to broad, holistic, local-level strategies and planning.

Notes

1. Other key related external initiatives in 2015 included the Twenty-First Conference of the Parties ("COP21") to the United Nations Framework Convention on Climate Change, which resulted in the Paris Climate Agreement—a commitment to keep global temperature change below 2 degrees Celsius by 2050.

2. In 2007, Mayor Bloomberg released the first PlaNYC (*A Greener, Greater New York*), which focused on responsibly meeting the city's growing population and infrastructure needs. It included the city's initial sustainability strategy and became the model for other large global cities. PlaNYC 2011 expanded on the previous plan by strengthening the city's commitment to environmental stability and livable neighborhoods. In 2013, after Hurricane Sandy, the city released *PlaNYC: A Stronger, More Resilient New York*, which documented the lessons learned from Sandy and developed recommendations to adapt the city to the projected impacts of climate change, including rising sea levels and extreme weather events. For a fuller description, see OneNYC, pp. 11–12.

3. Based on IDEO's Human-Centered Design Approach. More information available at https://www.ideo.com/post/design-kit. Accessed May 25, 2017.

4. Comments provided by Daniel Zarrilli, Senior Director of Climate Policy and Programs and Chief Resilience Officer, New York City, at roundtable discussion hosted by SDSN on July 25, 2016. Meeting report is available at http://unsdsn.org/news/2016/07/25/localizing-the-sdgs-from-a-global-agenda-to-city-action. Accessed May 25, 2017.

5. Survey is available at http://data.myworld2015.org. Accessed March 1, 2017.

6. Downloadable at https://www1.nyc.gov/site/sustainability/codes/80x50.page.

7. Interview of February 18, 2016.

8. Progress Reports are available at https://onenyc.cityofnewyork.us. Accessed May 25, 2017.

9. These cities are key partners in SDSN's USA Sustainable Cities Initiative. More information is available at http://unsdsn.org/what-we-do/solution-initiatives/usa-sustainable-cities-initiative-usa-sci. Accessed March 17, 2017.

10. City administrators from each of these cities have contacted SDSN to learn more about the USA SCI program and lessons from New York's experience. Partly, it is this interest that spurred the production of this case study.

References

Abeywardena, Penny, and Nilda Mesa. 2016. "How New York Is Embarking on a Local Journey to Meet the UN's New Global Goals." *Huffington Post*, October 19. http://www.huffingtonpost.com/penny-abeywardena/how-new-york-city-is-emba_b_8330104.html.

Biron, Carey L. 2017. "How Baltimore Is Using the SDGs to Make a More Just City." *Citiscope*, March 9. http://citiscope.org/story/2017/how-baltimore-using-sustainable-development-goals-make-more-just-city.

City of New York. 2004. *New York City Charter: As Amended Through July 2004*. Accessed March 17, 2017. http://www.nyc.gov/html/records/pdf/section%201133_citycharter.pdf.

——. 2015a. *One New York: The Plan for a Strong and Just City*. Accessed March 25, 2017. http://www.nyc.gov/html/onenyc/downloads/pdf/publications/OneNYC.pdf.

——. 2015b. *Open Data for All*. Accessed March 25, 2017. http://www1.nyc.gov/assets/home/downloads/pdf/reports/2015/NYC-Open-Data-Plan-2015.pdf.

Cuthill, Michael. 2001. "Developing Local Government Policy and Processes for Community Consultation and Participation." *Urban Policy and Research* 19:2.

de Blasio, Bill. 2014. *One New York: Rising Together*. Accessed May 25, 2017. http://www.danagoldstein.com/images/2013/06/OneNewYork,RisingTogether.pdf.

Donoghue, David. 2016. "My Perspective on the SDG Negotiations." *Deliver 2030*. Accessed March 1, 2017. http://deliver2030.org/?p=6909.

Halseth, Greg, and Annie Booth. 2003. "What Works Well; What Needs Improvement: Lessons in Public Consultation from British Columbia's Resource Planning Processes." *Local Environment* 8:4.

NYC Planning. 2016. *Employment Patterns in New York City: Trends in a Growing Economy.* Accessed May 30, 2017. http://www1.nyc.gov/assets/planning/download/pdf/data-maps /nyc-economy/employment-patterns-nyc.pdf.

Sustainable Development Solutions Network. 2014. *Deep Decarbonisation Pathways Project.* Accessed May 25, 2017. http://deepdecarbonization.org/.

——. 2016. *Getting Started with the SDGs in Cities: A Guide for Stakeholders.* Accessed May 25, 2017. http://unsdsn.org/wp-content/uploads/2016/07/9.1.8.-Cities-SDG-Guide.pdf.

United Nations. 2015. *Transforming Our World: The 2030 Agenda for Sustainable Development,* A/RES/70/1, October 21, 2015. Accessed November 9, 2017. http://www.un.org/ga /search/view_doc.asp?symbol=A/RES/70/1&Lang=E.

——. 2016. *Report of the Inter-Agency and Expert Group on Sustainable Development Goal Indicators,* Statistical Commission, E/CN.3/2017/2, December 15, 2016. Accessed May 10, 2017. https://unstats.un.org/unsd/statcom/48th-session/documents/2017-2-IAEG -SDGs-E.pdf.

Vergragt, Philip, and Jaco Quist. 2011. "Backcasting for Sustainability: Introduction to the Special Issue." *Technological Forecasting and Social Change* 78, no. 5: 747–55.

CHAPTER 2

THE MAYOR'S OFFICE OF DATA ANALYTICS

Institutionalizing Analytical Excellence

CRAIG CAMPBELL, *Harvard University*

STEPHEN GOLDSMITH, *Harvard University*

Executive Summary

This chapter explores the inception and operating model of the New York City Mayor's Office of Data Analytics (MODA)—a young government unit whose story is fraught with identity crisis, having been variously termed New York City's "civic intelligence center" and City Hall's "skunk works," said to have been staffed by the "Mayor's Geek Squad" or, alternatively, a team of "data therapists."[1] These varying epithets reflect changes in leadership, staff makeup, and institutional design in the eight years since its inception. What persists throughout these changes, however, is that MODA is foundationally an in-house consultancy helping city agencies use data and analytical techniques to improve how they deliver on their missions. By combining a shared service model for public-sector analytics with a broad data stewardship mandate, MODA represents a structural innovation in the way municipal government uses data analytics to produce public value.

The term "data analytics" has been deployed in a variety of competing contexts; here, we define "operational data analytics" as the protocols for producing actionable knowledge at the intersection of two discourses. The first is *operations research*, a discipline with a long history in government that is primarily concerned with using data to conduct deep analysis into a specific logistical activity or area of service delivery (Pollock & Maltz 1994). The other is *data science*, the scientific inquiry into the technology and methods of data analysis (Donoho 2015).

MODA provides New York City government a unique set of capabilities through its three programmatic areas: providing advanced analytics services to other city agencies; facilitating data-sharing among city agencies; and administering the city's open data program. Its footprint in various projects has ranged from light-touch advisory roles to large-scale interventions in municipal operations, in areas from economic development (see chapter 4) to sustainability (see chapter 1) to tenant protections and emergency response.

Before it was formally coined "MODA," though, it was a small team pulling together data sets on mortgage fraud under the supervision of the mayor's criminal justice coordinator. A few key factors—executive support, early successes in inspections-use cases, and a message well suited to a swelling nationwide interest in data-driven government—led to MODA's official instantiation by then-mayor Michael Bloomberg in a 2013 executive order. In 2014, in a new administration and under the direction of a new chief analytics officer, MODA moved into the Mayor's Office of Operations and realigned its portfolio around a new set of administrative priorities (see figure 2.1).

Although the use of data analysis is certainly not a new phenomenon in municipal government, the organization of an analytics capacity in an agile internal-consulting model, combined with a data-stewardship responsibility for making information reusable across the city, represents a compelling approach to leveraging data analytics as a force multiplier in the production of public value.

Key Takeaways and Actionable Insights

- *Institutionalizing analytics as a service improves knowledge management across policy areas.* By building analytics into the city's institutional architecture, outside any single policy area or operating vertical, MODA creates capacity for leveraging analytical insights in one domain across other institutional functions and subject areas.
- *Internalizing data intelligence provides cost reductions across the enterprise.* Complicated data or analytics questions faced by governments are often outsourced to outside consultants. MODA provides this expertise at no cost to city agencies, while ensuring that all processes are transparent and well-documented.
- *Operational focus and rapid prototyping ensures high-value service delivery.* Because of the "actionable" posture of its analytics work, MODA prioritizes projects that have a high likelihood of resulting in changes that optimize city processes. Because of its penchant for piloting new ideas, MODA provides client agencies an experimental sandbox where failure and rapid iteration are built into the analytics process.
- *Analytical excellence within government drives civic engagement externally.* MODA is not only a center of excellence for the use of data within government; through its implementation of the de Blasio administration's *Open*

Data for All vision, MODA also serves as a model for connecting government-transparency initiatives with data-literacy efforts, empowering those outside of government to use city data to take action on their own behalf.

- *Public interest in open data drives better use of data internally.* Pairing data analytics with open data program administration in the same office, MODA channels public interest in open data to improve the quality of the data sets that are also used for analysis within the city.

Theoretical Background, Contextual Environment, and Problem Definition

How does a city decide to improve? In this case study, we will not attempt to answer this question wholesale, but instead explore it through the lens of one key part of the twenty-first-century government innovation agenda: data analytics.

Data analytics, as a field, can be defined as the rough art of making sense of a morass of information to improve how decisions are made. The case for data analytics in the private sector is clear: quantifying information and organizing an institutional aptitude to understand poses clear benefit to profit-seeking firms that define success in the empirical terms of a monetary bottom line. In the public sector, clear measures of success can be less straightforward. The question of what is valuable for a public administration to produce—and what costs are acceptable for realizing these goals—is more complex, clouded with ideology and often determined by more qualitative measures of success (Moore 1995). For government, the opportunity for data analytics is at once more promising and more difficult to effectively organize at the institutional level.

We will examine the Mayor's Office of Data Analytics as an example of an institutional innovation that sits at the center of several recent trends in public administration, including an increased understanding of the capacity of data science, a growing appetite for organizational innovation, and more sophisticated data management strategies.

The Analytics Opportunity for City Government

City agencies and offices collect and maintain data on a variety of activities, including operational information on licenses, service requests or complaints from the public, and capital planning and investments; administrative data on revenue and procurement, performance indicators, and survey data; and more recently, embedded-sensor, social-media, and crowdsourced data.

Taken as a whole, a municipality has an enormous amount of data at its disposal. It naturally follows that data analytics—the means to derive actionable insight from otherwise latent information—has the potential to make a significant impact in public administration. At a more granular level, however, the way in which data analytics can be deployed is complicated by the institutional culture, bureaucratic design, real and imagined legal challenges, and legacy information-technology systems common to city governments.

When the organizational structures prevent information from being socialized with other units, it is commonly labeled a "data silo"—the information-storage equivalent to "service silos" that are seen as anathema to streamlined customer experience and internal collaboration in a variety of organizational contexts.[2] A frequent assumption is that by creating lines of access across these silos, the enterprise at large is suffused with the data maintained by each of its constituent pieces. As information is socialized, analytical insight and decision-making can, from any organizational locus, operate with a complete picture of the city.[3]

Silo-breaking alone, however, does not result in operational improvement. For its data to be used effectively, a city also requires a culture that identifies high-value use cases by challenging long-standing procedures and norms. This culture is constituted by technical capabilities enabling analysis of data, a formal capacity for identifying patterns in this information, and a delivery strategy that allows for pattern-finding to be acted upon.

One salient example in New York City is municipal emergency management. Preparing for and responding to major emergencies is a primary objective of several city government agencies. Emergencies activate city resources in often novel ways, forcing the creation of new data and operational workflows that may not have existed previously. They prompt unanticipated questions—for example, where are all commercial cooling towers in New York City?—that the city, prior to that moment, had never needed to systematically ask.

Accessing high-quality data to answer these new questions, in the face of rapidly evolving circumstances and conflicting or incomplete information, is precisely the kind of situation that demands the creation of new infrastructures, protocols, and organizational units—and a way to make sense of it all.

Enter the Mayor's Office of Data Analytics.

Inception, Development, and Rollout: From Ideation to Implementation

From the Financial Crimes Task Force to MODA

Former New York City mayor Michael Bloomberg, a leader in technological innovation in both business and government, recognized the importance of harnessing data and analytics to improve how the city operates. Throughout his three-term tenure, a number of units across city government brewed their own

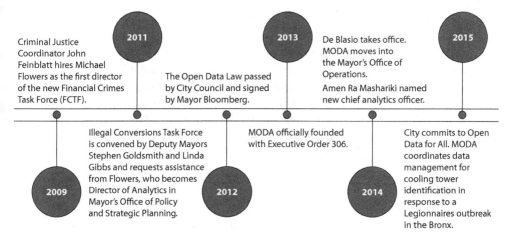

FIGURE 2.1 MODA timeline.

TABLE 2.1 Stakeholder Table

Stakeholder group	Goals	Role played	Opportunity for MODA
City leadership (mayor and deputy mayors)	Deliver on mayoral platform priorities more effectively and coordinate service delivery across institutional units using data and analytics	Supplied political will to found and fund an office of data analytics and a chief analytics officer	Allow leaders to "query" their city by using data to create better situational awareness; coordinate multiagency data efforts that fall outside any single domain
City agencies (e.g., Department of Buildings and City Commission on Human Rights)	Deliver value to New Yorkers based on their missions	Served as clients to MODA and supply data for analytics-use cases	Add measurable value to agencies' operations by applying advanced data analytics to improve service delivery
Local data and tech community (e.g., BetaNYC, businesses using city data)	Create information products and services for New Yorkers	Provided feedback to improve city data through the Open Data initiative	Expand value proposition of city data by publishing it for public reuse through Open Data

data-centric solutions to government problems.[4] One of them was the city's administration of the criminal justice system, managed by John Feinblatt, who served as the city's criminal justice coordinator and Bloomberg's chief liaison to district attorneys and the state criminal justice system from 2002 to 2013.

In 2009, Feinblatt hired Michael Flowers, a former Manhattan district attorney and Department of Justice military crimes investigator in Iraq, as the first-ever director of the newly formed Financial Crimes Task Force. The task force was created to coordinate the city's response to the 2008 financial crisis and started with no staff and no budget, just a mandate: Flowers was to identify and combine data from across city agencies to better understand the potentially criminal activity that contributed to the financial crisis, and then to hand this information off to the city's law enforcement agencies such as the district attorney's office.

Over the course of his first year on the job, Flowers built a small team of analysts and mapped out which agencies held relevant data, identifying in the process a use case prime for an analytical solution. Integrating and analyzing data—including property-deed transactions, various permits, and construction data—Flowers's team stitched together a picture of mortgage fraud that had contributed to irrational growth of the real-estate market. But while the model showed compelling evidence of illegal activities, the victims of fraud were big banks. Prosecuting on behalf of the major financial institutions was not, at the time, an urgent policy goal of the district attorney's office, and the mortgage-fraud project concluded without a single indictment.

This was a learning experience for the incipient analytics team. The process they had followed—identify a broad issue area, locate relevant data, specify a use case, and then match the evidence to an implementation pathway—needed to be reversed. Data analytics did not fix problems outright; for analytical solutions to be effective, the group needed to actively align incentives across a variety of stakeholders (table 2.1) to ensure that analytics deliverables would be acted on.

Meanwhile, other city leaders were pursuing their own data and analytics agendas. By mid-2010, the deputy mayor for operations was working to build a data analytics center and charged agency commissioners with surfacing analytical questions that, if answered, would change their operations. The deputy mayor for health and human services was developing a data and legal infrastructure to allow caseworkers to make decisions with a more holistic picture of a given constituent's encounters with different city agencies. Data-driven innovation was a shared goal of top officials, which brought needed visibility and support to Flowers' team.

Building inspections presented Flowers an opportunity ripe for analytics. The Department of Buildings (DOB), which is responsible for ensuring the structural stability of the city's built environment, oversees inspections. One aspect of this mandate is identifying apartments that unscrupulous landlords have illegally renovated to accommodate more tenants than their city-sanctioned capacity. Known as "illegal conversions," these properties were not only a potential quality-of-life problem; they also presented an outsize fire risk. After five people were killed in fires during the summer of 2011, Feinblatt, along with the deputy mayors for operations and health and human services, convened an interagency task force to address the issue (Moore et al. 2011).

Flowers seized the opportunity to provide quick and valuable data insights into strategies that might preempt future fires. He eventually became the director of analytics for the Mayor's Office of Policy and Strategic Planning, bringing with him the young analytics team he had developed. His team provided the analytics support to the Illegal Conversions Task Force, creating indicators for high-risk conversions from data on tax and bank foreclosure records and 3-1-1 complaints. The result was a model prioritizing which buildings to inspect. According to MODA's 2013 annual report, the model allowed DOB to identify up to 70% of the illegally converted buildings by sending joint teams of building and fire inspectors to just 30% of the complaints (Mayor's Office of Data Analytics 2013).

This strategy gained enough traction that the team, still operating as the Financial Crimes Task Force, was reconstituted as its own mayoral office. In April 2013, Bloomberg formalized the team as the city's "civic intelligence center" through Executive Order 306, which establishes the Mayor's Office of Data Analytics as the unit where data from across agencies is aggregated, analyzed, and turned into actionable insights. The order mandates MODA to address five areas of work: "Collaborative, Data-Driven Solutions, Citywide Data Platform, Oversight of Data Projects, Data Liaison Duties, Implementation of the Open Data Law" (City of New York 2013). It also created the chief analytics officer position, which Flowers stepped into.

The executive order, in short, chartered an office to create a formal institutional function for providing insight into city data sources, guiding the development of the infrastructure to share it, and enabling stakeholders across the city to leverage an advanced analytics capacity for rendering the data usable.

From Bloomberg to de Blasio

Late in 2013, Flowers stepped down from his post as chief analytics officer, leaving behind a legacy of an analytics office styled as a consulting unit—a long way from his original charge of investigating financial crimes.

Not long after, in January 2014, Bill de Blasio took over the mayoralty. De Blasio ran a campaign promising to bridge the gap in a "Tale of Two Cities," contrasting the New York City of the privileged elite with the city experienced by "everyday New Yorkers" (Chen 2013). The equity focus of the incoming administration was surrounded by a very different rhetoric of technology than the business-oriented pragmatism of Bloomberg. How this would apply to MODA was uncertain.

Among de Blasio's first political appointees was Mindy Tarlow. A seasoned expert in both public administration and nonprofit leadership, Tarlow was named the director of the Mayor's Office of Operations, a large team that provides project management support to interagency initiatives, researches and evaluates innovative programs, and measures city agencies on their commitments and key performance indicators. Among Tarlow's primary charges from the mayor: "bring the Mayor's Office of Operations back to the center of government" (Tarlow 2017).

Soon after Tarlow took the helm at Operations in January 2014, an auspicious turn of events brought some of the city's most advanced data and analysis functions within her purview. The deputy mayor for health and human services agreed to move the Center for Economic Opportunity—the city's in-house antipoverty think tank and a center of excellence for economic research and program evaluation—into Operations. Not long after, the research director of the Mayor's Office of Criminal Justice similarly pivoted MODA into Operations.

Structurally, this represented an opportunity to improve data use citywide by leveraging Operations' tactical toolkit. Through its performance-management role, Operations has a broad, lateral view of the city, providing a picture of how well the city is meeting its goals at any moment. Through a number of specialized "service" units—such as its project-management team and CEO—Operations engages tactically on a project basis as in-house consultants. Within this structure, MODA's focus, given its small size and sharp mission, is to engage on those projects where advanced analytics can have the biggest impact.

With MODA in Operations in mid-2014, Tarlow began a search for a new chief analytics officer, looking for "someone who could combine an analytic mindset with an equity-orientation" (Tarlow 2017). She found a match in Amen Ra Mashariki, a Brooklyn native who brought to the role a doctorate in engineering, data-intensive roles in the telecommunication and biomedical fields, and a background in technology leadership in federal government as the chief technology officer of the federal Office of Personnel Management (McEnery 2014).

One of Mashariki's first orders of business when he took the position in October 2014 was working with a small but astute set of holdovers from Flowers's team to hire a set of four "aggressive analytical thinkers."[5] In light of a different staff makeup, a different set of administrative values, and a different organizational location in Operations, the team had to prove its value in a new administrative climate. Mashariki's strategy: start small, collect "wins," and show how the cross-functional analytics team could thrive not only under the technology-driven management style of Michael Bloomberg, but in any environment (Mashariki 2017b). "We wouldn't be successful if we jumped into the scrum battles over the sexy tech projects," Mashariki said. "MODA could work with agencies on small things and get small wins."

In the summer of 2015, two pivotal events came to pass that would define MODA's future. The first was a deliberate act, in collaboration with the Department of Information Technology and Telecommunication (DoITT), to define a new direction for the Open Data program. The next was an unexpected public-health emergency that unearthed a deep need for a federated data-governance model and an analytics environment to support it.

Open Data for All

New York City began publishing administrative and operational data sets maintained by city agencies in 2009 with the inaugural NYC BigApps, a competition designed to spur community data science and app development with city data. NYC Open Data, from its inception, was seen as an opportunity to engage the technology community as a key resource for local entrepreneurialism. Two years later, the initiative was written into the administrative code when City Council passed Local Law 11 of 2012, also known as "the Open Data Law," which added an aggressive transparency provision to the overall mandate of open data. With the 2013 executive order establishing MODA, the role of the chief analytics officer also captured the responsibilities of the chief open platform officer—leader of the Open Data initiative (Campbell 2017).

In July 2015, three years and 1,300 data sets into the program, the de Blasio administration charted a new direction for the program. MODA and DoITT published *Open Data for All*, the strategic document that redoubled the program's focus on everyday New Yorkers and aligned the city's data-publishing program with the de Blasio equity agenda (City of New York 2015). Open data for the local technology elite was, by 2015, a well-understood use case. *Open Data for All* marked the start of the administration's effort to make open data a part of its community empowerment and digital literacy toolkit.

The *Open Data for All* strategy committed to building feedback into the data-disclosure process. It also set a course to make explicit the abstract idea of who was benefiting from public data. Starting with a Citywide Engagement Tour and segueing into a number of other user-research and community-engagement initiatives, MODA committed to doing more to understand who was actually using city data while simultaneously spurring greater use.

Cooling Towers and Legionnaires' Disease Response

The following month, several New Yorkers were killed during an outbreak of Legionnaires' disease, a respiratory infection caused by Legionella bacteria (Hu and Remnick 2015). When the Department of Health and Mental Hygiene (DOHMH) learned that these bacteria were incubating in cooling towers (HVAC systems on top of some buildings), the city suddenly encountered an urgent need to locate, count, and track inspections on all cooling towers. It was the kind of crisis the city had not encountered before (Chamberlain, Lehnert, and Berkelman 2017).

By early August, the initial outbreak in the South Bronx had been contained and the public-health emergency declared resolved by a quick response from the DOHMH. Although the crisis had subsided, it became a priority to mitigate the risk of Legionella bacteria in other cooling towers across the five boroughs. City leadership needed to locate all of the places where the bacteria might be incubating, test them for the bacteria, and then register that they had been cleaned. Time was in short supply: several New Yorkers' lives had already been lost.

A legislative solution was fast-tracked through City Council: Local Law 77 of 2015 required any building owner with a cooling tower to register and verify it had been inspected. With the statutory mandate in hand, the city deployed its "boots on the ground"—a combination of inspectors from the Department of Buildings and the Fire Department—and conducted proactive outreach to building owners through outbound calls and a site on nyc.gov to register buildings with cooling towers.

Given the breakneck pace at which the crisis was unfolding and the many moving parts of city government activated to respond, maintaining an accurate and complete picture of the status of inspections, in addition to routing new inspections efficiently, was imperative. What had started as an epidemiological problem became a data-management one. It was clear that infrastructure and protocol for handling a problem this complex and quickly evolving were not in place.

MODA, which was originally involved in providing information on landlord addresses, stepped in to help manage the data. Relevant agencies sent data to MODA, which acted as an analytics hub for the duration of the event. MODA analysts built a machine-learning model that reconciled counting methodologies from the various agencies involved and reported results back to City Hall within hours of receiving incoming data.

This emergency work, which necessitated immediate access to data, made it clear after the crisis subsided that MODA needed to help prepare the city for more coordinated data-sharing in response to emergency events. This included developing an emergency-data model and accompanying data standards, as well as a protocol for mobilizing access to information in emergency situations—a mandate that came to define MODA's interagency data-sharing strategy in the years that followed.

Results and Lessons Learned

With its coordination of the cooling-tower-counting during the Bronx Legionnaires' outbreak, MODA demonstrated to the de Blasio leadership team the value of a data-analytics office outside any single agency or subject area. With *Open Data for All*, MODA gained visibility with the community of public users and created a message resonant with the mayor's equity agenda. These two formative actions created space to take the ad hoc nature of project-specific analytics work and formalize it into a coherent, consistent strategy for citywide data and analytics.

Data at the Speed of Thought

Data-management issues that surfaced during the Legionnaires' crisis prompted a new outlook on the role the Mayor's Office of Data Analytics should play in facilitating interagency data access. Tarlow (2017) observes:

> Coming out of Legionnaires, we needed to have a way to build a foundation of all the information we have and a means to share it . . . so that when an emergency happens, we can focus just on the emergency itself. When it was cooling towers—or in the case of Zika, still or standing water—we should have all of the foundational information already and only be focusing on sharing relevant information we have and collecting any new information specific to the issue at hand.

According to Tarlow, a citywide crisis should never be an information crisis. Relevant information should be furnished at the "speed of thought,"[6] meaning that as soon as a need for information is articulated, the infrastructure and protocol are already in place to furnish it immediately. Mashariki explains further that, while one-to-one agency data exchanges were common, the challenge lay in creating an integrated, citywide view.[7]

Early efforts in New York City to integrate data across a variety of sources were focused in the areas of health and human services and criminal justice. The value of data integration for these subjects is clear: matching records on a single person who accesses city services across a variety of departments and information silos enables better coordination and more efficient service delivery. It also creates linked data ripe for analytics. "The same process we used with Health and Human Services, we could use with Emergency Management" (Tarlow 2017). Under Tarlow's leadership, the Mayor's Office of Operations led the effort to standardize policy and protocol, creating an omnibus policy for interagency data collaboration called the Citywide Data Integration Framework. In parallel, Mashariki set out to build the Citywide Intelligence Hub, a data-sharing platform that agencies across the city could use to share data and use collaborative applications.[8]

Among the city's core data infrastructure assets is DataBridge, a central data warehouse managed by MODA, DoITT, and the Mayor's Office of Operations that stores data sets shared between city agencies. The core innovation of DataBridge, when it was designed and implemented for citywide data retention and analytics, was that it enabled MODA and other key analytics teams to access data that was already being shared out of its source system. Its implementation and functional architecture resulted in a first-of-its-kind centralization effort.

Originally coined "DataBridge 2.0," the hub strategy takes a federated, rather than centralized, approach to citywide data-sharing. The hub system does not store any data itself but provides a view directly to agency data systems, allowing users to search for and share data with each other through a user interface oriented around geographic tools. According to Mashariki (2017a), this approach better accommodates the fluidity of data assets: "If we got every single data set that exists in the City in [DataBridge], then by tomorrow there would be ten more that we are missing," Mashariki said. A hub, alternatively, accommodates the fact that new data are created constantly, allowing data to be seamlessly drawn into other tools as soon as a need arises so that, as Tarlow put it, the data work happens in the background while officials "focus on just the emergency itself" (Tarlow 2017).

In collaboration with MODA, New York City Emergency Management (NYCEM) created an exercise modeled after emergency tabletops and live operational drills for the city's data and analytics personnel, which leveraged the Intelligence Hub prototype to test the system's functionality outside the context of an actual emergency. The first "data drill," as the exercise came to be known, took place in July 2016 and simulated a large-scale power outage in Brooklyn. Agencies shared relevant data sets, which MODA analyzed to answer questions on how the boundaries of the blackout zone would be identified and how data could be organized to provide situational-awareness reports to city leadership. The drill showed that the hub was not only an effective data-sharing platform but also a good governance approach, convening relevant stakeholders at agencies while fostering a culture more prone to collaboration on data operations.

Beyond Data Publishing

Just as MODA helps make data accessible to city employees, it also supports efforts to provide that same data to a community of public users. MODA has encouraged and supported several implementations of *Open Data for All* as a force multiplier for existing agency initiatives. In 2015, for example, NYC Parks facilitated a participatory mapping campaign known as TreesCount! 2015, which mobilized 2,300 volunteers and more than sixty local organizations to count every curbside tree in the city. One year later, the NYC Parks analytics team worked with MODA and BetaNYC, a local civic hacker group, to host the TreesCount! Data Jam. Five of the community groups that collected data presented challenges to civic hackers, and the resulting projects were presented back to Parks leadership to consider taking on as operational solutions. The event also included a workshop for Parks volunteers and Open Data newcomers to develop skills to analyze TreesCount! data themselves—linking data stewardship with Parks' long history of tree stewardship. Parks used the *Open Data for All* framework to convene a coalition of stakeholders around a data set that had personal significance to a variety of existing affinity groups, including Parks staff, nonprofit volunteers, and civic tech partners.

In addition to empowering community users, Open Data serves a valuable function for city employees and citywide data management. The chief analytics officer is also the chief open platform officer, meaning the analytics principal also enjoys the organizational role of the city's director of open data. According to Mashariki, public interest and pressure foster a virtuous cycle that contributes to better data quality and governance in the city at large (Mashariki 2017c). MODA has used this position strategically, leveraging the community interest in the city's open data sets to advance an agenda for better data quality internally. For instance, an amendment to the city's Open Data Law required MODA to standardize street addresses and other geospatial attributes for locational data sets. MODA solicited public feedback on the standard and received a rich collection of expert opinions and actionable insights on ways to optimize geospatial data—not just for open data, as the law mandated, but also for internal use cases.

Advanced Analytics in Action

Sharing data—publicly or internally—is not inherently valuable. Analytics render data assets into the knowledge that, when acted on, creates public value. To this end, MODA structurally includes oversight roles over citywide data-sharing and open data (see figure 2.2).

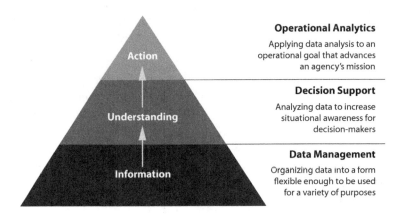

FIGURE 2.2 MODA project types.

MODA's analytics methodologies support the full span of a project, rather than isolating the "analytics" phase as a particular step in the process, and include not just programing, statistics, and other data-modeling methods but also business analysis, project management, stakeholder engagement, and policy analysis.

MODA's analytics process, which resembles the iterative techniques of agile project management, builds key benchmarks into the scoping, data management, analytics, and pilot stages of the project.[9] These benchmarks pose simple questions—Is the problem solvable? Is there enough information? Is the model good enough?—which the MODA analysts and agency clients work together toward consensus.

According to Simon Rimmele, a MODA data scientist:

> Each of these steps provides something of value. Just because a project doesn't go from one-to-five does not make it incomplete, and does not make it a failure. We encourage ourselves and others not to think that way. Projects may not begin at one and may not end at five, but provided we're completing each step in a way that's airtight, we've added value. Even if [a project] just reaches the scoping phase, if we help clients decide if a problem is solvable or unsolvable, we've helped the City. (Rimmele and Zirngibl 2017)

Many engagements start with an agency requesting data. In MODA's model, a data request represents a deeper need at the agency level and is an opportunity to investigate how analytics could add value. "We call it data therapy," says Rimmele. "The best way to start a project is to get everyone in the room. They state 'I want data set x.' Then we ask: is it just a data ask, or is there a deeper problem? We go back and forth, asking probing questions to get to the real issues."

In one example, MODA partnered with the City Commission on Human Rights (CCHR) to optimize where inspectors search for landlords who are illegally rejecting tenants on the basis of their source of income.[10] CCHR first reached out to MODA for an exploratory conversation on data sets that could be applicable to the project. But working with MODA was an iterative process. According to Sapna Raj (2017), assistant commissioner for the Law Enforcement Bureau at CCHR, "We had many meetings where we said, 'Oh this is not working, let's tweak it a little bit.' There was a lot of back and forth."

The collaborative process paid off. Before MODA was involved, inspectors had to physically walk, block to block, building to building, to see where landlords were accepting new tenants. With the data, "there was a huge difference." With the resulting analysis, the testers "didn't have to do all that research to kind of figure out who owns it, who gets the tax bill. All those things became much more simplified than what they were doing before" (Raj 2017). These results were presented in straightforward maps that the eventual testers could understand without special training.

The analytics process is MODA's framework, not only for delivering results, but also for familiarizing its partners and clients with analytical thinking. According to MODA data scientist Ryan Zirngibl, "a lot of what MODA does is not what the data was collected for—so you need smart people to give it the disclaimer" (Patel and Zirngibl 2016). The role of the MODA staff is "to challenge assumptions about the data as we massage data into being useful," said Deena Patel (Patel and Zirngibl 2016), another data scientist at MODA. "It's not just the outcome that matters—it's a back-and-forth with the client where decisions are made and insights are gained from exploring the data."

Challenges

"Should MODA be an *epicenter* of everything, or a *center of excellence*?" asks Mashariki (2017b). This question—whether MODA should administer the city's collective analytics agenda or instead encourage innovation at the agency level—points to a core tension in MODA's makeup and organizational placement, as illustrated in figure 2.3.

Data alone cannot drive operational innovation: a challenge facing any analytical organization is its ability to move data-driven insight into actual process change (Wiseman 2017). Clients interested in engaging a resource such as MODA may tend to be innovative thinkers who already see the value of data analytics. While this process, MODA analysts say, results in better uptake of analytical results, it may also result in fewer engagements with low-performing

Strengths	Weaknesses
Advanced analytics extract business value from otherwise latent information assets. Free in-house consultancy model with citywide focus allows for knowledge retention across subject areas, allowing the City as a whole to become more "intelligent" as more use cases are developed.	In-house consultancy may attract high performers, not areas where data and analytics could make the biggest impact. Institutional inertia in government creates barriers to moving projects from ideation and analysis to implementation.

Opportunities	Threats
Open Data opens co-production opportunities. Data issues and analytical insights delivered by public users can improve data upstream. MODA's insight into data needs across City government allows the office to broker external data sources for internal use cases.	Risk-averse agencies may be reluctant to share data for citywide analytics projects. MODA's placement in Mayor's Office makes its existence and agenda subject to political lifecycle of the mayoralty. City data is accompanied by a complicated regulatory environment.

FIGURE 2.3 MODA SWOT analysis.

operations where analytical solutions may deliver outsized value—creating an open question as to whether MODA should ideate and pursue analytical questions before the relevant city agency generates one. Striking a balance between maintaining trust with clients and changing agency processes proves difficult, MODA's data scientists say.

Culture Change: Conceptualizing Data as an Asset

MODA data scientists also described challenges guiding clients to see analytics as a problem solving tool, rather than a more facile view of "data analytics" as a particular technology or software product. Good technological tools can help, but they are always a means rather than an end. In the words of Zirngibl, "The agencies' data is so useful that tech companies come to them all the time, trying to convince them that *their technology* will solve all of their problems. What they are really trying to sell you is the fact that *your* data and information is valuable—and that their tool can make sense of it" (Zirngibl 2016). This underscores the broader challenge in empowering agencies to manage their data as an analytical asset, rather than technology overhead.

Balancing Tactical and Strategic Priorities

In addition to its tactical work analytics projects, MODA plays a strategic role in advancing the analytics agenda of the city by allocating staff to advise on agency data strategy and build capacity for agencies to do their own analytics work. The balance between these tactical and strategic activities is a challenge, though, especially since indicators of success in "capacity building" significantly lag behind upfront investments. It is tempting to attribute the growing analytics culture throughout the city to MODA: several other city agencies have adopted MODA's analytics model, including the Fire Department, the Parks Department, and the Department of Buildings. In reality, however, the growth of analytics in city agencies parallel's MODA's growth in a symbiotic way.

Conclusion

Several other cities in the United States and abroad have followed the model that MODA has pioneered. NOLAlytics, an analytics unit situated in the Office of Performance Management followed in MODA's footsteps in 2014. The idea for a London Office of Data Analytics (LODA) was directly inspired by MODA (Copeland 2015). And the Johns Hopkins Center for Government Excellence, as a consortium member of the Bloomberg Philanthropies' What Works Cities program, assists some of the network's one hundred midsize cities in developing their own dedicated data and analytics capacity in the style of MODA. Despite its lean team, MODA has become the standard-bearer in municipal analytics.

MODA's success owes to a well-honed repertoire of analytics tools that often avoid the cutting edge of data science techniques—the neural nets, cellular processes, artificial intelligence, and evolutionary algorithms that excite those unschooled in the specific policy instruments available for change—through no shortcoming of technical skill. Rather, MODA's techniques are deceptively simple, asking questions such as: What goes with what? How much? Where to look? What if? Data analytics, for MODA, is less about cultivating a black box of data science than making a growing body of civil servants comfortable with asking analytical questions and using analytical tools to drive policy and operational decisions. Analytics deliver sustained value only when it is embedded in the institutional fabric of the city—a lesson learned that has been reflected in the organizational strategy of MODA over the course of two mayoral administrations.

Mashariki says that MODA's long-term theory of change for the city is expanding analytics capabilities of city agencies through its analytics and data-sharing portfolio, ultimately building capacity to enable its own obsolescence. While that future is not yet in sight, MODA's institutional model has demonstrated that raising the analytical tide floats all boats. From its beginnings as a niche innovation wedged between existing functions in city government, through its sustained delivery of value across different political environments, MODA's continued existence offers evidence that decision-making informed by advanced analytics is becoming standard fare in New York City government.

Notes

1. "Civic intelligence center": www.nyc.gov/analytics, accessed March 20, 2016; "Skunk works in City Hall": Michael Flowers, quoted in Stephen Goldsmith, "Digital Transformations: Wiring the Responsive City," Manhattan Institute Papers, June 2, 2014; "Mayor's Geek Squad": Alan Feuer, "The Mayor's Geek Squad," *New York Times*, March 23, 2013; "Data therapists": Amen Ra Mashariki, quoted in "Digital Technology and the City: Leveraging and Managing Technology to Improve Services," NYU Wagner Graduate School of Public Service, December 3, 2015.
2. On analogizing data silos to service silos, see Wilder-James 2016. Specifically, the rhetoric of breaking down data silos has been frequently discussed in the context of business analytics (Duncan, Selvage, and Judah 2016), public health informatics, and centralized government management (Lubell 2017).
3. Media historian Shannon Mattern (2017) writes that to boosters of data-driven cities this perspective "appeals because it frames the messiness of urban life as programmable and subject to rational order." She argues, however, that this approach risks overlooking "data's human, institutional, and technological creators, its curators, its preservers, its owners and brokers, its 'users,' its hackers and critics"—that is, the imperfections and political instrumentality of information.
4. For a full account of MODA's inception and early work, as well as the other data-driven initiatives happening in New York City government at the time, see "The Data-Smart City," chapter 6 of *The Responsive City: Engaging Communities Through Data-Smart Governance* (Goldsmith and Crawford 2014).
5. Mashariki (2016) added: "I hire people based less on how well they match a profile of technical skills, more on whether they are curious and aggressive analytical thinkers."
6. Mashariki attributes the idea of "emergency data at the speed of thought" to Henry Jackson, chief information officer at New York City Emergency Management. It references Bill Gates's *Business @ the Speed of Thought: Using a Digital Nervous System* (Grand Central Publishing 1999), which explains how managers should view technology not as overhead, but as a strategic asset.
7. Mashariki elaborates: "You have people who have been in government for 20, 30 years who've worked at four different agencies. And because they've worked at four different agencies they know the people to call at those agencies when they need stuff. So there is a mechanism that exists, [which is] 'Oh I know that guy at the agency, let me call him.' But there wasn't a framework or an infrastructure across the board" (quoted in Deleon 2017).
8. The core of the agile approach, which was proposed and refined in the software-development context, is adaptability to process that follows value, as opposed to protocol-driven process where value production is secondary to a plan and role. (Agile Alliance 2001 and Flora and Chande 2014).

9. For a more in-depth discussion of the interagency data hub approach, and its incarnations in different cities, see chapter 5 in *The New City O/S* (Goldsmith and Kleiman 2017).
10. For more information on the MODA-CCHR partnership, see McKenzie 2017.

References

Agile Alliance. 2001. "Manifesto for Agile Software Development." Accessed October 1, 2017. http://agilemanifesto.org/.

Campbell, Craig. 2017. "New York City Open Data: A Brief History." *Data-Smart City Solutions*, March 8, 2017. http://datasmart.ash.harvard.edu/news/article/new-york-city-open-data -a-brief-history-991.

Chamberlain, Allison, Jonathan Lehnert, and Ruth Berkelman. 2017. "The 2015 New York City Legionnaires' Disease Outbreak: A Case Study on a History-Making Outbreak." *Journal of Public Health Management and Practice*, March 25. doi: 10.1097/ PHH.0000000000000558.

Chen, David. 2013. "De Blasio, Announcing Mayoral Bid, Pledges to Help People City Hall Forgot." *New York Times*, January 27. http://www.nytimes.com/2013/01/28/nyregion /bill-de-blasio-kicks-off-campaign-for-mayor.html.

City of New York. 2013. "Executive Order 306: Establishing the Mayor's Office of Data Analytics." Signed by Mayor Michael Bloomberg on April 17, 2013.

——. 2015. "De Blasio Administration Releases Open Data for All, the City's New Open Data Plan." Press Release, July 15.

Copeland, Eddie. 2015. "Big Data in the Big Apple: The Lessons London Can Learn from New York's Data-Driven Approach to Smart Cities." Capital City Foundation, June 2015. http://eddiecopeland.me/wp-content/uploads/2015/11/Big-Data-in-the-Big-Apple -Report.pdf.

Deleon, Nicholas. 2017. "How Data Can Stop Your City from Burning to the Ground." *Motherboard*, May 10. https://motherboard.vice.com/en_us/article/data-can-stop-your -city-from-burning-to-the-ground-smart-cities-nyc.

Donoho, David. 2015. "Fifty Years of Data Science." Proceedings of the Tukey Centennial Workshop, Princeton University, September 18, 2015.

Duncan, Alan, Mei Yang Selvage, and Saul Judah. 2016. "How a Chief Data Officer Should Drive a Data Quality Program." Gartner Research, October 14. https://www.gartner.com /document/3471560.

Flora, Harleen, and Swati Chande. 2014. "A Systematic Study on Agile Software Development Methodologies and Practices." *International Journal of Computer Science and Information Technologies* 5, no. 3: 3626–37.

Goldsmith, Stephen, and Susan Crawford. 2014. *The Responsive City: Engaging Communities Through Data-Smart Governance*. Hoboken, NJ: Jossey-Bass.

Goldsmith, Stephen, and Neil Kleiman. 2017. *A New City O/S: The Power of Open, Collaborative, and Distributed Governance*. Washington, DC: Brookings Institution Press.

Hu, Winnie, and Noah Remnick. 2015. "A Belated Look at New York's Cooling Towers, Prime Suspect in Legionnaires' Outbreak." *New York Times*, August 4. https://www .nytimes.com/2015/08/05/nyregion/new-york-officials-move-to-regulate-towers-tied-to -legionnaires-disease-outbreak.html?_r=0.

Lubell, Sam. 2017. "Virtual Singapore Looks Just Like Singapore IRL—but with More Data." *Wired*, February 21. https://www.wired.com/2017/02/virtual-singapore-looks-just-like -singapore-irl-data/.

Mashariki, Amen Ra. 2016. Remarks at the Inaugural Convening of the Civic Analytics Network. Cambridge, MA, April 11–12, 2016.

——. 2017a. Interview by Craig Campbell. New York, March 7.

——. 2017b. Interview by Craig Campbell. New York, April 20.

——. 2017c. Testimony before City Council at Oversight Hearing on Open Data Examination and Verification. January 22, 2017.

Mattern, Shannon. 2017. "A City Is Not a Computer." *Places*, February. https://placesjournal.org/article/a-city-is-not-a-computer/.

Mayor's Office of Data Analytics. 2013. "NYC by the Numbers: Annual Report—2013." December 2013. https://civicio.files.wordpress.com/2016/07/annual_report_2013.pdf.

McEnery, Thornton. 2014. "De Blasio Names New Chief Analytics Officer." *Crain's New York Business*, October 22. http://www.crainsnewyork.com/article/20141022/TECHNOLOGY/141029947/de-blasio-names-new-chief-analytics-officer.

McKenzie, Jessica. 2017. "How the NYC Commission on Human Rights Uses Open Data Against Discriminatory Landlords." *Civicist*, July 13. https://civichall.org/civicist/how-the-nyc-commission-on-human-rights-uses-open-data-against-discriminatory-landlords/.

Moore, Mark. 1995. *Creating Public Value: Strategic Management in Government*. Cambridge, MA: Harvard University Press.

Moore, Tina, Brian Kates, Benjamin Lesser, and Greg Smith. 2011. "Recent Fatal Fires at Illegal Apartments Forcing City to Aggressively Attack Problem in Courts." *New York Daily News*, May 22. http://www.nydailynews.com/new-york/fatal-fires-illegal-apartments-forcing-city-aggressively-attack-problem-courts-article-1.143141.

Patel, Deena, and Ryan Zirngibl. 2016. Interview by Craig Campbell. New York, December 18.

Pollock, Stephen, and Michael Maltz. 1994. "A Brief History of Operations Research in the Public Sector." *Handbooks in Operations Research and Management Science* 6: 1–23.

Raj, Sapna. 2017. Interview by Craig Campbell. New York, May 25.

Rimmele, Simon, and Ryan Zirngibl. 2017. Phone interview by Craig Campbell. February 22.

Tarlow, Mindy. 2017. Interview by Craig Campbell. New York, April 10.

Wilder-James, Edd. 2016. "Breaking Down Data Silos." *Harvard Business Review*, December 5.

Wiseman, Jane. 2017. "Lessons from Leading CDOs: A Framework for Better Civic Analytics." Ash Center for Democratic Governance and Innovation White Paper, January 2017. http://ash.harvard.edu/files/ash/files/leasons_from_leading_cdos.pdf.

Zirngibl, Ryan. 2016. Interview by Craig Campbell. New York, September 22.

CHAPTER 3

LinkNYC

Redesigning Telecommunication to Activate the Twenty-First-Century Creative City

MAREN MAIER, *Pratt Institute*

MARY McBRIDE, *Pratt Institute*

PAUL McCONNELL, *Pratt Institute*

Executive Summary

Finding good Wi-Fi today is just as important as finding a payphone twenty years ago. As people today rely heavily on smartphones to communicate, the City of New York wondered what it should do with the thousands of physical payphone structures dotting city streets. As the old payphone franchise was coming to an end in 2014, the city seized the opportunity to rethink its communication infrastructure and innovate on the franchise model and bidding process itself.

In the process, they tapped the joint creativity of public and private innovation to push the boundaries of what was possible and uncover a strategic design and revenue model that could self-support this effort. The result was a grid of new Links that would provide a free Wi-Fi signal, as well as other city and user amenities, at regular intervals throughout the city. As it rolls out, LinkNYC is laying the foundation to give residents and visitors access to free high-speed public broadband on city streets and in many ground-floor commercial and residential buildings by 2025 with minimal use of taxpayer money (NYC Information Technology & Telecommunications 2016a).

By strategically repurposing existing infrastructure (old payphones, street conduits, etc.), encouraging strong collaboration across agencies (DoITT, DOT, and Mayor's Office) and with the private sector (CityBridge), and actively involving local communities and their elected officials through the build-out process (borough board meetings, street teams, targeted PR and marketing campaign, etc.), the city was able to kick off this transformative twenty-first-century communications infrastructure project at unprecedented scale within a reasonable time frame.

As the first phase of deployment comes to an end, it is still too early to determine the exact scale of its impact and revenue potential, but the signs are pointing in the right direction. This case study will show the feasibility of building a profitable public broadband network in New York City without taxpayer support. It will provide a map for city decision-makers interested in replicating and amplifying the impact of this model in other dense urban environments. Finally, it will highlight how technological innovation, when applied correctly, can generate larger cultural benefits and activate the full potential of a twenty-first-century creative city.

Key Takeaways

1. Broadband is a twenty-first-century communications-infrastructure necessity to ensure democratic and equitable access and opportunity for all citizens.
2. A public broadband network can be built without using taxpayer money.
3. The revenue enters the city's general fund but may be earmarked to support citywide broadband inclusion initiatives, as well as public-service communication capabilities for the city.
4. Building strong collaboration in public/private partnerships is a valuable asset.
5. A community-first approach can help bring equity and inclusion into every step of the process (i.e., hiring from communities, communities owning part of the process, etc.).
6. A design-driven approach can push the boundaries of what is possible and ensure the experience of Links is meeting people's real desires and needs (see chapter 9).
7. A coordinated and aligned broadband infrastructure strategy for the entire city is crucial.
8. Link technology can open up a whole new layer of entrepreneurship in the city.
9. Technology is more than its utility value. It influences culture, and that culture can be intentionally designed. LinkNYC is an invaluable public-culture-shaping opportunity around inclusion.
10. Technology can be designed strategically to activate the full potential of a twenty-first-century creative city.

Problem Definition

The Origin Story

In 2014, the existing payphone franchise was coming to an end. Yet with so many people carrying phones in their pockets, payphone use had dwindled dramatically. As of March 2015, there were only 8,178 active public pay telephones on the city's sidewalks (NYC Information Technology & Telecommunications 2016c), down from 35,000 at its peak in the late 1990s (see figure 3.1) (Badger 2013). The New York City Department of Information Technology and Telecommunications (DoITT), which administered the franchises that brought public payphones to New York City sidewalks, wondered what to do with the leftover physical infrastructure related to "street furniture" (physical amenities affixed to the sidewalk). DoITT took the initiative to find a model that would replace the city's payphone network with an updated communication platform more suitable for today's needs.

With the DoITT commissioner's approval, in 2012 DoITT initiated a Request for Information (RFI) and a Wi-Fi pilot at ten payphone locations to test the feasibility of using the infrastructure for free broadband service across the city. They received considerable responses to the RFI and positive feedback, but many of the proposed scenarios lacked creativity. Through this process, they recognized a need to stimulate more resourceful ideas for repurposing the city's payphones.

FIGURE 3.1 Map of existing New York City payphone locations.

Source: New York City Independent Budget Office 2013.

Rethinking City Innovation

Seeing an opportunity to innovate, DoITT decided to pivot away from its traditional franchise approach. Instead of using a multiple-vendor model that only drew 36% of revenue from advertisements, they decided on a single franchise system with a 50% revenue share similar to another street-furniture model, the Department of Transportation's (DOT) coordinated street-furniture franchise (which includes bus stop shelters, newsstands, and public toilets) (Shor 2016).

At roughly the same time, the general counsel of the NYC Taxi and Limousine Commission transitioned to a new role at DoITT. As he came onboard, he shared his positive experience with the Taxi of Tomorrow design competition a few years earlier. He explained how the design-competition model helped to inject fresh perspectives and more extraordinary responses to the agency's Request for Proposal (RFP) process. DoITT decided to host a design competition as a way to unlock creativity in the bidding process for its new franchise. In this new "innovation cycle," they would use the RFI insights to frame a formal, independent, public design competition, which would in turn inform the criteria of the official RFP.

Inception, Development, and Rollout: From Discover to Deliver

DISCOVER: Catalyzing Possibilities Instead of Prescriptions: Reinventing Infrastructure (2012–2013)

DoITT partnered with the Mayor's Office to announce the design challenge at the end of 2012. The city decided to host the competition externally to avoid any bias and to protect itself if the city chose to move in a different direction. Four leading creative professionals sat on the panel of jurors, including John Borthwick (founder and CEO of Betaworks), Majora Carter (founder of Startup Box), Jason Goodman (CEO and cofounder of 3rd Ward), and former United States Deputy Chief Technology Officer Beth Noveck. Submissions were rated against each of the following criteria: connectivity, creativity, design, function, and community impact.

The Reinvent Payphones Design Challenge attracted hundreds of imaginative designs, and six winning prototypes were selected based on the criteria. The design competition proved a successful way to energize the creative community, a sector that historically has not participated actively in public bids because of a lack of awareness about the RFP process. The success of this challenge was attributed to the way it was initially launched. At a tech meet-up

FIGURE 3.2 LinkNYC rendering of a "Link" on a New York City street.

Source: Intersection 2016

at NYU, the city's chief digital officer presented a playful video of Mayor Bloomberg confronting a payphone and inviting urban designers, planners, technologists, and policy experts to propose physical and virtual prototypes for the Payphone of the Future.

The results of the design competition confirmed several initial decisions the DoITT team had made in the RFI. For instance, rather than maintaining a physical shelter with three-panel advertising, many of the proposals offered elegant solutions for a thinner, taller, two-panel structure to reduce its footprint and gain public space. The design competition proved an effective method to test and affirm these initial considerations and generate inspiring insights from the field. A few months later, one of the finalists went on to submit the winning bid in the official RFP process with a modified design, called LinkNYC (see figure 3.2).

Learnings

Design matters. If our megacities are to thrive, they will need to be designed to encourage inclusion, equity, and cultural participation. The city was intentional about broadening the audience for the RFP to encourage creative submissions founded on these values. As Colin O'Donnell, chief innovation officer at Intersection, described, "One of the things the City said in the initial meeting was 'you're free to propose.' They didn't say you need a certain bandwidth or a certain this or that. But we decided that going from 100 megabytes to one gigabyte [Wi-Fi speed] wasn't a significant cost compared to the effect it could have on people's imagination."

Let criteria emerge. RFPs often prescribe criteria up front and in some cases may be written with a veteran bidder or the lowest-cost bidder in mind. DoITT offered a very inclusive process without demanding specifications, such as a specific bandwidth, dimensions, or cost. The parameters were loosely framed around community impact, quality of the technology solution, and the financial calculation, allowing the bidders to fill in the details.

City Collaboration (2014)

The design competition also helped city agencies expedite and design communication and coordination around the new franchise. Prior to the design competition, DoITT formed a planning team with relevant agencies including the Department of Transportation, the Department of City Planning, and the Public Design Commission, among others, to define the scope and parameters of the new payphone structures. This early interagency coordination helped to address key considerations up front, such as land-use impacts and historic preservation, that were tested during the design competition. It also set the foundation for a strong interagency working relationship throughout the course of the franchise process.

As DoITT moved to release the official RFP, they vetted their plans through every agency that had a stake in the payphone franchise. This saved DoITT time in the long run by avoiding lengthy reviews, such as the Uniform Land Use Review Procedure (ULURP) process, with the Department of City Planning. The project's success also hinged on the ability to create space for disagreement. For example, the Department of City Planning advocated for reducing the concentration of installations on the streets, whereas DoITT advocated for clustering in certain areas because it was important to subsidize Links in locations that would not sell advertising as well. The agencies gave DoITT their input, which informed the final competitive RFP.

This process also uncovered a need for cross-agency planning on the design of streetscape initiatives. According to Stanley Shor (2016), assistant commissioner of franchise administration at DoITT, "If we hadn't talked to the Department of Transportation (DOT) early, we wouldn't have known of the Wayfinding initiative they were doing." DOT was in the process of installing physical panels with city maps on sidewalks across the city, and the agencies joined forces to coordinate placement of both across the city. With 24,000 bike racks, 3,500 bus shelters, and 300,000 streetlights, among other objects on sidewalks, a lack of agency coordination on street-furniture placement has real consequence for the user experience of city streets. It left agencies wondering what could be improved in the innovation process for cities to acknowledge density of independent activities that compete for space and attention. Perhaps there are ways to institute regular early-phase concept-sharing so that agencies can identify opportunities to combine projects before it is too late.

Learnings

Design engagement with other city agencies early. City agencies looking to launch a new public-service project can benefit from developing RFPs inclusively with other agencies. "You can't do new projects on the street well without involving other agencies early in the planning process. The worst thing is to be rushed in the process, and when it gets implemented it can no longer be changed," says Shor.

Integrate streetscape design and strategic planning. Many city agencies have a role to play in the New York City streetscape. Various objects have agglomerated on the street over time, some of which may not need to be there or have outlived their purpose. As Keri Butler (2016), deputy director at the Public Design Commission, stated, "The street can get really cluttered at a subconscious level, and coordination is really important. We need to understand the street and what our goals are." Wendy Feuer (2016), assistant commissioner of urban design, art, and wayfinding at the DOT, suggests a coordinated mapping effort across agencies to help identify all of the current assets and build a strategic organizing principle for the streetscape.

DESIGN: Engaging the Creative Sector: Moment of Opportunity

Crucial to LinkNYC's success was a finessed understanding of the converging social and political forces at play. DoITT understood that access to high-speed, affordable Internet service was no longer a luxury but a requirement for New Yorkers to function adequately in the modern world. Broadband provides communication about city services—including public health, transportation, and social services—and access to broadband can be lifesaving during emergencies. Broadband access also provides an opportunity for jobs and education and supports an active and participatory democracy (New York City Comptroller 2014a).

At the same time, DoITT also took advantage of a timely change in administration. In 2014, New York City transitioned from the Bloomberg to the de Blasio administration. The new mayor embraced the Payphone of the Future concept. Running on a platform of equity and inclusion, de Blasio saw its

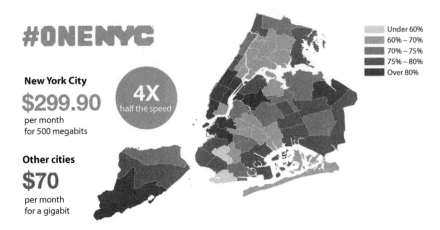

FIGURE 3.3 Percent of households with broadband access.

Source: New York City Comptroller 2014b.

potential to help close the digital divide in New York City in support of his new OneNYC plan to provide every resident and business with access to affordable, reliable, high-speed broadband service everywhere by 2025 (see figure 3.3) (NYC Information Technology & Telecommunications 2016a). While people in cities across the country and around the world spend less than $70 per month for a one-gigabit connection, the top speed available for most people in New York City is only half that (500 megabits), at a cost that is more than four times higher ($299.99 a month) (New York City Comptroller 2014b). De Blasio requested a quick timetable for a competitive RFP to repurpose payphone infrastructure with free Wi-Fi, phone calls, and advertising.

Excited to define the cutting edge of smart city infrastructure, a newly formed consortium called CityBridge answered the call. They saw the RFP as an opportunity to redesign and reinvent the city and provide public broadband in ways no other city had done previously. Their winning LinkNYC concept framed the city as a responsive computing platform, with physical devices on streets acting as an input/output layer for the city. Each "Link" would offer network activity as well as direct output on screens that was customizable to the communication needs of specific neighborhoods. CityBridge was awarded a twelve-year franchise for its innovative and community-first approach and its strong blend of expertise in the requisite areas of technology, media, user experience, and connectivity (NYC Office of the Mayor 2014). Shor (2016) noted that the CityBridge proposal offered services that went above and beyond the RFP, including gigabit Wi-Fi, free phone service nationwide, and an iconic design.

Learnings

Galvanize leadership from the top. The de Blasio administration provided a catalytic force for the new payphone franchise. It is often easy for one agency to obtain approval from above for a new project, but it is more difficult to coordinate across agencies around implementation. The new mayor's office quickly stepped in to ensure the process moved from approval to implementation in a timely fashion.

Design the right mix of expertise. A revolutionary project of this nature requires a strong team of professionals with the experience to handle innovation in the telecommunications space. Led by veteran payphone-franchise administrator, Stanley Shor, the city's team was able to guide the process forward by avoiding previous challenges with telecommunication street furniture, such as vandalism and high maintenance costs. Control Group, a design firm with expertise in mediated screens on MTA platforms, and Titan, the city's largest payphone advertiser, had initially collaborated on a submission for the design competition; named one of six finalists, they later formed CityBridge to apply for the competitive RFP. The design competition served to help the creative sector organize the right strategic partnerships in preparation for the official RFP process.

Stakeholder Alignment (2014–Ongoing)

A revolutionary project at unprecedented scale, LinkNYC was charged with an ambitious timeline to launch. CityBridge, comprised of several key partners including Intersection (design and media), Qualcomm (wireless technologies), and Civic Smartscapes (hardware manufacturing), required a climate of collaboration and an ecosystem of support among key stakeholders. From the beginning, the partners engaged in an inclusive process with community leaders, grassroots organizations, city agencies, businesses, technology companies, developers, and other civic leaders.

They designed and hosted gatherings in key neighborhoods and aligned with community-based organizations, such as Silicon Harlem, to work on a common vision of bringing broadband where it is needed most. The meticulously designed product and careful plan to find influencers and advocates for each constituent group paid off. DoITT won approval from the Franchise and Concession Review Committee in 2014 despite political wrangling, turbulent press, and a lawsuit from a competitor.

CityBridge has also prided itself on supporting the New York City creative economy through the creation of local employment in the media and technology sectors (see figure 3.4). Intersection took measures to intentionally staff the

LinkNYC FTE Employment, 2016

Employer	Direct	Indirect	Induced	Total
CityBridge	100	25	45	170
NYC-based vendors	250	80	115	445
Total	350	105	160	615

LinkNYC Employment Multiplier, 2016

Every 1 direct job of CityBridge and local vendors = Supports 1.8 total jobs in New York City

FIGURE 3.4 Employment snapshot.

Source: CityBridge.

project with particular attention to women and the underserved. In an ongoing partnership with Per Scholas, a local employment organization, they hired people from underrepresented communities in the city to bring various design perspectives to the process. Angie Kamath, executive vice president for social ventures at Per Scholas, attributes the company's initial success to designing inclusion into the organization itself.

Learnings

Design stakeholder engagement around an audacious goal. Good partners are the key to success in any project (see table 3.1). Politics handled by the de Blasio administration focused on lining up the interests of every player involved and orienting them around a shared end goal rather than discrete business terms. They also encouraged a willingness to iterate and learn among the team. As Colin O'Donnell (2016), chief innovation officer at Intersection, stated, "Be passionate about goal and flexible how you get there. Getting people behind a common vision and moving everyone forward is the hardest part of the work."

Design equity into the process. Find ways to build diversity and inclusion throughout the project. Hire from the communities that will benefit from your service, and empower those communities with a sense of ownership to customize the product in ways that serve them best. CityBridge hopes neighborhoods will eventually create inputs and outputs of its Links that are relevant to their local area.

Key Stakeholders

Given the size and scope of the projects, LinkNYC required strategic interfacing and planning among a suite of partners and stakeholders. Table 3.1 and figure 3.5 illustrate how the CityBridge consortium structured itself to leverage expertise, competencies, and stakeholder experience across various facets of the work.

TABLE 3.1 The LinkNYC Organization Structure

Stakeholder name	Description	Roles played	Interest in the program/incentives needed to engage
Intersection (core team)	*A merger between Titan and Control Group*	Titan: brings expertise in operations and advertising	Titan: relevant experience—was one of the largest NYC payphone franchisees
	Titan: The country's leading transit-media company and a large and experienced payphone franchisee working with municipalities		
	Control Group: A NYC-native technology, strategy, and user-experience design firm	Control Group: brings expertise in exceptional technology and user-experience design for all New Yorkers	Control Group: relevant experience— developed the interactive digital Wayfinding system with the MTA
Qualcomm (core team)	A world leader in Wi-Fi, 3G, 4G, and next-generation wireless technologies	Serves as technology adviser on wireless connectivity technology, to help ensure the LinkNYC network stays abreast with the latest developments in applicable communications technology	Fits into Qualcomm's smart-cities strategy to help municipalities reimagine city infrastructure and how to use technology to do more with less
Civic Smartscapes (formally Comark) (core team)	Specializes in the design and manufacture of interactive hardware solutions that withstand rugged environments	Designs, engineers, and manufactures the Links to create durable, robust, and reliable structures	Relevant experience— previously worked with Control Group on the MTA Wayfinding system

(continued)

TABLE 3.1 *(Continued)*

Stakeholder name	Description	Roles played	Interest in the program/incentives needed to engage
Antenna Design (extended team)	Award-winning NYC-based industrial-design team specializing in people-centered design	Responsible for the iconic physical design of the Link	Relevant experience—previously worked with Control Group on the MTA Wayfinding system
ZenFi (extended team)	NYC-based; the city's premier provider of connectivity and colocation delivered over a private dedicated fiber-optic network	Responsible for building out the LinkNYC fiber network infrastructure	The opportunity to build a network of neighborhood fiber networks, for neighborhoods to have their own fiber colocation facility, reducing fiber-cable congestion and prohibitive installation costs across the city
Per Scholas (community partner)	A nonprofit that provides tuition-free technology training to unemployed or underemployed adults for careers as IT professionals	Provides IT training and LinkNYC employment opportunities for residents from underrepresented communities in the city	The opportunity to connect residents from underserved communities to cutting-edge IT jobs in the city
Silicon Harlem (community partner)	A Harlem-based company providing leadership in sustainable, technology-led, economic development for emerging urban communities	Partnered with Intersection to prototype and test iterations of Link designs with local residents	The opportunity to bring digital technology to the masses in Harlem and transform the neighborhood into a technology and innovation hub
NYC public	NYC residents and tourists	LinkNYC audience and users	The opportunity to obtain high-speed broadband access for free

Source: NYC Information Technology & Telecommunications 2016b.

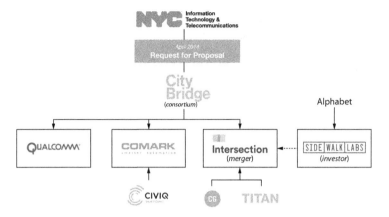

FIGURE 3.5 CityBridge consortium behind LinkNYC.

Source: Wikipedia 2016.

Design Overview

Business Model

- LinkNYC brings free, super-fast Wi-Fi to New York City.
- It is paid for by advertising revenue without using a dime of taxpayer dollars.
- Its groundbreaking digital OOH advertising network offers location-based, targeted advertising for small businesses and larger companies alike.
- LinkNYC advertisements are expected to generate a minimum of $500 million for the city over the first twelve years (LinkNYC 2016).
- The city directs more than $10 million of those revenues per year toward improving broadband access in the city (Shor 2016).

Broadband

- Each gigabit Link is powered by an all-new, purpose-built fiber-optic network that delivers speeds up to 100 times faster than average public Wi-Fi.
- CityBridge is investing more than $200 million to lay hundreds of miles of new fiber-optic cable that will deliver gigabit connectivity to Links in all five boroughs.

- Each Link can support hundreds of Wi-Fi users simultaneously.
- A total of 7,500 Link kiosks will be installed across all five boroughs over the next six years. CityBridge will also bring gigabit service to an indoor public center in each borough for New Yorkers to access educational opportunities and connect to their communities.
- LinkNYC offers an encrypted public Wi-Fi network for protection of personal data.
- New York City and CityBridge have created a customer-first privacy policy.

Hardware

- Links offer two 55-inch HD displays for digital advertising and public-service announcements.
- Every Link is also equipped with a dedicated 911 call button for direct access to a 911 emergency operator.
- Links include opt-in location services with Bluetooth beacon technology. Like GPS, beacons send one-way signals from Links to mobile devices of users who have chosen to receive them.
- Each Link features two free USB power-only charging ports to charge devices.
- Each Link is built to withstand extreme heat and cold, rain, snow, flooding, earthquakes, vandalism, and theft—all while conforming to ADA standards.
- Links also have the ability to include sensors to support the provision of Wi-Fi and phone services.
- Links provide more room on the sidewalk with Link's sleek, ADA-compliant physical design by Antenna.

Software

- From the Vonage app on the tablet, New Yorkers and visitors can make free phone calls to anywhere in the United States, including access to 311 and 411, using directional speakers or headphones.
- International phone calls can be made using calling cards.
- Links provide access to city services, maps, and directions from the tablet.
- Additional apps and services will be rolled out over the course of the franchise.

DEVELOP: Connecting the Community: Infrastructure Mapping (2015–Ongoing)

After contract approval from the FCRC, CityBridge began the product-development phase. One of the first steps was to figure out how and where Links could be deployed and create a plan for installing them strategically across the city. The city created a map of payphone locations using precise coordinates and shared them in Open Data in 2014, which was available during the RFP process. However, these locations are not always exact, and each location must again be confirmed by both CityBridge and DoITT during the construction process. In June 2016, the Landmark Preservation Commission amended its rules to allow the installation of Links in historic districts with further restrictions that needed to be taken into account when planning deployment routes.

CityBridge applied various filters on their maps to remove disqualified sites, such as protected streets (streets that had been reconstructed within the previous eighteen months) and vaults or basements under sidewalks (sites must be at least twelve inches deep). From there, they mapped fiber routes along the areas with the highest population density that also connected a viable number of remaining Link sites. Because highly commercial fiber routes subsidize the fiber routes in poorer neighborhoods, it is challenging to design a plan that balances economic viability, equity, desirability, and structural feasibility. The year-one maps were sent to the city for approval but were subsequently revised more than once.

Learnings

Build in extra time. New York City's public payphone infrastructure dates back more than fifty years. The network has expanded and contracted over time, and documentation of the changes in infrastructure over the decades can be difficult or impossible to locate. Foreseeing challenges in citywide infrastructure mapping can help create more accurate timelines or easier workarounds for franchisees.

Design Prototyping (2015–Ongoing)

While CityBridge devised an installation plan, the design team at Intersection tested and refined initial design prototypes. Typically, a design process spends considerable time understanding the end users and tailoring an approach to them. In this case, with such a diverse group of users, the team was presented with an interesting challenge of designing a product that had to appeal to literally everyone. As a way to tackle this, they focused first on what was there previously, such as contact emergency services, phone calls, and Wi-Fi, as well as compliance measures such as the Americans with Disabilities Act and siting requirements. They then designed a beta minimum viable offering that could be continuously iterated and improved upon over time to maximize the user experience.

Early on in their design research, the team met with marginalized communities to learn about what was working and not working in their neighborhoods and how design could play a role. They organized meet-ups with partner community organizations such as Silicon Harlem, Per Scholas, and Older Adults Technology Services (OATS) to prototype and test iterations of Link designs with locals. The process uncovered important insights, such as a desire to make all services available in multiple languages, simplifying the Wi-Fi login steps, and ensuring the designs look more like media machines than surveillance machines.

Later in the design process, Intersection also created street teams from marginalized communities to conduct user ethnography and education campaigns in the neighborhoods where Links were installed. This served to provide education and feedback for the community, but also to build a pipeline of talent that could eventually work inside Intersection at the support desk, as software testers, etc. All street-team members know their feedback flows directly back to the design department at Intersection and has a potential impact on the success of the project. As Tiernan Walsh (2016) at Per Scholas explains, "Every member of the street team would love to get inside Intersection to be a part of this. You can feel the enthusiasm. It's different than other IT jobs that are more behind the scenes and invisible. Links are so visible and so new. You can see them and talk about them with your kids or friends, so there is an intrinsic and social motivation to get hired." Practices like these have helped catalyze adoption in communities that need it most.

Learnings

Prioritize the community voice and human experience. In any design process, it is important to have a clear understanding of the needs and desires of users. Do we know enough of what people want to use a product for? Engaging in user ethnography, prototyping, and testing before a product is built is essential. As Clayton Banks (2016), CEO and founder of Silicon Harlem, stated, "It's important for the community to embrace the concept, because it will push the tech in the right direction. Without incorporating their voice, it will be a great technology for not the right civic reasons."

DELIVER: Activating the Twenty-First-Century Creative City:
Beta Installation (2015–2017)

Innovation assumes obstacles, and only some of these can be anticipated. Marking the beginning of the rollout, the first beta LinkNYC was installed in December 2015. The goal of the beta phase was to unveil a stable product that provided New Yorkers an early opportunity to try out Link's features and provide feedback as additional apps and services are developed during the next several years. Understanding the susceptibility of digital networks, Intersection focused heavily on hacking security and building a stable product out of the starting gate.

They encountered regular installation issues in the early stages of rollout. For instance, a Verizon strike blocked manhole access for the LinkNYC installation team, the holiday construction embargo in Manhattan slowed work on key avenues, and street-paving schedules delayed fiber cable laying along key fiber routes for months. Many of these hurdles required constant back-and-forth with various city agencies.

As a result, the installation timeline agreed to in the initial franchise contract was not met. In some ways, this was not entirely surprising given the groundbreaking nature of this project. While the CityBridge team may have underestimated the construction-permitting realities that accompany large-scale urban projects, the team adapted quickly to the initial hurdles and is now well underway to successfully connecting Links across the city.

Learnings

Overestimate the complexity. CityBridge devoted a lot of time and planning to get the first Link into the ground. This was important, but the bigger challenge was establishing a process to get ten, twenty, or fifty Links into the ground every week. Most of the hurdles were uncovered in the repetition. Spend time up front and start conversations with the city permitting agency early to devise a plan for the long-term complexity, seasonal nature, and uncertainty of ongoing installation.

Streamline the permitting process. Many of the installation hurdles were due to the complexities of coordinating with the city's permitting agencies. A well-coordinated permitting process can make it easier for the franchisee to submit and update completed applications or line up construction with city street-paving schedules. Additionally, installing a seasoned permitting point person at the franchisee early on could help smooth the submission process and avoid duplicative efforts or missing materials.

Use Data (2016–Ongoing)

In spite of the rollout realities, initial public reactions to the first Links were largely positive, and broadband use has far exceeded expectations. CityBridge was surprised by the creative ways in which people were using them. Street teams documented people using the Wi-Fi to throw dance parties on the street or even using the power outlet on the Link to boil coffee. They discovered early on that people were generally using Links for longer stretches—on average three minutes—than expected.

They began receiving complaints about people loitering in front of Links and clogging sidewalks while charging their phones (see figure 3.6). A city agency was concerned about kids sitting on cars and hovering around Links to use the Wi-Fi. As Claudia Herasme (2016) from the Department of City Planning stated, this has raised larger questions about comfort in public space. Are Links changing people's behaviors and creating mini parks on city sidewalks? How can the user claim space and feel protected while also respecting passersby? How would these behaviors change if people had access to reliable Internet everywhere? Intersection has been exploring implications of convergence—single versus multiple use and short versus long sessions—as they iterate on the design.

Another unexpected phenomenon was the development of what has been described as homeless encampments around Links (Kanno-Youngs 2016).

FIGURE 3.6 Unexpected encampments around Link.

Source: Kevin O'Neil.

When Intersection explored potential scenarios of misuse in their design research, they did not consider people commandeering Links for weeks at a time. While there has been large public outcry around the home-less-encampment issue, a key premise of the LinkNYC project is to provide broadband to everyone. At one point, Nick Colvin (2016), interim head of product at Intersection, approached a man who identified himself as homeless using a Link. He explained how transformative this access had been in his life. He did not own a phone, and Links were the only way to communicate with his family outside of public library hours. In the end, local communities had a largely critical stance on this issue, giving the city and CityBridge clear direction to adjust the project features.

Perhaps one of the most egregious misuses of the Link tablet during this time was the attempts to access pornography through the web browser. This raised the question of public browser behavior. How can you filter content or nudge people toward positive screen uses, such as job searches, instead of music or other videos? The city and CityBridge eventually decided to remove the web browser from the Link tablet in September 2016. Since then, both entities have seen a dramatic decrease in community complaints of loitering or inappropriate public behavior near Links.

Learnings

Design for the street experience as well as individual users. With the quick development and deployment timetable (see figure 3.7), Intersection did not conduct a live street-level prototyping phase. In a public infrastructure project, use goes beyond the individual technology experience and affects behavior and experience of people in the entire streetscape. It is important to understand what people desire in a collective infrastructure experience as well as for their individual needs. Thoughtfully designing for both considerations is important from the outset. For instance, is designing for short-term usage more desirable, or does phone-charging capability make more sense on park benches than on Links? How can you bring out more creative uses of public space by fostering the right behaviors versus the less optimal behaviors?

Revisit the franchise regularly. With communication infrastructure projects of this scale, it is useful for the city and the vendor to regularly review, modify, and iterate on the design over time. Claudia Herasme (2016) from the Department of City Planning suggests that feedback loops are key, not only to reassess the technology but also to reassess the physical design and build a revision process into the contract. It is important to think through and even role-play what success even means, or what those extremes are. Embracing the X factor and

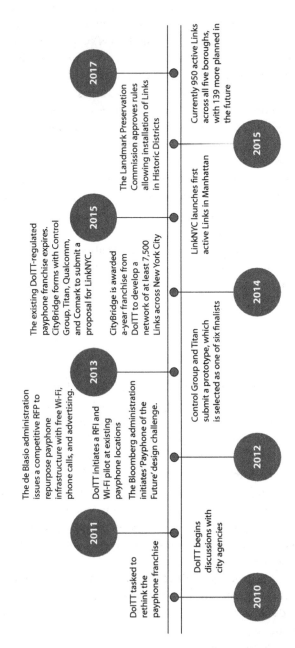

FIGURE 3.7 LinkNYC timeline.

remaining adaptable to expectations throughout the process can open up new and unexpected possibilities.

Design to encourage true collaboration. There is an inevitable culture difference between the public and private sectors. As Jen Hensley (2016), general manager of LinkNYC at Intersection, states, "Government has to retain its important oversight function, but where they can make processes smoother or quicker, where they can prioritize projects that will have a bigger impact, where they can make sure agencies are working together, and not at odds, they will be able to better foster that climate of collaboration." A good partnership requires the willingness to be flexible and the ability to strike a balance between agility and stability that successful public/private partnerships exhibit. It also requires both sides to work through problems together and stay united in the press, rather than blame sides for not meeting expectations. It is the difference between a vendor relationship and a true partnership.

Results and Impact

As of this writing, LinkNYC has celebrated its two-year anniversary on New York City streets and reached more than two million users across the system (Fasoldt 2016). While it would be premature to draw any definitive conclusions, adoption rates have exceeded initial projections. Soon after launch, CityBridge measured the penetration of LinkNYC in the public consciousness (see "LinkNYC by the Numbers"). Using a third-party perception survey conducted by Sachs Insights, they learned that New Yorkers from all boroughs have already come to know and enjoy LinkNYC.

This poses a larger question about measuring the long-term impact of LinkNYC on New York City life without compromising privacy. Currently, LinkNYC only requires email information when users sign up for LinkNYC. Though CityBridge owns the data outright, it ensures that all data are only analyzed in an anonymized and aggregate form—for instance, to measure login data by time of day or location. To date, the city's most popular Link stands in Herald Square (at 699 Seventh Avenue); it serves more than 400,000 Wi-Fi sessions each month all by itself (LinkNYC 2016).

While it is beyond the city's scope and obligation to track specific use data, LinkNYC provides an interesting opportunity to measure the increase in broadband access across New York City. How can LinkNYC measure its reach into key demographics? CityBridge has already recognized that tablet use is extremely popular in the Bronx, so geographic location of specific Links can over time help determine if underserved communities are lit up in ways they never were before.

LinkNYC by the Numbers

LinkNYC use (as of July 20, 2017)

- Total Wi-Fi subscribers: 2,027,640
- New Wi-Fi signups per week: 40,000–50,000
- Wi-Fi sessions per week: 8,500,000
- Data downloaded by LinkNYC users since launch: 1,820 TB
- Busiest day by users: January 4, 2017: 125,756 unique users
- Busiest day by data transferred: December 31, 2016: 4,656 GB

LinkNYC penetration (from November 2016)
Of more than one thousand New York residents surveyed, 71% are aware of LinkNYC, and of those:

- 92% believe it has positive benefits for New York City.
- 78% have a favorable opinion of the network.
- 89% believe LinkNYC makes New York more innovative than other cities.
- 89% appreciate that LinkNYC's services are free thanks to advertising, which reaches more than 11 million people weekly.

Source: LinkNYC 2016.

Strengths, Weaknesses, Opportunities, Threats

In reviewing the incubation and development of the LinkNYC franchise, four main factors emerge as contributing to its early successes:

- City leadership: a veteran and visionary DoITT assistant commissioner whose influence helped to align agency partners to rethink city telecommunications infrastructure and the agency's franchise model
- Intrapreneurship: DoITT's willingness to experiment with a new franchise-contracting process in the form of a design challenge to help bring fresh ideas to the table
- Creative talent: an invitation to the local creative sector to participate in the design challenge by submitting innovative proposals and business models
- Collaboration: a stipulation that the winning proposal include the critical competencies and partnerships required to design, develop, and deploy such an unprecedented franchise

Strengths	Weaknesses
DoITT point person with over a decade of experience overseeing the payphone franchise	Lack of interagency streetscape strategic planning
Creative sector participation through the Design Challenge	Infrastructure mapping and installation hiccups
Franchisee strategic partnership with the right breadth of competencies and expertise for the transformative project	Short street-level design prototyping and testing phase
Interagency collaboration from the onset of the RFI process	Franchisee with insufficient experience in NYC construction and permitting
Early and ongoing stakeholder engagement with community groups	Broadband penetration is limited to the streetscape and second-floor building levels.

Opportunities	Threats
Reduction in underserved populations without access to broadband Wi-Fi	Unintended use and/or lack of public acceptance of LinkNYC
NYC regarded as an innovator in free public communication infrastructure	Privacy and security concerns with free public Wi-Fi network
Range of communication design options from micro-targeted campaigns in neighborhoods to citywide campaigns and cultural initiatives	Speed and complexity of deployment
Redesign of the public advertising model	The potential of less advertising revenue than expected to fund the deployment pace
Free broadband on street-level and second-floor businesses could unlock more entrepreneurial activity in the city	Less revenue could reduce the number of Link deployments in less-lucrative advertising neighborhoods and near populations who need it most

FIGURE 3.8 LinkNYC SWOT analysis.

These success factors, along with the strengths and opportunities listed in figure 3.8, position CityBridge to continue its rapid and responsive deployment of Links throughout the New York City boroughs.

However, as LinkNYC further expands its deployment phase, a key potential threat for the franchise relates to its broadband penetration. Since the City of New York presents LinkNYC as an effort to help bridge the "digital divide" and bring broadband to its residents, integral to LinkNYC's long-term success is its ability to measure those intended impacts and, over time, course-correct to expand and improve the impact of broadband penetration in areas that need it most. Yet this is largely dependent on the franchise's obtaining enough advertising revenue in lucrative advertising locations, or wealthy parts of the city, to support the development of Links in underserved neighborhoods. Finally, LinkNYC does not take into account vertical broadband penetration above second-floor building levels, leaving a large swath of residential and business units out of range of potential free broadband access. There are opportunities for LinkNYC to expand free broadband use beyond public spaces and city streets.

Challenges and Replicability

1. *Infrastructure mapping.* The installation of new fiber cable routes relies on precise historical telecommunications-infrastructure maps that document the changes in infrastructure over the decades. These can often be difficult to obtain.
2. *Equity/revenue tension.* The LinkNYC business model relies on advertising revenue from Link kiosks to support expansion of the network. Therefore, the deployment of Links in underserved neighborhoods is dependent on the success of Links in the more lucrative advertising locations, such as wealthier neighborhoods and commercial districts.
3. *Speed and complexity of deployment.* Innovation is messy. An unprecedented large-scale infrastructure project such as LinkNYC requires buffers in deployment planning and scheduling to allow for the inevitable unanticipated challenges.
4. *Unintended use.* Even with robust early testing, it is hard to predict how new products will be received by their audiences and users. This requires the agility to adapt the designs quickly when necessary.
5. *Public/private partnership.* Managing a franchisor/franchisee relationship as a true collaboration across sectoral partners requires a delicate balance of shared intent, clear expectation, constant communication, and mutual adaptation.
6. *Impact measurement and online privacy.* The potential for data collection from citywide LinkNYC usage provides a wealth of impact measurement and analysis opportunities for the city, as well as obvious broadband security and user privacy issues.
7. *Messaging.* Under New York City's OneNYC campaign to provide every resident with affordable high-speed broadband by 2025, numerous broadband projects have sprouted throughout the city. However, coordinating the strategy and implementation of these projects and their cohesive impact across the five boroughs largely remains a challenge and a missed opportunity for the city.

NYC Advantages

- People generally accept the presence of advertising in public space (which is not the case in all cultures), so an advertising-based revenue model works well in New York City.
- New York City is a very dense urban environment, so there are many eyeballs on advertising and there is enough broadband signal range coverage from Links.
- New York City is renowned for its brand identity and public street culture, which can be tapped into for citywide public advertising campaigns.

- With a strong entrepreneurial culture and creative spirit, Links can be harnessed by people looking to build businesses off Link broadband, advertising, or app services (see chapter 4).
- There is a strong willingness among city agencies to act as a test bed for urban innovations.

NYC Disadvantages

- The city's aging infrastructure and complex underworld makes it hard to lay new cables.
- The dynamic between telecommunication players in New York City is strained.
- A complex city permitting process and inadequate infrastructure maps slow the project down considerably.
- Complexities of street-level operations—traffic, construction, safety, accidents, etc.—make it difficult to install and maintain Links.
- Residents who need access to broadband the most continue to be pushed, by the cost of living, farther out to where the density of old phone booths is less and reaching them with fiber is much more difficult.

Conclusion

Now that the official development and deployment phases have stabilized, the CityBridge team is collecting and sifting through initial data from beta Links. The question is, how can they embrace the unexpected and unlock the full potential of Links? How can the franchise help further expand economic growth, deepen inclusion, and amplify cultural participation across New York City? How can it serve as a model elsewhere as Links expand to London and other cities (Lunden 2016)?

Catalyzing the Infrastructure

LinkNYC has already begun to open up economic opportunities for city residents. As it reaches full deployment, the program expects to support up to 150 new full-time jobs in manufacturing, technology, and advertising, as well as an additional 650 jobs in support services in New York City (NYC Information Technology & Telecommunications 2016b). Beyond that, Links present a myriad of ways for budding entrepreneurs to use LinkNYC to build new businesses. Built on android properties, Link software and the improved accuracy of beacons could allow for a new array of opt-in, useful applications for users, such as job-training programs and targeted hiring or recruitment campaigns for specific neighborhoods, or improved navigation services for people with disabilities.

Telling the Inclusion Story

New York City also has the opportunity to converge its various broadband inclusion initiatives into a powerfully designed long-term strategic plan, and LinkNYC is a transformative cornerstone project. According to Walsh (2016) from Per Scholas, the people who are really getting excited about Links are those who live in communities that historically have not had access. His colleague Angie Kamath (2016) states, "There are about a dozen really cool digital inclusion initiatives happening, including local tech talent initiatives, mesh networks, and Wi-Fi library pilots that lend to 10,000 users across the library system, not to mention LinkNYC. By connecting the dots and sharing a common agenda, vision, and metrics across city agencies, the city can tell a better story around inclusion that galvanizes and delivers for all city residents."

Activating the Cultural Potency

Technology is a tool. Tools should serve the purpose for which they were designed. Innovators need to ask, "What behaviors do we want to encourage or discourage? What values do we want to reinforce?" The power of creative cities is their ability to intentionally design community-using technology as a facilitator, not as the end goal. How can LinkNYC infrastructure enable and embed intentional values in our city? The city's new network of Links can help New Yorkers connect with one another better and even communicate as a single city. Its immediate feedback loops amplify a common New York City pride. Whether as culture hubs that create safe and inviting gathering points as a kind of third space in the city, as local-community information hubs displaying a marathon route through Queens or a parade route through Harlem, or as culture mash-ups that offer artists in residence digital displays as canvases for community arts projects, LinkNYC has the ability to thread creativity and inclusion into the social fabric of the city.

Looking Forward: Amplifying the Impact

New York City is constantly redesigning itself. As cities try to keep pace with global innovation and growth, they look for new ways to catalyze industries and update aging physical infrastructure. Conversations around infrastructure modernization are more pertinent now than ever in light of the 2016 U.S. presidential election. In an unprecedented project, CityBridge and the City of New York have illustrated how an innovative franchise model can build much-needed twenty-first-century municipal communications infrastructure without costing a dime to taxpayers.

City innovation is never perfect. Just as Broadway shows test off-Broadway first before they premiere on the bigger stage, transformative urban infrastructure projects of this magnitude require enormous creativity and adaptability to navigate uncharted territory. They also require a public/private partnership focused on deep collaboration and community engagement. With DoITT guidance, CityBridge stepped up to the plate and took on an extraordinarily ambitious project by activating the city's creative potential.

As this case study shows, successful creative cities not only use technology to engage and enliven, they also use technological innovation to intentionally shape the attitudes and values that make up the city fabric. The real innovation of LinkNYC is that its design enables it to harness the creative economy for better citizen services, urban growth, *and* cultural enrichment. It is a model for other cities hoping to turn infrastructure upgrades into thriving cultures of inclusion for the twenty-first-century city.

Note

The authors wish to thank Ruth Fasoldt (Intersection) and Stanley Shor (DoITT), who were critical allies in the development of this report. The authors also wish to thank the following people, who were kind enough to answer questions and provide feedback on early versions of this case study: Clayton Banks (Silicon Harlem), Corrine Brown (Intersection), Keri Butler (NYC Public Design Commission), Nick Colvin (Intersection), Colin O'Donnell (Intersection), Daniel Engelmann (Intersection), Wendy Feuer (DOT), Jen Hensley (Intersection), Claudia Herasme (NYC Department of City Planning), Angie Kamath (Per Scholas), Stacey Levine (Intersection), Tiernan Walsh (Per Scholas).

References

Badger, Emily. 2013. "How New York Is Reinventing the Phone Booth." *Atlantic*, May. http://www.theatlantic.com/magazine/archive/2013/05/immobile-phones/309291/.
Banks, Clayton. 2016. Interview by author. Transcript. New York, September 2.
Butler, Keri. 2016. Interview by author. Transcript. New York, September 16.
Colvin, Nick. 2016. Interview by author. Transcript. New York, August 30.
Fasoldt, Ruth. 2016. Interview by author. Transcript. New York, July 25.
Feuer, Wendy. 2016. Interview by author. Transcript. New York, September 16.
Hensley, Jen. 2016. Interview by author. Transcript. New York, September 5.

Herasme, Claudia. 2016. Interview by author. Transcript. New York, October 13.

Kamath, Angie. 2016. Interview by author. Transcript. New York, August 24.

Kanno-Youngs, Zolan. 2016. "New York City's Wi-Fi Plan Faces Delays, Criticism." *Wall Street Journal*, July 22. http://www.wsj.com/articles/new-york-citys-wi-fi-plan-faces-delays-criticism-1469234058.

LinkNYC. 2016. "Free Super Fast Wi-Fi. And That's Just the Beginning." Accessed October 15, 2016. https://www.link.nyc/.

Lunden, Ingrid. 2016. "LinkNYC's Free WiFi and Phone Kiosks Hit London as LinkUK, in Partnership with BT." TechCrunch, October 25. Accessed November 6, 2016. https://techcrunch.com/2016/10/25/linknycs-free-wifi-and-phone-kiosks-hit-london-as-linkuk-in-partnership-with-bt/.

New York City Comptroller. 2014a. "Comptroller Stringer Report Reveals the Scope of Internet Inequality in New York City." December 7, 2014. Accessed November 12, 2016. http://comptroller.nyc.gov/newsroom/comptroller-stringer-report-reveals-the-scope-of-internet-inequality-in-new-york-city/.

——. 2014b. "Internet Inequality: Broadband Access in NYC." December 2014. Accessed November 12, 2016. https://comptroller.nyc.gov/wp-content/uploads/documents/Internet_Inequality.pdf.

New York City Independent Budget Office. 2013. "New York City Public Payphones: How Many Are Left?" October 21, 2013. Accessed November 6, 2016. http://ibo.nyc.ny.us/cgi-park2/2013/10/new-york-city-public-payphones-how-many-are-left/.

NYC Information Technology & Telecommunications. 2016a. "Broadband." Accessed November 6, 2016. https://www1.nyc.gov/site/doitt/initiatives/broadband.page.

——. 2016b. "LinkNYC: Say Goodbye to the Payphone." Accessed November 6, 2016. https://www1.nyc.gov/site/doitt/initiatives/linknyc.page.

——. 2016c. "Pay Phones." Accessed November 6, 2016. https://www1.nyc.gov/site/doitt/residents/pay-phones.page.

NYC Office of the Mayor. 2014. "De Blasio Administration Announces Winner of Competition to Replace Payphones with Five-Borough Wi-Fi Network." November 17, 2014. Accessed November 6, 2016. http://www1.nyc.gov/office-of-the-mayor/news/923-14/de-blasio-administration-winner-competition-replace-payphones-five-borough.

O'Donnell, Colin. 2016. Interview by author. Transcript. New York, July 28.

Pollicino, Joe. 2013. "NYC Awards Six Reinvent Payphones Finalists, Asks Public to Select Favorite via Facebook," Engadget, March 6. Accessed November 6. https://www.engadget.com/2013/03/06/nyc-reinvent-payphones-finalists/.

Shor, Stanley. 2016. Interview by author. Transcript. New York, August 9.

Walsh, Tiernan. 2016. Interview by author. Transcript. New York, August 3.

Wikipedia. 2016. "LinkNYC." Accessed December 12, 2016. https://en.wikipedia.org/wiki/LinkNYC.

PART II

CITY SERVICES AND
DOMAINS OF LIFE

CHAPTER 4

THE NEW YORK CITY BUSINESS ATLAS

Leveling the Playing Field for Small Businesses with Open Data

ANDREW YOUNG, *New York University*

STEFAAN VERHULST, *New York University*

Executive Summary

While retail entrepreneurs, particularly those operating in the small-business space, are experts in their respective trades, they often lack access to high-quality information about social, environmental, and economic conditions in the neighborhoods where they operate or are considering operating. The New York City Business Atlas, conceived by the Mayor's Office of Data Analytics (MODA) and the Department of Small Business Services, is designed to alleviate that information gap by providing a public web-based tool that gives small businesses access to high-quality data to help them decide where to establish a new business or expand an existing one. The tool brings together a diversity of data, including business-filing data from the Department of Consumer Affairs, sales-tax data from the Department of Finance, demographic data from the census, and traffic data from Placemeter, a New York City startup focusing on real-time traffic information.

The initial iteration of the Business Atlas made useful and previously inaccessible data available to small-business owners and entrepreneurs in an innovative manner. After a few years, however, it became clear that the tool was not experiencing the level of use or creating the level of demonstrable impact anticipated. Rather than continuing down the same path or abandoning the effort entirely, MODA pivoted to a new approach, moving from the Business Atlas as a single information-providing tool to the Business Atlas as a suite of capabilities aimed at bolstering New York's small-business community.

Through problem- and user-centered efforts, the Business Atlas is now mak-ing important insights available to stakeholders who can put it to meaningful use—from how long it takes to open a restaurant in the city to which areas are most in need of education and outreach to improve their code compliance. This chapter considers the open data environment from which the Business Atlas was launched, details the initial version of the Business Atlas and the lessons it generated, and describes the pivot to this new approach.

Key Takeaways

- Data-driven government initiatives benefit from partnerships and collab-orations both with other government actors and with private businesses. MODA's work on the Business Atlas (and other initiatives) is more targeted as a result of collaborations with domain experts in city agencies like Small Business Services. Additionally, the use of the startup Placemeter's data in the initial version of the Business Atlas is an example of a "data collaborative"—a new form of collaboration, beyond the traditional public/private partnership model, in which multisector participants exchange data to solve public prob-lems (Verhulst and Sangokoya 2015).
- Although a large number of early-stage open data projects around the world focus on simply pushing information out, the next stage should revolve around a targeted, user-centered release. In the example discussed in this chapter, the Business Atlas offerings consistently grew more user-centered, moving beyond the simple provision of information toward a targeted suite of data-driven capabilities aimed at addressing the biggest challenges faced by the New York small-business community.
- The sharp change in focus for the Business Atlas after its initial launch dem-onstrates the importance of agility in city-level open data projects. After the Business Atlas was launched in 2013, MODA determined that the "if you build it will they come" approach was not having the intended impact on the city's business community—or if it was creating such an impact, they could not meaningfully measure it. Rather than abandoning the project or contin-uing down the same path, MODA pivoted to an entirely new approach for achieving the same goal: arming New York small-business owners with the data-driven tools that can help them succeed.

Theoretical Background, Contextual Environment, and Problem Definition

In recent years, there has been growing recognition that life in cities is being transformed by data. From Chicago to London to Singapore, city administrators and planners are turning to data to help plan the future and address mundane, everyday issues like potholes and waste collection. Underlying such trends is an awareness of the vast amounts of data being generated (often passively) in urban centers, through devices like smartphones and sensors. In the words of the *Economist*, cities today are "open-air computers" and "data factories" ("Open-Air Computers" 2012).

In 2002, Michael Bloomberg assumed office as the 108th mayor of New York City. Bloomberg had made his fortune providing data and sophisticated analytics to financial traders. It was probably inevitable that, under his administration, New York would join the many cities around the world seeking to extract greater value from the terabytes of data being created every day by their citizens.

As discussed in chapter 2, in 2013, through Executive Order No. 306, New York City created the Mayor's Office of Data Analytics (MODA). The stated goal of the office was "leveraging City data for more effective, efficient, and transparent government" (Flowers 2013). Bill de Blasio, who became the 109th mayor of New York in 2014, replacing Mayor Bloomberg, has continued the city's work on open data initiatives.

Today the Mayor's Office of Data Analytics comprises a team of analysts, based in City Hall, who collect and analyze data from a wide variety of sources. Among other areas, MODA works on crime prevention, disaster response, improvement of public services, and economic development. MODA also played a key role in setting up New York's Open Data portal (figure 4.1; https:// opendata.cityofnewyork.us/), which houses more than 1,700 data sets related

FIGURE 4.1 New York City's Open Data portal.

to health, business, public safety, and much more. In addition, MODA helped establish DataBridge, a single, unified repository of information that aims to enhance data-sharing and interoperability among various New York City organizations (Yasin 2013). The de Blasio administration passed two laws in 2014 dedicated to transparency, essentially announcing a "public partnership that will enable NYC to unlock and analyze municipal decision-making information stored in the City Record" (NYC Office of the Mayor 2014). In July 2015, the city released its updated "Open Data for All" strategy document (City of New York 2015), which focuses on two central "beliefs": that every New Yorker can benefit from open data, and that open data can benefit from every New Yorker.

Because of these and other efforts, New York City is generally considered a leader in open data initiatives in the United States (itself the fourth-ranked country on the 2017 Open Data Barometer from the World Wide Web Foundation). In particular, MODA, as discussed in more detail in chapter 2, is a pioneering and increasingly emulated entity in the open data ecosystem. It has played an important role not only in releasing open data to increase accountability and innovation, but also in doing analytical work on those data. This work includes measuring the efficiency of city services, providing data-driven predictions, and, as with the Business Atlas, combining high-value data sets from a diversity of sources to provide new insights and capabilities to government agencies and the public.

MODA's analytics efforts, led at the time of writing by New York City's chief analytics officer Amen Ra Mashariki, are deployed to aid disaster response and recovery, improve delivery of city agencies and services, enable data-sharing among city agencies, crystallize best practices in data analysis, and, as evidenced in the case described here, spur economic development (Flowers 2013). Within these domains of focus and types of analytical work, MODA subscribes to four central, overarching goals: improving awareness, measuring success, maximizing impact, and increasing engagement ("NYC MODA Presentation" 2015).

Mike Flowers, Mashariki's predecessor and the first New York City chief analytics officer, described the integral role played by MODA in the city's data operations in an annual report released after MODA's first year of operations:

> Over the last three terms, our agencies have developed information systems that they use to make our streets safer, our businesses vibrant, and our parks cleaner. Through a blend of statistical analysis, engineering skills, and deep investigation of the missions and organizational structure of the agencies—the why, what and how of city government—MODA ties these systems together, enabling the City to tap into our collective knowledge and experience to tackle our thorniest challenges. (Flowers 2013)

According to MODA officials, its mission and projects are focused on the "thorny" challenges at hand for New Yorkers while its efforts are using new analytical capabilities. Lindsay Mollineaux, director of analytics at MODA, for instance, notes that "[addressing real need] is very much how we think about things at MODA—every project is addressing need. We want to make sure what we're doing is useful" (Mollineaux 2015).

Design, Piloting, Development, Implementation

The New York City Business Atlas, initiated in 2013, is part of a broader effort by MODA aimed at "driving small business growth with analytics" (Flowers 2013). Such an initiative fills a clear need for the small-business community in New York City. Commercial rents have risen dramatically in recent years: rent for one café in the West Village rose by $26,000 per month in 2014; another establishment found its rent increased by $20,000. Both businesses have since closed (Wu 2015). This trend is consistent across the city, evidenced by a 2015 report that found that the average commercial rent in Manhattan rose 34% in the decade from 2004 to 2014 (Schlossberg 2015). Increases of this magnitude can be difficult for any business to withstand, but small businesses are less equipped to handle them than large competitors. The Business Atlas was thus designed to help small businesses make more informed decisions and help close the gap between large corporations and smaller entities.

MODA's broader effort toward using data analytics to benefit small businesses also includes the Comprehensive Business Census, which arose in the aftermath of Hurricane Sandy, when the city struggled to assess the storm's full impact on businesses and the economy. Before MODA began working in this area, there existed no comprehensive record of businesses in the city. MODA sought to fill this information gap by working with PLUTO, a database of land use and geographic data, to assemble a more complete picture of businesses and business activity in New York City.

The New York City Business Atlas grew out of a recognition among city officials across agencies and departments that, when it comes to data, large businesses often have an edge over smaller ones. While large businesses can afford to hire expensive consultants and commission data-driven research, smaller businesses must rely on "gut feeling" to make important business decisions, such as where to open a new location or how to navigate regulatory challenges. Mike Flowers explains the advantages held by large businesses: "In many parts of Manhattan, you can't swing a dead cat without hitting a Starbucks. Those guys have robust infrastructure and a capacity to help them figure out two things: a) where to open up in the first place; and b) the piece of this about navigating the regulatory challenges of opening a place" (Flowers 2015). He adds that, for

FIGURE 4.2 New York City Business Atlas with population and demographics sidebar.

small businesses in particular, data paucity is a "chronic" problem, and "probably [has] been chronic since Emperor Augustus was trying to incentivize small business in Rome."

Work on the Business Atlas (figure 4.2) began following a discussion within MODA on how small-business owners often feel under siege from the city government, rather than supported by it. Flowers noted that the city restaurant-rating system, which assigns letter grades to restaurants based on their compliance with health regulations, tends to benefit large chains and restaurants, which typically have "the wherewithal and institutional experience and institutional resources to bake into their infrastructure code compliance" (Flowers 2015). Over its life span, Business Atlas initially pivoted away from this specific inspiration regarding code compliance, but interestingly, compliance has more recently reemerged as a focus for the Business Atlas as a result of a more user-centered approach, discussed below.

In the words of John Feinblatt, chief policy adviser to Mayor Bloomberg, the Business Atlas "democratizes" information, "putting quality research into the hands of small business owners" (Schweidel 2015). It is important to note that much (but not all) of the data included in the Business Atlas already existed—for example, through the city's Open Data portal—and was at least theoretically available to small-business owners. As noted, however, it was often in fragmentary form and lacked the sophisticated analytics and visualization layer contained within the Business Atlas, both of which make the data far more accessible and useful for entrepreneurs. To use the tool, businesspeople visit maps.nyc.gov/businessatlas and select a neighborhood. The app pulls up

FIGURE 4.3 New York City Business Atlas with Placemeter pedestrian activity mapped.

data including population, population distribution by age, median household income, how many households have children, homeowners versus renters, and much more, specific to that neighborhood. Not only is the Business Atlas free to use, but users can also sign up for free training sessions, held in city business centers, to help them derive the most from the tool (Furman 2013).

One of the platform's most important pieces of data is the foot traffic in various neighborhoods. To collect this information, New York partnered with a unique local startup, Placemeter, a self-styled "urban intelligence platform" (Peyre 2015). Placemeter uses cameras (including existing municipal street-traffic cameras and sensor-laden IP cameras) to assess population movement through neighborhoods. The resulting information includes both pedestrian- and vehicular-traffic data (figure 4.3). While much of the analytical work is done algorithmically, Placemeter relies on humans to analyze videos and perform random quality checks of the work being done by the algorithms. The resulting data give businesspeople an indication of prospective customer numbers, thus helping guide location-relevant business decisions.

Although Placemeter's work is an important, if not critical, piece of the Business Atlas, quantifying public spaces could lead to privacy concerns directed at the city down the road. To the credit of both New York City and Placemaker, they have taken specific steps to mitigate crucial privacy concerns by (a) processing video in real time so that less than 0.01% of all video is recorded or stored—and only for processing and quality-assurance purposes and (b) providing only anonymized counts of pedestrians, with no specific identities attached. Former U.S. deputy chief technology officer

Nicole Wong, an accomplished Silicon Valley privacy lawyer, acts as a privacy adviser to the company.

In addition to Placemeter data, the Business Atlas platform incorporates data from a variety of government departments and agencies, including the Department of Consumer Affairs and the Department of Finance (e.g., sales tax information), as well as demographic data from census results. The Atlas supplements these data with information shared by the New York City Department of Health and Mental Hygiene (DOHMH), Business Integrity Commission (BIC), Department of Environmental Protection (DEP), Department of City Planning (DCP), and Department of Buildings (DOB), as well as state and national open data ("NYC MODA Presentation" 2015). In many cases, MODA's task involved combining and analyzing data sets that were already open and accessible to the public through the city's Open Data portal. In other cases, additional effort was required to secure the release of data. Sales-tax data from the Department of Finance, for example, are protected because they include personally identifiable information. In order to include the data in the Atlas, MODA first had to strip away personal information through an anonymization process (Flowers 2015).

In order to combine all the data in a single place, the team creating the Atlas had to overcome several technical and conceptual challenges. For example, while as much information as possible was pulled from the city's DataBridge (described in more detail in chapter 2), issues inevitably arose concerning the compatibility of data sets. Differences between data standards and formats create a major, time-consuming challenge in the effort to combine multiple data streams into one usable tool. In addition, finding accurate data for local businesses proved more challenging than anticipated. As Mollineaux (2015) explained, each industry has its own particular licensing regulations (and some businesses, such as bookstores, have no licensing requirements at all), making it difficult to accurately represent and synthesize local business information across sectors.

Ramping Up User-Centered Design and Targeted Interventions

In addition to the partnership with Placemeter described above, MODA and the Business Atlas leverage partnerships with city agencies to ensure that interventions are targeted at addressing the real needs of city actors and the citizens they serve. MODA's central partner in the Business Atlas effort is the New York City Department of Small Business Services (SBS). As Mollineaux (2015) noted:

> Some of the needed data in designing the Atlas was obvious to us, but the question was what is useful to entrepreneurs versus information overload? SBS served as our subject matter experts who interfaced with actual entrepreneurs (for example, people might come to them about opening a bakery) and could use

the Atlas to directly serve these needs. . . . We always partner with client agencies who are subject matter experts and can help define what success looks like.

Through ethnographic research and interviews, SBS was able to help MODA determine what was most relevant for various types of users. For example, MODA originally focused on displaying some of the business and demographic information as a score for a given geographic location. User feedback, gathered with the assistance of SBS, helped MODA to recognize that, in fact, entrepreneurs would be more interested in less-aggregated data; most business owners wanted the underlying data rather than a one-size-fits-all score (Mollineaux 2015). Rather than a simple score or grade, therefore, the data are now mapped in a disaggregated, "raw" form, allowing users to draw their own conclusions.

In addition to partnering with SBS to supplement the platform's informational base, MODA partnered with the New York City library system to drive use. Research had indicated to MODA that many entrepreneurs rely on their local library to gain insight into how to start a new business. With this audience of potential users in mind, MODA worked with and trained library staff to introduce the platform to potential entrepreneurs and essentially serve as "small business counselors" (Flowers 2015).

Overall, MODA's approach of partnering with different agencies and institutions has proven remarkably fruitful. According to Flowers, it is part of a well-thought-out strategy to ensure the longevity of the Business Atlas. As Flowers (2015) puts it, "You have to get the civil service on board. . . . If you don't have them on board as major participants, then in the next election everything you worked on is gone."

In more recent years, this focus on user-centered design and targeted interventions has greatly accelerated. The online Business Atlas 1.0 platform represented a pathbreaking effort to arm small businesses with the data and data-driven insight needed to thrive in New York City. Following the initial launch of the Atlas and the change in leadership at MODA from Mike Flowers to Amen Ra Mashiriki, the Business Atlas has evolved (figure 4.4) into a more targeted initiative, representing a suite of capabilities, rather than a single, somewhat top-down, information-provision web application. While the flagship online platform still exists, recent efforts at MODA falling under the Business Atlas banner are more focused on directly engaging with city government actors responsible for aiding small businesses and providing them with purpose-built tools and insights to solve their identified challenges.

Mashariki (2017) has described the goal of MODA under his leadership as "consistently user-centered analytics." In an interview with *Motherboard*, he went on to say, "We lead with people and not data. It's all about whom you engage, how you engage them, and what tools you give them with which to respond" (Deleon 2017).

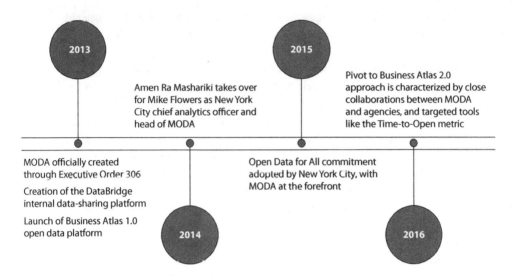

FIGURE 4.4 NYC Business Atlas timeline.

One important example of the new, more targeted Business Atlas approach is the Time-To-Open (TTO) initiative. As part of the Business Atlas suite of activities, MODA is working with SBS to leverage multiple sources of municipal data—some but not all of it formally open data—to calculate the time it takes for new restaurants to open across the city. MODA is also partnering with the Department of Buildings and Department of Housing as the primary data sources for the project.

With a clear understanding of how long it will take to open a new restaurant, actors at SBS can give entrepreneurs a better and more realistic understanding of the time and resources required to open a successful restaurant in the city. While the ultimate beneficiary of this arm of the Business Atlas initiative remains largely the same as in the original version of the Atlas, the TTO effort works through SBS, rather than simply placing the information online and hoping the right people access and use it. As a result, SBS can engage with entrepreneurs through a variety of mechanisms, bringing knowledge and insight to the small-business owner rather than relying on the reverse.

Beyond the goal of enabling SBS to provide useful information to the small-business community, the TTO initiative was formulated in such a way as to provide SBS with a "measuring stick" for the effects of its Small Business First commitments. Small Business First is an "interagency initiative focused on reducing the burden of regulation on small businesses by making it easier for business owners to interact with the City."

The TTO measuring stick provides an initial baseline against which to test the effects of new small-business-focused interventions. TTO represents one of many examples where MODA is leveraging data with an eye toward creating evidence of what actually works in practice.

Also demonstrating the expansion of Business Atlas's user focus, MODA is using data on where health and other business violations are prevalent to target education and compliance outreach. In particular, these data-driven efforts are aimed at identifying areas with a high incidence of violations, particularly in low- and middle-income areas, as well as areas with a high percentage of foreign-born New Yorkers. This effort is aimed not only at benefiting the citizens of those areas by helping increase compliance by businesses in their area, but also at ensuring that outreach and education efforts are targeted at business owners who are more likely to lack relevant information to enable better compliance, rather than those that are simply delinquent or cutting corners.

The education and outreach initiative is another close partnership with SBS. In this line of activity, SBS rather than MODA employs the team responsible for providing support to those business owners that data analytics have shown to be out of compliance. Armed with an understanding of whom to target, SBS's outreach efforts include "direct, one-on-one engagement with business owners, local informational events, and informational guides—all with the goal of helping small businesses better understand City regulations in order to reduce the future incidence of violations" (*Small Business First* n.d.). This arrangement ensures that MODA can focus on what it does best—targeted data analytics—while SBS puts the domain expertise of its staff into action informed by these analytics.

Impact and Results

Over its life span, the Business Atlas has produced benefits for small-business owners in New York City, influenced similar data-driven efforts abroad, and provided a blueprint for problem-focused data initiatives and partnerships. Like many data-driven urban projects around the world, the Business Atlas has benefited from the existence of copious amounts of data, a team of public-minded experts working within government, the agility to change course over time, and a keen focus on user-centered design and development.

Leveling the Playing Field for Market Research

The most important impact of the initial version of Business Atlas is the way in which it levels the playing field between large and small businesses. MODA's 2013 annual report points out: "When a major national retailer looks to open

TABLE 4.1 Key Stakeholder Table

Stakeholder name	Role played	Interest in the program	Positive/negative effect on program	Incentives needed to engage
Mayor's Office of Data Analytics	Project creator	Driving force behind both Business Atlas 1.0 and Business Atlas 2.0	*Positive*: the central actor in the Business Atlas program, providing both strategic and technical expertise	Conforms to MODA's mission to leverage data analytics to improve the lives of New Yorkers, in this case small businesses
Department of Small Business Services	Provides MODA with domain expertise and insight into the needs of the New York City small-business community	Leveraging new tools and capacities provided by MODA to improve its work	*Positive*: especially following the move toward Business Atlas 2.0 with a closer focus on collaboration and more targeted interventions to benefit the business community	Access to new tools and insights to benefit its mission of bolstering the city's small-business community
New York City small businesses and small-business owners	Target audience of the Business Atlas offerings	Access to new insights related to market research, time-to-open, and other information not usually accessible to smaller businesses	*Neutral*: does not appear as though Business Atlas 1.0 reached a large audience of small businesses with its initial web-based platform; the move toward more targeted Business Atlas 2.0 offerings and a focus on collaboration should lead to more engagement and opportunities for the small-business community to provide feedback to MODA	Awareness of the tools and insights on offer through the Business Atlas, and a clear understanding of their operational value

a new storefront, they often commission sophisticated neighborhood market research that helps the company decide where to locate the new business" (Neubauer 2014). That type of research is often too expensive for smaller businesses.

Even when small businesses do have access to data (for example, through public feeds or other sources), they may lack the analytical skills to process and understand it. Here, too, the Business Atlas plays a powerful role, its sophisticated analytics and visualization tools further leveling the playing field between larger and smaller players. At a meeting of municipal chief data officers, Mashariki pointed out the many ways in which such data and analysis can empower small businesses. He cited the example of an entrepreneur approaching a bank for a loan. With the information contained in the Business Atlas, the entrepreneur can make a far more compelling case, backed by real evidence, for the sustainability and potential of the business (*Towards Data Driven Cities* 2015).

Targeted Analytical Insights for the New York City Government

More recently, the effects of the Business Atlas have been felt more directly by the city government itself, with benefits to the citizens of New York to follow. While the initial version of the Business Atlas was focused on providing information to citizens and entrepreneurs, more recent efforts under Mashariki are aimed at getting useful information into the hands of city government actors who can then help improve the city's small-business community.

With information like the Time-To-Open metric and granular insights into areas with low levels of code compliance, MODA is helping the Department of Small Business Services and other business-focused city agencies benchmark their interventions to determine what is truly having an impact on business development in the city and what is not, and thus to direct its outreach and education efforts to the areas where they are likely to have the greatest impact.

More specifically, SBS is using data from the Business Atlas to aid in the analysis of how Business Improvement Districts (BIDs) are fueling economic growth in New York. BIDs are public/private partnerships "in which property and business owners elect to make a collective contribution to the maintenance, development and promotion of their commercial district" (New York City Department of Small Business Services 2003). The data now in place, thanks to the Business Atlas suite of capabilities, will allow SBS to compare BID neighborhoods in terms of economic change, commercial investments, and business activities; this will in turn permit SBS to identify which BIDs have been most effective to date and develop best practices to replicate their success across the city.

The deployment of the Business Atlas to fuel the growth of BIDs, as well as the targeted outreach and education efforts, points to another particular community that stands to benefit from new availability of market-research data: residents of underserved neighborhoods. In addition to the SBS efforts to improve code compliance in low- and middle-income areas and areas with a high percentage of foreign-born New Yorkers, Mashariki has pointed out, "city agencies can also use Business Atlas to address large businesses and show them that there is good reason for them to open locations in neighborhoods which they may have otherwise avoided" (*Towards Data Driven Cities* 2015). Instead of making location-based decisions based purely on intuition (or media-driven biases), companies can now take a closer look at data and find underserved areas that offer a compelling business case. This is just one more way in which the Business Atlas holds potential to level the playing field—for consumers as well as for businesses.

Influencing Data Analytics Innovation in New York and Abroad

MODA's work has had important ripple effects, spurring the development of other similar open data projects. Flowers (2015) notes that the original Business Atlas "certainly has this burst through the wall capacity to show that open data can mean a lot more than simply building a Yelp app." Recently, for example, the Fire Department of New York (FDNY) set up its own analytics unit modeled on MODA's analytics team. The FDNY team's efforts have included the development and use of a Risk Based Inspection System (RBIS), which "enables the Department to identify buildings most at risk for fire and prioritizes those for fire inspections" (Roth 2014). Data are pooled using DataBridge from an FDNY data warehouse and other city databases, including City Planning, Buildings and others (Yasin 2013). In setting up the unit and its analytics platform, FDNY worked directly with MODA, providing an example of a constructive partnership and synergy across city departments (Flowers 2013).

Another example of MODA's ripple effects within the city can be found in a Buildings Department project to manage complaints about illegal building conversions, a "311 City Pulse" program that live-feeds city 311 activities, and a data collection and sharing mechanism on disaster response (Yasin 2014). All of these programs used lessons and principles that had been applied and tested by MODA.

Other cities have also taken notice of New York's open data efforts. The London-based Capital City Foundation has suggested, for instance, that London should look to projects like the Business Atlas in its efforts to become a "smart city." In a 2015 report, the foundation argued:

> If a business wanted to appeal to customers from certain parts of London, data from Transport for London (TfL) shows exactly where people touch in

and touch out of the transport network. Maps can thereby be created showing where people move from and to. This could be helpful to know which tube or bus stops to place a business near. Creating an online tool to make these kinds of data sets available would build on ideas started in New York City. (Copeland 2015)

It is likely that the appetite for similar data-analytics teams will continue to spread, as the lessons learned and best practices from MODA are increasingly shared with innovators and policymakers around the world (Flowers and Talbot 2014). The City of London in 2014 launched a similar-style map with specific information on neighborhood demographics. The respective LSOA and MSOA Atlases' data are available to download as zipped Excel file or viewable as an interactive map in the style of the Business Atlas (Mayor of London and London Assembly n.d.). Although London's maps do not seem to be directly targeted at business owners, much of the same information is provided to researchers: a range of data on population, diversity, households, health, housing, crime, benefits, land use, deprivation, schools, and employment, all of which are useful when starting a business in a new neighborhood.

An initiative similar to the New York City Business Atlas can also be found in Spain, in the form of InATLAS, although there is a crucial difference: InATLAS is a privately developed mobile app that requires registration and a fee. Nevertheless, since 2014 it has offered users the ability to parse through government data within 500 meters of a chosen location, allowing clients to access population breakdowns/demographics, economic status, spending by commodity, and tourist visits alongside likely competitors. Although both London and InATLAS differ from the NYC Business Atlas, it is clear that the goals and interface are quite similar to those first developed by New York— and a sign of the replicability of a data-driven approach to small-business development.

Challenges and Lessons Learned

MODA in general and the Business Atlas in particular represent pathbreaking efforts to improve governance and people's lives in New York City. It's no surprise, then, that the Business Atlas has experienced a number of challenges along the way, and that agility and a willingness to pivot toward new approaches have been paramount for creating a positive impact. Here we discuss some of the key challenges experienced since Business Atlas's launch in 2013, as well as some of the key lessons learned that have helped address those challenges.

Communicating Opportunity and Building a User Base

A tool is only useful if people actually use it. While the initial version of the Business Atlas presented a major opportunity for giving more businesspeople an understanding of the contexts in which they might consider opening a business, communicating that opportunity to the public to widen its use was a central challenge. As Mike Flowers (2015) put it, the original version of the Business Atlas was part of an effort to give (a hypothetical) "Nadine's Burritos" the type of market-research insights and capabilities that have been enjoyed by the likes of McDonald's and Subway for years. But making sure that Nadine—and thousands of small entrepreneurs like her—was aware of the availability of this information was something of a challenge. To that end, awareness-raising and the types of outreach already conducted with city libraries will be essential. In addition, Flowers believes that the creation of an application program interface (API) to enable developers to take the data housed on the Business Atlas and create new apps could also help disseminate the data more widely.

Addressing Technical Challenges

In order to achieve its many ambitions for continuing Business Atlas's transition from an information-providing tool to a robust suite of capabilities, MODA will need to address a number of technical challenges that could serve as stumbling blocks. For example, as noted previously, different types of businesses typically have different licensing requirements. As Mollineaux (2015) points out, this is just one instance of a more general issue—the different "data contexts" that exist for different categories of businesses, and that make it challenging to pull together and meaningfully analyze data from disparate sources.

In the past, MODA has written a number of proprietary algorithms to overcome such difficulties. But challenges remain, and as the agency plans to operationalize more data toward more ends, these challenges could possibly grow. Finding new ways to synthesize and harmonize large sources of data, pulled from different agencies and groups, is one of the key tasks confronting the agency as it seeks to expand its reach and scale up its efforts.

A Model of Agility and User-Centricity

The most important lesson learned through the Business Atlas effort to date is one of agility and a focus on users and problems rather than on data. The initial iteration of the Business Atlas—a web-based information-providing platform—played an important role in providing useful data to entrepreneurs who accessed it. A few years into its life span, and after a leadership change at MODA, however, the office took note of the difficulty in capturing the real-world impact of the Business Atlas. While the original version was clearly useful at a theoretical level, newly installed chief analytics officer Mashariki and his team could not identify much evidence that the small-business community was actually putting the information to use, beyond a few anecdotal examples.

Rather than continuing down the same path or abandoning a good idea entirely, MODA pivoted toward a new approach. While the initial version of Business Atlas remains accessible, MODA's efforts of late have been more focused on identifying the clearly demonstrated problems felt by the small-business community and the actors within the city government capable of addressing those problems if only they had the information and insight to target their efforts. So, instead of continuing to focus efforts on increasing the supply of data available to entrepreneurs who might not even be aware that the information is available to them, MODA has pivoted toward enabling actors like SBS—the people who know the city's small-business community and its needs better than anyone—to make evidence-based decisions and undertake data-driven interventions.

Strengths	Weaknesses
Problem-oriented approach	Original platform might not have reached the New Yorkers who would benefit most from it
Keen focus on partnership inside and outside government	
High-level commitments to open data and data-driven problem solving	Lack of clear metrics of success for original open data platform approach
Expert team of data scientists and domain experts	
Agile approach defined by willingness to pivot and abandon less impactful strategies	
Opportunities	**Threats**
Closer collaboration with the Department of Small Business Services and other relevant agencies can help get tools into the hands of people who need them most	Lack of clearly demonstrable "wins" could create issues around resource availability and agency focus
Business Atlas 2.0 has clearer target goals, likely leading to improved ability to meaningfully measure success	Ballooning New York City real estate prices could overshadow any benefits to the small business community
	Leadership changes at MODA could again fundamentally change the Business Atlas approach or alter its level of priority

FIGURE 4.5 NYC Business Atlas SWOT analysis.

Although, for example, providing a baseline of how long it currently takes to open a restaurant in New York City might be less sexy and less in line with the traditional understanding of what open data can do than a flashy web application, it is clear that the Time-To-Open metric is exceedingly well-positioned to address actual problems experienced by stakeholders with a clear appetite for acting on that information.

Conclusion

As evidenced in figure 4.5, the NYC Business Atlas illustrates a number of key lessons related to the use of (open) data to generate public value in general, and to create economic opportunity in particular. Through its efforts to bring together data sets from diverse sources to make them more useful to more people, its partnerships with important actors within and outside government, and its agility evidenced by a pivot toward a more multifaceted and user-centered approach two years into the Business Atlas's existence, MODA provides a blueprint for leveraging data analytics at the city level to address public challenges in a strategic manner.

Going forward, MODA is seeking to deepen and expand on its user- and problem-focused efforts in relation to the Business Atlas and beyond. In 2016, for example, MODA began working with Columbia University's School of International and Public Affairs (SIPA) "to assess existing and future opportunities for Open Data to advance the goals of the city's many Community-Based Organizations (CBOs)" (City of New York 2016). The key insight gained from this engagement was that though city data can clearly provide value to CBOs, these organizations lack the capacity to put the data to use in a meaningful way. With this in mind, MODA is focused on increasing the usability of data made available to CBOs (and others) by including data dictionaries defining key attributes in data sets made accessible through the city's Open Data portal.

In the same vein, also in 2016, MODA began a citywide engagement tour, meeting with New Yorkers to "spread the word to those unfamiliar with Open Data" (City of New York 2016). This effort to gain insight into the actual problems and needs of New Yorkers made it clear to MODA that open data initiatives can only be truly successful if there are consistent feedback loops connecting the supply (government) and demand (citizens) sides of the equation. Consistent with the wider focus on user-centricity and providing "open data for all," MODA is organizing "in-person office hours" to create more touchpoints and conversations between those providing information and those who use (or could use) it.

References

City of New York. 2015. *Open Data for All*. July 1, 2015. http://www1.nyc.gov/assets/home /downloads/pdf/reports/2015/NYC-Open-Data-Plan-2015.pdf.

———. 2016. *Open Data for All: 2016 Progress Report*. July 1, 2016. http://www1.nyc.gov/assets /analytics/downloads/pdf/Open-Data-2016-Progress-Report.pdf.

Copeland, Eddie. 2015. *Big Data in the Big Apple*. Capital City Foundation. http://www .spatialcomplexity.info/files/2015/06/Big-Data-in-the-Big-Apple.pdf.

Deleon, Nicholas. 2017. "How Data Can Stop Your City from Burning to the Ground." *Motherboard*, May 10. https://motherboard.vice.com/en_us/article/data-can-stop-your-city -from-burning-to-the-ground-smart-cities-nyc.

Flowers, Mike. 2013. "NYC by the Numbers Annual Report." New York City Government. December 2013. http://www.nyc.gov/html/analytics/downloads/pdf/annual_report_2013 .pdf.

———. 2015. Interview by GovLab, August 14, 2015.

Flowers, Mike, and Lauren Talbot. 2014. "Building a Gov Data Skunkworks." Code for America. February 18. http://www.codeforamerica.org/peer-network-training/02-18-2014/.

Furman, Phyllis. 2103. "Map This! New City Tech Tool Lets Small Businesses Compete with the Big Guys by Dishing Data." *New York Daily News*, December 16. http://www.nydailynews .com/new-york/map-new-city-tech-tool-lets-small-businesses-compete-big-guys-dishing -data-article-1.1559044.

Mashariki, Amen Ra. 2017. Interview by GovLab, March 1.

Mayor of London and London Assembly. n.d. *MSOA Atlas*. https://data.london.gov.uk /dataset/msoa-atlas.

Mollineaux, Lindsay. 2015. Interview by GovLab, July 2.

Neubauer, Miranda. 2014. "With Business Atlas, NYC Analytics Office Looks to 2014." TechPresident, January 2. http://techpresident.com/news/24635/business-atlas-nyc-analytics -office-looks-2014.

New York City Department of Small Business Services. 2003. *Starting a Business Improvement District: A Step-by-Step Guide*. http://www.nyc.gov/html/sbs/downloads/pdf/bid_guide _complete.pdf.

———. 2015. "Small Business Services Launches Proactive Education and Outreach Efforts to Help Ease Regulatory Burden on New York City Small Businesses." May 27, 2015. http:// www.nyc.gov/html/sbs/html/pr/2015_05_27_SB1.shtml.

"NYC MODA Presentation Federal Summit." NYC Analytics, February 2015. http://lnwprogram .org/sites/default/files/NYC_MODA_Presentation_Federal_Summit.pdf.

NYC Office of the Mayor. 2014. "Mayor Bill de Blasio Signs Two Transparency Bills into Law, Announces Public-Private Partnership to Release City Record Data." August 7, 2014. http://www1.nyc.gov/office-of-the-mayor/news/393-14/mayor-bill-de-blasio-signs -two-transparency-bills-law-public-private-partnership-to#/0.

"Open-Air Computers." 2012. *Economist*, October 27. Accessed July 14, 2015. http://www .economist.com/news/special-report/21564998-cities-are-turning-vast-data-factories -open-air-computers.

Peyre, Florent. 2015. Interview by GovLab, August 19.

Roth, Jeff. 2014. "FireCast: Leveraging Big Data for Mitigating Fire Risks." Innovation Enterprise, January 22. https://ieondemand.com/divisions/big-data/events/4/presentations /firecast-leveraging-big-data-for-mitigating-fire-risks#sthash.FidXBzgc.dpuf.

Schlossberg, Tatiana. 2015. "Bodegas Declining in Manhattan as Rents Rise and Chains Grow." *New York Times*, August 3. http://www.nytimes.com/2015/08/04/nyregion /bodegas-declining-in-manhattan-as-rents-rise-and-chains-grow.html?_r=1.

Schweidel, David A. 2015. *Profiting from the Data Economy: Understanding the Roles of Consumers, Innovators, and Regulators in a Data-Driven World.* Upper Saddle River, NJ: Pearson Education.

Small Business First: Better Government. Stronger Businesses. n.d. http://www1.nyc.gov /assets/smallbizfirst/downloads/pdf/small-business-first-report.pdf.

Towards Data Driven Cities? Meet Up with Chief Data Officers. 2015. Proceedings of Paris Seminar, La Fabrique de la Cité. March 23, 2015. http://www.lafabriquedelacite.com /fabrique-de-la-cite/data.nsf/FDD3CB2E8CEA41D2C1257E0F00324482/$file/actes_cdo _02062015_def_web.pdf.

Verhulst, Stefaan, and David Sangokoya. 2015. "Data Collaboratives: Exchanging Data to Improve People's Lives." *Medium*, April 22. https://medium.com/@sverhulst/data -collaboratives-exchanging-data-to-improve-people-s-lives-d0fcfc1bdd9a.

Wu, Tim. 2015. "Why Are There So Many Shuttered Storefronts in the West Village?" *New Yorker*, May 25. http://www.newyorker.com/business/currency/why-are-there-so-many -shuttered-storefronts-in-the-west-village.

Yasin, Rutrell. 2013. "How Analytics Is Making NYC's Streets and Buildings Safer." *GCN*, October 4. http://gcn.com/articles/2013/10/04/gcn-award-nyc-databridge.aspx.

——. 2014. "NYC Geek Squad Stays on Mission to Liberate Data." *GCN*, February 19. https:// gcn.com/articles/2014/02/19/new-york-city-geek-squad.aspx.

CHAPTER 5

DEMAND RESPONSE

Incentives for Smarter Energy Management

ANDRÉ CORRÊA D'ALMEIDA, *Columbia University*

CHRISTOPHER LEWIS, *Independent Consultant*

Executive Summary

Since 2013, the City of New York has been participating in an energy-management and resiliency program called "demand response." Overseen by the city's Department of Citywide Administrative Services (DCAS), demand response utilizes a range of innovative technology—including real-time electricity-metering equipment and a web-based monitoring system—to curtail building electricity use at peak times, helping to prevent failures in the city's power grid. City agencies wanting to participate in the program work with NuEnergen, a third-party vendor contracted by DCAS to enroll city buildings and other facilities in demand response. The agencies reduce their electricity use during peak times, when required by the program, and earn revenue from the state's regulated electricity market for every kilowatt (kW) reduced. Twenty-three of the city's agencies and organizations had enrolled by 2017 (twenty-five are expected by summer 2018), and they contributed more than 75 megawatts (MW) of power (80–85 MW expected by summer 2018), earning more than \$12 million in that year alone. Since 2013, when it was launched, the program has already generated more than \$23 million in revenues for the city. Program success has been achieved through a high level of collaborative effort and engagement between the DCAS energy-management team, NuEnergen, and various agency program managers and facility managers. This case examines how that effort has unfolded, highlighting transferable practical lessons.

Key Takeaways and Actionable Insights

- A high level of collaboration was essential for program initiation. Proactive efforts taken by personnel at DCAS and NuEnergen to build their client/vendor relationship and align their objectives helped to get the program off the ground.
- The alignment of incentives, contractually for NuEnergen and programmatically for city agencies, helped program growth.
- Additionally, advocacy on the part of DCAS, NuEnergen, and energy-management personnel within city agencies was vital for the program's growth. Enrollment required significant recruitment efforts both between and within agencies.
- Adaptability in program structure and rollout was also important for program growth. NuEnergen's absorption of potential penalty risk helped address operational constraints and unique challenges that each agency presented for program enrollment. In order to improve participation in demand response, it was also important to understand and respond to agencies' incentives, which varied based on the particular needs and objectives of city agencies.
- Recognizing achievement among program participants helped to ensure the continued success of demand response. Honoring participating agencies and individuals among their peers fostered program ownership, pride, and positive competition, leading to improved participation.
- Finally, the use of real-time metering in demand response confers benefits other than system resilience and revenues. It promotes energy consciousness among facility managers, leading to improved energy management.

Problem Formulation, Contextual Environment, and the Innovation Opportunity

A Primer in Demand Response

As demand for electricity increases—for instance, during a summer heat wave when everyone starts cranking up air conditioners—it puts the entire state electricity grid under stress. That added stress can destabilize the delicate systemwide supply/demand balance and cause brownouts or blackouts. In order to ensure the reliable provision of electricity during such times, the New York Independent System Operator (NYISO), New York State's grid manager, increases capacity by incorporating additional power plants into the grid, boosting power production to meet demand. Those additional plants are costly to operate, and they pass along that higher marginal electricity production cost to the state's end users. Furthermore, those additional plants are not as efficient to run, producing more greenhouse gases than the state's primary power generators. The state's grid manager therefore has an incentive to prevent city electricity demand from reaching the point where those more expensive power plants would need to be turned on. To that end, it is willing to pay electricity users in the state to reduce their load when overall power demand increases.

This is the essence of demand response. Electricity users in the state enroll in a program where they agree to reduce consumption when demand begins to peak. Although demand-response events may only be triggered for a dozen or so hours over the span of an entire year, the potential savings run into the millions of dollars. Participants are informed of these demand-response events by the state's grid manager, which monitors electricity-consumption trends and forecasts increased consumption. The state's grid manager offers participants a financial incentive to reduce their load, paying the going market rate per kilowatt reduced, essentially treating the freed-up capacity made available by the participants as equivalent to electricity production for the state. In summary, the state's grid manager shares a portion of the averted marginal costs with the partnering end-use customers, such as city agencies, in the form of monetary compensation, which provides an additional economic and behavioral incentive to participate in the program.

The Opportunity: Demand Response in NYC

In New York City, demand response has existed in some form since utilities were deregulated in the 1990s. Working with the state's grid manager (NYISO), the state's public power authority (NYPA) oversaw a peak-load-management

Key Players in New York's Electricity Market

NYPA, the New York Power Authority, is the state's main electricity producer, selling low-cost power to public and private clients through the state's electricity market. Independent power producers also exist in New York.

NYISO, the New York Independent System Operator, manages the New York State electricity market, ensuring competitive wholesale prices to facilitate the flow of electricity across the state, including into New York City.

Con Edison, New York City's regulated utility, is like the city-level version of NYISO. Con Edison owns the city's meters and wires and is responsible for distributing electricity throughout the city.

system in the 2000s that was basically a rudimentary demand-response program. However, NYPA was principally focused on generating and supplying
power, not in overseeing a demand-response program in New York City. City
enrollment during this period therefore never exceeded twenty megawatts, and
revenue to the city capped out at about $750,000 per year. For the City of New
York, which has a municipal peak electricity load of around 950 megawatts and
an annual electricity bill of $600 million, demand response had the potential to
be a large, untapped revenue stream (Shabalin 2015).

The Entrepreneurial Role of DCAS

As the city's administrative backstop, the Department of Citywide Administrative Services (DCAS) is responsible for a range of support functions. This
includes coordinating the payment of the energy utility bills of New York City's
eighty municipal agencies and organizations, comprising city departments,
mayoral offices, public schools, universities, and cultural institutions. All told,
that encompasses some 10,000 bill accounts in more than 4,600 facilities spread
out across the city's five boroughs and in some upstate counties (Shabalin 2015).
DCAS was therefore in a prime position to identify the demand-response gap
for those facilities and to do something about it. However, in deciding to take
on and expand demand response for the city, DCAS was faced with an overwhelming task. How would its energy-management team enroll such a huge
number of municipal facilities—ranging from offices to firehouses to ferry
terminals—operated by the city's many different agencies, each with its own
internal processes, systems, and technology? Furthermore, there was no mandate requiring the agencies to join the program. So how would they convince the
agencies' facility managers and building staff to take on more work? The team at
DCAS decided to engage an industry leader that could manage the city's massive
portfolio, maximize revenues, and generally take the city to the next level with
demand response.

Inception, Development, and Rollout: Ideation to Implementation

Finding a Partner in the Private Sector

There are nearly twenty demand-response service providers offering energy-management solutions to public and private entities in the New York City
area (New York Independent System Operator 2017). To find the best match
for city government's various demand-response needs, in 2012 DCAS issued a
detailed call for proposals. The proposal called for an appropriately qualified

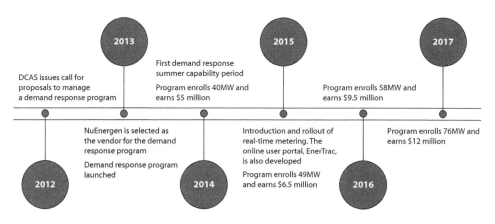

FIGURE 5.1 Energy demand-response timeline.

vendor to manage and expand demand-response enrollment and to analyze the citywide portfolio for long-term program potential. DCAS also established an interagency selection committee to review responses and whittle them down through three selection rounds before deciding on a final winner (Hamilton 2015). Quantity and quality of successful relevant experience, demonstrated level of organizational capability, and quality of proposed approach, as well as price proposals, were all taken into account. The committee received fourteen proposals and finally selected NuEnergen as the winning bidder. NuEnergen is an energy-management firm based in White Plains, New York, that had been providing energy-management solutions in the region for nearly ten years. Skippered by president and CEO Kevin Hamilton, the company had a proven track record in working with public and private organizations in the New York market. In the end, getting a contract signed with NuEnergen took eighteen months from the time the call for proposals was issued (see figure 5.1). For the DCAS energy-management team, this proved to be a defining first achievement for the demand-response program (Shabalin 2015). The important task of leading the newly minted program was assigned to Sergey Shabalin, director of billing programs and analytics at the energy budget, supply, and reporting group directed by Susan Cohen, assistant commissioner at DCAS for energy management.

City Agency Recruitment: Aligning Incentives for Citywide Collaboration

Now that a contract was finally signed with NuEnergen, DCAS had to recruit city agencies into the program. DCAS's role in managing the city's utility bill would be central to the success of this effort, and that role was centered around

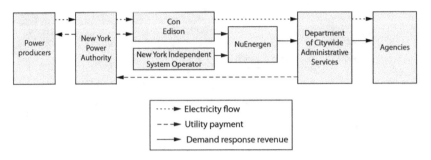

FIGURE 5.2 Electricity generation, payment, and demand-response (DR) flows for the city.

the DCAS energy-management team. Shabalin and his colleagues already had relationships with the various city agencies, and it would be their responsibility to advocate for program participation with each of those agencies. Thankfully, they had a very engaged ally in their vendor, NuEnergen. Hamilton and his team at NuEnergen were understandably anxious to help expand the demand-response portfolio; the company's profits would be directly tied to the city's total demand-response revenue (see figure 5.2). However, Hamilton saw his firm's budding relationship with DCAS as more of a collaborative partnership than a mere business association. Indeed, NuEnergen would be ready to work hand in hand with DCAS to educate, recruit, and train as many agencies as possible. Their goal would be to make enrollment as straightforward and effortless as they could, keeping any administrative complexities within DCAS, thereby relieving city agencies of much of the burden of implementing a new program (Hamilton 2015).

As the agency responsible for coordinating payment of the city agencies' utility bills, DCAS already knew who the biggest electricity consumers were. They targeted those users first, focusing on agencies with large portfolios of buildings in excess of 500 kW, the threshold that Con Edison, the city's primary utility power distributor, had set for outfitting buildings with upgraded interval meters which autonomously provided regular electricity-usage data. There were a couple of benefits to this approach. First, because Con Edison already had the interval-metering technology installed in these facilities, NuEnergen could tap into those data to track a building's performance once it was enrolled. Second, starting with the largest facilities would bring the highest potential earners on board from the beginning, showcasing the program's value and jump-starting its expansion across city agencies.

However, enrolling a building in the program was not a straightforward task. Some of the city's buildings are extremely old, and most—about 80%—don't have a modern, automated building management system (BMS) but instead rely on manual management. That is, in a demand-response event, the facility manager would likely need to coordinate building staff to physically turn off equipment in order to meet the building's energy-reduction target, sometimes even having building personnel return to the workplace after hours. Convincing agency personnel to sign up for this would be a tough sell, especially in agencies where building personnel were unfamiliar with the concept of demand response. DCAS needed to convey to them the importance of demand response, explaining why the agency should stretch its resources and personnel with the extra responsibilities.

While the DCAS team was determined to present a simple, straightforward, and convincing case for enrollment in the program, it also had a couple of additional incentives for agencies to join. Even though DCAS was administering the program, support from the city's central Office of Management and Budget enabled them to pass on all revenues earned by the city agencies from demand response in the first two years. DCAS would channel the semiannual payments from NuEnergen to each agency in accordance with how much those agencies earned. NuEnergen would also work directly with each agency at the facility level to develop site-specific protocols. Anton Nicaj, NuEnergen's director of field operations, would personally visit each of the agencies' facilities to establish what equipment would be switched off and in what sequence during a demand-response event, tailoring the program specifically to each agency's facility needs (see figure 5.3). This was no simple task. While some agencies are housed in a single facility, most operate multiple facilities across the five boroughs and beyond. The Department of Education (DOE) alone operates more than 1,200 schools and other facilities across the city. This level of scope and complexity would have to be matched by a high degree of specificity in the development of protocols, requiring Nicaj to tailor each protocol to each

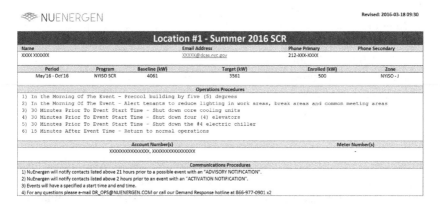

FIGURE 5.3 Sample demand-response protocol for a single facility, detailing operations and communications procedures in the lead-up to and during a demand-response event.

facility. NuEnergen also committed to informing the facility managers of a demand-response event up to twenty-one hours in advance, as well as keeping them updated on the duration of the event while it was underway (Hamilton 2016). The level of attention that NuEnergen paid to each agency really helped to differentiate itself among demand-response service providers in the city in terms of client involvement.

Advocating Within City Agencies and Strengthening Ties

Managers within some of the agencies also played a crucial role in promoting demand response. Tami Lin, senior energy policy adviser at the Department of Environmental Protection (DEP), tells how she and the team at DEP's Energy Office created their own demand-response material to help facilitate their agency's involvement. She points out that facility managers at DEP were already very operationally driven, and they just needed the appropriate information and protocols for their facilities in order to get excited about the initiative. Lin worked closely with Nicaj in this regard, together visiting each of DEP's facilities in order to develop site-specific protocols. Once she had the protocols in hand, Lin turned them into user-friendly visuals for the facility managers' convenient use in a demand-response event (Lin 2016).

Adapting the Program to Agency Needs

However, the incentives and collaborative efforts outlined above were sometimes not enough to entice every agency with buildings of 500 kW or above into joining the demand-response program. Some facility managers were simply concerned that the revenue generated by demand response in their agency would not filter down to the facility level. Why should a facility participate in a sometimes labor-intensive program if the financial benefit of that program was not being felt at the facility level?

Some city agencies were already enrolled in separate programs and had little incentive to switch. A number of companies, including NRG Curtailment Solutions, EnerNOC, and others, provide their own demand-response services in the city. The Department of Education (DOE), which also happens to be the city's largest energy user, was already enrolled in one of those programs. Energy managers at DOE were well aware of the benefits that demand response engendered, but they did not see any added value in switching to a new program managed by DCAS. Joe Chavez, sustainability coordinator at DOE, was especially concerned that DCAS and NuEnergen might not fully appreciate his agency's unique requirements. DOE's facilities make up about

25% of the city's total energy use across agencies, and its demand-response program encompassed 300 separate accounts (Chavez 2015). Would DCAS and NuEnergen have the right expertise, tools, and software to manage that portfolio?

Other agencies and organizations were initially resistant to the DCAS program because of their unique operational restrictions. The Metropolitan Museum of Art, one of the city's most famous cultural institutions, is required to maintain an indoor temperature of 75 degrees Fahrenheit with 50% humidity in order to preserve its art collection (Kellermueller 2016). Would NuEnergen be able to work with the museum's energy personnel to find energy cuts that would not jeopardize those strict parameters? The city's Health and Hospitals Corporation (HHC)—with eleven hospitals, six diagnostic and treatment centers, and dozens of clinics—presented a similarly challenging case (Lewis 2016). Could a program that requires electricity-use reductions be adapted to any of those health facilities without compromising patient care?

A final challenge was what to do about penalties for nonperformance. Demand-response resources—in this case, city facilities enrolled in the program—need to be reliably available when called on to act as generation plants. Therefore, both NYISO and utility programs have stringent rules that penalize participants if their load reductions do not meet their commitments. Those penalties would include participation restrictions on NuEnergen as well as reduced earnings for city facilities in future cycles. As NuEnergen would not be able to transfer the cost of penalties to the city, would they be willing to accept the risk of noncompliance among city facilities? Additionally, would the reduced earnings for noncompliance discourage facilities from continued participation in the program?

Each of these hurdles had to be addressed distinctly. DCAS and NuEnergen worked extensively with the city's art preservation institutes, including the Metropolitan Museum of Art, to try to find creative ways of introducing demand response, given their complex humidity and temperature requirements. Meanwhile, significant progress was made with a number of city hospitals. Joining the program does not compromise health-service delivery when power reductions are found in hospital facilities and offices dedicated to administration or clinical work rather than patient care (Hamilton 2015).

Where agencies were enrolled in alternate demand-response programs, as with DOE, the DCAS team sold their case from an efficiency standpoint. Having all the agencies under a single umbrella program would improve service delivery by centralizing the program. On top of that, DCAS was willing to take on most of the administrative burden of the program, thereby freeing up agency staff to focus their attention elsewhere. Susan Cohen (2015) points out that when it comes to paying the utility bill, it does not make sense for eighty different agencies to write eighty different checks every month, especially considering that the city's annual energy budget is developed centrally. A single demand-response program overseen by DCAS would similarly benefit from centralized administration; that included assistance from DCAS's own central fiscal office to create the budget structures and provide the support to make it as easy as possible to transfer earned funds to each agency twice a year. Program participants have already felt that benefit. Marcus Lewis, corporate energy analyst at HHC, points out that since DCAS takes care of all the legal and administrative aspects of the program, his agency's energy staff are freed up to spend more time on facility operation and on improving energy efficiency (Lewis 2016). Additionally, NuEnergen would be absorbing much of the risk associated with program participation. Indeed, NuEnergen's business model is to absorb risk that participants' nonperformance might impose. The company does this in a couple of ways: through carefully analyzing how much load a facility should commit to the program, and by introducing facility-specific reviews and communication systems to help minimize the risk of nonperformance.

Finally, DCAS worked with NuEnergen to ensure that the enrolled agencies could maximize revenues. Some demand-response programs only offer a summer participation option, although extreme winter weather (think polar vortex) can trigger demand-response events as well. Under the DCAS-administered program, agencies would be able to participate in both a summer (May–October) and a winter (November–April) period, allowing agencies to accrue demand-response revenues throughout the year. The DCAS energy team worked closely with NuEnergen, seeking to address each of the agencies' concerns and finding ways to maximize their benefits under the new program. They knew that success in their first summer period—the summer of 2014— would be essential for proving the program's potential (Shabalin 2015).

The Critical Role of Real-Time Metering

The summer of 2014 was the first full summer under the city's demand-response contract with NuEnergen. DCAS was hoping to enroll between fifteen and twenty megawatts in the program that summer. In the end, they doubled that enrollment, exceeding forty megawatts and generating more than $5 million in revenue for the city. The demand-response program was a resounding success! However, by the end of the summer, the DCAS energy-management team already had on board most of the large, energy-intensive facilities. Where could the program go from here? It was at this point that Susan Cohen and Sergey Shabalin at DCAS realized that the real bottleneck was the metering infrastructure. Con Edison, New York City's regulated electricity-delivery company, freely provides meters that collect interval-pulse data to buildings using 500 kW or more. However, most municipal buildings operate below that threshold and only register their energy use once a month. This precludes the enrollment of smaller facilities in demand response, a program that requires data collection at a level granular enough to capture electricity use as it occurs during a demand-response event. If DCAS was going to enroll smaller facilities, the meters in those facilities would need to produce energy readouts more frequently. The meters would also need to communicate remotely, wirelessly transmitting their readings to a central location. Sergey and his team realized this equipment was an essential missing piece. They worked with Con Edison to find a way to upgrade metering periphery, allowing facilities of all sizes to capture their electricity use. Additionally, the team opted for meters that would provide data every five minutes, yielding a much higher level of precision in energy-use data collection across city agencies (Shabalin 2015).

Because real-time metering was outside the purview of the original contract with NuEnergen, the contract was updated with an amendment to incorporate this development. More than a simple contract amendment, however, real-time metering ended up being the most important feature in terms of enrollment among city agencies. Tapping into its budget for energy efficiency and greenhouse-gas-reduction programs, DCAS would now cover the cost of new metering equipment for city agencies, at least for an initial two years of program rollout. At up to $3,000 per real-time monitor—the market rate for such equipment—this would be a major and expensive undertaking, but the added demand-response revenues would recoup those costs to the city within a couple of years. Additionally, NuEnergen agreed to develop an online user portal, called EnerTrac. Agencies would now be able to have their facility managers log in and access their real-time energy data on a user-friendly dashboard (see figure 5.4). For Joe Chavez at DOE, this piece really added value to NuEnergen's service and was indicative of the company's commitment to understanding and responding to agency needs (Chavez 2015).

The streamlined dashboard would provide alerts on building energy-use thresholds, notifying building managers of any issues. The information would be provided in such a way that facility managers could literally watch their buildings' energy use live. When it comes to building energy management, this presented a new level of accessibility and usability. A successful first summer, plus the benefits outlined above, would hopefully make demand response an easier sell among the city's agencies moving forward. DCAS started integrating real-time metering equipment in January 2015, adding fifty facilities to the demand-response portfolio in time for the summer 2015 capability period (Shabalin 2016).

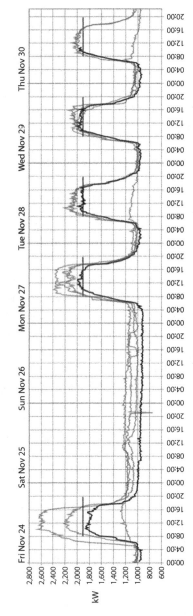

FIGURE 5-4 EnerTrac portal screenshot indicating rolling kilowatt load for four weeks.

Results and Impact

Unprecedented Enrollment and Revenues

By summer 2018, nearly 500 facilities will be enrolled across twenty-five agencies and organizations, including six cultural institutions, committing more than eighty megawatts to demand response, and accounting for around 8.5% of the entire municipal peak load. Agency participation over the summer of 2017 resulted in revenues of $12 million to the city in that year alone—more than $23 million in revenue since the program was launched in 2013 (Shabalin 2017). Hamilton (2015) at NuEnergen estimates that the city is by far the most active participant in the demand-response space nationally, with more buildings enrolled than any other municipality in the country.

The DCAS energy-management team strongly encourages city agencies to use demand-response revenues for energy sustainability and efficiency goals. The city's Department of Education (DOE) has been active in this regard, funding its entire Sustainability Office with demand-response funds. DOE also uses the revenues to retrofit schools and administrative facilities with greener and more efficient technology and infrastructure (Chavez 2015). Danny Donovan, an energy manager at DCAS, notes that his agency created a separate fund for demand-response revenues that they use for further energy-management programs. His goal is to set up an energy-management toolkit—software applications, guidelines, and benchmarks—that DCAS facility managers can access to improve their efficiency (Donovan 2016).

Some agencies, however, have other more pressing priorities or simply incorporate their demand-response revenues into a general operating budget. For the Department of Environmental Protection (DEP), revenues are

The Energy Bucket Challenge at DCAS

Energy manager Danny Donovan relates how the introduction of real-time metering into the demand-response portfolio at DCAS resulted in some friendly competition. He and his team at DCAS organized an Energy Bucket Challenge (think Ice Bucket Challenge, but about energy and without the ice). The competition pitted facility managers against one another to see who could run their facility most efficiently in a given time frame. While that challenge had its winners, it brought energy-reduction efforts to the fore of the agenda among all participants, further enhancing a spirit of collaboration.

almost beside the point, even though they have some of the city's largest and most energy-intensive facilities enrolled in demand response. Among other things, DEP is in charge of managing the city's water supply and controlling its wastewater treatment. A power failure in any one of those processes would have catastrophic effects for city residents. The agency is therefore primarily concerned with grid reliability and resiliency, outcomes that provide more than adequate incentive for DEP's active participation in demand response (Lin 2016).

Improved Energy Consciousness

Aside from the benefits of a more reliable power grid and all the revenues accrued through the program, participation in demand response has also had a positive impact in the form of improved energy consciousness. One major positive development is that facility managers have become more engaged with energy-use trends in their buildings. The availability of real-time data that the new meters afford through the demand-response program gives those managers another tool to increase their effectiveness. In one case, a facility manager was watching his building's energy use on the online portal during a demand-response event. Seeing that the building wasn't reaching 100% response, even with the protocols established for that building, he went and physically turned off a few extra bits of nonessential equipment. Checking the portal again several minutes later, he saw it was just what was needed to get his building to the 100% mark (Shabalin 2015).

Furthermore, facility managers have begun to understand energy use in their buildings much better at all times, not just during demand-response events. According to Joe Chavez (2015) at DOE, demand response has been "a way to keep [facility managers] engaged in energy management. Sort of like a reminder that you need to be aware of your building's energy use." Chavez points out that this awareness has helped facility managers understand building occupancy and equipment schedules throughout the year, identifying inefficiencies in building operation. Marcus Lewis (2016) at HHC notes that energy managers can even tailor NuEnergen's web-based dashboard to a facility's specific needs, setting up threshold alerts to catch inefficiencies, which in turn helps improve routine facility performance. In sum, the impact of real-time data availability on facility managers' energy consciousness has been ubiquitously positive, which is a significant win for energy efficiency. This is especially so given how infrequently demand-response events actually occur; New York City only faces grid-reliability issues for between eight and twelve hours over the course of a year (Hamilton 2016). The fact that the demand-response program, designed to kick in for just a few hours a year, has resulted in more engaged energy management at the facility level for all 365 days is therefore quite impressive.

Recognizing Achievement, Encouraging Participation

Every year DCAS hosts a Demand Response event, inviting all program participants for a morning of presentations, updates, and discussion surrounding demand response, as well as additional face time with NuEnergen. DCAS also takes the opportunity to highlight key successes of the program, as well as top performers during the preceding year. For instance, the agency with the highest percentage of buildings participating in demand response, or with the highest number of kilowatts enrolled in the program, will be recognized and applauded. The energy-management personnel representing those agencies are presented with certificates of achievement during the event (Shabalin 2016). This ceremony has at least two positive effects. First, it provides an opportunity for the people who are making demand response happen to receive recognition for their efforts, helping to foster pride among those who are celebrated for their agency's achievements. Second, it helps to build positive competition among peers, incentivizing agency personnel to improve their own participation and competitive edge into the following season. Both of these benefits ultimately result in improved engagement among agency personnel, positively affecting the city's overall involvement in the demand-response program (Hamilton 2016).

Along with the benefits of participating in demand response once enrolled, there are penalties for signing up and not participating. When facilities underperform during a demand-response event, their revenues are prorated at a higher than one-to-one ratio. That is, failure to perform results in a discriminatory loss of revenue, deducting reimbursement at a higher rate per kilowatt than the rate reimbursed when in compliance. The significant loss of revenue for noncompliance is therefore a real motivating factor for facility managers to participate in demand response once enrolled (Hamilton 2016).

Alignment with GHG Reduction Efforts

Demand response in New York City has been tied to the city's greenhouse gas (GHG) reduction efforts since at least the Bloomberg era (see chapter 7). Mayor Bloomberg's city plan explicitly called for increased participation in the program, pushing for fifty-megawatt enrollment among city agencies by 2030 (City of New York 2011, 117). Mayor de Blasio's revised city plan subsequently brought that target date to 2018 (City of New York 2015, 306) (see chapter 1).

While the city has already surpassed that goal, quantifying and demonstrating the effects of demand response on GHG reductions is not a straightforward task. This is partly because some facilities actually increase their energy use in preparation for a demand-response event. Other facilities exchange municipal power for local generation; they switch on their own generators during a demand-response event to make up for the loss of city power. Both situations seriously complicate net GHG-emission measurements.

As explained earlier, in order to meet higher demand in the absence of demand response, NYISO would need to bring on board additional power production in the energy market. That additional production typically comes in the form of power plants of last resort called "peaker plants." Peaker plants are deemed a last resort because they are expensive to run and often the least efficient and the most environmentally polluting. Preventing them from being turned on likely has a net positive effect in terms of GHG emissions. However, NYISO is not currently measuring GHG emissions on a real-time basis for those plants, so the GHG reduction benefits of demand response can only be made at a system level.

Regardless, the DCAS energy-management team is more focused on power-infrastructure resilience, the ability to generate revenue to reinvest in energy efficiency, and the opportunity to use real-time metering for hands-on energy management over more hours of the day. This reduces the city's carbon footprint no matter what is happening on the power-generation side. The general push at DCAS is always toward curtailing overall energy use. As Susan Cohen (2015) says, it's all about "bringing down the average." Demand response is bringing down that average and shrinking the city's carbon footprint, regardless of how that affects GHG emissions from power generation.

Challenges and Lessons Learned

The Problems Posed by Smaller City Agencies

Despite all of the benefits conferred by demand response, a number of facility managers and agency heads are not interested for various reasons. In some cases, participation could require altering room temperatures to an uncomfortable level. Take a courtroom, for example. The majority of its energy use is committed to air conditioning, but a judge might not want to let the temperature rise too much in a packed court on a hot summer day. Some agencies lease floors within large office buildings and therefore cannot control whether the building is enrolled in a demand-response program. Among smaller agencies, with lower energy use, some simply don't find the level of effort required for demand response worth the payoff. However, this might change with increased awareness. Danny Donovan, the energy manager at DCAS, says that in his experience with demand response, education "has been the key motivator of getting everybody on board and buying into the program of energy reduction" (Donovan 2015). The energy-management unit at DCAS has sponsored key staff to complete semester-long certificate programs at the City University of New York (CUNY), which have helped building operators connect their facility-level efforts to citywide energy-reduction targets. This has been a motivating factor for energy-conscious facility management, and it may be a worthwhile initiative for other agencies to consider as well.

Competing Interests: New York's Independent Power Providers

As noted previously, when demand for power begins to peak, it usually requires that NYISO bring peaker plants on board. Those plants are run by independent power producers, represented by an advocacy group called the Independent Power Producers of New York (IPPNY) that lobbies against artificial pricing in the state's electricity market. IPPNY members who run peaker plants operate a business model that depends on NYISO's needing extra capacity for energy production. Ostensibly this would put them in direct competition with demand-response participants. However, because citywide demand-response enrollment is so low (accounting for just 6% of municipal load to date) and because demand-response events are so infrequent (around five times per year), the program does not yet pose a significant threat to IPPNY members. Indeed, IPPNY has not seriously considered demand response as being a significant solution to grid-reliability problems (Independent Power Producers of New York 2010, 4). A recent Supreme Court ruling, however, is opening up the demand-response market to more consumers (Tweed 2016). This decision may put pressure on inefficient power producers in the New York electricity market, as real-time meters become more ubiquitous at the consumer level, allowing more consumers to participate in demand response. As one of the state's largest participants in demand response, the City of New York could find its demand-response program curtailed if action on the part of IPPNY were to precipitate legal blockades affecting program participation at the state level.

Is Demand Response a Band-Aid, Not a Cure?

One could argue that demand-response programs may divert the city's attention from a deeper problem—namely, an aging power-delivery network. The greater metropolitan area of New York City consumes two-thirds of the state's total power, of which more than half is imported from remote power plants,

TABLE 5.1 Key Stakeholders Table

Stakeholder name	Role played	Interest in the program	Positive/ negative effect on the program	Incentives needed to engage
DCAS	Recognized the opportunity in NYC; initiated and coordinated the demand response program	*High*: responsible for the success and continued growth of the program	*Positive*: a citywide demand-response program would not have occurred without DCAS	None
NuEnergen	Provided most attractive proposal for program management; worked with DCAS and city agencies to facilitate enrolment	*High*: the level of participation among city agencies directly affected NuEnergen's revenues	*Positive*: expedited and simplified agency participation at the facility level	Contract with NYC in which the company is compensated per kilowatt enrolled
City agencies	Enrolled their facilities in the program; championed the program among facility managers	*High*: the demand-response program offered a new revenue stream	*Positive*: increased the demand response portfolio and improved program revenues	Variable; revenues provided some incentive, as did the benefit of participating in a program administered by another agency (DCAS)
IPPNY	Lobbied for stake in New York electricity market, including NYC	*Low*: does not consider the city's nascent demand-response program to be a threat	*Negative*: demand-response programs undermine IPPNY's business model	A larger demand-response program could precipitate their engagement

creating significant reliance on power transmission to the city. More than 80% of the state's high-voltage transmission lines went into service before 1980, and more than 40% of the transmission lines will need to be replaced within the next thirty years, at an estimated cost of $25 billion (New York Independent System Operator 2015, 6). Will these transmission lines be able to keep pace with the energy needs of a city that is still growing economically and in population? While demand response is a significant and growing revenue source for many city agencies, it could distract the city from working with state-level authorities to make capital investments in power transmission.

Conclusion

Replicability

There is still a lot of room for efficiency improvements in the city's demand-response program. Newly constructed buildings are typically outfitted with advanced, automated building management systems (BMS) that can accommodate complex demand-response programs (Hamilton 2015). However, most of the buildings in the city's portfolio are relatively old and rely on manual management. The St. George Ferry Terminal in Staten Island is an outstanding exception, where demand response can be managed with the push of a button (Shabalin 2015). Ideally, much of the city's portfolio would be similarly automated. At least, this is the perspective of Danny Donovan. Having worked in a modern building with a state-of-the-art BMS prior to joining DCAS, Donovan cannot emphasize enough the value of these systems. As he points out, why not use demand-response revenues to increase building-management automation? The result would improve demand response and again increase revenues (Donovan 2015). Short of retrofitting city buildings with new management systems, there are other technical improvements that could have significant impacts as well. In some cases, it is simply an equipment-maintenance issue. According to Art Fasolino, director of energy and facility sustainability at CUNY, one of the university's colleges could probably triple its enrollment in demand response if adequate resources were available to maintain some of the college's larger equipment (Fasolino 2015). In many cases, the maintenance and improvement costs would likely pay for themselves with increased demand-response revenues.

DCAS and NuEnergen will continue to expand the demand-response program in New York City. They had hoped to break sixty-five-megawatt enrollment by summer 2017, pushing city revenues to $10 million. They handily topped that target and are continuing to expand, bringing on board additional facilities that had initially been a challenge. The Health and Hospitals

Strengths	Weaknesses
A demand response program offers an additional revenue stream for city governments. An additional and perhaps more impactful result in the long term is that implementing a demand response program increases energy consciousness at the facility level, leading to more efficient energy use and more cost savings.	Some agencies operate facilites that are not conducive to joining a demand response program due to their function (i.e., hospital, courtroom, etc.), complexity (i.e., the agency only owns one floor in a multistory building), or size (the facility does not consume enough energy to warrant the effort required to participate).

Opportunities	Threats
Power reductions and outages affect any major urban center with grid reliability issues. Demand response is an effective tool to mitigate negative outcomes stemming from that unreliability. Advances in real-time metering technology will enable increased participation.	A centralized demand response program requires a prerequisite degree of administrative centralization in city government. This type of program may not function as efficiently in municipalities that lack that centralization. A demand response program may discourage capital investments in aging power grids.

FIGURE 5.5 Energy demand-response SWOT analysis.

Corporation (HHC), an agency with particularly complex facilities, has already enrolled facilities at nine of its eleven locations. Marcus Lewis at HHC only sees that enrollment continuing to grow (Lewis 2016). Larry Kellermueller, senior manager of engineering services at the Metropolitan Museum of Art, is also optimistic. Working with NuEnergen, Kellermueller and his team have found creative ways to enroll nonessential equipment in demand response, and their institute will likely join the program at a later date. Meanwhile, DCAS is on track to increase the total number of facilities using real-time metering equipment from fifty in 2015 to nearly 300 in 2017. Institutes and agencies already enrolled will work to improve their facilities' performance in order to maximize their revenues over the summer. NuEnergen is working with them in this regard, raising thresholds if buildings are far exceeding their mark, or reducing those thresholds if buildings are underperforming, all with a view toward ensuring efficient participation.

Looking Forward

The success of the City of New York's demand-response program hinged on such key structural elements as ease of administration, revenue pass-throughs, and risk mitigation, along with the enthusiasm of individuals who were actively engaged in the city's energy space. They recognized an unmet need and mobilized broad participation, implementing a responsive program that harnessed available technology. While program participation has contributed to improved reliability and resiliency in the city's power grid, a key tangible benefit has been the financial earnings for many of the city's agencies, revenues that often go to additional sustainability efforts. The program has also resulted in increased awareness of energy use both for its own sake and within the framework of the citywide energy-reduction efforts. The city's proactive involvement in the demand-response space is indicative of the ability of its people, agencies, and systems to adapt and respond to a new technological environment for the betterment of New York City as a whole.

References

Chavez, Joe. 2015. Interview with authors, December 10.

City of New York. 2011. *PlaNYC: A Greener, Greater New York*. http://s-media.nyc.gov/agencies /planyc2030/pdf/planyc_2011_planyc_full_report.pdf.

——. 2015. *One New York: The Plan for a Strong and Just City*. http://www.nyc.gov/html /onenyc/downloads/pdf/publications/OneNYC.pdf.

Cohen, Susan. 2015. Interview with authors, November 13.

Donovan, Danny. 2015. Interview with authors, December 17.

——. 2016. Roundtable discussion with demand response stakeholders, March 24.

Fasolino, Art. 2015. Interview with authors, December 8.

Hamilton, Kevin. 2015. Interview with authors, December 21.

——. 2016. Roundtable discussion with demand response stakeholders, March 24.

Independent Power Producers of New York. 2010. "Memorandum: IPPNY Response to NYISO Demand Curve Questionnaire." http://www.nyiso.com/public/webdocs/markets _operations/committees/bic_icapwg/meeting_materials/2010-02-12/IPPNY_Response _to_NYISO_Demand_Curve_Questionnaire.pdf.

Kellermueller, Larry. 2016. Interview with authors, April 19.

Lewis, Marcus. 2016. Interview with authors, May 3.

Lin, Tami. 2016. Interview with authors, April 7.

New York Independent System Operator. 2015. *Power Trends 2015: Rightsizing the Grid*. http://www.nyiso.com/public/webdocs/media_room/press_releases/2015/Child _PowerTrends_2015/ptrends2015_FINAL.pdf.

——. 2017. "Demand Response Service Providers." http://www.nyiso.com/public/webdocs /markets_operations/market_data/demand_response/Demand_Response/General _Information/dr_providers.pdf.

Shabalin, Sergey. 2015. Interview with authors, November 13.

——. 2016. Email correspondence with authors, March 18.

——. 2017. Email correspondence with authors, April 6.

Tweed, Katherine. 2016. "US Supreme Court Rules in Favor of Demand Response." *Greentech Media*, January 25. https://www.greentechmedia.com/articles/read/supreme-court-rules -in-favor-of-demand-response.

CHAPTER 6

GREEN INFRASTRUCTURE PLAN

Opportunities for Innovation in Climate-Change Resilience

BERNICE ROSENZWEIG, *City University of New York*

BALAZS FEKETE, *City University of New York*

Executive Summary

The New York City Green Infrastructure (GI) Plan demonstrates how innovative, engineered systems that mimic natural water-cycling processes can be utilized to improve water management in an ultra-urban setting. The use of green infrastructure for combined sewer overflow (CSO) reduction represented a paradigm shift in New York City's stormwater management, and the city faced many challenges in its implementation because of its age, density, and physical setting. Although New York City was not able to meet anticipated stormwater-management milestones, the city demonstrated that green infrastructure could be successfully deployed in even its densest communities and that the use of green infrastructure could be institutionalized into city operations. Collaboration among various city offices, environmental organizations, and community groups was key to this advance.

New York City has emerged as a leader in climate-change-resilience planning, and this is reflected in the GI Plan, which employs an adaptive management approach, making it more resilient to projected changes in precipitation patterns caused by climate change over the coming decades than conventional urban water-management approaches that rely on large-scale, centralized infrastructure. Beyond the utilization of green infrastructure for CSO abatement, the lessons learned through the implementation of the GI Plan currently inform the development of future city initiatives to use green infrastructure to reduce pollutant loads conveyed directly by stormwater and to mitigate flooding from extreme rain.

Key Takeaways

- The use of green infrastructure represents a paradigm shift in stormwater management for New York City.
- Citizen groups played a key role in encouraging the city to utilize green infrastructure rather than continue to rely on conventional centralized ("gray") stormwater infrastructure.
- New York City's dense development presents distinct challenges for the deployment of green infrastructure compared to less-dense urban areas.
- Collaboration among agencies at multiple levels of governance was critical to the implementation of the Green Infrastructure Plan.
- Engagement with the general public and community organizations is essential to ensure that green infrastructure operates as intended and provides community benefits.
- The case of the New York City GI Plan provides important lessons for the intensive utilization of green infrastructure by other dense "megacities" worldwide.

Theoretical Background, Contextual Environment, and Problem Definition

This case study focuses on the NYC Green Infrastructure Plan (GI Plan) of 2010 (NYCDEP 2010), the first broad-scale implementation of green infrastructure in the city. As one of the most densely developed urban centers in the world, the City of New York faces critical challenges in the conveyance and treatment of sanitary (sewage) and stormwater flows. More than 70% of the city's land area is impervious and is drained by 12,000 km (7,500 mi) of sewers. Although the city receives an average precipitation of 1,017 mm/yr (42 in./yr), it imports an even greater volume of water—1.4 billion m³/yr, or the equivalent of another 1,700 mm/yr over the city's 783.84 km² (302 sq mi) land area—from upstate reservoirs to provide the municipal supply. All of this water must be managed to minimize the transport of pollutants to the city's surrounding harbor and prevent flooding of the city's communities and subterranean infrastructure (NYCDEP 2013b).

Through its history, New York City's approach to water management has evolved with the city's urban expansion, advances in civil engineering, and federal regulatory requirements. The design and operations of the sewer and wastewater system are also highly dependent on climate, and the challenges of water management in the city will be augmented by projections of more extreme precipitation patterns with climate change in the coming decades (Fischer and Knutti 2015; Kharin et al. 2013). Although water management during the twentieth century relied primarily on the use of centralized, large-scale "gray" infrastructure, innovative "green" infrastructure can provide opportunities for the city to develop climate-change-resilient systems for water management while providing ecological, social, and economic co-benefits.

One of the most important water-management challenges currently facing New York City is the management of combined sewer overflows (CSOs). As is the case with many older U.S. cities, the majority of New York City's sewer system is *combined*, with both sanitary sewage flows and stormwater conveyed by the same distribution pipes. Under most conditions, this combined flow is treated by wastewater-treatment plants before being discharged into waterways. However, during heavy rain events, the combined stormflow and sanitary baseflow may exceed the maximum treatment-plant capacity. When these CSO events occur, the excess flow is diverted directly into the city's waterways. Although CSO discharges are predominantly composed of stormwater, the fraction of raw sewage they contain can be a significant source of pathogens, nutrients, and other pollutants to receiving waters.

To address their water-quality impact, the U.S. Environmental Protection Agency (EPA) has regulated CSOs under the Clean Water Act since 1994 (EPA 1994). In New York State, these regulations are administered by the New York State Department of Environmental Conservation (NYSDEC), which issues National Pollutant Discharge Elimination System (NPDES) permits associated with mandated CSO-control practices to municipalities in the state that have combined sewer systems. Until recently, the mitigation of CSOs has relied primarily on the use of large centralized infrastructure, such as retention tanks, that store large volumes of combined flow until it can be treated by wastewater-treatment plants. However, these approaches are often costly and disruptive, requiring either very large amounts of land or underground tunneling. As an alternative, green infrastructure distributed throughout the landscape has been increasingly recognized as an effective option for CSO control, and is central to the NYC Green Infrastructure Plan (GI Plan).

While most of the city's sewer system is combined, sections of the system that were developed more recently are *separate*—stormflow and sanitary wastewater are conveyed in separate pipes, with only sanitary flows transported to the wastewater-treatment plant. This approach prevents overflow discharges of untreated sewage during wet weather, but the continuous discharge of untreated stormwater runoff can also contribute to impaired water quality. As a result, municipal separate storm sewers (MS4s) are also regulated under the U.S. Clean Water Act, and the NYSDEC also administers the MS4-permitting program through the NPDES. In 2018, the city will be required to submit a Stormwater Management Plan (SWMP), describing how the city will use green infrastructure and other best management practices to reduce pollution conveyed to receiving waters through the city's separate storm sewers to meet the requirements of its MS4 NPDES permit.

Although GI can provide a variety of benefits for the management of urban stormwater (Voskamp and Van de Ven 2015), the NYC GI Plan of 2010 was developed as a strategy for the city to control CSOs. In 2005, the New York City Department of Environmental Protection (NYCDEP) agreed to an administrative consent order (CSO Consent Order) with the NYSDEC, which mandated the preparation of Waterbody/Watershed Facility Plans (CSO Facility Plans) for the areas of New York City with combined sewer systems. These original CSO Facility Plans were released by the NYCDEP in 2007 and relied exclusively on centralized, large-scale infrastructure projects, such as the construction of large tanks and underground tunnels to store CSO flow and the expansion of wastewater-treatment plants.

However, the release of the initial CSO Facility Plans in spring 2007 coincided with a growing movement in support of the use of GI at both the national and city levels, along with several key events that greatly affected the perception of stormwater management by city managers and stakeholders. In March 2007, while the CSO Facility Plans were in preparation, the EPA, in collaboration with nongovernmental environmental organizations, issued a memorandum to encourage the use of GI in Clean Water Act programs. This memo defined green infrastructure approaches as those that "infiltrate, evapotranspirate or reuse stormwater, with significant utilization of soils and vegetation rather than traditional hardscape collection, conveyance and storage structures" (EPA 2007). It also emphasized that green infrastructure is most effective when supplemented with decentralized storage and infiltration approaches such as cisterns, rain barrels, and permeable pavement.

While smaller and less dense cities throughout the United States began to utilize GI to meet Clean Water Act requirements in response to this memorandum, the widespread utilization of GI was still assumed to be infeasible in a city as densely developed as New York. It took considerable advocacy by community organizations for GI to be seriously considered as a strategy to meet New York City's Clean Water Act CSO-reduction requirements. Under the CSO Consent Order, the NYCDEP was advised by Citizens Advisory Committees, which included nongovernmental environmental organizations, community groups, and local universities. These stakeholders advocated for the widespread utilization of *source controls*—the use of a decentralized approach to detain or retain stormwater rather than conveying and collecting it. These organizations formed the Storm Water Infrastructure Matters (SWIM) coalition in March 2007, developing demonstration GI projects throughout the city and engaging the Mayor's Office in the development of water-quality initiatives.

On Earth Day (April 22nd) 2007, the city released PlaNYC (City of New York 2007), its first long-term sustainability plan, which included a stated goal of improving water quality to support recreational use in 90% of the city's waterways by 2030. PlaNYC included initiatives to construct "Greenstreet" parks at intersections, incentives for the construction of green roofs, and requirements to include green infrastructure in parking lots. In response to stakeholder advocacy, PlaNYC also specifically recommended the formation of an interagency task force to develop a Sustainable Stormwater Management Plan for the City.

When this Sustainable Stormwater Management Plan (City of New York 2008) was released in 2008, a key finding of the report was that decentralized GI could actually be more cost-effective than large-scale gray infrastructure projects. The plan thus adopted a goal to create a "network of source controls" to reduce the volume of runoff entering the city's sewer system. It recommended a three-part strategy to achieve this goal, which included implementing cost-effective GI, resolving the feasibility of promising technologies through demonstration projects and analyses, and exploring funding options for stormwater source controls.

In response to these recommendations, the New York City Department of Environmental Protection released the NYC Green Infrastructure Plan (GI Plan) in September 2010 (table 6.1). The plan would result in greater reduction in annual CSO discharge volume compared to the all-gray strategy detailed in the Watershed Facility Plans, while providing energy-demand reduction (see chapter 5), habitat creation, and city beautification co-benefits. However, the widespread utilization of green infrastructure would be a paradigm shift in New York City water management; implementation of the plan (figure 6.1) would require close coordination among a variety of city agencies, along with close engagement with the city's nongovernmental stakeholders (table 6.2).

TABLE 6.1 Events That Set the Stage for the NYC Green Infrastructure Plan

Date	Event
1990s	New York City initiates the Staten Island Bluebelt Program for stormwater management and flood amelioration in low-density neighborhoods at the edge of the city.
April 19, 1994	The EPA issues the CSO Control Policy (59 FR 18688), which establishes a nationally consistent approach for controlling CSO discharges through the National Pollution Discharge Elimination System (NPDES) permit program.
May 15, 2000	Congress amends the Clean Water Act to require NPDES CSO discharge permit-holders to conform to the CSO Control Policy (65 FR 30886).
March 9, 2003	NYC311 launches as a gateway to New York City nonemergency services. The system includes water system service requests to the NYCDEP, which can be used as a geospatial indicator of nuisance flood occurrence or other problems with the sewer system.

TABLE 6.1 (*Continued*)

Date	Event
January 14, 2005	The NYCDEP agrees to an administrative consent order (CSO Consent Order) with the New York State Department of Environmental Conservation (DEC File CO2-20000107-8). The CSO Consent Order requires the preparation of CSO Watershed Facility Plans by June 2007.
March 5, 2007	The EPA issues a memorandum titled "Using Green Infrastructure to Protect Water Quality in Stormwater, CSO, Nonpoint Source and Other Programs," encouraging the use of green infrastructure to meet NPDES permit requirements (EPA 2007).
March 22, 2007	Storm Water Infrastructure Matters (SWIM), a coalition of nongovernmental environmental organization, local community groups, architects, and universities, launches with an event in Stuyvesant Cove, Manhattan.
April 22, 2007	The New York City Mayor's Office of Long Term Planning and Sustainability releases PlaNYC.
June 30, 2007	The NYCDEP submits CSO Waterbody/Watershed Facility Plans pursuant to the 2005 CSO Order.
August 8, 2007	A cloudburst rainstorm causes widespread urban flooding and transit disruptions throughout New York City. The storm's occurrence during a weekday rush hour exacerbated its impacts on New York City's critical infrastructure and awareness of the issue of extreme rain.
April 28, 2008	The City convenes a Flood Emergency Response Task Force.
December 1, 2008	An Interagency BMP Task Force releases the PlaNYC Sustainable Stormwater Management Plan. This plan concludes that green infrastructure is feasible in some areas and can be more cost-effective than large-scale, conventional, gray infrastructure projects.
February 21, 2009	As part of the American Recovery and Reinvestment Act of 2008, 20% of the Clean Water and Drinking Water State Revolving Funds are targeted toward green infrastructure and related environmentally innovative projects.
February 1, 2010	Archived 311 service requests are made accessible through the New York City Open Data Portal.
September 28, 2010	The New York City Green Infrastructure Plan is released by the Department of Environmental Protection.

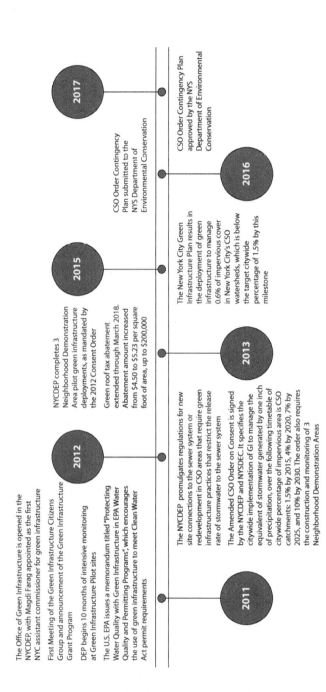

FIGURE 6.1 New York City's GI Plan timeline.

TABLE 6.2 Implementation of the New York City Green Infrastructure Plan

Date	Event
January 2011	The Office of Green Infrastructure is opened in the NYCDEP, with Magdi Farag appointed as the first assistant commissioner for green infrastructure.
February 2011	First meeting of the Green Infrastructure Citizen's Group is held and Green Infrastructure Grant Program is announced.
October 2011	NYCDEP begins ten months of intensive monitoring at green infrastructure pilot sites.
April 20, 2011	The EPA issues a memorandum titled "Protecting Water Quality with Green Infrastructure in EPA Water Quality and Permitting Programs" (EPA 2011), which encourages the use of green infrastructure to meet Clean Water Act permit requirements.
January 4, 2012	The NYCDEP promulgates regulations ("stormwater performance standards") for new site connections to the sewer system or redevelopment in CSO areas, requiring green infrastructure practices that restrict the release rate of stormwater to the sewer system (New York City, N.Y., Rules, Tit. 15, § 31).
March 13, 2012	The Amended CSO Order on Consent is signed by the NYCDEP and NYSDEC. This order specifies the citywide implementation of GI to manage the equivalent of stormwater generated by one inch of precipitation, over the following timetable of citywide percentage of impervious area in CSO catchments: 1.5% by 2015, 4% by 2020, 7% by 2025, and 10% by 2030. The order also requires the construction and monitoring of three neighborhood demonstration areas (NDAs).
June 3, 2013	NYCDEP completes three NDA pilot green infrastructure deployments, as mandated by the 2012 Consent Order.
December 18, 2013	Green roof tax abatement is extended through March 2018. Abatement amount is increased from $4.50 to $5.23 per square foot, up to $200,000.
December 31, 2015	The New York City Green Infrastructure Plan has resulted in the deployment of green infrastructure to manage 0.6% of impervious cover in New York City's CSO watersheds, which is below the target citywide percentage of 1.5% by this milestone.
June 27, 2016	CSO Order Contingency Plan is submitted to the NYSDEC.
July 5, 2017	CSO Order Contingency Plan is approved by the NYSDEC.

Implementation of the GI Plan

GI Plan Approach: What Is "Green" Infrastructure?

New York City adopts a broad definition of "green" infrastructure (GI), encompassing all decentralized stormwater source controls—including those that do not actually utilize vegetation, such as porous pavement or rain barrels. This definition reflects a more holistic, watershed-focused view of green infrastructure that centers on restoring features of the natural water cycle such as detention storage, evapotranspiration, and recycling of precipitation. While New York's GI definition differs from that of the EPA, it reflects the EPA's recommendation that vegetated infrastructure should be integrated with decentralized, engineered source controls (figure 6.2). It also reflects the view of the EPA that GI "facilitates or mimics natural processes that also recharge groundwater, preserve baseflows, moderate temperature impacts and protect hydrologic and hydraulic stability" (EPA 2007).

Cost-effectiveness and optimization of the existing gray stormwater system are a central feature of the GI Plan. The plan preserved several large retention-tank projects included in the 2007 CSO facility plans that were determined to be cost-effective, but eliminated planned gray infrastructure projects where an equivalent volume of combined sewer flow could be managed more efficiently with GI. At the release of the 2010 GI Plan, the original all-gray strategy of the CSO facility plans was estimated to cost $6.8 billion over twenty years, while the GI Plan was expected to cost $5.3 billion over the same time

(a)

FIGURE 6.2 Integrating gray and green infrastructure at the Paerdegat Basin CSO Facility: (a) gray CSO retention-tank facilities; (b) green roof installed at the retention facility (vegetated "green"); (c) porous pavement (unvegetated "green").

(*Images*: NYCDEP)

(b)

(c)

FIGURE 6.2 (*Continued*)

period, with $2.9 billion of the GI Plan costs resulting from the construction of already planned centralized gray infrastructure that was determined to be cost-effective.

Optimization of Existing Gray Stormwater Infrastructure

To support the optimization of the existing gray stormwater system, NYCDEP relied heavily on the use of newly available sensor technologies and communications media. For example, clogging of sewers by debris, sediment, and improperly disposed cooking oil results in reduced capacity for stormwater storage and conveyance and increased frequency of CSOs and sewer-backup flooding. Under the GI Plan, the NYCDEP conducted regular video and sonar surveying of the sewer system to identify sewer lines that require cleaning, rehabilitation, or repair (NYCDEP 2010).

The use of "smart" water metering is another example of the use of information technologies in support of the GI Plan. NYCDEP invested in an Automated Meter Reading (AMR) network, which consists of low-power radio transmitters connected to individual water meters that send daily readings through a network of rooftop receivers located throughout the city. The AMR network allows customers to regularly track their water use, supporting more efficient use and reduced demand. It also allows NYCDEP to identify leaks in the municipal distribution system and to track usage trends over time. Reduced water demand results in reduced sanitary baseflow in the sewer system and an increased capacity to convey and store stormwater without additional gray infrastructure construction (NYCDEP 2010).

Green Infrastructure Siting, Construction, and Maintenance

While optimization of existing gray infrastructure was critical for the implementation of the GI Plan, the core of the GI Plan was the use of novel GI to slow down—or entirely prevent—stormwater from entering the city's combined sewer system. The plan included specific targets for stormwater management (figure 6.3), depending on the amount of impervious surface present within a CSO watershed. Thus, future land development in CSO watersheds that increased total impervious cover would require additional deployment of green infrastructure to meet volume-control targets. The GI Plan targets do not prescribe the type of source controls to be implemented, but instead can be met from a "toolbox" of GI options, based on demonstration projects that had been piloted by the NYCDEP. These infrastructure options employ one or more mechanisms to *retain* stormwater, preventing it from ever entering the sewer

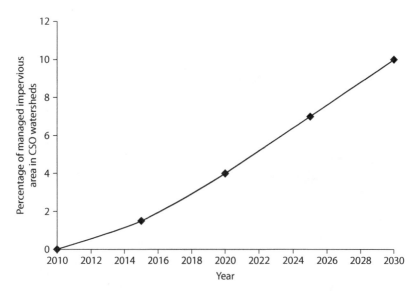

FIGURE 6.3 Schedule of milestones for GI Plan implementation under the 2012 Amended Consent Order.

system, or *detain* stormwater, storing it temporarily with only slow releases to the sewer system to prevent exceeding capacity.

By their nature, conventional sewer systems operate out of sight and mind of city residents and independently of other critical city systems. In contrast, GI distributed throughout the city can influence many aspects of city life and function, with the potential to provide numerous co-benefits, but also disruptions if not sited or maintained properly. The NYCDEP analyzed geospatial tax-lot and land-use data to identify potential opportunities for siting green infrastructure. These types of sites can be divided into three major categories:

1. *Right-of-way*: Includes New York City's public streets and sidewalks. In 2010, 27% of the area of CSO watersheds were in the public right-of-way.
2. *Public onsite*: This area includes property lots owned by the City of New York, such as public housing developments, schools, facilities, and parks.
3. *Private onsite*: More than half of the area in CSO watersheds is privately owned. Direct support and incentives are incorporated into the GI Plan to encourage the use of GI on these properties.

During the first few years of implementation of the GI Plan, construction of GI in the right-of-way was prioritized (figure 6.4). The procedure for siting right-of-way GI is as follows. Each year, priority CSO areas are identified based

FIGURE 6.4 Right-of-way bioswale in Bushwick, Brooklyn.

Source: NYCDEP.

on CSO volume and frequency, water-quality conditions, and outfall proximity to existing or planned public waterfront access locations (NYCDEP 2017b). Once these areas have been determined, the DEP then works with the New York City Department of Parks and Recreation (NYCDPR) and the New York City Department of Transportation (NYCDOT) to conduct neighborhood "walkthroughs" to identify sites that would provide minimal disruption to pedestrian or road traffic while providing needed greenspace in underserved communities. After potential sites are identified, field investigations are conducted to ensure that the sites have suitable geophysical conditions and are not contaminated by legacy pollutants (NYC Geotechnical Guidance Document). If sites meet these criteria, the New York City Department of Design and Construction (NYC-DDC) supervises bidding to private contractors for construction.

Regular maintenance is critical in ensuring that GI functions as intended and provides maximum co-benefits. For example, right-of-way GI provides water-quality benefits by allowing suspended solids and floatables to settle while water is detained, rather than being conveyed directly into receiving waters during CSOs. However, this process, along with direct littering and dumping, can result in the collection of debris or garbage in the right-of-way swales. Regular maintenance prevents potential accumulation of this debris. In addition, cleaning and maintenance ensure that water completely drains between storm events to prevent breeding of mosquitoes or other vectors (EPA 2005).

In 2012, the NYCDEP developed an agreement with the NYCDPR establishing agency roles for maintenance of green infrastructure in the public right-of-way. Under this agreement, DEP staff would perform basic cleaning and maintenance while NYCDPR staff would maintain the trees, plants, and landscaping. In addition, the DOT would maintain the original grade to the extent possible, performing regular resurfacing operations. Beyond this regular maintenance, citizens can request additional maintenance service directly through the stormwater outreach coordinator in the Office of Green Infrastructure (NYCDEP 2013a).

As right-of-way green infrastructure construction continues, more recent efforts have focused on siting green infrastructure projects on public property ("public onsite"). In January 2012, the NYCDEP signed a partner agreement with the New York City Housing Authority (NYCHA) to site green infrastructure in publicly owned housing developments, with the DEP providing needed maintenance. Much of New York City's publicly owned housing was developed as "superblocks," with multistory residential buildings surrounding open plazas that are often fenced off and underutilized. Although public housing communities are among the most densely populated in the city, they still provide opportunities to create a variety of different types of green infrastructure that would not be feasible with a conventional street grid, while providing needed amenities for local residents. These have included retrofitted playgrounds with permeable pavement, rain gardens (figure 6.5), and green roofs.

As with the right-of-way GI, the city has also had to overcome feasibility challenges with the siting of project on NYCHA property. In addition to encountering inappropriate geophysical conditions, some otherwise suitable sites were found to have existing subterranean infrastructure, hazardous materials, or facilities-maintenance issues that prevented the safe construction of planned green infrastructure. These obstacles have delayed the

FIGURE 6.5 Pilot rain garden installation at NYCHA Hope Houses in the Bronx.

Source: NYCDEP.

widespread implementation of onsite GI on publicly owned properties to date (NYCDEP 2016a).

In addition to the partnership with NYCHA, the city has maintained ongoing efforts to site GI in public parkland and playgrounds. NYCDEP is partnered with the New York City Department of Parks and Recreation Green Infrastructure Unit to implement green infrastructure retrofits in city parks. Along with this ongoing collaboration, in fall 2014 the NYCDEP committed $36 million to fund green infrastructure as part of a new City Parks Initiative (CPI). This funding will support a variety of types of green infrastructure while providing increased access to greenspace for underserved communities. Construction on the first CPI site will begin in summer 2018 (NYC Department of Parks and Recreation, personal communication).

Public/private partnerships also play a key role in facilitating the siting and construction of green infrastructure on public properties. In 2011, the NYCDEP joined the "Schoolyards to Playgrounds" program, an existing collaboration between the Trust for Public Land (a private nonprofit organization), the New York City Department of Education (NYCDOE), and the New York City School Construction Authority (NYCSCA) to renovate schoolyards in neighborhoods with inadequate access to parks. Through this partnership, the NYCDEP provides funding for green infrastructure components in playground projects. Then, the Trust for Public Land identifies potential sites in CSO priority areas based on the community need for access to open space.

Once suitable sites are identified, the design of these playgrounds is developed in close coordination with local schoolchildren and then tailored to suit the sites' geophysical conditions in collaboration with NYCDEP engineers (NYCDEP 2014). As maintenance for these projects is ultimately provided by the school custodial staff, the Trust for Public Land consults with them in advance to address concerns about design features that could create maintenance difficulties. Once the playgrounds are completed, the Trust for Public Land conducts school assemblies with lessons on the how the playground regulates the water cycle, protects harbor water quality, and makes the city more resilient to climate change. To date, GI installed in public playground sites through this partnership includes rain gardens to drain asphalt ballfields, permeable synthetic turf, and areas of permeable pavement (figure 6.6). According to Mary Alice Lee, director of the Trust for Public Lands' New York City Playgrounds Program, "The Trust for Public Land feels that the Green Infrastructure partnership supports our mission completely—we're creating safe places to play while protecting the environment."

As more than half of the land area in CSO watersheds is privately owned property, incentivizing private deployment of green infrastructure will ultimately be critical to the effective use of GI for CSO mitigation. However, the deployment and maintenance of GI on private property presents distinct challenges; the DEP must be able to ensure that the GI utilized is designed to effectively manage stormwater and must be able to gain regular access for direct maintenance or ensure by some other means that private GI continues to operate as intended.

FIGURE 6.6 Playground at Public School 65K in Brooklyn, New York, before (*left*) and after (*right*) retrofit through a public/private partnership with the Trust for Public Land.

Source: NYCDEP.

FIGURE 6.7 Agricultural green roof at the Brooklyn Grange Urban Farm. The green roof was funded by the NYCDEP GI Grant Program.

Source: NYCDEP.

To begin to address these challenges, the NYCDEP has administered a grant program since 2010 to provide funding to community organizations, academic institutions, and other private property owners to develop a variety of different GI projects (figure 6.7). The NYCDEP also sponsors a Rain Barrel Giveaway program, which provides fifty-five-gallon rain barrels free of charge to thousands of New York City homeowners each year. The rain barrels connect directly to the downspout draining the roof and can be used to store water for irrigating lawns and gardens (figure 6.8). During giveaway events, recipients receive training on their proper operation and maintenance. The rain barrels deployed to date on private properties throughout the city have the potential to prevent up to 2,270 m^3 (600,000 gallons) of stormwater from entering the sewer system during a rain event (NYCDEP 2016c).

Green infrastructure on private property is also incentivized by tax and fee abatements and rules for new development. Since 2007, private properties are eligible for a tax abatement based on the area of green roofs. In order to qualify, property owners must prepare a maintenance plan as part of their registration process. Beginning in 2011, New York City has also piloted an area-based stormwater fee for existing large parking lots that do not receive municipal

FIGURE 6.8 Rain barrel connected to a downspout. Water stored in the rain barrel can be used for watering lawns and gardens.

Source: NYS Soil and Water Conservation District.

service. Although parking lot owners that implement GI would be exempt from this fee, no green infrastructure exemptions have been awarded in the first five years of implementation of this pilot program.

In addition, in 2012 the NYCDEP amended city rules governing connections to the sewer system to limit the release of stormwater from new development throughout the city and alterations to existing development in CSO areas. To support the implementation of the new stormwater-release standards by the city's development community, the NYCDEP collaborated with the Department of Buildings to develop Guidelines for the Design and Construction of Stormwater Management Systems (NYCDEP 2012c). This document provided guidance for the use of a variety of types and combinations of green infrastructure to meet stormwater-release standards.

Community Outreach and Engagement

Community organizations played an integral role in the initial development of the GI Plan, and outreach with the community remains an essential component of the plan's implementation (table 6.4). The NYCDEP has dedicated stormwater outreach staff that meet regularly with local community organizations and address residents' concerns. In addition, the NYCDEP holds an annual public forum with a GI Citizens Group, an open group of interested individuals,

TABLE 6.3 Federal and State Agency Stakeholders

Stakeholder	Role	Interest	Effect	Needed incentives
United States Environmental Protection Agency	Promulgates regulation under the U.S. Clean Water Act	Fishable/swimmable U.S. waterways; water management that provides sustainability co-benefits	Encouragement and guidance for the use of green infrastructure to meet water-quality requirements	Support in the federal budget and by all three branches of the U.S. federal government
New York State Department of Environmental Conservation	Administers Clean Water Act regulation in New York State	Ensuring that New York municipalities meet NPDES requirements	Enforces Clean Water Act–mandated green infrastructure planning	Support integrated water management that goes beyond regulatory requirements; engage nongovernment stakeholders in the regulatory process

TABLE 6.4 NGOs, Community Groups, and the Private Sector

Stakeholder	Role	Interest	Effect	Needed incentives
Engineering/design and environmental consulting firms	Participate in the Water Infrastructure Steering Committee; design, construct, and monitor green infrastructure	Profit through providing technical expertise	Play a critical role, along with city agencies, in the actual implementation of the GI Plan	Increased public and private funding for GI
Trust for Public Land	Partner with NYCDEP to incorporate GI in public school playgrounds	Equitable access to high-quality public space; sustainable and resilient cities	Support the NYCDEP in onsite GI implementation	Increased public and private funding for GI
Green infrastructure grant recipients	Propose the development of GI in their communities	Improved water management and co-benefits	Provide demonstrations of GI use on private property	Increased public and private funding for GI
Property owners and residents	Fund and implement GI on their property; deploy rain barrels	Improved water management, reduced water bills, GI co-benefits	Support meeting stormwater-management targets under the CWA	Financial incentives through rate structure and tax abatements
Community organizations	Participate in GI Citizens Committee and/or the GI Steering Committee; advocate for citizen concerns; conduct education and outreach	Sustainable and resilient communities	Advocate for GI utilization, funding, and maintenance; facilitate citizen participation in GI Plan development and implementation	None

TABLE 6.5 New York City Agencies and Public Benefit Corporations

Agency/public benefit corporation	Role	Interest	Effect	Needed incentives
Department of Environmental Protection (DEP)	Development and implementation of the GI Plan and related city GI programs	Protection of public health and the environment of New York City	Oversees the construction and use of GI in New York City	Continued federal, state, and local political support for GI implementation
Department of Design and Construction (DDC)	Standing participant in the GI Technical Task Force; areawide contracts and construction, design standards development, grant application review	High-quality infrastructure in New York City	Supports implementation of the GI Plan	None
Department of Parks and Recreation (DPR)	Standing participant in the GI Technical Task Force; right-of-way and onsite site selection and design; maintenance of GI vegetation; Community Parks Initiative	Creation and maintenance of resilient and sustainable parks and recreational amenities	Supports implementation of the GI Plan	Increased public and private funding for GI; increased information on biodiversity and recreational co-benefits of GI
Department of Transportation (DOT)	Standing participant in the GI Technical Task Force; review of all areawide design, right-of-way site selection and design-standards development, grant application review	The safe, efficient, and environmentally responsible movement of people and goods throughout New York City	Supports implementation of the GI Plan	Increased public and private funding for GI

Agency	Collaboration	Mission	GI Plan	Benefits
Environmental Development Corporation (EDC)	Frequently meets with the GI Technical Task Force; areawide contracts design and construction	Inclusive innovation and economic growth in New York City	Supports implementation of the GI Plan	Increased public and private funding for GI; increased information on economic co-benefits of GI
Health and Hospitals	Frequently meets with the GI Technical Task Force	Health services for New York City residents	Supports implementation of the GI Plan	Increased public and private funding for GI; increased information on public health co-benefits of GI
New York City Housing Authority (NYCHA)	Collaborates with DEP to construct GI on public housing property	Safe housing and community for low-income New Yorkers	Supports implementation of the GI Plan	Increased public and private funding for GI
Department of Buildings (DOB)	Assists DEP in developing guidance for the use of GI in city buildings	The lawful use of buildings in New York City	Supports implementation of the stormwater rule, but the GI implemented is not counted toward GI Plan targets	Legal mandates to incentivize or require the use of GI
Department of Cultural Affairs (DCA)	Works with the DEP to identify appropriate sites on public properties	Support for and strengthening of cultural life	Supports implementation of the GI Plan	Increased public and private funding for GI; increased information on the cultural co-benefits provided by GI
Department of Education (DOE)/NYC School Construction Authority	Collaborates with the Trust for Public Land and the DEP to construct GI on public school properties	Safe, attractive, and environmentally sound schools for students in New York City public schools	Supports implementation of the GI Plan	Increased public and private funding for GI
NYC311—Mayor's Office of Operations (MOO)	Collaborates with the DEP to provide information on New York City's water systems to the general public and to facilitate the resolution of water-related service requests	Access to government services and information	Supports implementation of the GI Plan	Incorporation of GI service requests into the 311 system, along with "gray" infrastructure

organizations, businesses, and institutions. They are also advised by a GI Steering Committee, which is comprised of representatives from local environmental organizations, academic institutions, and architectural firms with expertise in stormwater management. Shino Tanikawa of the New York City Soil and Water Conservation District says, "We feel that we have a relationship with the New York City Department of Environmental Protection. They listen to us and respect our opinion."

Along with this broader outreach, the NYCDEP helps prepare communities for GI construction by deploying community construction liaisons (CCLs), who serve as resources for local stakeholders. The CCLs provide maps of all planned GI projects to community boards and elected officials prior to the start of construction work, distribute informational brochures and door-hangers to property owners, and provide regular updates during GI construction (NYCDEP 2016a). The NYCDEP has also worked to involve the community in GI stewardship. In collaboration with the NYCHA and Million Trees NYC, they launched the BioswaleCare Program, which has hosted workshops for public-housing residents, local church congregations, and other community groups. Participants in these workshops receive hands-on training in clearing inlets and outlets, removing weeds, and using tools to maintain the grading of right-of-way bioswales and have the opportunity to care for green infrastructure.

Adaptive Management and Institutionalizing the Use of Green Infrastructure

The GI Plan utilizes the strategy of *adaptive management*—an iterative process in which incremental measures are continually evaluated and refined. At the time of the initial development of the GI Plan in 2010, this approach was viewed as essential given the uncertainties about the future condition of various factors that could affect stormwater management, including climate change, population, water demand, technologies, and regulatory requirements, and the magnitude of investment required. It also supports the city's current strategy of building *resilience* (see chapter 1), or the ability to adapt to and quickly recover from changing circumstances and system-level shocks.

Monitoring and assessment to support adaptive management have been conducted in partnership with environmental consulting firms and academic institutions and take place at three scales:

1. *Monitoring of individual green infrastructure projects.* To support initial implementation of the GI Plan, the NYCDEP oversaw the design and evaluation of twenty-five pilot green-infrastructure projects of different technologies

and under different conditions throughout the city. These pilot sites were equipped with rain gauges, soil moisture sensors, piezometers, and flowmeters to continuously monitor water levels and stormflow. Plant survival and qualitative assessments of aesthetics, community perception, and maintenance requirements were also considered. Monitoring was conducted for a period of several months during 2011 and 2012, which included August 2011, the wettest month in the meteorological record of New York City. The results indicated that green infrastructure was effective in detaining stormwater to reduce peak flows—even during very intense storm events—and retaining stormwater from storm events with an inch or less of total precipitation (NYCDEP 2012a, 2012b). Data from this performance monitoring were used to represent green infrastructure in watershed-scale numerical modeling studies and cost/benefit analyses (NYCDEP 2013a).

The NYCDEP is also leading a comprehensive co-benefits study. Field site monitoring to quantify co-benefits has included observations of temperature, plantings, biodiversity, and soil chemistry. The initial results of this study suggest that while GI surfaces are cooler than nearby pavement, the current area of GI is insufficient for the cooler surfaces to translate to cooler ambient air temperatures. Soil respiration rates were found to be generally high, which may facilitate carbon sequestration, but additional study is necessary to clarify the role of green infrastructure in stormwater pollutant retention. Pollinators, which have experienced widespread decline throughout North America (Cameron et al. 2011), were present in vegetated green infrastructure sited in even the most highly urbanized communities (John McLaughlin, Personal Communication). The results of the co-benefits monitoring were incorporated into a software tool, which facilitates costs and benefits calculations for different types of green infrastructure.

2. *Monitoring of neighborhood demonstration areas (NDAs).* In fulfillment of the 2012 Amended CSO Consent Order, the NYCDEP developed three NDAs, consisting of multiple-block drainage areas that were instrumented to observe actual stormwater volumes entering the sewer system. A variety of green infrastructure was then deployed, covering 17.9%, 18.7%, and 5.1% of the impervious areas of each NDA, with an average of 14.1% of the impervious cover being managed across the three NDAs. This average percentage exceeded the citywide target for 2030 of 10% impervious-area management.

    Several dozen storms were monitored before and after deployment of GI in the NDAs to assess the catchment-scale effects of GI implementation. The results showed a decrease in stormwater runoff entering the combined sewers in all three areas with the implementation of GI. For storm events with total precipitation less than or equal to one inch (the 90th percentile of storm events in NYC), the runoff entering the combined sewers was decreased by 20–23% across all three areas. These results suggest that for such storms, the performance of green infrastructure is not a linear function of the percentage area managed or that there may be a threshold above which green infrastructure does not provide additional stormwater control for the majority of small storms. The role of green infrastructure in capturing runoff in large storms is less clear, because most of the large storms monitored in the NDAs occurred before the green infrastructure was deployed (NYCDEP 2014).

3. *Citywide monitoring and performance metrics.* The NYCDEP tracks the thousands of GI projects implemented under the GI Plan using GreenHUB, based on a geographic information system (GIS). For each GI project in the database, the system maintains information including location, type of GI, construction status, dimensions, data from the field geotechnical investigation, and calculated stormwater volume capacity. GreenHUB also includes information about potential sites that were found to be unsuitable so that these sites can be reconsidered as conditions change and new designs of green infrastructure are developed. Projects in the GreenHUB database are updated monthly to reflect current information (NYCDEP 2017b). The 2012 Amended CSO Consent Order required the city to develop CSO performance metrics representing the cumulative citywide CSO volume reduction associated with implementing the 2015 target of managing 1.5% of impervious cover in CSO watersheds, and the ultimate plan goal of 10% impervious cover management by 2030. NYC GreenHUB provides the data needed to represent the actual design and location of GI that has been implemented or planned for the near term under the GI Plan in distributed numerical models.

Impact

The implementation of the GI Plan has demonstrated that the constructed GI may be even more effective in mitigating CSOs in New York City than originally estimated, but this effectiveness will depend on full implementation of the plan through 2030. Using data on actual GI that has been deployed under the GI Plan, GreenHUB numerical modeling has shown that with the management of 1.5% of the impervious area in CSO watersheds planned for the very near term, 2.4% of the annual CSO volume would be reduced. Upscaling the pilot monitoring data to represent GI performance with 10% impervious cover management, full implementation of the GI Plan in 2030 would result in a citywide reduction in CSO volume of 8.1%, exceeding the original projection of 7.3% in the 2010 GI Plan (NYCDEP 2016a).

While work toward these regulatory objectives under the CSO program continues, the use of GI will also be critical in helping the city meet impending regulatory requirements under the Clean Water Act MS4 (separate storm sewer) program. To reflect this broader role, the original GI Steering Committee that advised the DEP on implementation of the GI Plan was restructured in 2013 as a Water Infrastructure Steering Committee and considers synergies among the MS4 program, climate change resiliency, and the CSO program.

To support implementation of the Stormwater Management Plan (SWMP), the NYCDEP has developed designs for several enhanced bioretention gardens that will be piloted in public onsite locations. Informed by the lessons learned through implementation of the GI Plan, these include a shallow alternative that can be used at sites with high water tables and a settling forebay that can be installed under a hardscape cover, concealing litter transported by stormwater between cleanings. To maximize treatment opportunities within areas designed for human use, the new bioretention designs can be connected underneath sidewalks, providing a treatment train for maximal stormwater quality improvement (NYCDEP 2017c). According to Alan Cohn, NYCDEP Climate Programs Office, "New York City has been a leader in resilience planning. Its Green Infrastructure Program uses an adaptive management approach, so exploring opportunities to use green infrastructure for flood mitigation is the next natural step."

Many city practitioners view climate change as the greatest threat to the successful implementation of the GI Plan and related stormwater programs; design and planning are based on the historical record of precipitation occurrence, which may not be representative of local precipitation conditions under climate change (Trenberth 2003). However, while climate change will make implementation of the GI Plan more challenging, GI itself brings great potential to support the city in building climate-change resilience (see chapter 1).

In dense cities, nuisance flooding can occur when precipitation rates exceed the ability of the city's engineered drainage system to convey stormwater. As it would be prohibitively expensive and impractical to design a sewer system to convey runoff from the most intense and infrequent storms, all sewer systems are constructed to convey the flow associated with a "design" storm. Most of New York City's sewer system (built prior to 1960) was designed to convey stormwater runoff corresponding to rainfall rates of 38 mm/hr (1.5 in./hr). Since 1960, stormwater sewers have been designed to convey runoff corresponding to 45 mm/hr (1.75 in./hr). During intense "cloudburst" rainstorms, rainfall rates can exceed these design flows and result in surcharging conditions, in which the sewer pipes are submerged and pressurized, ultimately leading to urban flash flooding (City of New York 2009). Based on the long-term record at the meteorological station in Central Park, these events can be expected at recurrence intervals of about five to ten years. The frequency of cloudburst rainstorms is expected to increase with unmitigated climate change (Westra et al. 2014).

While flood mitigation was not considered in the original 2010 GI Plan, the reduction of peak flows by GI has the potential to play a role in the mitigation of cloudburst rainstorms, and this opportunity is being actively investigated by the NYCDEP Climate Program Office. In collaboration with the Ramboll Group, an international engineering design consulting firm, they conducted a best-practice study on the use of GI to mitigate flooding from cloudburst rainstorms (NYCDEP 2017a). Through the use of high-resolution GIS data, numerical modeling, and community engagement, they developed a Cloudburst Masterplan for a pilot community in Queens that experiences chronic pluvial flooding. Like the GI Plan, the Cloudburst Masterplan relies on the construction of cost-effective gray infrastructure along with green infrastructure in the right-of-way and on publicly owned housing property.

Challenges and Lessons Learned

The GI Plan was successful in demonstrating that green infrastructure could be used for stormwater management in even the densest communities of the city. However, it failed to meet the first milestone (figure 6.3) of the 2012 Amended Consent Order, the management of 1.5% of impervious cover in CSO watersheds. This failure mostly resulted from challenges in siting GI, along with the complexity of coordination among the various agencies involved in GI implementation (NYCDEP 2016b).

The city's complex geology, which includes large areas with shallow bedrock, clay-rich soils, or high water tables, was recognized early as a challenge for the utilization of green infrastructure that relies on subsurface infiltration (City of New York 2008). In response to this challenge, detention-based green infrastructure, which is less dependent on subsurface conditions than bioswales, will be given greater emphasis in future implementation of the GI Plan (NYCDEP 2017b). Also, while there are comprehensive data on existing underground utilities in the right-of-way, the extensive presence of this infrastructure can greatly limit the availability of suitable locations for right-of-way green infrastructure. In response, the NYCDEP has developed revised design standards for GI that are protective of private service lines already sited in the right-of-way.

In light of the strong community advocacy in support of the initial development of the GI Plan, an unexpected challenge that has emerged is opposition by some property owners to GI construction in the right-of-way. This opposition has mostly been limited to a small number of neighborhoods and is often based on misconceptions about how the GI program operates prior to the actual construction of GI in their communities. Residents' concerns commonly reported in local newspapers include worries that GI will impede curbside parking, that property owners will be responsible for maintenance of GI in the right-of-way, that the GI will accumulate litter, or that standing water in the GI will support breeding of mosquitoes (Edmonds 2016; Nir 2017). In response, the city has expanded outreach to these communities, supporting increased education about how the GI Plan works and stormwater issues in general.

To directly address stakeholder concerns about inadequate GI maintenance, the city increased the number of dedicated maintenance staff. However, although GI maintenance is the responsibility of NYCDEP staff, under the existing rules of the City of New York property owners could still be fined by the New York City Department of Sanitation (NYCDS) for any accumulation of litter in the public right-of-way adjacent to their property. To alleviate this potential burden on property owners, the NYCDEP negotiated an agreement with the NYCDS to give it enforcement authority for illegal dumping in right-of-way green infrastructure. In addition, the NYCDEP has come up with an impervious pavement alternative for right-of-way bioswales and tree pits, to meet the preferences of property owners who do not want vegetated green infrastructure adjacent to their property.

The use of information technology, key to the initial implementation of the Green Infrastructure Plan, can also play a critical role in future use of GI to support water-quality improvement and climate-change resiliency. For example, NYC311, a comprehensive system to respond to nonemergency inquiries and service requests, includes more than fourteen years of geo-referenced, crowdsourced flood reports and is currently being used to support priority siting of GI in neighborhoods that experience chronic nuisance flooding. NYC311 also has the potential to provide important metrics of GI performance for future flood mitigation and will allow practitioners to compare changes in nuisance flood frequency with the deployment of GI tracked through GreenHUB. In addition, NYC311 is currently used to allow the public to request maintenance of gray stormwater infrastructure, such as clearing of clogged catch basins. The expansion of this system to support service requests for GI would enhance the NYCDEP's ability to provide efficient maintenance, engage the general public in basic GI operations, and enhance the institutionalization of GI as essential city infrastructure. According to Joe Morrisroe, executive director of NYC311, "NYC311 has provided useful data to improve a multitude of city operations. We're very interested in supporting its potential use as a resilience indicator."

Conclusion

New York City's Green Infrastructure Plan merges natural ecosystem processes, cutting-edge information technology, and engagement with local communities to enhance operations of the city's sewer system and improve water quality. Although green infrastructure has been increasingly adopted for urban water management over the past decade, its utilization in New York City presented

Strengths	Weaknesses
Early engagement with the community	Needs stronger incentives for the construction of GI on private property
Dedicated funding	
Performance monitoring	Needs stronger integration between programs supporting the use of GI for CSO reduction, stormwater quality enhancement, and cloudburst flood mitigation
Integrated approach to water management that recognizes the linkages between optimization of existing gray infrastructure and development of green infrastructure	

Opportunities	Threats
The availability of frequently updated, sub-parcel resolution on impervious cover and enhanced data on GI on private property could support the development of stronger incentives for GI construction on private property	Climate change presents the greatest threat due to projected changes in precipitation patterns for New York City that may affect GI performance
Continued collaboration among various city agencies and offices will support integration of the GI Plan with other city initiatives to develop GI	
Through collaboration with climate scientists, New York City can design GI not only to function through climate change, but also to enhance the city's resilience to climate change (through cloudburst flood and urban heat mitigation, etc.)	

FIGURE 6.9 NYC GI Plan SWOT analysis.

new challenges because of the city's density, age, and physiography. Strengths and weaknesses of the GI Plan, along with future opportunities and threats, are summarized in figure 6.9. Lessons learned from the initial implementation of the GI Plan can serve as a model for other global "megacities" and will be critical for the successful use of green infrastructure to support climate-change resilience in the coming decades.

Note

This case study is based upon work supported by the National Science Foundation under Grant Number SBE-1444755. Any opinions, findings, and conclusions or recommendations expressed in this material are those of the author(s) and do not necessarily reflect the views of the National Science Foundation.

References

Cameron, Sydney A., Jeffrey D. Lozier, James P. Strange, Jonathan B. Koch, Nils Cordes, Leellen F. Solter, and Terry L. Griswold. 2011. "Patterns of Widespread Decline in North American Bumble Bees." *Proceedings of the National Academy of Sciences* 108, no. 2: 662–67.

City of New York. 2007. *PlaNYC 2007: A Greener Greater New York.* www.nyc.gov/html /planyc/downloads/pdf/publications/full_report_2007.pdf.

——. 2008. *PlaNYC: Sustainable Stormwater Management Plan 2008.* http://www.nyc.gov /html/planyc/downloads/pdf/publications/nyc_sustainable_stormwater_management _plan_final.pdf.

——. 2009. *Natural Hazard Mitigation Plan.* March 2009. https://www1.nyc.gov/assets/em /downloads/pdf/hazard_mitigation/full_hmp_march_2009.pdf.

Edmonds, Lynn. 2016. "Bayside Residents Vow to Fight Bioswales." *Queens Tribune*, July 21. http://queenstribune.com/bayside-residents-vow-fight-bioswales/.

Environmental Protection Agency (EPA). 1994. "Combined Sewer Overflow (CSO) Control Policy." *Federal Register* 59, no. 75 (April 19): 18688–98. https://www3.epa.gov/npdes/pubs /owm0111.pdf.

——. 2005. "Stormwater Structures and Mosquitoes." EPA 833-F-05-003.

——. 2007. Memorandum from Benjamin H. Grumbles, Assistant Administrator, to EPA Regional Administrators. "Using Green Infrastructure to Protect Water Quality in Stormwater, CSO, Nonpoint Source and Other Water Programs." March 5, 2007. Accessed March 24, 2017. https://www.epa.gov/sites/production/files/2015-10/documents/green infrastructure_h2oprograms_07.pdf.

Fischer, E. M., and R. Knutti. 2015. "Anthropogenic Contribution to Global Occurrence of Heavy-Precipitation and High-Temperature Extremes." *Nature Climate Change* 5, no. 6: 560–64.

Kharin, V. V., F. W. Zwiers, X. Zhang, and M. Wehner. 2013. "Changes in Temperature and Precipitation Extremes in the CMIP5 Ensemble." *Climatic Change* 119, no. 2: 345–57.

New York City Department of Environmental Protection (NYCDEP). 2010. *NYC Green Infrastructure Plan: A Sustainable Strategy for Clean Waterways.* Accessed March 21, 2017. http://www.nyc.gov/html/dep/pdf/green_infrastructure/NYCGreenInfrastructurePlan _LowRes.pdf.

——. 2012a. *NYC Green Infrastructure Plan: 2011 Update.* Accessed March 21, 2017. http:// www.nyc.gov/html/dep/pdf/green_infrastructure/gi_annual_report_2012.pdf.

——. 2012b. *NYC Green Infrastructure Plan: 2012 Green Infrastructure Pilot Monitoring Report.* Accessed March 10, 2017. http://www.nyc.gov/html/dep/pdf/green_infrastructure /2012_green_infrastructure_pilot_monitoring_report.pdf.

——. 2012c. *Guidelines for the Design and Construction of Stormwater Management Systems.* July 2012. http://www.nyc.gov/html/dep/pdf/green_infrastructure/stormwater_guidelines _2012_final.pdf.

——. 2013a. *NYC Green Infrastructure:2012 Annual Report.* Accessed March 21, 2017. http:// www.nyc.gov/html/dep/pdf/green_infrastructure/gi_annual_report_2013.pdf.

——. 2013b. *The State of the Sewers 2013.* Accessed March 21, 2017. http://www.nyc.gov/html/ dep/pdf/reports/state-of-the-sewers-2013.pdf.

——. 2014. *Report for Post-Construction Monitoring: Green Infrastructure: Neighborhood Demonstration Areas.* Accessed March 14, 2017. http://www.nyc.gov/html/dep/pdf/cso _long_term_control_plan/post-construction-monitoring-report-gi-neighborhood -demonstration-areas.pdf.

——. 2016a. *NYC Green Infrastructure: 2015 Annual Report*. Accessed March 21, 2017. http://www.nyc.gov/html/dep/pdf/green_infrastructure/gi_annual_report_2016.pdf.

——. 2016b. "Green Infrastructure Contingency Plan." June 27, 2016. Accessed March 21, 2017. http://www.nyc.gov/html/dep/pdf/green_infrastructure/gi-contingency-plan-2016.pdf.

——. 2016c. "More than 11,000 New Yorkers Received a Free Rain Barrel in 2016." Press Release, November 17. Accessed April 4, 2017. http://www.nyc.gov/html/dep/html/press_releases/16-118pr.shtml.

——. 2017a. *Cloudburst Resiliency Planning Study: Executive Summary*. January 2017. http://www.nyc.gov/html/dep/pdf/climate/nyc-cloudburst-study.pdf.

——. 2017b. *Green Infrastructure Performance Metrics Report*. June 2016. Accessed March 21, 2017. http://www.nyc.gov/html/dep/pdf/green_infrastructure/gi-performance-metrics-report-2016.pdf.

——. 2017c. *NYC Municipal Separate Storm Sewer System (MS4): 2016 Progress Report*. Accessed April 4, 2017. http://www.nyc.gov/html/dep/pdf/water_sewer/ms4-progress-report.pdf.

Nir, Sarah Maslin. 2017. "To the City, a Pollution Fighter. To Some Residents, an Eyesore." *New York Times*, March 23. https://www.nytimes.com/2017/03/23/nyregion/bioswale-rain-gardens-new-york.html.

Trenberth, Kevin E., Aiguo Dai, Roy M. Rasmussen, and David B. Parsons. 2003. "The Changing Character of Precipitation." *Bureau of the American Meteorological Society* 84 no. 9: 1205–17.

Voskamp, I. M., and F. H. M. Van de Ven. 2015. "Planning Support System for Climate Adaptation: Composing Effective Sets of Blue-Green Measures to Reduce Urban Vulnerability to Extreme Weather Events." *Building and Environment* 83:159–67.

Westra, S., H. J. Fowler, J. P. Evans, L. V. Alexander, Peter Berg, F. Johnson, E. J. Kendon, G. Lenderink, and N. M. Roberts. 2014. "Future Changes to the Intensity and Frequency of Short-Duration Extreme Rainfall." *Reviews of Geophysics* 52, no. 3: 522–55.

CHAPTER 7

RESIDENTIAL CURBSIDE ORGANIC-WASTE COLLECTION PROGRAM

Innovation for Sustainability

ANA ISABEL BAPTISTA, *The New School*

Executive Summary

Organics diversion presents a unique opportunity to fulfill a vision of sustainability that encompasses economic, environmental, and equity goals (National Academies of Sciences, Engineering, and Medicine 2016). The New York City Department of Sanitation (DSNY) is the world's largest sanitation agency, collecting 3.8 million tons of residential and institutional waste annually, a third of which is composed of organic materials (Department of Sanitation 2016b). Diverting organic waste (including food scraps, yard trimmings, and food-soiled paper) from landfills and incinerators greatly reduces greenhouse gas (GHG) emissions released into our atmosphere. Diversion of organic waste has other environmental, economic, and social benefits, such as lessening the impact of pollution on vulnerable communities at the sites of disposal (environmental justice), increasing employment opportunities in the waste sector (composting is more labor intensive), improving soil quality, decreasing the use of chemical fertilizers, and increasing the GHG capture in soil enriched with compost.

In 2013, New York City piloted a residential curbside organics collection program, beginning with about 3,250 households in one borough. The pilot has since expanded (figure 7.1) and now services 190,000 households throughout the five boroughs, representing approximately 10% of the city's population

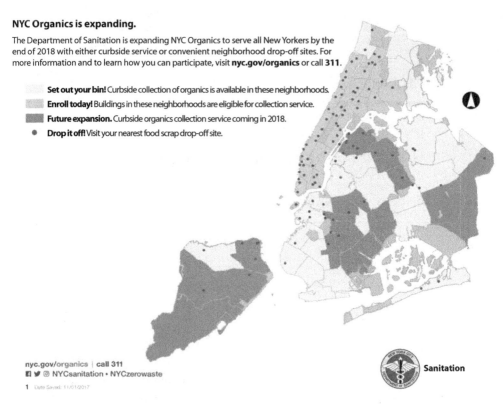

NYC Organics is expanding.

The Department of Sanitation is expanding NYC Organics to serve all New Yorkers by the end of 2018 with either curbside service or convenient neighborhood drop-off sites. For more information and to learn how you can participate, visit **nyc.gov/organics** or call **311**.

Set out your bin! Curbside collection of organics is available in these neighborhoods.

Enroll today! Buildings in these neighborhoods are eligible for collection service.

Future expansion. Curbside organics collection service coming in 2018.

● **Drop it off!** Visit your nearest food scrap drop-off site.

nyc.gov/organics | call 311
◼ ⬥ ⓐ NYCsanitation • NYCzerowaste

1   Date Saved: 11/01/2017

Sanitation

FIGURE 7.1 DSNY organics collection area map, 2017.

Source: DSNY website, www1.nyc.gov.

(Department of Sanitation 2016b). The expansion of DSNY's organics collection program was prompted in part by the 2013 enactment of Local Law 77 mandating that DSNY pilot a curbside residential organics collection program to improve on the existing system of collecting organic waste at designated city drop-off locations. The residential compost collection program is intended to leave the pilot phase and provide curbside pickup to all households within the five boroughs by 2018. Mayor de Blasio further accelerated the organics collection program's expansion with the 2015 OneNYC Plan that set the goal of zero waste to landfills by 2030 (see chapter 1). These efforts helped the DSNY's residential organics collection program become the largest in the country, serving 1.2 million residents and collecting more than 22,000 tons of residential organic waste annually (Goldstein 2017).

Key Takeaways

DSNY's residential curbside organics collection program is a model of innovation driven by key programmatic elements including:

- Ambitious *policy directives* to catalyze the program and a *phased piloting approach* to implement a program that embeds learning and flexibility into the program design;
- Utilization of *existing infrastructure and organizational capacity* to ease program expansion and manage costs;
- Leveraging *external and internal partnerships* to expand the reach, depth, and effectiveness of DSNY's program; and
- Strategic use of and experimentation with *technology* to improve the program's delivery.

Problem Definition and Contextual Environment

Waste management is one of the most critical components of a well-functioning city and one that the City of New York, as one of the most densely populated metropolitan areas in the world, has tackled for well over a century. As the birthplace of the public health (see chapter 8) and sanitation movements of the early twentieth century, New York City experimented with innovative approaches to managing its refuse. When the city's first sanitation department was formed in 1881 as the Department of Street Cleaning, Commissioner George Waring became famous for his white-uniformed crews, called the "white wings," that cleaned every street in the city. They pioneered the nation's first comprehensive recycling programs.

Since then, New York City's waste-management systems have undergone various configurations, from reliance on a chaotic collection of family-run

City of New York Organics Statistics

- 8.4 million people
- 14 million tons of trash/year
- 31% of waste is organic material
- 49 million CO_2 emissions/year

waste-hauling businesses to the nation's largest professional sanitation department. While the mantra "Reduce, Reuse, Recycle" has long been in use to encourage diversion of recyclable materials like plastics and glass, the collection of organics has been less well integrated into traditional residential waste-collection systems. Many of the earliest organics programs began similarly to New York City's program with links to local gardens or organics drop-off locations in neighborhoods participating in community-based composting efforts. Today, New York City's organics collection program is the largest in the country (figure 7.2).

New York City is a global leader in sustainability efforts aimed at reducing its climate impact and improving the quality of life of its residents. DSNY's organics collection program is a significant component of the city's overall sustainability initiatives. In 2013, DSNY estimated that waste in landfills emitted one million metric tons of greenhouse gases, and the organic-waste stream was a significant contributor to these emissions (City of New York 2012). DSNY's 2015 Organics Collection Report detailed this impact: "DSNY's organics recycling programs, including the organics collection pilot program and Christmas tree collection program, reduced NYC's overall carbon footprint by 0.01 million metric tons of carbon dioxide equivalent (MTCO2 eq)" (Department of Sanitation 2016a).

The benefits of organics collection programs extend beyond climate-change mitigation, including economic benefits like increased job creation and quality-of-life improvements. Composting generates approximately 7.4 jobs per 10,000 tons of refuse processed annually. In comparison, the same annual tonnage disposed of via landfilling generates 2.2 jobs and waste-to-energy only 1.2 jobs (Platt, Goldstein, and Coker 2014). The creation of new composting jobs may prove to be an important component in achieving the OneNYC goal of generating 4.9 million well-paid jobs by 2040 (see chapter 1). Additionally, the practice of disposing of organic waste in city-supplied rodent-resistant bins instead of typical plastic garbage bags helps deter pests.

Program Inception, Development, and Rollout

Organic materials can be diverted from the residential-waste stream and treated in a variety of ways. How this material is separated, collected, transported, processed, and ultimately disposed of is critical to understanding the challenges faced by DSNY's large and complex waste-management system. The DSNY delivers organic waste to contracted waste vendors who preprocess the organics and then haul it to final disposal sites. Once the organic materials are collected and sorted or preprocessed to remove contamination with noncompostable materials, they can be disposed of in a variety of ways. Two of the most common methods are aerobic composting and anaerobic digestion (AD).[1] Most of

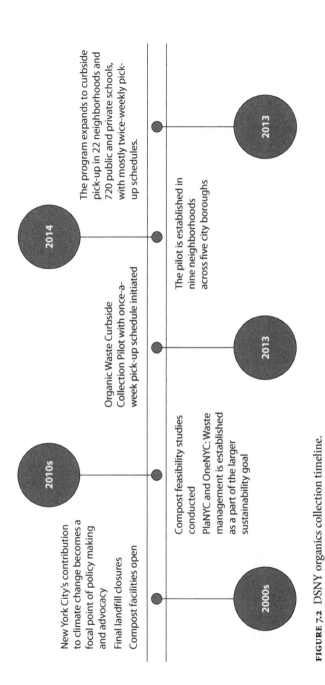

FIGURE 7.2 DSNY organics collection timeline.

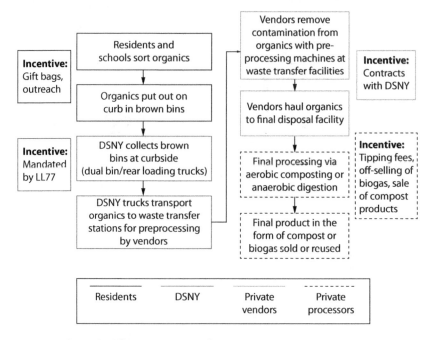

FIGURE 7.3 Organics collection process and initiatives.

the organic materials collected by DSNY's programs are processed using aerobic composting methods in locations around the tristate area. Figure 7.3 depicts the way in which curbside collection moves organics from the individual household to final disposal.

Evolution of Organics Collection

Early organics collection pilots in places like Park Slope, Starrett City, or Staten Island in the 1990s proved difficult to scale up because of issues related to cost, lack of participation, and contamination of the waste stream. So how did New York City go from these small-scale pilots to launching an ambitious campaign to collect organics curbside? The city first initiated mandatory curbside recycling in 1989, and by 1993 diversion rates for all recyclable materials (proportion of the total amount of waste collected that gets recycled) were around 14%. By 2001, the city was also experiencing a crisis of disposal with the closure of the Freshkills Landfill in Staten Island. The city had to consider how it was going to divert and dispose of approximately 6 million tons of refuse a year, a third of which was organic waste (see chapter 1).

Today almost all of the city's waste is exported to landfills and incinerators outside the city, some as far away as 600 miles. The diversion rates for all recyclable and recoverable materials hovers around 17%, with only 48% of the total recoverable materials being captured (Department of Sanitation 2016b). In the 2000s, concerns about New York City's contribution to climate change became a focal point of policymaking and advocacy. Waste was increasingly perceived to be a critical component of achieving a more sustainable city. These attitudes linking waste to larger sustainability goals for New York City are reflected in both Mayor Bloomberg's PlaNYC policies and Mayor de Blasio's OneNYC policies, with waste management and diversion prominently featured.

Organic Waste Curbside Collection Pilot 2013

In 2013, the New York City Council passed Local Law 77 (LL77) calling for a pilot program "to test the efficacy and cost-efficiency of the curbside collection and processing of organic material in our unique urban environment." This pilot mandated curbside collection of organics in a manner similar to regular garbage and recycling pickup by DSNY trucks (figure 7.4) directed at select residential areas with low-rise housing, select high-rise buildings, public schools, city agencies, and nonprofit entities. Residential low-rise buildings (nine units or less) and public schools in the designated areas outlined in LL77 were automatically

FIGURE 7.4 Rear dual-bin loader.

Source: DSNY vehicle & equipment website.

enrolled in the program and placed on a collection schedule and route for regular (weekly) pickup of organics. For high-rises (ten or more units) and nonprofits in these designated areas, DSNY partnered with the nonprofit organization GrowNYC to help recruit buildings voluntarily into the pilot. Pilot areas were selected based on a variety of factors, including high recycling participation rates, existing truck and personnel capacity, and ease of routing in the selected area.

From September 2013 through 2014, the pilot was established in nine neighborhoods across all five city boroughs. By 2015, the program expanded to curbside pickup in twenty-two neighborhoods, mostly with twice-weekly pickup schedules, and 720 public and private schools. When the program began in 2013, organics collection was done across all neighborhoods once a week, similar to other recycling schedules. In the second year of the program, DSNY experimented with introducing twice-a-week pickup of organics at the same time that regular trash pickup occurred, to test whether more frequent pickups increased participation in the program or the total amount of organic waste diverted. It was found that this more frequent pickup schedule increased participation in the program and volume of organics collected.

Challenges and Lessons Learned

A number of challenges were encountered and lessons learned in designing and implementing the curbside residential organics collection program. Some of the challenges included:

1. *Contamination* of the waste stream from poor source separation and nonbiodegradable waste, particularly plastic bags
2. *Capacity* of processing facilities to handle organics in the region
3. *Participation* in the diversion program
4. *Managing costs* of implementation

These challenges also presented opportunities for learning ways to improve the program over time as the city expands delivery of this service citywide.

Challenges: Contamination of Organic-Waste Stream

A key challenge facing the organics collection program is the issue of contamination in the organic-waste stream. Many composting and anaerobic digestion disposal facilities cannot process organic-waste streams with large proportions of contamination in the form of nonbiodegradable waste like plastics and mixed organics like woodier yard waste. For example, the compost facility at

McEnroe Farm, which accepts New York City organic waste, requires a contamination rate of less than 5% by volume to ensure that the end product is as clean as possible for use as fertilizer (Schwartz 2017). The anaerobic digestion (AD) facility at the recently opened Quantum BioPower in Connecticut accepts organic-waste streams with contamination rates of up to 10–15% but has not yet started receiving New York City organics (Ferguson 2017). The Newtown Creek Wastewater Treatment facility, where an existing AD facility handles New York City organics, only accepts wetter food scraps because their system cannot process woodier yard wastes. These contamination issues are significant obstacles in trying to increase the capacity of final disposal sites to accept the city's growing organic-waste stream.

The biggest contamination challenge in the DSNY program is the use of non-biodegradable plastic bags to contain organics. According to Brian Fleury from WeCare, who runs a composting facility for DSNY in Staten Island, "Plastic bags are troublesome for all composters. Contamination by plastic bags is costly for separation." He further elaborates on the problem of plastic-bag contamination:

Residents and schools that are successfully source separating and actively participating in the organics collection program, primarily still use non-compostable plastic bags to move their organic waste to a location suitable for pickup. As the technology for compostable products, including bags, continues to evolve we are hopeful these products will become more cost competitive and accessible and decrease the need for traditional plastic bags.

Fleury here presents the hope that the future adoption of alternatives to non-compostable bags may limit the scale of the plastic-bag contamination problem.

Removing plastic bags from the organic-waste stream requires significant investment in equipment at waste transfer stations before the organics can be transported to final disposal facilities. When DSNY first initiated the pilot program, vendors that hauled organic waste delivered organics with high levels of contamination to a compost facility in Delaware called the Peninsula. This facility was closed in 2014 by regulators because of problems with contamination. Vendors were left scrambling for disposal facilities that could handle the high levels of contamination in the organic-waste stream. DSNY learned from the initial round of contracts with vendors that preprocessing of organics at waste transfer stations prior to final disposal was an essential component of the program's infrastructure.

DSNY researched preprocessing machines (machines that remove plastic bags before chopping and churning the organic material; see figure 7.5) and invested in a machine at their Staten Island facility run by WeCare, where they could be assured that the technology was viable. Once they determined that the equipment worked and was widely available,[2] they required vendors to

FIGURE 7.5 Ecoverse Tiger HS 640 organics depackaging machine.

Source: Ecoverse.net.

have preprocessing machines in their next round of contracts. DSNY is also investing on the front end of the system by distributing compostable bags and educating residents, but until there is widespread acceptance of the practice of using compostable bags, or the elimination of bags altogether, sorting and processing equipment at the back end will be necessary to ensure that the final product is clean enough for disposal.

Challenges: Capacity for Waste Processing

The limited capacity of processing facilities in relatively close proximity to New York City is one of the key challenges to expanding the organics diversion program. Composting has large land requirements, and anaerobic digestion can be a costly capital investment, which can make development within city limits challenging. Most of the compostable materials collected by DSNY are processed at a handful of composting facilities in the region.[3] One of the limitations with respect to securing the necessary processing capacity close to the city is the volume of waste current facilities can accept. There are 106 viable facilities within 400 miles of the city, 26% of them within 100 miles; collectively, they can accept 200,000 tons of material per year. According to Kirk Tomlinson (2016), DSNY deputy director of composting, "Within the next few years we hope to add the capacity to process more material on [the] same footprint, therefore, we will need to look at technologies that will provide greater efficiencies and economy of scale, this could mean in-vessel processing or other mechanized systems." DSNY also estimates that they can extract increased processing capacity from current facilities, but the challenge of meeting the growing demand for organics processing remains a concern as the city expands its collection citywide and implements mandates for large commercial generators.

Kathryn Garcia, the DSNY commissioner, discussed the issue of processing capacity as a "chicken and egg" problem, describing the tension between investing in increased capacity before you can guarantee demand (Garcia 2017). Some composting disposal sites, such as McEnroe Farm, are limited in their capacity to take more organics by their existing permits and their own demand for the final product onsite (Schwartz 2017). Others see investment in disposal capacity as a risk if organic diversion cannot be guaranteed: "It is difficult to encourage the private sector to expand capacity when they can't guarantee tonnages because composting is still optional for residents" (Fleury 2017). While DSNY's goal is to provide access for all New Yorkers to curbside organics collection, there is no accompanying mandate requiring residents to participate in the separation of organics. Such a mandate could be implemented in the form of a requirement to separate organics, similar to those instituted for large commercial generators, or it could be implemented as a "pay as you throw" system in which financial incentives (or fees) are used to incentivize organics diversion.

Others in the industry see great potential for increased disposal capacity directly linked to the growth of DSNY's organics program. John Ferguson from Quantum BioPower recently developed an anaerobic digestion facility in Connecticut and reflected on the question of whether DSNY's organics program is driving investments or future business growth in the sector: "New York City is at the epicenter for organics diversion—many have their eyes on the City. The scale of what the city is producing in terms of organic waste is incredible . . . We are talking to vendors and haulers in New York City to educate them about AD and exploring the potential for AD facilities closer to the city" (Ferguson 2017). A 2017 article in the *New York Times Magazine* featuring Charles Vigliotti as the "Compost King" of New York seems to support this notion that the organics industry is booming. Vigliotti is constructing a $50 million AD facility in upstate New York to handle the city's organic waste (Royte 2017).

Challenges: Participation

A key challenge that the DSNY has proactively addressed is increasing participation in the program. "Our mandate about access to organic waste disposal is written into the law but for the system to really work, we need residents to participate" (Bruce 2016). The DSNY first selected neighborhoods to implement organics collection based on historical recycling diversion rates. High recycling diversion rates signaled a higher interest in recycling that could translate to organics diversion, but ultimately it was up to residents to opt in. "Organics is still voluntary, people who really like and want to participate, will participate. There are still people who refuse to source separate. Our goal is to capture those in the middle."

Perceptions of organic waste as messy and odorous means that many New Yorkers prefer not to handle this waste, making diversion challenging. Commissioner Garcia (2017) called this "the ick factor." DSNY's residential outreach manager, Andrew Hoyles (2016), also notes that many New Yorkers think organics collection is just "gross." Some of the most often cited concerns of New Yorkers with respect to source-separating organics include odor (16%), attracting rodents (13%), attracting insects (13%), it's too much trouble (4%), and it's messy and will leak (4%).[4] Hoyles wants to understand how the psychology of participant behavior affects current waste-disposal habits and how DSNY can use this knowledge to improve outreach and educational materials to increase participation in the program. DSNY is working to unpack these behavioral obstacles through targeted educational campaigns, public demonstrations, door-to-door outreach, and alternative marketing methods to realize more robust participation in their organics program. Incentives aim to increase participation as well: "We're framing organics as having intrinsic benefits and leveraging incentives. [These include] free starter kits including the bins, coupons for compostable bags, discounts with partnering agencies. There is no monetary incentive as of now" (Anderson 2016). The pilot phase demonstrated that educational campaigns help increase participation, resulting in a tenfold increase in tonnage and a 70% participation rate in pilot areas since the inception of the program in 2013. "Eventually, we want people to see how little trash there is once compost, paper, and MGP [metal, glass, plastic] is recycled correctly" (Hoyles 2016).

Challenges: Managing Costs

For most cities, budget considerations are a top priority for assessing the feasibility and viability of proposed recycling or organics collection programs. In fiscal year 2016, New Yorkers paid $1.7 billion for waste collection, transportation, and tipping fees (the charge levied on a given quantity of waste received at a waste-processing facility). A 2016 Independent Budget Office (IBO) report estimates the full citywide expansion of the organics collection program, including landfill savings from diversion, would cost $23 million annually by 2020, depending on tonnage captured (New York City Independent Budget Office 2016). The largest costs associated with the organics program are the capital investments required to purchase new garbage trucks, such as dual-bin and single-stream rear-loaders, and labor costs. Ultimately, the increase in organics diversion means increased costs, which DSNY must plan for as the program expands. Shari Pardini (2016), the director of operations in the Management Division, echoes this key issue: "Funding is important, how do we make this program sustainable in and of itself?"

In 2014, the first full fiscal year of the organics collection program, DSNY spent $6.01 million and collected 4,046 tons of organic waste. In 2015, DSNY spent $13 million and collected 11,066 tons of organic waste. The spending increase in 2015 included $1.8 million to hire twenty-four additional full-time employees within DSNY and $4.4 million in overtime pay for sanitation workers on organic collection routes that were more than one shift's workload (New York City Council 2015). In 2016, DSNY spent $16.9 million and collected 21,608 tons of organic waste. Spending increases from 2016 to 2017 were primarily due to expanding the program to include fourteen new neighborhoods and reinstating the fall leaf collection program (New York City Council 2016).

A 2016 report by the Citizens Budget Commission estimated that the organics pilot program had cost approximately $19 million for the residential and school-based initiatives since 2014, which amounts to about a $1,200/ton cost to divert 15,850 tons (includes education, bins, outreach, etc.). This is relatively high compared to recycling diversion costs of $721/ton, but these figures are expected to decrease as initial startup costs and capital investments decline and scale efficiencies kick in. DSNY is tracking costs and identifying creative ways to reduce costs, such as using efficient routing and scheduling strategies. DSNY expects that the implementation of increased commercial (privately hauled and privately funded) organics collection will lead to an increase in the scale efficiencies to help bring down the overall cost of organics diversion.

Replicability

The success of DSNY's curbside residential organics collection program reveals important elements for the replication of this program in other contexts. To expand and implement the organics collection program, the DSNY has utilized a phased-in piloting approach, leveraged novel policy initiatives, collaborated with internal and external partners, maximized existing infrastructure and staff capacity, and embraced technological innovation. These replicable factors provide important insight into the program's overall performance, as detailed in the SWOT (strengths, weaknesses, opportunities, threats) analysis in figure 7.6.

SWOT Analysis

The SWOT analysis lists some of the most critical opportunities and threats for the continued growth and sustainability of the organics collection program. The program was catalyzed by key policy mandates and capital investments, led by supportive city administrations and key partnerships. If political or economic conditions change significantly, it could represent challenges for this emerging

Strengths	Weaknesses
Supportive city and state policy directives Phased piloting approach	Voluntary status of resident participation may limit private investment in organics processing
Utilization of existing infrastructure and organizational capacity	
	High initial capital costs
Leveraging of external and internal partnerships	Limited processing capacity in the region
Experimentation with new technology	

Opportunities	Threats
Expansion of the private waste sector can catalyze scale efficiencies and increase capacity of organics infrastructure	Leadership changes may change the prioritization and/or support for city organics collection
New city/state mandates can support growth and decrease costs of program	Budget constraints may impede program growth
Growing interest in the program from residential and commercial sector	Private sector may limit investment until organics waste stream is guaranteed

FIGURE 7.6 SWOT Analysis of DSNY's Curbside Resident Organics Collection.

program. Nevertheless, the infrastructure and capacity that have already been developed, along with the partnerships with private vendors and interest from participating residents and businesses, are good foundations to build upon for future growth.

Piloting Approach and Policy Directives

To meet the city's ambitious waste-reduction targets, DSNY used a piloting approach that allows for reflective practice and phased growth. This ensured that the program could make adjustments before expanding citywide, reducing the risk of program failure or poor investments. According to Louise Bruce (2016), "Past pilots have taught us to not scale too fast. Things are on track and we are moving at a good pace and are going to have the impact we want to have." She described the implementation of the organics pilot as a means to scale responsibly and incorporate reflective practice into the program: "We want to maintain flexibility to be able to feed the market, let it grow and if things don't work out, we can shift our strategy. If things do work, we can keep expanding." The piloting approach utilized by DSNY mirrors the "backcasting" problem-solving framework guiding OneNYC's implementation of potential solutions for achieving the United Nations Sustainable Development Goals (see chapter 1).

DSNY's piloting approach, like OneNYC's backcasting framework, relies on intermediate actions based on achieving long-term quantitative targets. In the context of DSNY's organics collection program, the long-term quantitative goal is citywide access to organics collection services. The pilot program allows for incremental steps to be taken to achieve this ultimate goal.

Through this piloting approach, DSNY experimented with the deployment of different strategies to meet the needs of different types of neighborhoods. The DSNY was tasked with the challenge of delivering a viable curbside organics collection service to very different sectors of the city's residential sanitation end users. Louise Bruce (2016) underscores this challenge: "New York is many cities in one." The diversity of end users meant that a "one size fits all" approach would not work in New York City. "The diversity of the people and housing stock of the city make it necessary to have a variety of programs." One example of this differentiated approach is the way in which they rolled out the program to large apartment buildings. They understood that to recruit high-rises into the program, they would have to consult closely with building managers to develop plans for collecting and storing the waste prior to collection. To do this, DSNY contracted with partners like GrowNYC to work directly with building staff and residents to provide intensive technical assistance to buildings seeking to participate in the program. For lower-density residences, DSNY deployed door-to-door outreach, delivering brown bins and starter kits to each resident to encourage participation.

Policy Directives

Policy mandates were important catalysts for expanding the DSNY curbside residential organics program. One of the most critical policies for advancing the program was Mayor de Blasio's OneNYC Plan, which included an ambitious target to reduce waste sent to landfills by 90% by 2030. As part of this plan, the mayor prioritized the organics collection program as a signature initiative in efforts to achieve a more "sustainable and just city" (City of New York 2013). Although the organics pilot program was already in place, this mandate accelerated the program's expansion: "Having Mayoral support made it easier to decide to move forward with the initiative" (Bruce 2016). A study by Global Green USA (2015) credits policy directives like Local Law 77 and Local Law 146 with the growing movement toward organic-waste diversion and a more sustainable city: "The passage of this law [LL77] creates a significant opportunity to make the switch from investing resources in polluting assets toward those that support a cleaner, circular economy."

Table 7.1 lists of some of the critical pieces of legislation and policy at the state, city, and DSNY level that helped establish and complement the residential

TABLE 7.1 Critical Legislation and Policy Concerning New York City Organics Collection

Laws and policies	Date enacted	DSNY initiatives
New York State Solid Waste Management Act	1988	Established solid waste management priorities in New York State; included mandates for recycling and penalties for noncompliance
New York City Recycling Law	1989	Requires DSNY to collect and compost leaves and yard waste seasonally
DSNY Staten Island Compost Facility	1990	DSNY opens first yard-waste composting facility in Staten Island
Brooklyn Intensive Zone Pilot	1991–1996	A multipronged recycling program that included curbside collection of organic material; disbanded in 1996 when organics truck tonnage deemed too low to be sustained
New York City Compost Project	1993	DSNY project to raise public awareness of composting benefits and practices
Local Law 40	2006	Requires businesses to dispose of yard waste at a permitted compost facility; also requires residents to set out yard waste in bundles, paper bags, or rigid containers to minimize plastic bags at composting facilities
Local Law 42	2010	Requires DSNY to conduct a study of food-waste composting and to provide recommendations to City Council outlining possible methods for diverting compostable materials from the city's waste stream
PlaNYC	2011	Mayor's Office of Long-Term Planning and Sustainability mandates that 75% of New York City's solid waste be diverted from landfills by 2030
Local Law 77	2013	Requires DSNY to implement a voluntary residential organic-waste curbside collection pilot program and a school organic-waste collection pilot program; requires the sanitation commissioner to report the amount of organic waste diverted from participating households and schools

TABLE 7.1 *(Continued)*

Laws and policies	Date enacted	DSNY initiatives
Local Law 146	2013	Requires large generators of organic waste to ensure that their waste is composted or beneficially reused beginning July 2015; requires DSNY to evaluate processing capacity and cost-effectiveness at least once per year
OneNYC	2015	Mayor's Office commits DSNY to expanding organics collection to serve all residents by end of 2018, achieving zero waste to landfill by 2030
New York State Energy Research and Development Authority funding for anaerobic digestion	2016	Approximately $4 million in funding from the Clean Energy Fund (CEF) available in 2016 to support the installation and operation of anaerobic digester gas (ADG)-to-electricity Systems in New York State
Expansion of New York City organics program	2017	DSNY expands curbside food-scrap and yard-waste collection to 2 million more residents in the Bronx, Queens, and Brooklyn
New York State passes AD Bill S4770A	2017	An act to amend the real-property tax law regarding property-tax benefits for anaerobic digestion (AD) of agricultural waste
Curbside organics expansion	2018	DSNY expands curbside organics collection to all residents in New York City

curbside organics collection program (Department of Sanitation 2016a). These policy initiatives not only catalyzed the organics collection program but also helped shape the program by ensuring that evaluation and learning feedback loops were integrated into the program's design and implementation. "This is an incremental program in which learning occurs at every step" (Bruce 2016). For example, Local Law 42 required DSNY to conduct a study of food-waste composting in order to provide recommendations about methods for diverting compostable materials from the waste stream (Department of Sanitation 2012). The findings of the 2012 study included useful analysis such as waste-stream audits that established a baseline for understanding the amount of organics generated in the city's waste stream and the potential for diverting organics based on data about willingness to participate in composting efforts. Shari Pardini (2016) noted key lessons from Local Law 42 that helped shape the rollout of the program: "We're rolling out [the program] not only by districts, but by grouping districts who are geographically close together."

In addition to key policy initiatives, important stakeholders developed and implemented the organics program over time. Table 7.2 details the role that these stakeholders played. Each had a significant role in the evolution of the program and a unique interest in, impact on, and incentive to engage in the program's success.

Leveraging Existing Infrastructure and Organizational Capacity: Existing Infrastructure

Much of the initial organics collection program utilized existing infrastructure for curbside recycling. DSNY began the pilot by using existing sanitation trucks, collection routes, and schedules for organics collection. DSNY also learned that neighborhoods with twice weekly pickup schedules had higher diversion rates than districts with only once-a-week pickup schedules. But administering twice weekly pickup was significantly more labor intensive, costing the city additional overtime pay. To maintain the level of service necessary to sustain the increased participation with twice weekly pickups while also minimizing excessive labor costs, the DSNY decided to remap the organic collection routes to maximize the areas that could be cleared in less than eight hours while still meeting the designated productivity rates stipulated in the sanitation contract (10.7 tons of refuse/truck/route). "We are focused on maximum performance and making collection more productive. This includes looking at the [benefits of] dual bin trucks versus back-loading trucks depending on the district's needs" (Pardini 2016).

Organizational Capacity

One of the key ingredients in DSNY's ability to expand the organics collection program was investment in organizational capacity by increasing staffing and creating new strategic positions within the organization. One of the key leadership positions added was the organics senior program manager, located in the commissioner's office. This position was created to ensure clear coordination of the organics program across all of DSNY's bureaus and also with external city agencies. Louise Bruce (2016) explains her role in the DSNY as "mak[ing] sure we are expanding our abilities and capabilities, and rolling out this program together as one agency." The Bureau of Recycling and Sustainability also added

TABLE 7.2 **Key Stakeholders**

Stakeholder	Role played	Interest in the program	Positive/negative effect on the program	Incentives needed to engage
DSNY	Program development, testing, and operations	Responsible for the handling and oversight of waste-management systems in the city	*Positive*: DSNY piloted, conceptualized, and implemented the organics program	Conforms to department's mission to keep New York City healthy, safe, and clean by collecting, recycling, and disposing of waste
Private waste-transfer vendors	Handling and processing of organic-waste stream; technology testing	Under contract to DSNY to handle organics processing in the city; presorting of organics to make them suitable for final disposal	*Positive*: acted as partners to DSNY; identified technology and filled in processing needs	Business opportunity to hold contracts for a growing waste stream
New York City residents, businesses, and nonprofits	Participants and advocates in the organics program	Interest in contributing to sustainability goals	*Positive*: voluntary participation in the program allowed for growth in collection of organics	Improve quality of life and sustainability through management of organics
Regional processors	Final processing of organics (composting, anaerobic digestion)	Contracts to dispose of organic waste emanating from New York City	*Positive*: creating a regional market for sustainable disposal of organic materials	Reliable organic-waste stream and robust compost and AD market

twenty-four new outreach positions in early 2016, including positions specifically created for organics collection program outreach.[5]

The organics pilot program also leveraged the existing leadership, expertise,
and capacity of DSNY from the commissioner level down to the uniformed
sanitation workers. DSNY is the largest sanitation department in the country,
with a rigid organizational structure and the largest uniformed rank-and-file
staff in the city. These types of organizations are typically characterized as risk
averse, but despite this the program was able to produce major transformations
from within the department. Louise Bruce (2017) credits the willingness of the
department's leadership to take bold action for the program's ability to take on
"incubation, risk taking and professional development. . . . The leadership of
DSNY pushes very aggressive goals and they are ok with us making mistakes
sometimes, so we are able to learn from these mistakes and achieve our ambitious goals."

Also critical to the program's success were the buy-in and active engagement
of the employees on the ground. The organics program introduced new routes,
trucks, and equipment to sanitation workers. In some cases, this meant that
some sanitation workers experienced changes to familiar routes where they had
developed close relationships with the residents and neighborhoods they had
served for years. These changes had the potential to demoralize employees, so it
was important that the program invested in professional development, education, and hands-on encouragement about the benefits of the organics program.
Each time a new area was added to the organics collection program, the commissioner and program staff met with sanitation workers in the area garages
the morning of the rollout, before the collection routes began, to encourage
workers and reinforce the importance of their feedback to the success of the
program (Bruce 2017).

Partnerships

DSNY collaborates with partners both within and outside the city to implement
a successful organics collection program. Notably, public/private partnerships
were created to deliver key program components such as the preprocessing of
organics collected by DSNY. This relationship with processing vendors was part
of a larger effort to "reimagine the waste transfer station" as a critical lynchpin
in the organics program's infrastructure (Bruce 2017). DSNY partners with
vendors to help increase their organics-processing capacity and remove enough
contamination from the waste stream to deliver organics to a final composting
or AD facility. DSNY enters into contracts with vendors and agrees to pay tipping fees (cost per ton of waste delivered) to the transfer stations for handling
organics. Tipping fees stipulated in DSNY contracts provide an incentive for

vendors to bid on the organics contracts and make investments stipulated by the DSNY's contract requirements. There is no guarantee that the DSNY will deliver enough organics tonnage to make the vendors' investment profitable. Brian Fleury (2017) from WeCare notes that companies have to "take a leap of faith that there will be enough organics generated by the program to make it work . . . but there is no guarantee or built in 'put or pay' clause to protect them from the potential for low participation rates." Table 7.3 describes the vendor contracts that are handling New York City's organic-waste processing.

These relationships with vendors are critical to ensuring the infrastructure necessary to sustain the program. Kirk Tomlinson (2016), DSNY deputy director of composting, describes the DSNY relationship with WeCare, a vendor operating a DSNY composting facility in Staten Island: "We have a very good working relationship with the WeCare organization, they are experienced, knowledgeable and very responsive to the needs of the Department." These partnerships also help inform DSNY's practices, such as the type of preprocessing technology now mandated in vendor contracts. Brian Fleury (2017) explains DSNY's early investment in presorting technology: "Once we saw that this technology was out there and widely available, they [DSNY] purchased one of the available models to test out in Staten Island, and it has worked well over a relatively small sample size, now all the operators are required to have them."

TABLE 7.3 Organics Vendors

Vendor	Tonnage	Dollar amount awarded, DSNY five-year organics collection contract
Waste Management of New York, LLC	50 tons/day	$15.7 million
American Recycling Management LLC	90 tons/day	$12.93 million
Brooklyn Transfer LLC	50 tons/day	$8.21 million
WeCare Organics	20 tons/day	$6.57 million
Hi-Tech Resource Recovery Inc.	20 tons/day	$1.99 million
Regal Recycling Co.	20 tons/day	$1.6 million
Total	250 tons/day	$47 million

Source: Goldstein 2017.

While DSNY does not have direct contracts with final disposal sites, the partnerships with waste-transfer vendors ensure that the whole system for organics handling is viable. Louise Bruce (2016) comments, "By investing in our [vendors] through our contracts, we are creating a situation by which all of the commercial groups, who can also use these transfer stations, can contribute greater tonnage to the end user. It expands the private sector's ability to manage this material and create something that's really of high quality." These partnerships will help ensure the necessary infrastructure is in place to accommodate the citywide expansion of the organics program by 2018.

Other critical partnerships that have aided adoption and expansion of the DSNY organics collection program are those with nonprofits like GrowNYC that have years of experience promoting organics diversion across the city. GrowNYC (2017) expanded the city's ability to deliver important program elements like outreach and education that enabled the program to grow: "With our limited staff, we leveraged community partners to assist us in implementing programs and educating the public. Partners are also on the ground and immersed in the communities they serve, increasing their effectiveness. These partners include ones we fund and others that share the same mission" (Bruce 2016). Organizations such as these have also been key advocates for policies like zero waste, included in OneNYC, which further bolstered the organics program. Their network of volunteers, community gardens, and expert staff promotes the organics collection program through outreach campaigns and consultation services.

Technological Innovations and Experimentation

DSNY relies on the integration of new technologies to meet policy mandates regarding sanitation services. The organics collection program benefits from the agency's experience with and relative openness to new technology. One of the most important technological investments for expansion of the program was the Sanitation Management Analysis Resource Tracking (SMART) system. SMART transformed an antiquated sanitation operations system into an easy-to-manage scheduler system. The DSNY Bureau of Information Technology (2017) describes SMART as "a web-based mobile system that provides DSNY field forces with digital operations, scheduling, and reporting technology, and gives DSNY management instant access to real-time operational information. It is integrated with City-wide systems such as GIS mapping services, fleet management, building management, human resources, and purchasing and financial applications." The SMART system transformed the old paper system into digital boards that could capture performance data and allow for the analysis of route efficiencies. This innovative system will contribute to decreasing costs and improved operations in the organics collection program.

Conclusion

DSNY has proven that very large, complex sanitation systems can adapt their infrastructure and human assets to be innovative drivers of sustainability. Catalyzed by ambitious city sustainability goals, DSNY took up the challenge of curbside residential organics collection using technical acumen, a spirit of experimentation, visionary policies, leveraged partnerships, continuous learning, and a phased piloting approach to implement the country's largest organics diversion program. The resulting program provides useful insights on how to deliver a successful, large-scale organics collection program that contributes to a more just, sustainable, and smarter city.

Notes

I would like to thank the staff of the New York City Department of Sanitation who very generously shared their knowledge about the organics collection program, particularly Louise Bruce. Also, I am very grateful to the graduate students who helped prepare this research, including Lauren Fletcher, Ian Caddick, and Maxwell Barnett.

1. Anaerobic digestion is the breaking down of organics in the absence of oxygen to produce biogas (a renewable energy source) and digested solids suitable for composting and other end uses.
2. Preferred equipment includes Tiger, developed by Ecoverse; Turbo Separator, developed by Scott Equipment; and BioSeparator, developed by DODA.
3. McEnroe Farm, New York; New Milford Farms, Connecticut; Ag Choice, New Jersey; Delaware County Composting Facility, New York; Bedminster-Marborough, Inc., Massachusetts; DSNY Staten Island Compost Facility; some tonnage also processed at the Newtown Creek Wastewater Treatment Plant in Brooklyn (co-digestion).
4. Percentages reflect the percent of total respondents (500) surveyed about organics diversion; Local Law 77 Report, 2015, https://www1.nyc.gov/assets/dsny/downloads/pdf/studies-and-reports/OrganicsCollection-LL77-NYCOrganicsCollectionReport-2015.pdf.
5. Outreach staff are divided into groups determined by housing stock and agency type: residential (buildings with 1–9 units), high-rise (buildings with 10+ units), school, and commercial.

References

Anderson, Bridget. 2016. Personal interview by Lauren Fletcher, New York, October 31.
Bruce, Louise. 2016. Personal interview by Lauren Fletcher, New York, October 13.
———. 2017. New School Organics Collection Round Table Discussion, New York, March 23.
Citizens Budget Commission. 2016. *Can We Have Our Cake and Compost It Too?* February 2, 2016. https://cbcny.org/sites/default/files/media/files/REPORT_ORGANICWASTE_02022016_2.pdf.

City of New York. 2012. *PlaNYC: Inventory of New York City Greenhouse Gas Emissions.* December 2012. http://s-media.nyc.gov/agencies/planyc2030/pdf/greenhousegas_2012.pdf.

——. 2013. *PlaNYC: New York City's Pathways to Deep Carbon Reductions.* December 2013. http://s-media.nyc.gov/agencies/planyc2030/pdf/nyc_pathways.pdf.

——. 2012. *Local Law 42: A 2012 Assessment of Composting Opportunities in NYC.* https://www1.nyc.gov/assets/dsny/docs/about_2012-assessment-of-composting-opportunities_0815.pdf.

——. 2016a. *2015 NYC Organics Collection Report.* https://www1.nyc.gov/assets/dsny/downloads/pdf/studies-and-reports/OrganicsCollection-LL77-NYCOrganicsCollectionReport-2015.pdf.

——. 2016b. "New York City Municipal Refuse and Recycling Statistics: Fiscal Year 2016." https://www1.nyc.gov/assets/dsny/docs/about_dsny-non-dsny-collections-FY2016.pdf.

——. 2017. "NYC Food Scrap Drop-Off Sites." Accessed March 17, 2017. https://www1.nyc.gov/assets/dsny/docs/nyc-food-scrap-drop-off-sites.pdf.

Ferguson, John. 2017. Interview. Quantum BioPower, April 21.

Fleury, Brian. 2017. Interview. WeCare Organics, April 20.

Garcia, Kathryn. 2017. "The Future of Waste in New York." Lecture, New York, February 21.

Global Green USA. 2015. *Regional Food Waste Recovery Outlook 2015–2016.* http://thecorr.org/Regional_Food_Waste_Report_Global_Green_USA.pdf.

Global Green USA. 2015–2016, *Regional Food Waste Recovery Outlook.* http://thecorr.org/Regional_Food_Waste_Report_Global_Green_USA.pdf.

Goldstein, Nora. 2017. "Big Apple Goes Big on Organics Recycling." *BioCycle* 58, no. 1 (January): 38. https://www.biocycle.net/2017/01/12/big-apple-goes-big-organics-recycling/.

GrowNYC Compost Project. 2017. "NYC Food Scrap Drop-Off Sites." New York: Department of Sanitation. Accessed March 17, 2017. https://www1.nyc.gov/assets/dsny/docs/nyc-food-scrap-drop-off-sites.pdf.

Hoyles, Andrew. 2016. Personal interview. New York, September 9.

Intergovernmental Panel on Climate Change. 2013. *Climate Change 2013: The Physical Science Basis.* New York: Cambridge University Press.

Kuznitz, Todd. 2016. Personal interview. New York, October 21.

Manela, Marguerite, and Todd Kuznitz. 2016. Personal interview. New York, October 21.

National Academies of Sciences, Engineering, and Medicine. 2016. *Pathways to Urban Sustainability: Challenges and Opportunities for the United States.* Washington, DC: National Academies Press. https://doi.org/10.17226/23551.

New York City Council. 2015. *Fiscal Year 2016 Budget.* https://council.nyc.gov/budget/fy2016/.

——. 2016. *Fiscal Year 2017 Budget.* June 14, 2016. https://council.nyc.gov/budget/fy2017/.

New York City Independent Budget Office. 2016. "Organics Recycling Pilot Program to Expand with Additional Funds." March 2016. http://www.ibo.nyc.ny.us/iboreports/organics-recycling-pilot-program-to-expand-with-additional-funds-march-2016.pdf.

Pardini, Shari. 2016. Telephone interview by Lauren Fletcher. New York, October 24.

Platt, Brenda, Nora Goldstein, and Craig Coker. 2014. *The State of Composting in the U.S.: What, Why, Where, & How.* Institute for Local Self-Reliance. http://ilsr.org/wp-content/uploads/2014/07/state-of-composting-in-us.pdf.

Royte, Elizabeth. 2017. "The Compost King of NY." *New York Times Magazine,* February 15. https://www.nytimes.com/2017/02/15/magazine/the-compost-king-of-new-york.html.

Schwartz, Jason. 2017. Personal interview. McEnroe Farm, April 21.

Tomlinson, Kirk. 2016. Email correspondence with the author, November 20.

CHAPTER 8

SYNDROMIC SURVEILLANCE SYSTEM

The Science and Art of Using Big Data to Monitor the Health of New York City

MEGAN HORTON, *Mount Sinai Health System*

JOSEPH ROSS, *Columbia University*

Executive Summary

Seven days a week, the Syndromic Surveillance Unit (SSU) of the New York City Department of Health and Mental Hygiene (DOHMH) analyzes the previous day's data from emergency medical services (EMS) call requests, emergency department (ED) visits, over-the-counter (OTC) and prescription (Rx) pharmacy drug sales, and public school nurse visits to detect anomalies in disease patterns across the city. The capacity to collect, analyze, and act upon this information was developed entirely in-house within the DOHMH by a team of epidemiologists with coding abilities and knowledge of information and communications technologies (ICT) systems. The five-person SSU uses time- and geography-based algorithms that provide alerts or "signals" when there are increases in disease prevalence. These signals help the SSU identify public health concerns and provide the unit with analytical tools to support investigations into the sources and ramifications of outbreaks. The evolution of how the system collects, analyzes, and disseminates New York City's health data provides insight into the ICT infrastructure, human, and political resources required to generate and manage large, nonspecific data sets to inform public policy. The DOHMH's syndromic surveillance system illustrates how "big data" can be effectively leveraged by city authorities to understand citizens' needs, prioritize resources, and make more informed operational decisions.

Key Takeaways

1. *Timely and informative data help the city focus on the right things, routinely and in emergencies.* By establishing baseline trends for key syndromes, the DOHMH is better equipped to identify abnormal changes in the city's health profile. Collecting data daily from across the city allows for pattern identification and better public health needs analysis. During Hurricane Sandy in 2012, the DOHMH used the syndromic surveillance system to identify community needs for dialysis, medications, supplemental oxygen, and methadone maintenance. During the summer blackout of 2003, an increase in ED diarrhea and OTC sales of antidiarrheal medications occurred because perishable foods that had been without refrigeration and at more than 40 degrees Fahrenheit for more than two hours were consumed instead of discarded. The syndromic surveillance system enables the DOHMH to monitor the health status of New York City to inform resource allocation and response planning even in times of emergency.

2. *Syndromic surveillance data have given the DOHMH credibility and a bigger voice at the data-driven New York City policy table.* Extreme heat-mitigation initiatives are part of the city's new sustainability plan, OneNYC. The DOHMH's research into heat-related illness using syndromic surveillance data has enabled the city to shift the frame of thinking from responsive to proactive by providing insight into events occurring during a heat wave; including identification of subpopulations most at risk and a quantified assessment of increased morbidity and mortality by heat-index changes (DOHMH 2006). The syndromic surveillance system alerted city officials to the physical and socioeconomic factors that contribute to risk (e.g., cardiovascular disease, age over sixty-five, lack of residential air conditioning), providing insight into the underlying causal characteristics that contribute to heat-related disease vulnerability. This information can help the city plan new policies to mitigate adverse heat-related health outcomes.

3. *The syndromic surveillance system can provide advice or assurance if there is an abnormal risk of disease.* The DOHMH can inform New Yorkers if there is an elevated risk of certain communicable diseases (exogenous, or spread from person to person) and noncommunicable diseases (endogenous, or having an internal cause or origin). On normal days, the syndromic surveillance system confirms that there are no bioterrorism events or potential disease outbreaks. In their analysis of heat waves and mortality, the DOHMH identified who was most at risk and developed public messaging, including press releases and local meetings, to communicate the symptoms of heat-related illnesses and cooling-center resources to communities with heightened risk

profiles. Targeted public messaging can inform New Yorkers of their health risks and strategies for staying healthy.

4. *Administrative data, in addition to informing day-to-day trends, can provide a deeper understanding of human health-seeking behavior.* SSU analyses of historical administrative health data have provided the DOHMH with insight into how and when people seek certain types of medical treatment. Seasonal trends in flu and asthma are strongly associated with increased sales of certain OTC medications, and a spike in their sales precedes visits to primary-care physicians and outpatient clinics by a couple of days. The DOHMH uses flu and asthma OTC medication sales to inform the city's doctors when they can expect to see an increase in allergy, asthma, and flu symptoms among patients.

5. *Leverage preexisting electronic data sources to reduce the financial and operational burdens of building a sophisticated electronic data system from scratch.* A key approach to collecting sufficient data to develop the system while also minimizing resource investments was to use available administrative data instead of generating all new data. The DOHMH requested access to preexisting electronic data sets instead of trying to negotiate for partners to introduce new data-generation hardware and procedures. This method involved a simple request for engaging potential data partners, freeing up DOHMH resources to support partners to improve the quality and reliability of their electronic data records instead of building new systems.

6. *Advanced data-analysis techniques are powerful tools, but professional expertise, contextual knowledge, and critical reasoning are what make such tools effective.* The syndromic surveillance system provides the DOHMH with an incredible amount of information to understand changes in New York City's disease patterns, but this information can be nonspecific, and primary data analysis generates many false positives. For example, when foodborne illness signals activate, SSU staff evaluates the ED source data by age distribution, clustering of visits in space and time (minutes/hours), and similarity of chief complaints as indicators to confirm whether an outbreak is occurring and to determine the next steps of an investigation. The institutional knowledge and judgment of the SSU are critical to effectively understand and utilize syndromic surveillance data.

Introduction

Living in a dense, urban environment, many of us are keenly aware of the daily health patterns of family members, friends, colleagues, and even fellow New Yorkers. We see each other in our shared spaces and connect via phone calls, texts, emails, and social media on a daily basis. Knowledge of the health status of the people in our immediate social and physical proximities informs our own decisions regarding preventive health and lifestyle behaviors. Now imagine that the circle of people you interact with is the entire metropolitan area of New York City and your objective is to collect enough daily information to identify unanticipated changes in morbidity (disease) and mortality (death) across a number of high-priority syndromes (a group of symptoms associated with a particular illness). This is the work of the Bureau of Communicable Diseases (BCD) at the New York City Department of Health and Mental Hygiene (DOHMH). The system they developed and manage to complete this herculean data-management task is called the syndromic surveillance system, which is operated by a specialized Syndromic Surveillance Unit (SSU) of public health epidemiologists within the bureau.

Problem Definition and the Value of Syndromic Surveillance

Large, densely populated, and globally connected cities like New York City have unique health challenges but also opportunities to collect and analyze large data sets of population health indicators to inform health policy and improve resource management. Traditional urban public health surveillance focuses on identifying specific disease outbreaks and periodically taking measure of population health indicators. New York City's syndromic surveillance system differs from traditional surveillance by collecting and analyzing administrative data on health behaviors on a daily basis, providing the DOHMH and other city officials with situational awareness of the city's health status at the community level. This case study charts the evolution of the syndromic surveillance system from a bioterrorism defense system to a broader health-monitoring data platform that the DOHMH uses to study disease patterns and health-seeking behaviors of New Yorkers. The DOHMH has pioneered the practice of urban syndromic surveillance; its story provides empirical lessons and a practical framework for developing and deploying a robust urban health data platform to inform city health services.

Monitoring the health status of New York City is a large and growing task. As of July 2015, the New York State Census Bureau calculated that the population of the city was over 8.5 million, according to the city's online census database; meanwhile, the city's official tourism-marketing agency, NYC & Company, calculated a total of 58.5 million visitors for the year. PlaNYC, the city's first sustainability master plan forecasted the city's population to continue growing to more than 9 million by 2030, at which point its annual number of tourists was expected to exceed 65 million. The city's high population density and constant flow of visitors arriving from every part of the planet elevate the risk of an outbreak of infectious disease. Public health surveillance is a critical tool for improving health, both locally and globally, by reducing the burden of communicable diseases through the early identification of outbreaks and supporting the generation and use of data to guide effective response planning (Neiderud 2015). It is critical for the DOHMH to have accurate and reliable information on health issues as they develop across the city to identify emerging threats and determine appropriate responses.

Traditional Public Health Versus Syndromic Surveillance

Public health surveillance is defined by the World Health Organization (WHO) as "the continuous, systematic collection, analysis and interpretation of health-related data needed for the planning, implementation and evaluation of public health practice" (WHO 2018). Surveillance is closely integrated with the timely dissemination of these data to those responsible for preventing and controlling disease and injury (Thacker and Berkelman 1988). Authorities across municipal, national, and global health systems rely on public health surveillance to monitor for known and new types of infections, as well as to monitor population health, ascertain key issues, and set programmatic and policy priorities.

Traditional public health surveillance relies on diagnosis data, mainly from hospital records and laboratory results, collected through routine electronic laboratory reporting systems as well as periodic generalized population-health reviews. The use of diagnosis data for traditional surveillance is *specific*. Hospital records and laboratory data provide diagnoses, and public health officials assign a high degree of confidence to the information reported through traditional surveillance systems. Traditional surveillance works well for certain diseases with clear diagnostic criteria, such as hepatitis A, salmonella, or malaria. In contrast, syndromic surveillance data rely on alternative, nonspecific sources of health data (described at length below) to identify and characterize atypical patterns of disease. Each type of surveillance system (traditional versus syndromic) has relative strengths. The predominant strength of data used in New York's syndromic surveillance is its timeliness: health-related administrative data are collected and analyzed on a daily basis. The trade-off between the specificity of traditional surveillance and the timeliness of syndromic surveillance has important public health management considerations. For example, a traditional reportable disease surveillance system would confirm an outbreak of measles in an elementary school from the previous day, whereas a syndromic surveillance system might predict a measles outbreak for the following week. Syndromic surveillance, rather than traditional surveillance, can identify clusters of symptoms before diagnoses are confirmed and reported (Henning 2004).

Implementation

Origins of the Syndromic Surveillance System

A predecessor of the syndromic surveillance system in New York City relied on manual reporting of laboratory test requisitions that could portend outbreaks of waterborne diseases. Until the late 1990s, the DOHMH used this and other similar systems to comply with federal regulations to monitor for waterborne disease. However, this precursor system was limited in functionality and scope: manual reporting was slow, and the system monitored only a small subset of the population. Advances in disease surveillance at the national level were leveraging the speed of electronic data submission and the power of automated computer processing. As the DOHMH began exploring how to develop a public health surveillance system to protect against bioterrorism attacks, it became evident that the current approach to waterborne-disease tracking was inadequate for this larger task.

The city looked outward to identify existing models that could inform the design of this needed system. A model system would improve upon the data collection and analysis techniques of a traditional public health surveillance system to provide the early warnings required to counteract bioterrorism attacks. The template was found at the Centers for Disease Control and Prevention (CDC), which had developed one of the first electronic, computer-based surveillance tools: the Public Health Laboratory Information System (PHLIS). At the time, PHLIS identified salmonella outbreaks by collecting data from a large number of national- and state-level laboratory facilities, using preformatted data tools to provide automated analysis and messaging to key personnel within city and county health departments. The DOHMH had similar system requirements: to use automatic, electronic data collection and algorithmic analysis to track trends in disease incidence and quickly identify prevalence spikes that might indicate an outbreak associated with a bioterrorism event. Figure 8.1 provides an overview of the DOHMH's system development timeline, illustrating that the inclusion of new data sources and the expansion of functional capacities was a process that unfolded over ten years as their understanding for how to utilize syndromic surveillance evolved.

Syndromic Surveillance Version 1.0: Outbreak Detection

In the late 1990s, the DOHMH began collaborating with the New York City Fire Department (FDNY) to plan the development of a citywide surveillance system that would identify emerging disease patterns with enough sensitivity and

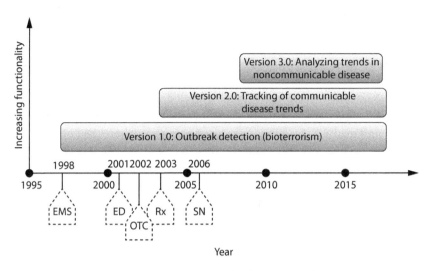

FIGURE 8.1 DOHMH syndromic surveillance development timeline.

precision to mobilize an immediate, targeted response. The DOHMH would serve as an intelligence provider to inform FDNY and other city first-responders of potential threats and help guide investigation and emergency response efforts. The original intention was to monitor and analyze 9-1-1 calls. However, the purposes of 9-1-1 calls are broad in nature, and it can be difficult to abstract the illness or syndrome associated with them. This pilot with FDNY revealed key challenges in developing the syndromic surveillance system: Data sources needed to be fast, reliable, and of sufficient size to provide for statistical analysis; 9-1-1 calls were fast, but the information provided was not necessarily reliable or relatable to the interests of the DOHMH.

The solution was discovered when the DOHMH learned that the FDNY had an ambulance-dispatch system tracking emergency medical service (EMS) requests in every borough of the city. This information was coded for standardization, electronically managed, and automatically pushed out to chiefs' beepers to help monitor the department's activities. However, these data were not centrally aggregated and systematically analyzed. The EMS system provided the reliable and timely health data fundamental to a syndromic surveillance system. It also established a key paradigm for the DOHMH: regular administrative data *already being collected* could flow into a surveillance system. By using the EMS system to identify disease patterns and flag potential outbreaks, the DOHMH was generating new intelligence from data the city already had at its disposal.

In 1998, the DOHMH operationalized EMS data into the city's first computerized syndromic surveillance system. Developed entirely in-house by the

Bureau of Communicable Diseases, the system collects data from EMS ambulance calls when patients display symptoms associated with an influenza-like illness (ILI). These symptoms are of particular interest as they correlate with early signs of anthrax exposure. EMS data provide coverage of a representative sample of the city's population, enabling DOHMH researchers to extrapolate the data to identify broader population trends. Of additional benefit, EMS calls are coded for standardization and stored in a centralized database for ease of retrieval and analysis. By leveraging this existing electronic data system, the DOHMH eliminated the time-consuming and costly process of developing an independent data-collection platform. There were of course challenges: data sets need to be transferred on time, securely, confidentially, and automatically to provide for daily disease monitoring. This type of data-sharing between city agencies was uncommon, and the effort was successful because of high-level support within both agencies that allowed for technical collaboration at the operational level.

As the system operates today, four EMS call types (codes) associated with influenza-like illness are collected: respiratory, difficulty breathing, sick, and sick pediatric. The SSU uses advanced algorithms,[1] or data models, to identify irregular patterns in these symptoms across the city. The models control for season, day of the week, holidays, positive influenza tests, and ambient temperature, all of which are known to affect fluctuations in the four symptoms. By controlling for these variables, the DOHMH improves the system's accuracy in detecting a true outbreak. The EMS syndromic surveillance system is able to identify widespread influenza epidemics in New York City two to three weeks before the DOHMH's traditional influenza surveillance systems (Mostashari et al. 2003). This early detection allows the DOHMH to advise primary-care physicians and outpatient clinics across the city to expect a higher influenza caseload, which in turn improves diagnosis and medicine supply planning. Over time, the DOHMH has used the EMS syndromic surveillance system data to analyze long-term trends in disease prevalence and develop a deeper understanding of the environmental and social determinants of influenza-like illnesses in New York City.

The Impact of 9/11

The terrorist attacks on September 11, 2001, confirmed the worst fears of many city officials and underscored the need for a rapid, automated surveillance system designed not only to identify disease outbreaks but also to provide situational awareness for what is happening across the city during times of emergency. In the immediate aftermath of 9/11, "second-wave" bioterrorism was the chief concern at the DOHMH. Second-wave bioterrorism is an additional attack launched after an initial successful terrorist attack when emergency-response systems are focused on responding to the unfolding crisis and may therefore be more vulnerable to further attacks. Because the EMS syndromic surveillance system could only detect bioterrorism attacks that manifested with influenza-like illness symptoms, the DOHMH established an emergency department (ED)–based system to have a broader range of detection capabilities. Within days of the 9/11 attack, the DOHMH had placed staff in sentinel EDs across the city to manually record patients' self-reported reasons for seeking emergency medical care, referred to as their chief complaint. By November, just two months later, this manual data-collection operation was replaced by an automatic electronic system providing reports of the previous day's patients, including date and time of visit, age, sex, residential ZIP code, and chief complaint.

A substantial challenge in developing and implementing the ED syndromic surveillance system was collecting and aggregating data from dozens of hospitals using multiple file formats and transmission protocols. To address these issues, the DOHMH provided direct technical assistance to hospitals to improve their data-sharing capacities. This direct assistance included training hospital administrators and IT staff to implement data-standardization protocols such as Health Level 7 (HL7) for the secure transmission of clinical data.

In addition to these investments to improve the inflow of data, the SSU explored and expanded analytical techniques. The use of free-text chief-complaint data allows for the modification of syndrome definitions easily and quickly to conduct event- or situation-based surveillance. For example, if city authorities wish to monitor gun violence, syndrome definitions of "gunshot wound" and "bullet" can be used to identify and track people seeking medical care likely related to gun violence. In 2012, the SSU introduced a new free-word text-analysis technique. This analysis identifies additional words not included in pre-identified syndromes. Free-word text analysis does not rely upon the SSU to set specific search terms; instead, the system can now identify patterns and present them to the unit staff. This functionality is important because it is not possible to conduct surveillance for all possible disease syndromes. New diseases and community health concerns sometimes arise without warning, and this new tool may help the unit identify such unexpected issues more effectively.

Use Case #1: Detection of Foodborne Illness

In 2002, a statistically significant increase in the number of ED visits for vomiting and diarrhea symptoms caught the eye of a DOHMH epidemiologist in the SSU because the surge in cases had a tight geographic cluster over a short time interval. The SSU called the involved hospitals—and learned that all patients had attended the same potluck dinner. In the case of this foodborne-illness out-break, the investigation required several steps: identifying a suspicious signal, verifying that the signal warranted further investigation, calling the hospitals, and discussing the cases with clinical staff to identify the source of the outbreak.

Syndromic Surveillance Version 2.0: Communicable-Disease Tracking

By 2003, the DOHMH had established four separate data systems to support the city's syndromic surveillance platform: EMS, ED chief-complaint data, and pharmacy sales of both over-the-counter (OTC) and prescription (Rx) drugs. OTC medication sales were used as proxy measures for reportable syndromes; for instance, medications used for treating influenza-like illnesses (ILI) or diar-rheal symptoms could be evaluated the same as an ED chief complaint of fever and diarrhea, respectively. The SSU could track communicable diseases across all of these data systems simultaneously, providing for cross-referencing and val-idation checks. If a spike in a symptom of interest was observed, the unit would launch an investigation (Heffernan et al. 2004a, 2004b). By integrating new data streams and exploring analytical tools, the SSU enhanced the functionality of the system while deepening their understanding of how to maximize its potential.

Driving this period of rapid expansion of data sources and functional capac-ity were three important factors. First, the strong collaboration across city officials and private-sector partners (including the pharmacy chain and some of the hospitals) was driven by the recent shared experience of the 9/11 ter-rorist attacks. Senior city officials recognized the importance of making New York City better prepared for future threats; this widely shared consideration lent weight to DOHMH requests for access to new data sources. Second, the DOHMH followed the EMS paradigm that all new data sources derived from preexisting administrative systems. This methodology kept system expansion costs low, while also making requests for additional information relatively easy to fulfill because the data were already on hand. Third, the system's improving accuracy in monitoring the city's health symptoms in near real-time made it increasingly valuable in a data-driven policy environment.

Use Case #2: The Impact of Tobacco-Control Policy on Health Behavior

In an effort to reduce smoking rates and lower associated chronic disease incidence among New Yorkers, a multifaceted smoking-control program was launched in the early 2000s. This included a state cigarette tax increase of $0.39 per pack in April 2002, a city tax increase of $1.42 in July 2002, sweeping smoke-free workplace legislation in March 2003, and a large nicotine-patch giveaway program in April and May 2003.

The DOHMH assessed weekly changes in the mean sales of twelve nicotine patches and nicotine-gum products during the weeks before and after the tax increases and policy changes, including the week prior to and four weeks following introduction of the new measures (Metzger et al. 2005).

Researchers found a 27% increase in nicotine-patch sales and a 7% increase in nicotine-gum sales during the week of the state tax increase, and a 50% increase in patches and 31% increase in gum sales during the week of the city tax increase. The week of the implementation of the Smoke Free Air Act saw a 31% increase in nicotine-patch sales and an 8% increase in nicotine-gum sales.

The syndromic surveillance system provided a mechanism to monitor and quantify the impact of smoking-control policies and programs by tracking pharmacy sales associated with smoking-cessation behaviors. Although these results do not provide evidence of people who successfully quit smoking, they do illustrate how the syndromic system can help evaluate policies designed to influence health-seeking behaviors.

Syndromic Surveillance Version 3.0: Expanding to Noncommunicable Disease Tracking

In the mid-2000s, the DOHMH conducted studies to expand use of the system's data. DOHMH researchers used time series and correlation analyses to examine historical data and develop predictive health-risk and health-seeking-behavior models. For example, researchers interested in health risks associated with heat waves for different population subgroups examined historical data on temperature and mortality patterns. This application of syndromic surveillance data generated predictive models of when risks for heat-related illnesses are elevated in New York City. The study provided insight into who is most at risk during heat waves (e.g., age, neighborhood, preexisting conditions), what constitutes a dangerous level of heat, and how to quantify the relationship between prolonged heat waves and mortality (DOHMH 2006). Results have informed public messaging and helped city officials decide where to place public cooling centers to align better with unmet demand. This example demonstrates how the syndromic surveillance system has provided actionable insights into underlying health-risk factors at the community and individual levels.

The functional capabilities of New York City's syndromic surveillance system grew over time as more data sources were integrated, analysis capabilities improved, and appetite for the data and outputs of the system grew within the DOHMH and among other city agencies. First launched in 1998, version 1.0 established that an electronic syndromic surveillance system could identify major flu outbreaks two to three weeks before traditional surveillance in New York City.

As demonstrated through the positive identification of foodborne illness example, by 2003 the system (version 2.0) could monitor communicable-disease patterns for large illness events in near real-time to provide a finger on the pulse of the city's health. By 2009, the DOHMH had extended the focus to noncommunicable diseases (version 3.0) by monitoring the health-seeking behaviors of New Yorkers, as illustrated in Use Case #2 on the effect of policy changes on smoking-cessation behaviors. Use Case #3, on synthetic marijuana, shows how the SSU continues to expand the system's capacities, including free-word text analysis, to provide actionable intelligence to city agencies and respond to new health issues facing New Yorkers.

Use Case #3: K2 (Synthetic Marijuana) Tracking

The DOHMH created a psychoactive-drug-related syndrome definition using twenty-five keyword terms found in ED chief complaints, including overdose, drug mention, and drug abuse. The syndromic surveillance systems sent daily alerts if counts were significantly different from expected values.

Between January 2014 and July 2015, the analysis detected a hundredfold increase in synthetic-cannabinoid-related ED visits, from three per week to more than 300 per week (Nolan et al. 2017). This acute increase prompted a public health investigation by the DOHMH, which included medical-chart reviews and qualitative interviews with medical providers and patients with a recent synthetic-cannabinoid-related ED visit.

Beginning in July 2015, the DOHMH began using aggregated syndromic data to generate priority neighborhood maps and coordinated with the New York Police Department (NYPD) to remove cannabinoid products from stores and seize raw materials from distributors. The syndromic system was also used to monitor the impact of the initiative: the number of synthetic-cannabinoid-related ED visits decreased 73% between July and December 2015 (Nolan et al. 2017).

Stakeholder Engagement

Implementing the syndromic surveillance system in New York City was only possible through the combined efforts of key stakeholders, including the DOHMH, the FDNY, other private data partners such as hospitals and pharmacies, the CDC, and New York City residents. The DOHMH intentionally engaged each of these stakeholders by identifying their key interests and incentives for playing a role in the system's development and expansion. Table 8.1 provides an overview of why and how the system's key stakeholders were engaged.

TABLE 8.1 Syndromic Surveillance Key Stakeholder Engagement

Name	Role	Key interest	Effects	Incentives
DOHMH	*System owner*: conceptualization, development, maintenance/ operation	Powerful *tool* that supports the organization's objective to track morbidity and mortality in NYC	*Positive*: the system provides large data sets and actionable analyses to help monitor health patterns in NYC; also creates new situational awareness capabilities	*NA*: the system was the DOHMH's initiative
FDNY	*Key partner*: early buy-in for concept, initial data-provider	Better and faster *intelligence* on disease outbreaks in NYC; enhances bioterrorism readiness	*Positive*: provides FDNY with analysis outputs; facilitates closer collaboration with experts at DOHMH to better utilize EMS data	*Clear value added* from partnership; additional incentive from post-9/11 sociopolitical factors
Private data partners (some hospitals and pharmacies)	*Data providers*: submit daily data reports in a specified file format and following HL7 transmission protocols	*None* confirmed	*Neutral*: requires minimal investment of time and resources to share data; some hospitals received valuable technical assistance from DOHMH to implement HL7	*Context* factors, including sociopolitical atmosphere in NYC after 9/11; personal relationships with senior DOHMH officials also contributed
NYC residents, businesses, and visitors	*Beneficiaries*: generate the health-seeking behaviors that are collected and analyzed by the system	Improved public health *service* and bioterrorism preparedness in NYC	*Positive*: the system generates intelligence that is used to improve the health and safety of NYC	None confirmed, involvement is *passive*
CDC	*Donor*: has provided financial support for system implementation, exploration/ enhancements, and operations	*Innovation* in syndromic surveillance technology and analysis methods	*Positive*: more data available for research, access to study results from the DOHMH, learning from implementation	*Research value* of the system's data and analysis outputs

How It Works: Technical Descriptions of the Syndromic Surveillance System

Overview

The current syndromic surveillance system analyzes data from five primary data sources, described in table 8.1. Data streams from each of these five sources are automatically analyzed by temporal and/or geospatial algorithms to identify aberrations. Algorithms are designed to identify atypical changes in both predefined syndromes and free-word text analyses. When a signal is detected, an epidemiologist analyzes the relevant data and compares it to the other data streams to determine whether the signal warrants further investigation. Signal investigation may include one or more of the following: checking for data-quality errors, phone calls to medical providers, interviews with patients, medical-chart review, more frequent analyses, consultation with regional public health partners, and site visits to determine if the findings are ongoing. Figure 8.2 illustrates the collection, two-stage analyses, and distribution of data by the syndromic surveillance system. The subsequent sections provide deeper explorations of each of these processes.

Data Collection

Data are transmitted through Health Level 7 and automatic file transfer protocol (FTP), which standardize the format, submission times, and processes of electronic information sharing. Received data are housed in databases managed by the SSU on DOHMH servers. The five syndromic surveillance data sources, key data field provided, daily transmission volume, coverage, and geographic resolution are described in table 8.2.

The Timeliness-Versus-Accuracy Continuum

A key characteristic of syndromic surveillance data is the balance between timeliness and specificity. All five of New York's syndromic surveillance data sources monitor health-seeking behaviors; they provide information about patients' symptoms but do not confirm disease through clinical or laboratory diagnosis. While lacking in specificity, such prediagnosis data are readily available and can be collected daily by the DOHMH using preexisting administrative systems. The SSU's sophisticated *primary* and *secondary* analysis techniques help officials evaluate the accuracy and reliability of the syndromic surveillance system's signals.

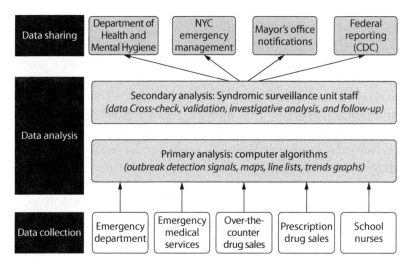

FIGURE 8.2 Syndromic surveillance data systems: Transforming big data to actionable information.

TABLE 8.2 Overview of the Five Syndromic Surveillance Data Systems

Data source	Key data field	Average daily volume	Coverage	Geographic resolution
Emergency department (ED) visits	Chief complaint	11,500	53/53 EDs; 100% of NYC ED visits	Hospital and patient zip code
Emergency medical service (EMS)	Call types	3,700	~75% of NYC fire stations	Zip code of incidence
Over-the-counter (OTC) drug sales	Drug name	70,000 OTC	757 of 2,500 pharmacies (~23%)	Store zip code
Prescription (Rx) drug sales		10,000 Rx	272 of 2,500 pharmacies (~10%)	
School nurse visits	Reason for visit	13,000	12,000 of 16,000 schools (~75%)	School location

Note: As of 2017, the DOHMH is negotiating with the city's private outpatient clinics to systematically collect their chief-complaint data.

Data Analysis: Methods and Processes

Every day, epidemiologists within the SSU spend about two hours reviewing the previous day's data. Automated data transmission is scheduled for the early morning hours, allowing the previous day's data sets to be available and ready for analysis by 11 AM. First, incoming data are checked for completeness: Have all data transmissions been received, and are records complete? Second, newly received data are appended to the syndromic surveillance archive. Third, the primary analysis algorithms are run to generate signals and line lists of reportable syndromes. When unusual data patterns are observed, the SSU drills down into the data to verify whether a full investigation is warranted.

Primary Analysis: Statistical Algorithms Organize and Contextualize New Data

Once transmitted to the DOHMH, the five syndromic surveillance data systems are analyzed independently, using software specializing in spatial and temporal data analysis such as SaTScan™. The DOHMH has developed its own algorithms, written in the data-processing and statistical-analysis language SAS, to identify patterns in twenty-two reportable infectious disease syndromes (e.g., antidiarrheal, coughing blood, fever, food poisoning, HIV exposure, vomiting) and about two dozen reportable noninfectious disease syndromes (e.g., alcohol, asthma, chest pain, gunshot wound, heat, K2/spice, tobacco cessation). New syndrome definitions are introduced regularly to reflect changing health concerns, as illustrated by the K2 Use Case. Primary-analysis algorithms identify statistically significant changes in reportable disease syndromes, which then generate signals. Signals are defined by thresholds set by the DOHMH based on experience, as well as the cost/benefit ratio of committing resources to investigate when a signal is identified. If signal thresholds are set too low, the primary analysis will return excess false positives. Alternatively, if a threshold is set too high, it may fail to signal when an outbreak is occurring.

Routine daily data analysis includes the generation of charts and graphs that examine temporal and geographic disease trends. These visualizations provide SSU staff with tools to assess changes in New York's health status. The system's algorithms are regularly reviewed and updated to enhance their sensitivity, specificity, and timeliness in detecting abnormal health patterns. In 2016, the DOHMH concluded a three-year review of the system's methods by exploring the utility of adopting alternative statistical methods reported in the literature (Mathes et al. 2015). The SSU continuously explores new methods to maximize the system's data. This curiosity, or professional diligence, has been the dominant driving force of systems expansion and improvement over the past twenty years.

Secondary Analysis: Critical Review of Data Reports by SSU Staff

Once primary analysis is complete, SSU staff review output reports for clustering and strength of p-values, within the broader context of current events in the city that could potentially affect information flowing through the system. *Primary analysis* processes what would otherwise be an overwhelming amount of data; *secondary analysis* then relies upon the institutional knowledge and critical thinking of the unit staff who review these data daily and are experienced in evaluating abnormal pattern characteristics such as age distribution, clustering of symptoms in space and time (minutes/hours), and similarity of chief complaints in the case of ED data. Primary and secondary analyses work in a sequential and complementary fashion to help the DOHMH make judgments based upon the scientific evidence and determine an appropriate course of action when there is a public-health event in progress.

Information Sharing

Syndromic surveillance data are shared daily through email with fourteen New York City DOHMH bureaus and seventeen external government agencies, including the CDC and New York and other regional public agencies at the state and community levels that monitor public health (see figure 8.3). The ED syndromic system reports are shared most broadly—with thirty-one internal DOHMH and fourteen external recipient groups. OTC drugs sales reports and school nurse visit syndromic data are shared with four departments/ agencies each, while prescription drug sales syndromic data are shared with just one other DOHMH department outside of the SSU. Across all systems and report groups, the Bureau of Communicable Diseases receives the most information from the syndromic surveillance system—sixteen syndromic data reports daily.

Interesting to note, the demand for communicable disease data is substantially higher than for environmental, drug and alcohol, and mental health data. Monitoring communicable disease is important for responding to emerging public health crises, whereas drug and alcohol use, mental health, and environmental health patterns are less relevant for emergency response and more relevant for longer-term policy planning. Although the SSU has demonstrated how data from the syndromic systems can be used to inform or monitor policy changes (see Use Case #2 on monitoring the impact of policy on tobacco-cessation behaviors), the principal use of these data remains for outbreak response and management. The syndromic surveillance system's original purpose was to monitor for bioterrorism threats. After twenty years of innovation and growth, it has the capabilities to do much more.

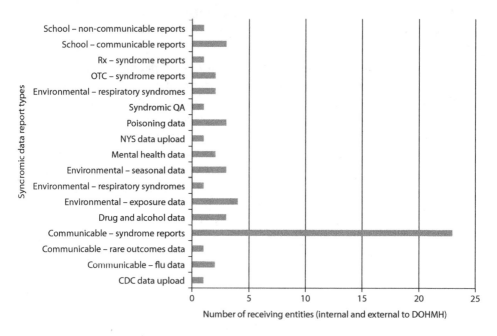

FIGURE 8.3 Demand from government agencies for syndromic surveillance data.

The ED syndromic surveillance system data are publicly available through the NYC.gov EpiQuery website (https://a816-healthpsi.nyc.gov/epiquery /Syndromic/index.html). Syndromic data dating from 2006 through yesterday are presented by patient date of visit, age group, geographic unit (citywide, borough, ZIP code area), and syndrome (e.g., asthma, diarrhea, influenza-like illness, respiratory, vomit). The website provides a brief description of the data and how the visualization software, EpiQuery, can be used to run queries and interpret results. The DOHMH also distributes syndromic surveillance data through press releases and targeted messaging on the radio and social media to notify vulnerable populations of critical health risks during emergency situations. For example, a heat-alert notification might include a description of heat-related illness symptoms and information on what resources are being made available, including the locations of public cooling centers.

Challenges and Lessons Learned

Finding the right data sources was an initial challenge for establishing syndromic surveillance, and fine-tuning the algorithmic approaches used during primary data analysis remains a work in progress. However, the system has achieved its primary objective of monitoring for bioterrorism threats in New York City. The daily collection of ED chief-complaint data from every hospital in the city was a major political and administrative accomplishment, but it required prolonged support to the hospitals to improve their technical capacities in electronic data collection and transmission. The system provides additional benefit to the DOHMH by increasing the department's abilities to monitor public-health events taking place across the city and to portend communicable and noncommunicable disease outbreaks. This is a powerful intelligence and planning tool for the city. Of even broader value, DOHMH staff study syndromic surveillance data and publish research on public health issues that contribute to the urban health policy and practice knowledge base.

A number of internal and external factors heavily influenced the DOHMH's experience in developing the syndromic surveillance system. These factors are grouped in figure 8.4 as strengths, weaknesses, opportunities, and threats, both

Strengths	Weaknesses	
Internal — In-house technical resources were sufficient to build and expand the system The system's effectiveness has been demonstrated. It can identify outbreaks (i.e., flu) before traditional surveillance	Low signal thresholds create many false alarms which take time and resource to investigate	**Internal**
External — Daily information reports are provided to other DOHMH bureaus, city departments, and other public agencies Functions as an effective bioterrorism monitoring system, which reaffirms key stakeholder buy-in	Reliant upon data partners to provide timely, complete, and high-quality transmissions on a daily basis Feedback mechanisms to data source partners are underutilized, reducing buy-in	**External**
Opportunities	**Threats**	
Internal — Add new data sources and signal reports to broaden the scope of diseases monitored Investigate the use of artificial intelligence/machine-learning algorithms to expand primary analysis capabilities	Heavy reliance on institutional knowledge of individual staff No strategic plan to guide investments in functionality	**Internal**
External — Identify city initiatives to support with monitoring and outcome data Partner with other cities interested in or already using syndromic surveillance to share best practices	Dependence on federal grant funding from CDC	**External**

FIGURE 8.4 Syndromic surveillance system SWOT analysis.

internal (within the DOHMH's control) and external (outside the DOHMH's control). These contextual factors are especially relevant when considering if and how to develop a syndromic surveillance system in another city.

Translating the SWOT Analysis Into Considerations for Replication

The DOHMH was able to develop the platform completely in-house, using staff that included software programmers, IT system architects, epidemiologists, and a program manager. These people developed the primary analysis algorithms, capacitated new partners in electronic data transmission, analyzed the daily reports, and investigated signals. In addition to having the technical and financial resources to develop the system, the DOHMH benefited from high-level buy-in from senior officials across city agencies to create a bioterrorism-monitoring system after 9/11. The imperative to detect and respond to a bioterrorist event remains a high priority within New York City and continues to facilitate data-sharing and collaboration to maintain and expand the system. In addition to bioterrorism monitoring, the system has proven effective in monitoring for routine disease outbreaks such as the flu. The DOHMH is able to identify such seasonal disease outbreaks sooner than when using traditional surveillance, and such data are being widely shared within the DOHMH and with external health and public agencies.

The system faces ongoing challenges, both in how it is designed and in its reliance on external data partners. The system is more sensitive than it is specific: signals are often false alarms, drawing the SSU's attention away from where it could be used more effectively. To mitigate this weakness, the SSU has continually tested and refined primary data-analysis methods to enhance the accuracy of signals. An additional challenge is that data quality and transmission from partners must be at the right time, in the right format, of the right quality, and complete in order for the system to function properly. This creates a strong reliance on current data partners, while also creating barriers to the integration of new data sources and partners. Feedback mechanisms with data partners are underutilized. Providing data reports and analytics to all data partners would provide incentives to improve the quality and accuracy of reporting and potentially enhance the external visibility and perceived value of the system to attract new data partners.

The amount of data collected, stored, and analyzed by the system is tremendous, and it can always be expanded to accommodate new data sources and analysis techniques. The DOHMH has only scratched the surface of what is possible with big data and has begun considering how artificial intelligence or machine-learning algorithms might be used to strengthen the system. A barrier to these opportunities is providing staff time to explore them properly and finding the resources to engage with external specialists. The SSU could do more to engage externally with other city agencies or thought partners outside of New York City. The system could be used to provide monitoring and outcome data relevant to citywide initiatives, such as the ShotSpotter and Vision Zero initiatives discussed in chapters 10 and 11, respectively. Supporting major city initiatives might help the DOHMH secure the funding support it currently lacks. While the SSU is active in communities of practice, including the International Society for Disease Surveillance, no partnerships have been formed with other cities using or interested in developing a syndromic surveillance system. Such partnerships could serve as conduits to share best practices and further scientific discovery and innovation in the field.

The SSU receives no funding from the city and relies upon grant support from the federal government, primarily through the CDC. The time spent applying for grant funding detracts from the small unit's ability to analyze and investigate signals. The development of a strategic plan would help the SSU map New York City's future data needs to plan investments in the system's functionality and could be executed collaboratively with other city agencies. Ultimately, the biggest threat facing the DOHMH syndromic surveillance system is losing the SSU staff who support secondary data analysis. The system is an effective health-monitoring tool because the SSU has the expertise to interpret and act upon the data and signals it generates. While some of this expertise is derived through academic training, as in epidemiology, much of it has been learned on the job through the daily review of syndromic data and experience investigating signals.

Conclusion

This case study aims to illustrate the value syndromic surveillance provides to the DOHMH and to the City of New York through the provision of timely and actionable information. Within the context of global urbanization, investments in syndromic surveillance data platforms at the city level can help identify local and global public health threats and systemic vulnerabilities. Of additional value, syndromic surveillance provides a framework for collecting and leveraging existing data systems to inform municipal policy. While these characteristics and the New York City example present a compelling case for replication, developing a syndromic surveillance system requires a very locality-specific approach. The DOHMH has benefited from readily available data sources, in-house access to the human and capital resources required to develop and manage the system, and high-level support across city agencies and partners. Other cities can motivate key stakeholders by identifying the high-priority capabilities and outputs that are most appropriate to the local context and design their system accordingly. Localized systems will maximize institutional and environmental strengths in much the same way the DOHMH has leveraged its highly skilled workforce and citywide interest in improving bioterrorism and emergency monitoring after 9/11.

Fostering an environment of ongoing improvement, where staff have the ability to explore, test, and improve data collection and use, has been fundamental for the long-term success of the DOHMH's syndromic surveillance system. A better-funded SSU with an expanded role in citywide information generation and dissemination would have positive effects across multiple city agencies, as health is closely interdependent with the focus areas of multiple city agencies. For instance, the syndromic surveillance system could monitor the impact of the Department of Transportation's Vision Zero policy initiative as described in chapter 11. For other cities interested in harnessing big data to improve city management, New York City will continue to provide a creative blueprint for the next generation of public health information systems.

Notes

The authors are grateful to the Syndromic Surveillance Unit, who generously shared their unique expertise and institutional knowledge during meetings and through email exchanges. We are especially indebted to Dr. Don Weiss, the unit's director since the early 2000s. Other key informants for this case, including current and former staff of the DOHMH, were Thomas Matte, Robert Mathes, Jay Varma, Kristina Metzger, and Farzad Mostashari. The knowledge and insights shared through this case study speak to their professional excellence and dedication to public service.

1. Based on the standard CDC algorithm for flu detection, the syndromic surveillance system runs a daily Serfling regression model (Serfling 1963) using a multiyear baseline to detect aberrations in the frequency of ILI.

References

Heffernan, Richard, F. Mostashari, D. Das, M. Besculides, C. Rodriguez, J. Greenko, L. Steiner-Sichel, S. Balkter, A. Karpati, P. Thomas, M. Phillips, J. Ackelsberg, E. Lee, J. Hartman, K. Metzger, D. Rosselli, and D. Weiss. 2004a. "System Descriptions New York City Syndromic Surveillance Systems." *CDC MMWR* 53 (Suppl.): 23–27.

Heffernan, Richard, Farzad Mostashari, Debjani Das, Adam Karpati, Martin Kulldorff, and Don Weiss. 2004b. "Syndromic Surveillance in Public Health Practice, New York City." *Emerging Infectious Diseases* 10, no. 5: 858–64.

Henning, Kelly. 2004. "Overview of Syndromic Surveillance What is Syndromic Surveillance?" *CDC MMWR* 24 (Suppl.): 5–11.

Mathes, Robert, Jessica Sell, Anthony W. Tam, Alison Levin-Rector, and Ramona Lall. 2015. "Building a Better Syndromic Surveillance System: The New York City Experience." *Online Journal of Public Health Informatics* 7, no. 1: e39.

Metzger, K., Farzad Mostashari, and Bonnie Kerker. 2005. "Use of Pharmacy Data to Evaluate Smoking Regulations' Impact on Sales of Nicotine Replacement Therapies in New York City." *American Journal of Public Health* 95, no. 6: 1050–55.

Mostashari, Farzad, Annie Fine, Debjani Das, John Adams, and Marcelle Layton. 2003. "Use of Ambulance Dispatch Data as an Early Warning System for Communitywide Influenzalike Illness, New York City." *Journal of Urban Health* 80 (Suppl. 1): 143–149.

Neiderud, Carl-Johan. 2015. "How Urbanization Affects the Epidemiology of Emerging Disease." *Infection Ecology & Epidemiology* 5, no. 1. Accessed November 10, 2017. https://www.ncbi.nlm.nih.gov/pmc/articles/PMC4481042/.

New York City Department of Health and Mental Hygiene (DOHMH). 2006. "Vital Signs Investigation Report: Deaths Associated with Heat Waves in 2006." *Special Report.* Accessed June 5, 2017. https://www1.nyc.gov/assets/doh/downloads/pdf/survey/survey-2006heatdeaths.pdf.

Nolan, M. L., H. V. Kunins, R. Lall, and D. Paone. 2017. "Developing Syndromic Surveillance to Monitor and Respond to Adverse Health Events Related to Psychoactive Substance Use: Methods and Applications." *Public Health Reports* 132, no. 1 (Suppl.): 65S–72S.

Serfling, Robert. 1963. "Methods for Current Statistical Analysis of Excess Pneumonia-Influenza Deaths." *Public Health Reports.* Jun; 78 (Suppl. 6): 494–506.

Thacker, Stephen, and R. L. Berkelman. 1988. "Public Health Surveillance in the United States." *Epidemiologic Reviews* 10: 164–90.

World Health Organization (WHO). 2018. "Public Health Surveillance." Accessed March 16, 2018. http://www.who.int/topics/public_health_surveillance/en/.

CHAPTER 9

SOLVING CITY CHALLENGES THROUGH NEIGHBORHOOD INNOVATION LABS

Moving from Smart Cities to Informed Communities

CONSTANTINE E. KONTOKOSTA, *New York University*

JEFF MERRITT, *World Economic Forum*

SANDER DOLDER, *New York City Economic Development Corporation*

Executive Summary

This case study of the New York City Neighborhood Innovation Labs, also known as NYCx Co-Labs, describes a new multisector collaboration model involving city agencies, industry, academic institutions, and local communities with the goal of making urban innovation processes more inclusive and responsive to the needs of city residents. Most urban information and communication technology (ICT) or civic technology implementation strategies today are characterized by a top-down, technocentric approach; innovative programs and products are often detached from the real needs of local communities and, therefore, do not achieve the promised benefits in practice. City agencies have become increasingly interested in bridging the gap between this top-down urban-innovation approach and community-led solutions by placing a higher emphasis on grassroots initiatives for identifying communities' needs and addressing them with new technologies and solutions. The Neighborhood Innovation Labs initiative aims to increase the effectiveness of city service delivery and improve quality of life by (1) enabling greater efficiencies through data and technology, (2) creating economic opportunities for entrepreneurs and the private sector by matching needs to solutions, (3) providing a data-enabled test bed for new innovations, (4) supporting new research opportunities for academic institutions to further the study of urban technology's impact on cities and communities, and (5) addressing specific neighborhood challenges through the support and advocacy of local community organizations. By providing a unique platform for collaboration, experimentation, feedback, and impact, the Neighborhood Innovation Labs hold the promise of an inclusive urban innovation and neighborhood development model of the future.

Key Takeaways and Actionable Insights

The Neighborhood Innovations Labs (NIL) initiative (also known as NYCx Co-Labs) is a multisector collaborative platform designed to bring benefits to its key stakeholders: city agencies, entrepreneurs and industry, academic institutions, local community organizations, and the general public. NILs are designed to produce clear, measurable results by leveraging problem-driven urban technology solutions guided by, and in close collaboration with, community organizations. Neighborhood Innovations Labs help city agencies achieve operational impact by increasing awareness and transparency of available "smart city" technology pilots and their outcomes; streamlining and shortening the timeline for identification, selection, testing, and deployment of new technologies; and improving equity, consistency, and efficiency in the way new technologies are deployed and used within and across the city. Just as important, the NILs provide actionable data for city agencies to measure the impact of technology, policy, or behavioral interventions in city neighborhoods and evaluate their effect on people's quality of life.

The economic impact of the NILs is driven by lowering barriers to entry for innovative tech companies with urban technology solutions and, as a result, leveling the playing field for smaller local firms to compete with large vendors. The NILs make city infrastructure accessible and ease permitting processes for prototype deployment and testing in municipal properties and public spaces, such as parks or sidewalks. This creates new opportunities for early-stage firms to validate proof-of-concept ideas in real-world test beds and verify their performance through analysis of collected neighborhood data.

Neighborhood Innovation Labs produce positive social impact for community stakeholders through a better alignment of community needs and technology investments and the facilitation of new skills and literacies to empower neighborhood stakeholders to be proactive agents in transforming their communities. NILs create opportunities for local economic development, including promoting science, technology, engineering, and math (STEM) career pathways and workforce development programs, through citizen science activities and hands-on learning opportunities in their own neighborhoods.

Finally, NILs allow for new research opportunities by connecting academic institutions with local communities to create experimental test beds supported by a comprehensive data infrastructure. The findings of such research can inform decision-making and ultimately benefit both neighborhood and city-wide operations, policy, and planning. This opportunity for shared learning and knowledge exchange extends beyond universities to support new mechanisms for engaging K–12 and community college students in impact-driven research and hands-on experiential learning with innovative urban technologies.

The key to the successful implementation of the NILs is the strong collaboration and alignment between the primary stakeholders in the urban technology implementation process. Advocacy on the part of local residents, supported by education and training of community members, is needed in order to produce meaningful results in addressing local challenges and needs. To enable effective community engagement, the government and academic partners are responsible for creating a feedback loop between local residents, technology providers, and data outputs through regular community discovery workshops and calls for innovations that are based on identified and prioritized needs. The management, transparency, and accessibility of collected data are paramount in order to ensure trust between partners and community stakeholders and to enable the long-term sustainability of the NILs.

Theoretical Case and Problem Formulation

The Neighborhood Innovation Labs seek to address the challenges of using urban technologies to solve meaningful, persistent problems facing cities and communities. From the public perspective, city agencies tend to identify potential urban technology solutions in an uncoordinated way, following different—and sometimes competing—strategies to tackle similar problems. The resulting emphasis, therefore, is less on comprehensive, integrated pilot studies to gain deeper insight into a particular issue, but rather on siloed efforts to find systemwide and typically enterprise-scale, vendor-reliant solutions in a particular vertical.

Often there is no overarching theory of change complementing the information and communication technology (ICT) or data solutions designed to address a specific underlying problem, one that takes into account local contextual factors and performance metrics. An example of this is the deployment of LED streetlights. The initial testing of this technology, in several cases, occurred on freeways rather than in dense residential environments, which precluded the need for community engagement or feedback. As a result, the large-scale deployment of LED street lighting has been met with some concerns about the impact on health and safety caused by glare and disruptions to circadian rhythmicity. In an extreme example, this community opposition resulted in the replacement of installed LED fixtures in the city of Davis, California. On the other hand, an example of effective ICT implementation has been the broadband expansion in the New York City neighborhoods of Harlem, Red Hook, and Queensbridge, where there was a concerted plan to demonstrate the value to local residents and community members. Therefore, there is a pressing need to streamline and shorten the timeline for identification, selection, testing, and deployment of new technologies that have proven benefits for community residents, particularly in low-income and underserved neighborhoods typically overlooked in the "smart city" discourse.

In the private sector, entrepreneurs and innovators often struggle to compete with large, incumbent vendors and to navigate a complex and lengthy procurement process when working with cities. At the same time, city agencies are looking to perform comparative testing and find scalable and cost-effective solutions to the challenges they face by creating competition among qualified providers. Compounding the problem of demonstration, investors require a field-tested proof-of-concept in order to provide next-stage funding. This circular challenge creates a recurring loop—urban tech entrepreneurs cannot scale and improve their products through real-world demonstrations without access to city infrastructure and local community support, but opportunities to test urban innovations are limited by existing procurement policies.

There is a need to build a process for standardized access to city infrastructure for technology testing and deployment. The level of complexity of city administration in large cities, including New York, requires transparency, safety, and coordination in managing municipal infrastructure to work through a labyrinth of regulations. Neighborhood Innovation Labs are designed around shifting the local regulatory environment to enable a streamlined process for using city infrastructure and to provide a data-enabled platform to test the quality and effectiveness of solutions in order to validate the proposed products. Through access to public infrastructure and objective testing of deployed technologies, the city will gain access to important data that can inform decision-making and provide necessary baseline information at the community scale. Currently, access to deploy technologies and sensors is largely restricted to privately held real estate assets or university campuses, rather than public space. This reliance on private infrastructure limits city governments' ability to manage such deployments and ensure that installation and data-management standards are in place to protect the public interest. The lack of government involvement in this testing and evaluation process limits a more iterative and incremental approach to scaling, which is generally regarded as a best practice for new technologies.

Another important consideration is that the rate of innovation in the private sector and in academia is far greater than the pace at which government solutions can adapt. Finding new models to expose city agencies to cutting-edge solutions, as opposed to legacy systems, is crucial. Creating dedicated environments to evaluate not only new technologies, but also policy and behavioral interventions, would aid in developing a more rapid process to test-evaluate-scale promising innovations.

More broadly, New York City, like most cities, faces several barriers to urban innovation. First, the city has historically been an "importer" of commercialized innovations. While there are numerous examples of urban technology innovation and startup ideas that were born in New York City, in many cases, only after technologies have been tested in other cities or regions do those technologies get deployed in New York. For early startups, it is hard to compete with larger vendors, while in smaller cities there can often be less competition. While New York City promotes idea generation, it is not yet a launchpad or early adopter of those ideas.

Second, urban innovation requires coordination and alignment of the public, private, and academic sectors. Large-scale programs such as the NYC Applied Science Initiative, and smaller efforts such as Town + Gown incubated in the Department of Design and Construction (DDC), have had a dramatic impact on the level of substantive engagement between the city and its universities. Similar efforts to build a startup and entrepreneurial ecosystem, such as incubators and accelerators, have helped to build connections between city government and industry.

Third, there have been few mechanisms for promising technologies and data solutions to demonstrate their effectiveness. Likewise, and compounding the challenge of developing problem-driven technology solutions, the city does not have a singular path to reveal its most pressing challenges and priorities. Recent efforts, such as NYC Big Apps, have started to provide a platform for city agencies to articulate specific challenges and areas where technology and data-driven approaches may be helpful. However, this is an ad hoc method, which does not address the persistent silos between city agencies and possible net gains from interagency cooperation. Finally, once problems are identified and potential solutions defined, the limited opportunities for comparative, objective testing and demonstration in situ constrain the ability to scale promising concepts. The need for independent evaluation of technology and data innovations is a critical component of widespread diffusion and adoption of effective tools and products.

The theoretical foundation for the NILs is situated between two movements prominent in technology innovation today: "smart city" initiatives, characterized by a predominantly top-down and technocentric approach to information technology, Internet of Things (IoT), and data management in cities; and the "quantified self" movement, driven by the desire to collect individual data and analyze it for personal health and other areas of improvement (Kontokosta 2016). However, across these two distinct movements there has been a call for a different urban innovation approach that is more grounded in participatory processes and in a data-collection strategy driven by community needs.

This approach has been operationalized through the Quantified Community (QC) framework, which is a key inspiration for the NILs initiative. The QC— a long-term neighborhood informatics research initiative—is a network of instrumented urban neighborhoods that collect, measure, and analyze data on physical and environmental conditions and human behavior to better understand how neighborhoods and the built environment affect individual and social well-being. This creates an "informatics" layer between the physical infrastructure and human systems represented in local communities. Launched by the Urban Intelligence Lab at New York University's Center for Urban Science and Progress and Tandon School of Engineering, this initiative creates a data-enabled research environment to rigorously study the complex interactions of physical, social, environmental, and economic systems in urban neighborhoods. The QC experimental environment, combining sensor deployment, data-mining, and citizen science, provides a testing ground for new technologies, allowing for unprecedented studies in urban engineering, urban systems operation, planning, and the social sciences (Kontokosta 2016). The goal is to use data to improve our understanding of cities, rather than for control or automation. There are currently five deployments of the QC across New York City in a diverse range of neighborhoods.

The QC approach is in many ways a hybrid of smart-city ICT initiatives and the "quantified self" movement as related to the use of technology in order to achieve certain goals or outcomes. The QC introduces a bottom-up approach to innovation processes and the use of technology to address collective community needs and challenges, which sets this approach apart both from the top-down view of urban life in the smart-city discourse and from the myopic focus on the individual of the quantified self (Kontokosta 2016).

Currently, there are only a few examples in the existing literature of holistic assessment frameworks that identify the effects of data and technology innovations in urban areas and that can be used to guide impact-driven deployments in communities. These urban innovations tend to be implemented sporadically, without an overarching strategy that takes into account systemic and interrelated economic, environmental, and social effects at various scales. This omission has resulted in a confusing and often superficial bevy of methodologies, rankings, benchmarks, and key performance criteria (Abdoullaev 2011). Additionally, the particular context of the city neighborhoods where technology is being deployed is rarely taken into account in practice, despite the importance of recognizing the uniqueness of place in community development. Several studies have shown that, for example, light-rail projects in some areas of the United States, such as Buffalo, New York, resulted in a 2–5% premium on home values near a station (Hess and Almeida 2007), while another study of light-rail impact in New Jersey showed that properties proximate to individual stations depreciated between 8% and 15% (Chatman, Tulach, and Kim 2011).

These divergent effects illustrate the importance of taking into account local context, including public perceptions in a specific neighborhood. In the previous example, homebuyers in New Jersey anticipated that light-rail projects would be associated with increased crime and noise near a station, while for the residents of Buffalo the project was an indication of an improved quality of life, hence the rise in home values around the new stations.

A stakeholder-driven and experimental approach in smart cities has already been highlighted in the literature. Technology can play a crucial role in mobilizing citizens' creativity and entrepreneurship and help to actively and effectively engage local residents; however, there needs be a governance framework that is open to citizen-driven initiatives (European Innovation Partnership on Smart Cities and Communities 2013). Research on "smart communities" in Japan has shown a difference between actual community participation and passive acceptance by local residents, when they are obliged to consent to smart-city technology rather than actively participate in its co-creation (Granier and Kudo 2016). Although not typical, the research does present a successful example of persistent citizen engagement in one of the cities, Kitakyushu, where the city administration, through multiple meetings and even door-to-door engagement, was able to get citizens' consent to use their private data on energy consumption and to install micro-generation units connected to the grid and remotely controlled by the utility. The result was an observed behavioral change among local residents, who agreed to shift their energy consumption from peak to off-peak periods when they were asked to. This points to the effectiveness of meaningful and persistent citizen engagement in order to achieve the successful adoption of technology innovations in local communities.

Another argument is that while investing in data and digital infrastructure may be an important step in improving city services, it will not achieve its fullest potential without sufficient adoption and use by city residents, which can only be secured by establishing trust through a regular and open feedback loop between stakeholders (Lea et al. 2015). A study of people's perception of a smart-city initiative in England has shown that for many citizens the term itself is somewhat distant, obscure, and abstract, while also raising concerns about the intersection of technology and privacy (Thomas et al. 2016). Such concerns need to be addressed in an open conversation, setting standards and procedures with local communities that create clarity around the role of technology and facilitate defining the necessary boundaries of control and ownership of data and infrastructure for a particular community.

Despite the strides in technology development and its implementation in cities, little has changed in terms of the rationale behind urban innovation— the call for an integrated learning approach in an experimental environment that recognizes and acknowledges local context and needs. In order to successfully translate a working technology prototype into a future city solution, opportunities to test and pilot the solution are critical. There is a significant need to build a simplified system to demonstrate the value of data and civic technologies in improving quality of life, to bring innovative and potentially scalable solutions to New York and other cities around the world, to give opportunities to entrepreneurs to work with the city and rapidly commercialize successful concepts, and most important, to engage the community at the neighborhood level to understand needs and challenges and bring solutions that can actually solve real problems. Here, we propose to utilize abductive reasoning to leverage data technologies to observe and understand the underlying phenomena that have an impact on the problems communities identify.

Contextual Environment and the Innovation Opportunity

In September 2015, the Obama White House announced a new smart-city initiative to support community-led solutions for tackling local challenges: "Every community is different, with different needs and different approaches. But communities that are making the most progress on these issues have some things in common. They don't look for a single silver bullet; instead they bring together local government and nonprofits and businesses and teachers and parents around a shared goal" (White House, Office of the Press Secretary 2015). The initiative is focused on the importance of multiparty collaboration among city leaders, universities, the private sector, and local residents, as well as among cities across the United States and internationally, to use data and technology to improve the quality of life in cities.

As technological advances continue to reduce the costs of IT infrastructure, one of the initiative's strategies has been to create test beds for Internet of Things (a ubiquitous network of connected devices and smart sensors, enabled by big-data analytics) applications and to develop new multisector collaborative models (White House, Office of the Press Secretary 2015). As part of its initial launch, New York City announced its intention to create a series of NILs across all five city boroughs. The concept is rooted in Mayor de Blasio's central focus on New York City neighborhoods: "We must innovate for the future in all our neighborhoods, always pushing the envelope for new ways to keep New York the greatest global city of the 21st century" (NYC Office of the Mayor 2016).

The approach of the NILs is particularly relevant in a city like New York, which is often described as a "city of neighborhoods," with its distinct neighborhood characteristics and cultures and high levels of local activism and advocacy. At the time of the White House announcement, NYU's Urban Intelligence Lab launched an independent partnership with Hudson Yards to create its first QC, with Red Hook, Brooklyn, and Lower Manhattan following soon after (figure 9.1). At the same time, the city felt there was a need to redirect the

The Neighborhood Innovation Labs Initiative is announced by the White House as part of the Obama administration's "Smart Cities" Initiative

Expansion of the program to create one neighborhood lab in each borough

Announcement and rollout of first Neighborhood Lab in Brownsville, Brooklyn

Launch of first two challenges in Brownsville: zero waste, and safe and thriving nighttime corridors

FIGURE 9.1 Neighborhood Innovation Labs timeline.

private sector's innovative solutions from private developments, where residents are already early adopters of technology, to underserved communities, where residents often push back on innovations, as they may be skeptical of government or corporate interference in their daily lives. There was a need to better understand differences between neighborhoods that were pushing away the technology and those that embraced it.

Background Information on Hudson Yards

Hudson Yards . . . will be a model for the twenty-first century urban experience—an unprecedented integration of buildings, streets, parks, utilities, and public spaces that combine to form a connected, responsive, clean, reliable, and efficient neighborhood.

Communications will be supported by a fiber loop, designed to optimize data speed and service continuity for rooftop communications, as well as mobile, cellular, and two-way radio communications. This will allow continuous access via wired and wireless broadband performance from any device at any on-site location. . . .

Hudson Yards will harness big data to innovate, optimize, enhance, and personalize the employee, resident, and visitor experience. Supported by an advanced technology platform, operations managers are able to monitor and react to traffic patterns, air quality, power demands, temperature, and pedestrian flow. . . .

Hudson Yards makes organic-waste collection convenient and space efficient by utilizing grinders and dehydrators to reduce food-service waste to 20% of its initial weight and volume.

Additionally, nearly 10 million gallons of stormwater will be collected per year from building roofs and public plazas, then filtered and reused in mechanical and irrigation systems to conserve potable water for drinking and reducing stress on New York's sewer system. . . .

Hudson Yards will have the onsite power-generation capacity to keep basic building services, residences and restaurant refrigerators running. . . .

Hudson Yards' first of its kind microgrid and two cogeneration plants will save 24,000 MT of CO_2 greenhouse gases from being emitted annually (that's equal to the emissions of ~2,200 American homes or 5,100 cars) by generating electricity as well as hot and chilled water for the neighborhood with over twice the efficiency of conventional sources.

Source: Hudson Yards, n.d.

Of course, an initial challenge was simply defining what is a "neighborhood." Traditionally, the definition has two important components. First are territorial boundaries. A neighborhood can be defined as a specific physical space with which local residents identify themselves and that serves as the basis for their attachment to the area (Coulton et al. 2001). The second characteristic is social connectivity, which can be viewed as the strength of local relationships in a defined geographic area. This self-identity with physical space and the established social relations in a community are what make local residents such important stakeholders for lowering barriers to entry and adoption of urban innovations in city neighborhoods. As a result, a large emphasis of the NILs is on facilitating an ongoing dialogue and a substantive feedback loop with local community organizations and residents. In this way, the NIL can be defined as a physical space or specific location where the community engages in identifying needs and challenges to improve quality of life, optimize city operations, and drive capital-planning decisions through the deployment of new technologies. The goal is to provide scalable solutions to solve pressing problems facing a particular community, while supporting new jobs, local economic development, and community engagement between local organizations and city government.

Through NILs, both researchers and industry can obtain insight into the challenges cities face and direct their research and development (R&D) and product innovations to target actual, resident-defined problems (table 9.1). Companies gain insights on new opportunities, as well as access to local talent and potential collaborations and partnerships with community organizations. Startups get the chance to refine their products, mission, and vision and gain

TABLE 9.1 R&D Pipeline Problems, Solutions, and Outcomes for NIL Key Stakeholders

Problem	Intervention	Outcomes
Entrepreneurs lack opportunities to prove the efficacy of their technologies on city assets and do not pursue government as a customer because of prohibitively long sales cycles	Partner with city agencies to enable access to New York City's physical and digital infrastructure (parks, buildings, streets, databases, etc.) for innovative demonstration projects	• Customer validation to New York and other cities around the world • Enhanced fundraising prospects and investor confidence • Encouragement for smaller firms to compete for government contracts, spurring local job creation
City agencies have imperfect information about available technology solutions and their validity	Demand-driven challenge briefings that source and facilitate A/B testing of various technologies before running full-scale procurements	• Informed, data-driven procurement decisions with third-party validation • Safe space for New York City to consider innovative solutions
Communities do not have a voice in shaping their neighborhoods, may be wary of new technology deployments, and are disconnected from educational and job opportunities	Involve community members in neighborhood challenge definitions; incorporate educational and workforce development programs	• An identified set of local needs specific to a particular neighborhood • Community-led technology-driven solutions to the identified local challenges
Universities require access to city-owned infrastructure to conduct research on critical urban issues	Build a singular digital platform on which all technologies can be evaluated, and offer city infrastructure for select research projects	• New academic research study opportunities • Findings of those studies further inform policy and decision-making

Strengths	Weaknesses
Better public services and improved operational efficiency through the use of private sector technology and innovation.	Risk averseness to using new technologies/processes.
Supplementing limited public sector capacities to meet the growing demand for infrastructure development.	Backlash from citizens due to a lack of transparency and communication with communities.
Extracting long-term value-for-money through appropriate risk transfer to the private sector over the life of the project, from design/construction to operations/maintenance.	Lengthy and administratively intense procurement process favors large private sector companies with dedicated staff (many truly innovative solutions come from smaller companies).
Opportunities	**Threats**
Exposure to new innovation and products.	Budgetary constraints on new projects and/or maintenance of urban systems.
Co-creating solutions to current challenges.	
Enabling comparative testing and identification of optimal scalable solutions.	Political agenda might not correlate with private sector objectives/desires.
More effective and less costly purchase decisions.	Procurement process and government policies on doing business with the city.
Increase adoption speed of technology and adaptability to innovation.	

FIGURE 9.2 Neighborhood Innovation Labs SWOT analysis.

access to the expertise of larger corporations and domain knowledge of city agencies, along with the opportunity to demonstrate their own technologies and capabilities. Figure 9.2 provides a SWOT analysis of the NILs initiative.

Program Inception, Development, and Rollout

The NILs initiative was jointly conceived and launched by a partnership of the Mayor's Office of Technology and Innovation, the New York City Economic Development Corporation, and the Urban Intelligence Lab at the NYU Center for Urban Science and Progress. The NILs build on the QC research facility, leveraging data-enabled IoT and ICT technology to enhance our understanding of urban dynamics and the impact of neighborhoods on quality of life for residents and communities. Currently, there are five QC sites: at Hudson Yards, in the Financial District of Lower Manhattan, in Red Hook and Brownsville in Brooklyn, and Governor's Island. The new NILs initiative will leverage the technology and data-analytics approach pioneered in these neighborhoods,

TABLE 9.2 Key Stakeholders of Neighborhood Innovation Lab in Brownsville, Brooklyn

	Research institutions	Public sector	Private sector	Community institutions
Direct (Primary)	NYU Center for Urban Science and Progress (CUSP)	Mayor's Office of Technology and Innovation (MOTI), New York City Economic Development Corporation (EDC)	Private companies (ICT vendors/startups)	Brownsville Justice Center and members of the Brownsville Community Technology Advisory Board
Indirect (Secondary)	Wider research community, other local colleges and universities	Other city agencies relevant to a particular problem (e.g., public safety— Mayor's Office of Criminal Justice)	Local businesses, entrepreneurs, incubators, and accelerators	Wider local community and other grassroots organizations

including sensor design and field deployment, large-scale data-mining and analysis, and visualization tools, developed by researchers at NYU.

To ensure that the NILs are connected together as part of a citywide network, there is a fixed, four-part governance structure, described below and in table 9.2:

- The government partner, the Mayor's Office of Technology and Innovation, acts as a hub for activity around the coordination of agency engagement.
- The private sector liaison, the New York City Economic Development Corporation (NYCEDC), ensures the ability to streamline the deployment of connected devices using city assets. The NYCEDC is integral to the operations and sustainability of the program, serving as an important connector for partnerships with the private sector, bringing its experience with deploying demonstration projects across the city and running challenge-based competitions, along with its direct project management experience. It is also an important financial contributor to the project.
- The academic partner, the NYU Center for Urban Science and Progress (CUSP), acts as the hub for activity around the specific instrumentation and data collection and liaises with academic and research entities.

- The community partner, which could be a community-based organization (CBO), anchor institution, or business improvement district (BID), anchors each NIL in the community. The community partner works with the government and academic partners to identify use cases and technologies and to operate the lab.

As part of the NILs program, there is a plan to develop at least one lab in each of the five boroughs of New York City. Locations are selected based on (1) community interest, (2) the presence of community partners, and (3) the applicability of technology solutions to provide benefits in the areas of need identified by community residents. Labs can range in size from a small community park to a cluster of buildings and common areas or larger collection of streets and public space. The labs are funded by the City of New York, operating through the Mayor's Office of Technology and Innovation and the NYC Economic Development Corporation. The labs will leverage a variety of funding sources and in-kind support—private, grant-based, public, and research—to fund the technologies, their operation, and urban science research.

An important part of the vision of NILs is that community residents can learn how urban civic and data technologies can help to improve quality of life and city service delivery. Together with city agencies, local residents will be able to try out new technologies and provide feedback before large-scale investments are made. Companies—established and startups—will have a place to launch new products in a real-world environment based on community and agency needs. Local academic institutions can explore how public spaces are used and better understand changes to the urban environment. Thus, the NILs create a "center of gravity" to weave together tech initiatives across agencies and sectors, enabling greater interagency connectivity and cross-sector engagement.

Neighborhood Innovation Lab in Brownsville

The first pilot project of the NIL initiative has been launched in the Brownsville neighborhood in Brooklyn—a neighborhood distinct from many of the typical smart-cities deployment sites across the globe. Brownsville was selected, in part, because it is home to a wealth of strong neighborhood organizations and a budding community of tech entrepreneurs; it represents an opportune place to explore how new technologies can improve quality of life, enhance city services, and modernize public infrastructure, while also creating new opportunities for local economic development. Brownsville has one of the highest rates of poverty in New York City, with a significant diversity

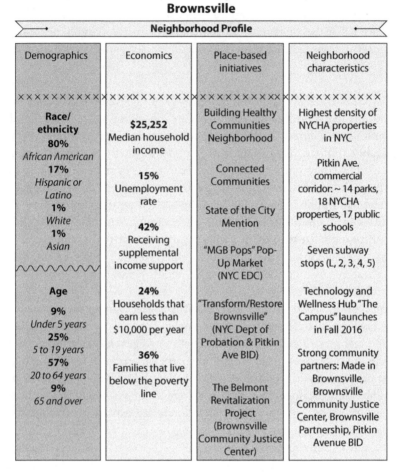

Brownsville

Neighborhood Profile			
Demographics	Economics	Place-based initiatives	Neighborhood characteristics
Race/ ethnicity **80%** *African American* **17%** *Hispanic or Latino* **1%** *White* **1%** *Asian*	**$25,252** Median household income	Building Healthy Communities Neighborhood	Highest density of NYCHA properties in NYC
	15% Unemployment rate	Connected Communities	Pitkin Ave. commercial corridor: ~ 14 parks, 18 NYCHA properties, 17 public schools
	42% Receiving supplemental income support	State of the City Mention "MGB Pops" Pop-Up Market (NYC EDC)	Seven subway stops (L, 2, 3, 4, 5)
Age **9%** *Under 5 years* **25%** *5 to 19 years* **57%** *20 to 64 years* **9%** *65 and over*	**24%** Households that earn less than $10,000 per year **36%** Families that live below the poverty line	"Transform/Restore Brownsville" (NYC Dept of Probation & Pitkin Ave BID) The Belmont Revitalization Project (Brownsville Community Justice Center)	Technology and Wellness Hub "The Campus" launches in Fall 2016 Strong community partners: Made in Brownsville, Brownsville Community Justice Center, Brownsville Partnership, Pitkin Avenue BID

FIGURE 9.3 Snapshot of Brownsville neighborhood characteristics.

of public assets, numerous innovation-focused place-based initiatives, and strong community partners that focus on creative ways to engage residents in uplifting their community (figure 9.3). Brownsville was chosen as the first NIL for several reasons. There were existing complementary city investments in the neighborhood, evidenced by the mayor's Brownsville Plan, and strong local community organizations to engage with and support. It was also an area of interest for the New York City Housing Authority (NYCHA), which provides housing for low- and moderate-income residents throughout the five boroughs of New York City and has significant concentrations of housing in the neighborhood.

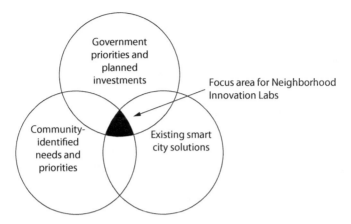

FIGURE 9.4 Venn diagram depicting the Neighborhood Innovation Labs as bringing together local community needs, government priorities, and smart-city technology capabilities.

Program Components

As in the case of Brownsville, once community partners have been engaged, each lab identifies priority areas (e.g., nighttime public safety) that are most relevant to the community, and technologies that address those topics are selected through requests for information (RFIs) or challenges (figure 9.4). Connected devices and systems that address community and city priorities are prioritized for inclusion in the NIL. Some examples of technologies include

- Temperature and air-quality monitors to quantify changes throughout the city
- Tools that quantify pedestrian or vehicle traffic
- Building energy-management systems
- Enhanced infrastructure that can provide Wi-Fi connectivity

The academic partner will develop a baseline analysis for each NIL, using low-cost in situ environmental sensors and an extensive array of data from city administrative records, social media, and participatory sensing programs. This analysis will focus on understanding the typical patterns of neighborhood activity and conditions (e.g., frequency, type, and location of 311 service requests and complaints) and various aspects of regular neighborhood dynamics (such as mobility and neighborhood health indicators). The utility of the baseline analysis is twofold: First, identification of these baseline patterns and their variance provides some measure of neighborhood that can be supplemented with data generated from demonstration projects.

Second, it enables validation of technology deployments, such as ICT interventions, through measurement of changes in the neighborhood conditions and/or dynamics associated with the specific intervention. In order to identify the effectiveness of NIL deployments, every technology implemented in the neighborhood labs follows an experimental evaluation framework with set goals and timelines. Community feedback is incorporated at regular intervals, through both qualitative and quantitative data-gathering. If the technology successfully meets the goals of the pilot and has the potential to address similar challenges in other communities, the city will explore other opportunities for implementation in additional NILs and, potentially, citywide.

Community access to, and ownership of, collected data is a critical aspect of the NILs structure. Data collected in the NILs will be made available to the community in an aggregated and anonymized manner so as not to compromise individual privacy. City agencies or researchers who wish to gain access to more granular data follow defined protocols on data sharing, management, and use in order to ensure the protection of privacy. All technology deployments, including any sensors, will follow the *NYC Guidelines for the Internet of Things.* Data transparency and strict controls on use and access are the foundations of the NILs. Without these requirements, it will be difficult to gain and maintain trust with community partners and ensure that local entrepreneurs have the chance to benefit from investments and initiatives in their neighborhoods.

A capable lead community partner and suitable anchor site are also vital aspects of the NIL framework. In Brownsville, the primary community partner is the Brownsville Community Justice Center (BCJC)—a nonprofit social-service organization dedicated to building off-ramps for young people who come into contact with the justice system. BCJC's programming includes promoting local tech entrepreneurship and becoming a leading voice in Brownsville advocating for local economic revitalization. In 2016, BCJC was awarded a contract with the New York City Department of Transportation to manage one of its high-need pedestrian plazas. Osborn Plaza has been chosen as an anchor site for the NIL, as it connects the Belmont Avenue business corridor with NYCHA's Langston Hughes affordable housing complex and is a site of multiple place-making programs and public events led by BCJC, Made in Brownsville (MiB), and other local community allies. Osborn Plaza was also designated as a "high-need plaza" under the OneNYC plaza equity program (figure 9.5).

A cohort of local leaders guides the NIL implementation as innovation advisers, representing a diverse mix of representatives from local nonprofits and foundations, elected officials, and agency outreach staff. In Brownsville, these innovation advisers include BCJC, Made in Brownsville, Brooklyn Community Board 16, Brownsville Partnership, Dream Big Foundation, and Friends of Brownsville Parks. This direct engagement with community representatives supports the goal of the NILs to bring together local expertise

FIGURE 9.5 Osborn Plaza, anchor site of a Neighborhood Innovation Lab in Brownsville, Brooklyn.

(empowering local leaders with the skills and capacities to drive technological change in their neighborhood) and tech partnerships (challenging technologists to develop and demonstrate new solutions to respond to community and government needs).

Local expertise is created and leveraged through (1) the formation of community advisory boards, which consist of civic leaders who are empowered to serve as strategic advisers involved in the local governance of the initiative; (2) the provision of learning incentives to build capacity of local leaders, which includes an intensive eight-session program to understand and drive technology change in their neighborhood, as well as other training opportunities; and (3) priority-setting to drive private-sector challenges, in which a series of workshops guide community advisers through a process of defining the most pressing neighborhood problems and focus areas where smart-city technologies can have the greatest impact.

Tech partnerships are strengthened through (1) establishment of a community baseline analysis led by the academic partner to collect, analyze, and visualize useful data about a given neighborhood; (2) calls for innovations (CFIs) that, in partnership with the relevant city agencies, turn the strategic priorities defined by community advisers into problem-based challenges that solicit proposals for new technology solutions to address local needs; (3) demonstration of technology solutions in public space, where selected technologies are piloted

Key components of our approach

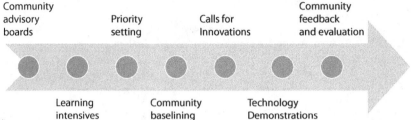

FIGURE 9.6 Neighborhood Innovation Lab workflow.

in and around public spaces, or anchor sites, including plazas and parks; and (4) community feedback and evaluation of technology impact, which supports the empirical evaluation by research teams of the deployed technology in relation to the goals and challenges defined in the CFI (figure 9.6).

Challenges and Lessons Learned

One of the main challenges to the deployment of data-enabled IoT and ICT technologies in cities stems from what has been an unclear return on investment (ROI). Innovative solutions tend to have little or no previous real-world demonstration to establish a viable proof-of-concept, while traditional city agency decision-making is risk-averse, relying primarily on solutions that have a long operational history and clear ROI. Consequently, this heavily favors solutions from large corporations rather than emerging players that are often inexperienced working with the public sector. Large cities such as New York tend to rely on smaller markets to be first-movers before adopting a technological trend or innovative solution. If an urban technology deployment does occur, key performance indicators (KPIs) and metrics to measure its efficacy and ROI are difficult to create and often not standardized at the city level. Large, dense cities face greater risks, including possible impact on the budget (financial risk) and the large number of people affected (human risk), creating the need for a platform to test innovations at a smaller scale.

Privacy and the use of personally identifiable information emerge as another challenge. While much can be learned from mobility tracking of smart devices, for instance, the potential infringement on personal privacy cannot and should not be ignored. Instead, a balance must be found between the sensitivity of the data collected and their use. Cities must develop use cases that clearly demonstrate the benefits of more widespread data collection, while at the same time ensuring that the least sensitive data needed are used to provide that benefit. This is an ongoing debate—on legal, technical, and moral grounds—and a discussion that needs to be handled in an open, transparent dialogue among city representatives, technology and data providers, data analysts, and the community. The NILs provide an environment in which use restrictions and controls can and will be explored, ranging from "opt-in" voluntary data-collection standards to individual and community ownership of personal and neighborhood-level data (Kontokosta 2016).

Another challenge relates to management and analysis of sensor-derived data. It is important to define the parameters of the data needed and to develop processes to balance data quality, resolution, and frequency with storage and computing capacities in order to address specific urban challenges and answer specific research questions. The challenge is to identify the appropriate data points needed to support neighborhood planning and community empowerment. By extension, how this information is conveyed to community members is a nontrivial challenge.

Finally, a significant challenge emerges in the implied responsibility of city agencies to respond to the new knowledge created through increased data collection, evaluation, and analysis. For instance, the NILs will collect high-resolution air-quality data across the selected communities. If readings show unhealthy levels of particulate matter, and these data are made available and accessible to community residents, it follows that the community will want action taken to improve air quality in the neighborhood. City agencies will need to modify and evolve methods of operational decision-making and governance to respond to these real-time data and new information about previously unmeasured quality-of-life indicators.

At a more micro level, a number of challenges stem from multistakeholder collaboration attempting to implement "living lab" models like the NILs. There can be ambiguities about when legal agreements are needed between partners, for instance, which can slow the process down, as well as challenges in identifying and agreeing to a "common language" when each of the key partners has different audiences and specific objectives. Questions about governance and how funding and expenses are handled can also cause delays and add to the complexity of the partnership. These challenges can be overcome, but doing so requires a dedicated team that is committed to the initiative and capable of understanding the needs, constraints, and goals of each of the partners. It is important to acknowledge that it took eighteen months from the announcement of the concept (September 2015) to the launch of the first lab in Brownsville (March 2017), in large part due to working out these issues in real time. But once these initial hurdles were overcome, the pace sped up dramatically, with community priorities released in July 2017 and the first challenges (CFIs) launched in October 2017.

Replicability and Looking Forward

The NILs initiative represents a model that is designed to be scalable and replicable across neighborhoods and cities. This model is especially useful for large cities, as smaller cities do not face the same constraints in testing and scaling potential solutions, given that they are often nimbler in their ability to explore new ideas. While there will be particular stakeholders with different strengths and weaknesses in certain areas, the overall governance structure and goals remain the same: city agencies, industry, academic institutions, and local community organizations working together to utilize data and urban technologies to solve problems identified by neighborhood stakeholders.

An important prerequisite, however, is strong local activism and the ability of local residents to formulate shared collective needs within a given neighborhood. While New York City represents a well-known example of distinct neighborhood identities and strong community advocates, this is not necessarily true for other U.S. cities, and is certainly not the case in many international cities with very different local, regional, and national institutions. In such cases, the role of local government, assisted by academic institutions, in providing efficient avenues and mechanisms for ensuring a feedback loop from local communities becomes crucial. The community engagement of the NILs model can also be used to develop community advocacy capacity by connecting neighborhood organizations around the shared goal of improving local conditions and quality of life.

The nature of participation in existing community engagement platforms, such as social media and cities' 311 complaint systems, is rather one-dimensional, ad hoc, and often superficial (Kontokosta 2016). The NILs provide a model for dynamic community engagement and community-led solutions by creating inclusive spaces where urban technology responds to targeted community needs and priorities. The NILs can be viewed as a means to improve citizen engagement and empower residents in urban decision-making.

Once several NILs are created, those communities can be linked and a common measurement baseline created to allow for community benchmarking across spatial and temporal dimensions (Kontokosta 2016). The shared learnings across neighborhoods, tied to the standardized infrastructure, data management, and technology engagement protocols, will serve to enhance the replicability of the model to other areas. The foundations of a multisector collaboration, community-led problem-solving, data management and transparency standards, and a data-enabled experimental environment constitute the key ingredients of success that can be translated and shared with cities across the world.

Conclusion

The NILs provide a scalable model for testing and deploying urban data and civic technologies, while leveraging data analytics to support community empowerment, neighborhood planning, urban research, and technology evaluation in real-world experimental environments. The neighborhood scale allows for communities to identify their unique needs and priorities and to meaningfully engage in the process from problem identification to technology evaluation. The multisector collaboration is designed to align goals and provide benefits for each of its stakeholders, including city agencies, the private sector, research institutions, and local communities, and create a more inclusive process for conceptualizing and deploying urban technologies at scale. The NILs provide a coordinated mechanism to accelerate the testing and deployment of new technologies and innovations with the aim of improving quality of life; optimizing city operations; increasing positive economic impact through job creation, training, and support for private-sector innovation; bolstering community engagement; and empowering residents to solve real challenges facing their neighborhoods.

Acknowledgments

The authors would like to thank the many people and community organizations who have made the NIL initiative possible and who were instrumental to its definition and launch. Specifically, we would like to recognize the contributions of Lindsey Paige-McCloy and Jose Serrano-Mclain in the Office of the Chief Technology Officer, David Gilford at the NYC Economic Development Corporation, and Ekaterina Levitskaya, Nicholas Johnson, Bartosz Bonczak, Kimonia Alfred, and Caryn Knutsen at New York University. Their dedication and commitment, and that of the NYC Mayor's Office, multiple city agencies, and numerous community leaders in Brownsville, demonstrate the potential for multisector and interagency collaboration to support community-led innovation.

References

Abdoullaev, Azamat. 2011. *A Smart World: A Development Model for Intelligent Cities.* Eleventh IEEE International Conference on Computer and Information Technology.

Chatman, Daniel G., Nicholas K. Tulach, and Kyeongsu Kim. 2011. "Evaluating the Economic Impacts of Light Rail by Measuring Home Appreciation." *Urban Studies* 49, no. 3: 467–87.

Coulton, Claudia J., Jill Korbin, Tsui Chan, and Marilyn Su. 2001. "Mapping Residents' Perceptions of Neighborhood Boundaries: A Methodological Note." *American Journal of Community Psychology* 29, no. 2: 371–83.

European Innovation Partnership on Smart Cities and Communities. 2013. *Strategic Implementation Plan.* Accessed June 26, 2017. http://ec.europa.eu/eip/smartcities/files/sip_final_en.pdf.

Granier, Benoit, and Hiroko Kudo. 2016. "How Are Citizens Involved in Smart Cities? Analyzing Citizen Participation in Japanese 'Smart Communities.'" *Information Polity* 21, no. 1: 61–76.

Hess, Daniel Baldwin, and Tangerine Maria Almeida. 2007. "Impact of Proximity to Light Rail Rapid Transit on Station-Area Property Values in Buffalo, New York." *Urban Studies* 44, no. 5–6: 1041–68.

Hudson Yards. n.d. "Maps & Graphs: Engineered City." Accessed August 12, 2017. http://www.hudsonyardsnewyork.com/press-media/images/maps-graphics/.

Kontokosta, Constantine E. 2016. "The Quantified Community and Neighborhood Labs: A Framework for Computational Urban Science and Civic Technology Innovation." *Journal of Urban Technology* 23, no. 4: 67–84.

Lea, Rodger, Mike Blackstock, Nam Giang, and David Vogt. 2015. "Smart Cities: Engaging Users and Developers to Foster Innovation Ecosystems." *Adjunct Proceedings of the 2015 ACM International Joint Conference on Pervasive and Ubiquitous Computing, Osaka, Japan, September 7–11,* 1535–42.

NYC Office of the Mayor. 2016. "One New York: Working for Our Neighborhoods." State of the City Remarks by Mayor de Blasio as Prepared for Delivery. February 4, 2016. Accessed June 28, 2017. http://www1.nyc.gov/office-of-the-mayor/news/133-16/state-the-city-remarks-mayor-de-blasio-prepared-delivery/.

Thomas, Vanessa, Ding Wang, Louise Mullagh, and Nick Dunn. 2016. "Where's Wally? In Search of Citizen Perspectives on the Smart City." *Sustainability* 8, no. 3: 207–19.

White House, Office of the Press Secretary. 2015. "Fact Sheet: Administration Announces New 'Smart Cities' Initiative to Help Communities Tackle Local Challenges and Improve City Services." September 14, 2015. Accessed June 14, 2017. https://obamawhitehouse.archives.gov/the-press-office/2015/09/14/fact-sheet-administration-announces-new-smart-cities-initiative-help/.

PART III

SAFETY AND MOBILITY

CHAPTER 10

NYPD ShotSpotter

The Policy Shift to "Precision-Based" Policing

TAMI LIN, *Independent Consultant*

MAŁGORZATA REJNIAK, *Columbia University*

Executive Summary

ShotSpotter (SST) is a wide-range gunshot-detection technology that can detect, locate, and alert law enforcement agencies of gunfire incidents in real time, using a network of acoustic sensors placed on rooftops. The New York Police Department (NYPD) worked to implement SST after Mayor Bill de Blasio was sworn into office in January 2014. The pilot, which became operational on March 16, 2015, at a cost of $3 million, comprised fifteen square miles of coverage in the Bronx and Brooklyn and was expanded to another nine square miles by the end of the following March, for a total of twenty-four square miles. In June 2016, NYPD entered into a five-year, $12.5 million contract with ShotSpotter Inc. (SST Inc.) that expands the coverage area to a total of sixty square miles (about 20% of the total area of New York City) across five boroughs.

SST was piloted to improve response to gunfire by the Police Department in the city. According to NYPD statistics, some 70–80% of gunshots are not reported (Freer 2016a). With SST, officers are now responding to gunshots with no associated 911 call, which translates to four to five times more gunshot responses. Overall response time to gunshots is also faster by two to three minutes and enables a more prepared response by officers. Moreover, SST alerts are incredibly valuable to police detectives. All shots are integrated into the city's Domain Awareness System (DAS), NYPD's proprietary crime-data aggregation platform, and detectives can overlap SST alerts with other crime data in a map. This spatial analysis leads to improved investigative work, enables deeper insights about the crime situation in a neighborhood, and helps NYPD target resources to the worst crime areas—i.e., "precision-based policing." Most important, the presence of officers responding to and investigating gunshots, especially in high-crime areas that may not usually report these incidents, sends a message that gun violence is not tolerated.

Key Takeaways and Actionable Insights

1. Initiative from top leadership enabled program inception in 2015. Use of SST was initiated by top leadership in the Police Department, including Commissioner William Bratton, and had the support of Mayor de Blasio. This enabled rapid organization and implementation of a pilot program, and eventual expansion, avoiding traditional budgetary and political hurdles.

2. A regular internal communication feedback loop enabled officers to maximize use of the technology. From the pilot onset, the use of SST was discussed during monthly leadership and weekly borough-based NYPD staff meetings. These discussions enabled peer-to-peer learning, helping police commanding officers share best practices on how to respond and follow up on SST alerts, how to carry out investigations, and how to improve the technology and the department's use of it. These knowledge-sharing feedback loops allowed officers to converge their ideas for designing response protocols and effectively leveraging the technology to combat crime.

3. A strong relationship and established feedback loop between the government client and technology vendor speeded up technology improvements. NYPD is in frequent communication with SST Inc., providing regular status updates on where the technology is working and where accuracy could be improved. SST Inc. responds quickly to service requests and other issues by updating its software algorithms and integrating improvements to its hardware (i.e., sensors).

4. Outsourcing technology implementation to a third-party vendor accelerated project rollout and conserved government resources for core agency mission. With the exception of a few key NYPD stakeholders who served as program manager and decision-makers on which precincts would receive sensors, SST Inc. was fully responsible for all aspects of technology implementation— determining sensor locations, installing sensors on buildings, licensing with property owners, maintenance, data integration, and upgrades to hardware and software. Additional public resources such as new hires and/or additional staff time at NYPD were not needed to execute the project; NYPD staff was able to keep focus on their core mission.

5. Integrate new technologies into existing systems wherever possible to produce more robust analyses. NYPD required SST Inc. to integrate its data into NYPD's existing crime data aggregator, the Domain Awareness System (DAS), which makes it easier for officers to access the data through a familiar user interface and software platform. Consequently, New York became one of the only cities that has integrated SST with other crime-related data. Alerts from SST can be overlaid with other crime statistics to paint a more comprehensive picture of crime patterns in a neighborhood. This helped enable more effective investigations by showing potential relationships between data from different sources.

6. Investments in new technology (e.g., investment in organization capacity) can help boost morale. NYPD invested in new technology, including SST and mobile devices for all 35,000 officers so they could access DAS from anywhere rather than just from the office. The officers felt they had cutting-edge technology that helped them in their work and were now at the forefront of their industry. They also understood that the technology was meant to increase officer safety by providing them with more data when responding to gunshots. The investment in the organization and its employees was recognized and helped to boost morale.

7. New technological tools can be particularly effective if used as part of a larger policy shift. NYPD was undergoing a policy change that shifted focus from "stop-and-frisk" to "people and geography"—that is, having officers become very familiar with the individuals and neighborhoods of the community they serve. This means getting to know community leaders and advocates, as well as known offenders and hotspots of crime. To do so, NYPD complemented the technological tools, such as SST and DAS, with a training program for new officers and new roles and responsibilities that focused on community engagement and outreach.

Problem Definition, Contextual Environment, and Innovation Opportunity

Gun violence and crime are closely interlinked in the United States. According to research by the FBI, firearms were used in 68% of murders, 41% of robberies, and 21% of aggravated assaults nationwide in 2011 (National Institute of Justice 2017). In 2015, 72% of New York City's murder victims died of gun violence, and 13% of violent crimes were committed with a firearm (Cuestas, Parascandola, and Moore 2015; New York State Division of Criminal Justice Services 2017). As Sergeant Joseph Freer (2017a), the day-to-day project manager for the SST rollout at NYPD, points out, "For every 328 gunshots fired, there is a homicide."

Reducing gun violence as a means of fighting crime has always been New York City's priority. This involves investigating all reported gunshot activity and repossessing illegal firearms. Traditionally, for the police to respond to gunfire, someone in the affected community needs to call the police and report a gunshot. Sergeant Freer remarks, "A gunshot alert is only as good as someone who responds, calls, looks out the window and says something, that's what makes a difference" (Freer 2017a). However, nationally, approximately 80% of gunshots are not reported to the police.[1] In New York City, approximately 74% are not reported (Freer 2016b). Reasons may include apathy in communities that live with gunfire on a regular basis, people not wanting to talk to the police and involve themselves in an investigation, and/or people preferring to handle the matter on their own (e.g., retaliation between gangs) (Iglesias 2016). According to Inspector Miguel Iglesias, who has used SST, "People are desensitized in certain areas; they may think it's firecrackers around the Fourth of July, they may think that the gunfire is far away from them and may think that someone else will call" (2017). The low incidence of reports enables unlawful gunfire to continue and illegal guns to be present on the streets, contributing to overall crime rates and homicide numbers.

Between 1960 and 1990, crime in America grew thirteen times faster than population. Crime in New York City followed this national trend. It was very high in the 1980s, partly due to the crack cocaine epidemic that hit major U.S. cities. The crime rate peaked in 1990, when New York experienced a record 527,257 reported crimes, including 2,262 murders, 3,126 rapes, 100,280 robberies, and 122,055 burglaries (NYPD 2017). The crime rate has been decreasing since 1990, and a large part of that is ascribed to the implementation in 1991 of Mayor David Dinkins's "Safe Streets, Safe Cities" program, which increased the number of police officers from 31,000 to 38,000 (Firestone 1996). Crime continued to drop at a slower rate during the administration of Mayor Rudolph Giuliani (1994–2001) and almost leveled off under Mayor Michael Bloomberg (2002–2013).

Since the 1990s, NYPD's strategy for fighting crime, reducing gunfire incidents, and repossessing illegal firearms was a policy called "stop-and-frisk." Introduced by Mayor Giuliani, stop-and-frisk was a practice of temporarily stopping, questioning, and at times searching civilians on the street for weapons and drugs; the individuals were arrested if drugs or weapons were discovered (Naspretto 2012). The number of stop-and-frisks increased rapidly in the 2000s and peaked at about 686,000 in 2011 (Grawert and Cullen 2016; New York Civil Liberties Union 2017; see figure 10.1).

Stop-and-frisk became a central issue in the 2013 New York City mayoral election because of a concern that the program stopped individuals without reasonable suspicion and disproportionately targeted people of color—more specifically, Latino and African American males. Indeed, in 2012, of those stopped and frisked, 89% were innocent, 55% were African American, 32% were

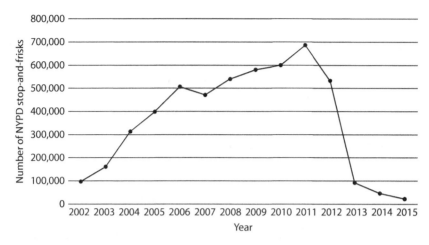

FIGURE 10.1 Number of NYPD stop-and-frisks.

Source: New York Civil Liberties Union 2017.

Latino, and only 10% were white (New York Civil Liberties Union 2017). In August 2013, Federal District Court Judge Shira Scheindlin found that stop-and-frisk was unconstitutional (Goldstein 2013). Mayor Bloomberg tried to appeal the verdict, but ultimately lost the case in November 2013 (Weiser 2013).

Around the same time as the federal district court issued its ruling, Bill de Blasio, then New York City public advocate, campaigned on a pledge to end the practice of stop-and-frisk if he were elected mayor. As part of an interracial family, with an African American son, de Blasio's message of concern for his son becoming a potential target of stop-and-frisk and his pledge to end the practice resonated with many city residents of color. Once elected, Mayor de Blasio named William Bratton to serve as the NYPD police commissioner and carry out their shared vision of building better relationships with the community. Commissioner Bratton had previously served as NYPD commissioner under Mayor Giuliani in the late 1990s and subsequently served as commissioner of the Los Angeles Police Department. In January 2014, Mayor de Blasio settled the stop-and-frisk litigation and formally ended the stop-and-frisk program.

As the stop-and-frisk program drew to a close, the dominant question in the administration and in the press became what would take its place and whether crime would continue to stay low or, better yet, decrease further. Mayor de Blasio's administration decided to shift toward a policy of what NYPD called "precision-based policing," or "intelligence-led policing," which works to target the worst offenders by taking advantage of new technologies and data integration. Commissioner Bratton shifted the department to using the vast amount of integrated data available to them to target serious offenders; rather than "casting a wide net," as was done under stop-and-frisk, they would use more "precision-based" policing. Mayor de Blasio and Commissioner Bratton were both keen on ending stop-and-frisk, restoring relationships between the police and the community, and investing in new technologies for the department, including gunshot-detection technology.

ShotSpotter: Gunshot-Detection Technology

Gunshot-detection technology, ShotSpotter, is one technological tool used to support the NYPD's policy shift toward precision-based policing. SST is a wide-range gunshot-detection technology that can detect, locate, and alert law enforcement agencies to gunfire incidents in real time. The technology detects outdoor gunfire using a network of acoustic sensors placed on rooftops. When a shot is fired outdoors within the geography of the sensors, the sound is recorded, sent to a SST Inc.–operated Incident Review Center in California, reviewed, and verified by an expert (usually former officers in the military or police forces). The system then generates a digital alert that is sent to NYPD's twenty-four-hour Operations Unit, NYPD-issued smartphones, and desktop applications. The time it takes to generate an alert is less than 60 seconds after the shot. The alert includes the location where the shots were detected, providing a precise location on a map (latitude/longitude) with corresponding metadata such as the address. This is possible because sensors detect shots within a certain radius and work together to calculate the geolocation of the shot (figure 10.2). The alert also pinpoints if the sound came from the rooftop or the side of a building and indicates the speed of travel, direction of travel, number of shots fired, whether there might be multiple shooters, and even the speed and direction of travel if the shooter is moving (figure 10.3). The information is also stored in a database of incidents, and police officers can listen to the stored gunshot recordings prior to responding to an alert.

ShotSpotter Inc., founded in 1996 and based in northern California, is the company that owns the SST hardware and software. To date, more than ninety cities globally have installed this technology, with sixty-two cities in the United States including Washington, D.C., Boston, and Newark.

Program Design and Development Phase

NYPD was a late adopter of gunshot-detection technology compared to other major cities in the United States (Washington, D.C., for example, has had the technology for a little over a decade). In 2011, during the Bloomberg

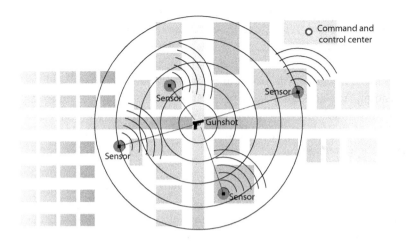

FIGURE 10.2 SST sample sensor network.

Source: Gagliardi 2016.

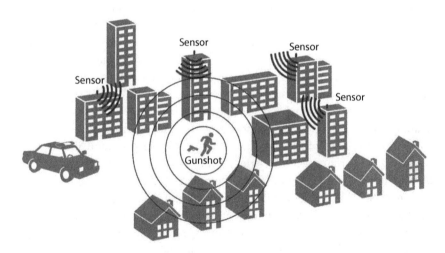

FIGURE 10.3 SST sensor diagram.

Source: ShotSpotter Sensor Diagram. Accessed May 3, 2017. http://www.shotspotter.com/system /content-uploads/mediakit/ShotSpotter_Sensor_Diagram.jpg.

administration, NYPD tested a gunshot-detection technology by another vendor, Safety Dynamics, for three months. The test yielded inaccurate geolocations, with up to 98% false alerts through the mistaken identification of other loud sounds (Freer 2017a). NYPD did not proceed with full implementation.

In late 2013, Mayor de Blasio and Commissioner Bratton were both keen on ending stop-and-frisk, restoring relationships between the police and the community, and investing in new technologies, including gunshot-detection technology, as part of an overall shift to precision-based policing. As Sergeant Freer (2017b) puts it:

> We were coming off the heels of the stop-and-frisk controversy, which led to huge problems, lawsuits, and deteriorated our relationship with the communities we serve, and created mistrust between the citizens and the police. So we wanted to take a step back and look at how else can we stop gun violence and protect our citizens, without broad-based stops. We wanted to see if there was a technology out there that could let us know about the gun violence that was going underreported, a kind of smoke alarm for gunfire.

The NYPD convened a group of officers, including those from the information and technology section, to evaluate gunshot-detection hardware and software. As Sergeant Freer (2017a) points out, other stakeholders, especially some commanding officers (COs), were not immediately aligned: "Institutionally, getting the internal people over the bias of the first failed experiment in 2011 took a lot of research and was a challenge." For example, Inspector Miguel Iglesias had participated in testing the Safety Dynamics gunshot-detection technology in 2011 and approached SST with apprehension. As Inspector Iglesias (2016) recalls, "This technology was going off when a car was backfiring. One time we had someone beating a drum and it went off, and then when we had actual gunfire on that same corner it wasn't going off. This is what led to my skepticism around ShotSpotter."

NYPD researched technologies from multiple companies, including ShotSpotter, Raytheon Boomerang, Shooter Detection Systems, and Safety Dynamics SENTRI. Other companies offered technologies designed for former military uses or SWAT team applications that used single-point sensors to detect when a known target is being shot at from a specific point. The detection radius of these other technologies was smaller (about 0.06–0.12 miles around a single sensor) than that of SST. SST was the only company to offer wide-area acoustical gunshot detection (i.e., gunshots are detected at distances as far as one mile or more from individual sensors, and more than one sensor may be involved in determining whether a sound qualifies as gunfire). As Sergeant Freer (2017b) remarks, "ShotSpotter's model was entirely different. With any given alert, ten to twelve sensors may be involved in determining that it's gunfire." This proved to be the critical determinant for choosing it over other solutions.

After narrowing in on SST, NYPD officers visited other cities that had installed the technology, including Washington, D.C., Camden, Newark, Atlantic City, and a few others, and asked their police departments about their experiences. When accuracy was a concern, SST Inc. stressed that it strives to constantly improve on its commitment to 80% accurate detection and regularly upgrades its technology and machine-learning algorithms. As Sergeant Freer (2017b) pointed out, SST Inc. has human verification of detected sounds that may be gunfire: "They do not just send us everything that they get—they have thousands more alerts than they sent us, but they determine them not to be gunfire." The validation of the sounds helped SST stand out among its competitors. NYPD selected SST for the pilot program to test their hardware and software to make sure the system met NYPD's needs. City Hall agreed to fund the $3 million pilot demonstration project.

NYPD Deputy Commissioner of Information Technology Jessica Tisch worked to secure and manage the contract with SST Inc. She was previously closely involved in the contract negotiations and development of DAS with Microsoft for counterterrorism purposes and is a key proponent of "democratizing" police data— i.e., providing police officers with access to information using current technologies (Goldman 2015). Deputy Commissioner Tisch's experience and vision to change how NYPD used and accessed data aligned with Commissioner Bratton's vision, which made her a prominent and high-level proponent of piloting SST. She executed the sole-source contract with SST Inc., which was originally for three years: one year for the pilot with two optional single-year extensions.

Program Pilot Phase

Sergeant Joseph Freer serves as the day-to-day project manager for SST rollout and use at NYPD. He previously served in the Chief of Department's office as part of the Strategic Analysis section, which is responsible for coordinating and evaluating major initiatives in the NYPD, and then moved to the Office of the Commissioner. Sergeant Freer and his former team from Strategic Analysis worked with SST Inc. on pilot development—i.e., defining the technical requirements of the technology.

One such requirement was that the data must be integrated into NYPD's existing big-data aggregator. SST Inc. has its own software called ShotSpotter Flex, which is a software portal that allows users to access alerts or a historical database of incidents. However, NYPD does not use this portal. Instead, in New York, SST data is accessible only through NYPD's proprietary DAS, which is a Microsoft-based big-data aggregation platform. Originally developed as part of the city's counterterrorism efforts, DAS presents aggregated crime information to provide a big-picture view of criminal activities. It serves as NYPD's centralized data warehouse that includes, but is not limited to, information from cameras, license-plate readers, history of 911 calls, mapped crimes, and arrest records. According to Sergeant Freer (2017a), who oversaw the integration of SST data into DAS, "The integration work went smoothly, aided by the fact that SST Inc. had worked with Microsoft in other places so there was already some familiarity with the Microsoft database framework." Consequently, New York became one of the only cities to fully integrate SST data with other crime-related data. The integration enables officers, when they receive an alert, to quickly pull up comprehensive information about the location they are going to, such as persons of interest in the area, so they are more prepared when responding to an incident.

SST Inc. was responsible for the technology implementation and operation. They own, install, maintain, and upgrade the sensors and software. The network of sensors must be located outside, ideally situated at least five stories above ground level, and properly spaced apart for accurate detection. SST Inc. worked with the NYPD and a variety of other city agencies to ask for and determine which public buildings would be most suitable for the sensors. For any remaining sensors that had to be located on private property, SST Inc. was responsible for reaching out to the property owners and getting signed agreements from them. Property owners with sensors do not receive compensation in any form. At times, property owners expressed pushback, as Sergeant Freer (2017a) notes: "We'll hear, 'There's no gunfire in my neighborhood—my block is safe.'"

With regard to how SST Inc. is compensated, NYPD does not pay per installed sensor, but rather according to the size of covered areas in square miles. It is up to SST Inc. to determine the number of sensors and the location of each sensor to ensure accurate gunshot-sound detection in that area. Through late 2014, SST Inc. installed sensors in seventeen select police precincts covering fifteen square miles in the Bronx and Brooklyn as part of the pilot program. To choose the area for the pilot rollout, NYPD devised a ranking of the most violent neighborhoods over the past ten years and targeted those areas first. Sergeant Freer (2017b) recalls:

> We looked at the murder rate, the shooting rate, and the 911 calls for shots fired, over a ten-year period. Some areas just didn't have the numbers to justify the expense to put ShotSpotter in that zone. Since SST sensors are not readily moved as crime trends shift, we needed to focus our efforts on the most historically violent areas of NYC to ensure we had the most success from this program—which ultimately is the goal of reducing gun violence.

The coverage areas where SST has been installed is strictly confidential to the NYPD and SST Inc. to prevent vandalism of the sensors. Additionally, Sergeant Freer (2016b) explains, "We don't want the criminal to wait until their target goes outside the SST detection area to carry out the shooting." Furthermore, information on which private buildings have sensors installed on them is confidential to SST Inc. Even the NYPD does not have access to it, partly to remove pressure to disclose the information publicly:

> When our precinct commanders first got the system in their commands, they were initially asking for sensor locations. We explained to them that individual sensors do not matter, the coverage of the array itself does. We explained that . . . SST is contracted to cover the area, and we leave it up to them where to put the sensors. We want to keep these confidential to protect the system. (Freer 2017a)

Human Learning from Technology: Pilot Phase Results and Full Rollout

The SST pilot became operational on March 16, 2015 (figure 10.4). Any skepticism toward SST started shifting once officers began recovering evidence from the incidents, recovering guns, and making arrests of the perpetrators—actions that supported the organization's primary goal of reducing crime and that might not have occurred if they did not have SST. Inspector Iglesias (2017) explains, "I was initially equally skeptical of SST. Once I started to see the benefits that we're getting, I love it, I really do. The last two to three years have been eye-opening."

A primary factor contributing to the success of the pilot was the internal communication between precincts and with top leadership about SST. Commanding officers (COs) of precincts where the sensors were installed were given a written order in December 2014 about SST. However, it was not detailed, particularly about how the officers were expected to respond to the alerts. The COs with SST came up with their own policies for their respective precincts on how to respond to the SST alerts and how to document the activities and results. Eventually, the response protocols among the precincts converged because of the discussions during weekly borough-wide precinct meetings as well as CompStat meetings. (NYPD CompStat meetings, which started in 1994, involve COs from different precincts and other high-ranking NYPD officers meeting monthly. In these meetings, COs are responsible for reporting on and responding to any questions about the crime statistics and trends in their respective precincts.) Top leadership emphasized SST during these meetings, which reaffirmed that this tool and its outcomes were important. From these meetings, COs with SST sensors in their precincts could learn from their peers about how best to respond to the alerts, discuss the protocols they tried and which worked, and how they could improve their response. Inspector Iglesias (2017) explains, "Whatever best practices I had, I'd share it with the other guys.

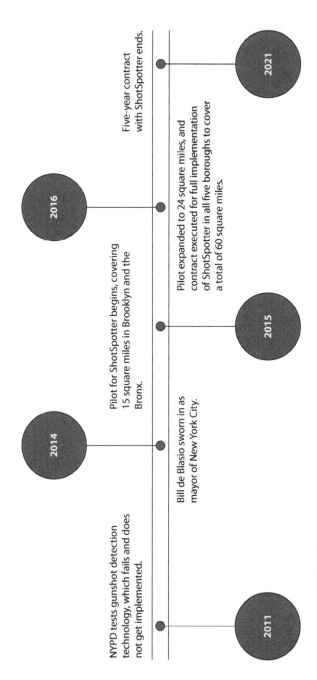

FIGURE 10.4 SST timeline.

It's a good thing to have and to share, because helping prevent these shootings is what we do." The sharing of success stories—of finding ballistics evidence and/or arresting the perpetrator, especially when there were no 911 calls associated with the gunfire—helped to bolster confidence in the use of SST.

Less than one year into the pilot, in January 2016, NYPD announced that it would expand the SST coverage area from twenty-four square miles to sixty square miles, spread across all five boroughs. In June 2016, NYPD went to the City Council and asked for funding for the additional thirty-six square miles. City Council approved funding of $2.5 million annually, and the original three-year contract was changed to a five-year agreement for the full expansion, which went into effect on June 16, 2016. The ranking of most violent neighborhoods was used to determine further rollout locations.

The decision to expand the coverage area was based on an analysis carried out by NYPD's data group, which found evidence of SST's effectiveness. Specifically, SST led to firearm and ballistic recoveries when there were no 911 calls associated with them, and SST alerts contributed useful detective evidence. The pilot (from March 2015 to January 2016) yielded more than 1,600 SST alerts, which led to eight arrests and thirteen gun recoveries. For 2015 and 2016 combined, there were eighty-nine incidents in which the NYPD recovered weapons. According to Sergeant Freer, about 20% of those weapons would never have been discovered had it not been for SST—there were no 911 calls associated with those weapons, so the police would have never known about the shootings. SST alerts also provided valuable evidence for detectives. As Sergeant Freer (2017a) explains, "When we found those ballistic recoveries, for the first year, one in five were matching with other cases we found in the city. So now you're starting to put together larger pieces of the puzzle. We're finding evidence that we wouldn't have normally found. That evidence is then matching to other shootings, so it's not disparate information anymore."

Installation in the last thirty-six square miles was completed in summer 2017. NYPD has SST installed in every borough, across sixty square miles (about 17% of the city's total area). NYPD does not foresee adding or shifting coverage before the end of the five-year contract in June 2021. It determined that the cost-effectiveness of implementing SST beyond the current coverage area may begin to decline. This has to do with the requirement that coverage must be a minimum of three contiguous square miles to be effective. As Sergeant Freer (2017a) explains:

> The issue we're getting into is that the violent areas that are left aren't really three square miles, they are a lot tighter and smaller. For example, would we need to deploy a whole three square mile zone on the Lower East Side, when we only have pockets of violence in concentrated areas? That may not be the best use of the technology or use of funding, and there are other traditional resources that may be better suited to address the violence in those smaller areas.

TABLE 10.1 Key Stakeholder Table

Stakeholder group	Role played	Interest in the program	Incentives needed to engage
City leadership (e.g., mayor, NYPD commissioner)	Recognized the opportunity in New York City; initiated pilot and coordinated with NYPD	*High*: program is part of larger policy change on how NYPD will address crime in the city (i.e., focus on precision-based policing)	None
New York Police Department (e.g., commanding officers, neighborhood coordinating officers, detectives)	Implemented the pilot and expanded the program; handled coordination with SST; responded to and investigated SST alerts	*High*: program serves to further NYPD's objective of reducing gun violence in the city	Pilot was needed to convince NYPD officers of SST's effectiveness
ShotSpotter Incorporated	Provided sensor coverage and gunshot reporting to NYPD	*High*: New York is SST's largest municipal customer	None

The NYPD is constantly evaluating the effectiveness of its current rollout in terms of successful firearm and ballistic recoveries and additional detective evidence and, upon completion of the five-year contract, will decide (1) whether to continue working with SST, (2) whether to shrink or expand coverage, and (3) whether to shift the coverage around to different zones. This will depend on changes in patterns of gun violence in the city.

The key stakeholders involved in the development, pilot, and eventual successful rollout of SST are summarized in table 10.1.

Program Impact

Impact on NYPD Response to Gun Violence

With SST, officers are now responding to significantly more gunfire incidents; responding faster; and responding more safely. The NYPD is now responding to four to five times more gunshots, because it allows the police to respond to gunfire that would not have been reported through 911 calls. Inspector Iglesias (2017) offers a telling illustration of the effectiveness of SST in this regard, "In November 2014, there was a machine gunfire coming out of the roof of one of our buildings in the command and I heard that and then it showed up on my phone. We didn't have a single 911 call reporting that those shots were being fired." Sergeant Freer (2017a) summarizes, "Shotspotter is really effective at filling in those gaps when people aren't calling."

Furthermore, average response time to gunshots is faster by two to three minutes, for two reasons. First, officers do not need to wait to respond until shots are reported through 911 and then dispatched to the field, which can sometimes take up to five minutes. With SST, officers get alerts directly on their mobile devices within sixty seconds of the shots being fired. Inspector Iglesias (2016) emphasizes that "two to three minutes can be a lifetime for a police officer." He recalls an incident in his precinct "where SST came on and, luckily, we had a police unit right there. Lo and behold, they come up on this guy shooting at the other guys. They apprehended him in real-time and got the gun" (2017). Second, the geolocation of the technology has shrunk the area that the police may need to search. The sound of a gunshot outside echoes and ricochets around, making it difficult for a person's ear to know where the sound came from. If someone called the police about the shot and gave an address, officers typically would need to search at least a three-block radius for where the gunfire occurred, providing additional time for the perpetrator to escape. SST can pinpoint exactly where the shot is coming from—whether it's the roof of the building, the backyard, or the front yard.

Moreover, SST enables a safer response by officers by equipping them with more situational information. Responding officers now know exactly how many shots were fired and where they occurred. This information is combined with other information from DAS, such as building information, past crimes, and known past offenders in the area. When officers arrive at the shooting scene, they have a better idea of what to expect, and a better chance of finding the shooter and/or recovering evidence. Inspector Iglesias (2016) recounts, "By the time you get a 911 call and a dispatcher sends you to a job, you already have the entire job on your [smart]phone. You don't have to ask: what's the description, who's the complaint from, etc. It's something that makes you more of an independent thinker as far as a police officer is concerned."

Impact on Detectives

Key support for the tool came from plainclothes detectives who conducted investigations. SST Inc.'s performance guarantee is that they will detect 80% of all outdoor shootings. According to Sergeant Freer, they are at about a 90% accuracy rate—missing about 10% of gunshots. A gunshot is considered "missed" by SST if an alert does not go off but someone calls 911 and officers discover evidence at the scene confirming that a shot was indeed fired within the SST geographic radius. Of the remaining 90% of gunshots, NYPD is able to find full ballistic evidence in 25% of the incidents. The remaining 75% are "unconfirmed," meaning the NYPD is not able to find any evidence confirming that a shot was fired or not fired (Freer 2017b). Nonetheless, all such incidents are treated as true and valuable, unless proven otherwise. Sergeant Freer (2017b) explains, "If you get to the scene and don't find anything, and there's no video or eyewitness available, is the shot confirmed or unconfirmed? Statistically we're putting them all in one bucket of 'unconfirmed' category because we don't know what happened but, realistically, they probably are true."

This information on all shootings, including the unconfirmed ones, is very helpful to the detectives. Since all shot alerts, including historic and unconfirmed incidents, are integrated into the DAS system, the detectives can produce a more holistic view of crime in an area. They can also track gun activity in neighborhoods over time and can see if ballistics evidence, if recovered, from one area matches with evidence from any other areas.

Impact on Organization Policy and Policing Strategy

As discussed previously, Mayor de Blasio and Commissioner Bratton wanted to improve NYPD–community relations after the end of stop-and-frisk. It is critical to note how use of new technology, such as SST, and new policies reinforced each other. SST helped enhance NYPD's responsiveness to public needs and enabled increased police engagement with the community, as part of NYPD's larger policy shift toward a focus on "people and geography" and use of intelligence-led, precision-based, data-driven policing. As figure 10.5 shows, the policy change pushed for more use of technology and data, and for changes in officer training and interactions with the public. SST was not the only technology to support NYPD's policy shift. It was an addition to a growing toolbox of technologies, coupled with human interactions to collect information to help officers do their jobs. Information is most essential to officers in testing or verifying hypotheses in deterring and solving crimes. Information or intelligence gathered by officers and technological tools were combined to enable more data-driven and precision-based policing.

The aim of NYPD's neighborhood policing program is to "support forming connections with communities and to serve as complementary to the technological tools and available data" (Freer 2017a). Implementation of a "people and geography" policy for policing involves officers having a strong understanding of the neighborhoods they serve and of the people within a community. They become familiar with community leaders and businesses,

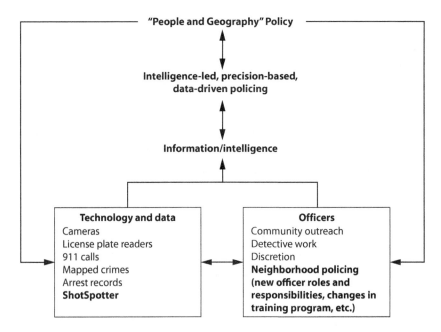

FIGURE 10.5 NYPD policy change.

as well as recognize areas with known gangs, and are familiar with individuals who have been past aggressors or victims of crime (individuals who are more likely to be involved with a criminal incident in the future). Importantly, officers are assigned to the same areas every day. An important goal of neighborhood policing was to restore and build relationships with members of a community, and provide different and positive types of encounters with police. As Sergeant Freer (2017a) states, "You really get to know the officer. We like to think that there is a lot more trust [in NYPD] after we launched this program," based on increased reporting and willingness of community members to speak with the police.

To enable the neighborhood policing model, the NYPD introduced changes to its organization structure, responsibilities of officers, and how new officers are trained. In the past, once cadets graduated from the police academy, they were often sent to perform "operation impact" work, which involved foot patrol of high-crime areas. In effect, rookie officers, who may never have set foot in these neighborhoods and had little to no understanding of its people or geography, were tasked with patrolling the area for crime.

Under the new training program, modeled after the Los Angeles Police Department's program, the typical career path for new officers involves formal field training for the first year, where they get to know the community.

Led by community members who volunteer as part of the Community Partners Program (CPP), new officers are shown around their neighborhood and have an opportunity to get to know the area and the people, such as by visiting local churches and stores. The new cadets then serve their second year in response automobiles, the third year in steady sector (answering calls in the area), and eventually move up to Sector Officers (SOs) and Neighborhood Coordinating Officers (NCOs) and then to a specialized squad. NCOs and SOs are new officer designations implemented under the neighborhood policing model. Each precinct now has at least two NCOs who are responsible for finding out community issues and for coming up with community outreach strategies. Sector Officers, at least one per sector, are patrol officers who assist the NCOs.

Furthering the goals of the neighborhood policing model, SST helps enable increased police engagement with a community because it improves responsiveness to criminal activity in neighborhoods. Improved responsiveness takes the form of increased immediate police response to gunshots, NCO and SO follow-ups, and keeping the community informed of incidents of crime. SST aids officers to more effectively follow up on shootings and inform the local community that gunfire took place. NCOs and SOs are often the ones who knock on doors and follow up on gunfire incidents from SST reports. The responsiveness of police to all shootings encourages reporting by the community, discourages criminal activity, and increases trust in police and perceived safety. The police seek to form relationships with community members to get more information and help to deter or solve crimes. When the pilot started, on average citywide, 20% of gunshots were reported to the police through 911 calls. The NYPD began to see gunshot-reporting metrics improve in 2016 in some neighborhoods, to a point where 34% of shootings detected by ShotSpotter resulted in 911 calls (Freer 2017b). NYPD ascribes this improvement in part to SST. Sergeant Freer (2017b) explains, "We're seeing an increase in the number of people calling, which is very good because we want people to be engaged—every time I get an alert, I want someone calling in on it with more information. Community members see that the police is responding to alerts and, therefore, doing something themselves about gun violence."

In an interview with the *New York Daily News*, Deputy Commissioner Jessica Tisch provides a good summary of SST's effect on neighborhood policing efforts:

> SST is affecting the way New Yorkers think about the NYPD. We know that based on neighborhood policing that the NYPD is making significant efforts to partner with the communities and we also know that cops are responding more to shots fired jobs because they know about more shots being fired. The numbers show more people are engaging with police. (Cuestas 2017)

Challenges and Lessons Learned

Challenges

Throughout the development, pilot, and full rollout phases, NYPD encountered three key challenges. An ongoing challenge for NYPD and SST is accuracy in locations that are more topographically diverse. The minimum sensor density requirement is at least twenty-five sensors per square mile. However, sensors need to be installed much more densely in a city like New York with a lot of ambient noise, and SST Inc. has had to move sensors around. Areas around outdoor sports stadiums, high-traffic highways, and airports have experienced some accuracy issues. NYPD relays these issues to SST Inc., which then investigates and recalibrates the sensors. This feedback loop and responsiveness on both sides makes this partnership successful.

A second challenge, particularly at the later stages of the full rollout, was NYPD's choosing coverage areas that maintained the cost-effectiveness of the program. As pointed out earlier, the remaining pockets of gun violence that did not receive coverage were much smaller than three square miles. The consideration for NYPD was whether it made sense to deploy SST to cover those small areas, or whether more traditional gun-violence prevention measures were more appropriate. As Sergeant Freer pointed out (2017b):

> We're getting down to these smaller pockets and asking ourselves—what's going to be more effective? Is SST going to be effective in an area that's only one square mile, or should we do something more traditional, for example, increase police deployment and engagement, implement a gun violence suppression or recidivism program?

The third challenge for the NYPD in the future will be deciding whether patrolling police are the most effective unit to respond to SST alerts, as is the current practice. The alternative strategy would be to shift the response to an investigative unit that would respond to aggregated gunshot alerts with detective teams once certain criminal activity patterns emerge. Sergeant Freer (2017b) described it as "taking a step back, aggregating all the dots [crime incidents], and seeing how you can help the people in that area." The District of Columbia implemented a limited patrol response to SST alerts. The NYPD will soon need to decide whether to undergo a similar transition without compromising the improved community relationships. It is important to remember that a primary goal of precision-based policing is being able to target the use of available resources in a more strategic way and in smaller, more specific locations. The successful implementation (and buy-in by officers) of SST has enabled leadership to now reassess human resource allocation and continue to find ways to be more effective and efficient. Additionally, as illustrated earlier in figure 10.5, the feedback loop of learning between people, technology, and policy adjustments is constant. The ability of participants in the feedback loop to identify issues and find ways to address them is a key factor in the success of the implementation of SST.

Lessons Learned

Many factors led to the successful implementation of SST. The most important were several feedback loops and institutionalized sharing of best practices involving SST Inc., NYPD, and other cities with the technology. As discussed earlier, peer-to-peer learning first took the form of formal monthly CompStat and weekly borough-based meetings, where COs and executive leadership discussed the use and impact of SST. These meetings provided a forum to share best practices, converge on alert response protocols, and help prioritize the worst crime areas and shift resources accordingly.

Communication between cities has helped NYPD incorporate certain best practices around SST. This communication is facilitated by NYPD or SST Inc. SST Inc. enables peer-to-peer learning between cities by sponsoring and hosting an online forum "where communities can come together and communicate best practices among each other without any oversight from us," as Mike Will (2017), vice president for customer support at ShotSpotter Inc., explains. SST Inc. also organizes international seminars and symposiums for agencies to exchange best practices. Moreover, annual police conferences and police chief conferences have also given cities opportunities to share their experiences with using SST. For instance, the follow-up process incorporated by NCOs was borrowed from Camden, New Jersey, and has proven to be very effective. As Sergeant Freer (2016a) explains, "Coordination with other cities and sharing of best practices has been happening since day one." Because the SST system is a machine learning system, every city has an incentive to work with other cities to get SST's detection as accurate as possible because it benefits every participant down the road.

Continuous support from SST Inc. directly to NYPD, in the form of SST Inc's customer support team, has contributed to the successful rollout of the technology. These customer support teams are assigned to and deal directly with the agencies, teaching best practices and sharing ways in which agencies of a similar size use the technology. These teams are instrumental to the onboarding process, "laying the ground work for these agencies to prepare for the technology and providing training on how to use," as Mike Will (2017) explains. These teams remain involved with an agency throughout the rollout to provide customer support. In the case of New York City, the customer support team for NYPD is of special importance to SST Inc. "because it's a very large agency. It's our largest customer. The success team is made up of a number of executives including our Chief Technology Officer. We treat them a bit differently due to their size."

Throughout the rollout, there were continuous feedback loops in the form of communications between Sergeant Freer and SST Inc., related to the technology's effectiveness. Mike Will (2017) said, "My team is in continuous communication with the NYPD. I meet with them weekly in person. My team interfaces with them daily. We report to them with metrics daily." NYPD also provided weekly, sometimes daily, reports to SST Inc. on the results from the alerts. Specifically, NYPD tells SST Inc. whether the alert was "confirmed" (evidence found confirming gunshot was fired), "unconfirmed" (no evidence found confirming gunshot was fired), "missed" (confirmed gunshots did not yield SST alerts), or "mislocated" (the geolocation was off). NYPD is providing these reports back to SST Inc. on a voluntary basis. This feedback loop helps both entities continue to improve the technology and its use. As Sergeant Freer (2016a) points out, "Unless you tell them [SST Inc.] whether they are right or wrong, they don't know. It's in our best interest to tell them."

Another factor that contributed to the success of SST was the buy-in from officers, partly achieved from NYPD investing money in new technologies and advancing the organization to the forefront of the industry. NYPD previously operated with older equipment and software technologies. The new investment in SST, along with investments in computers, laptops for cars, smartphones for all 35,000 officers where they can access DAS, and spending on research and development into other technologies, was very well received by officers and also helped boost morale since these technologies are meant to improve officer safety.

It is important to stress that the implementation of SST was successful largely because it was not implemented as a stand-alone technology; the existence of DAS coupled with a major policy shift in policing helped to support and drive the project. Since 2014, Mayor de Blasio and Commissioner Bratton have worked to change how policing is done through the neighborhood policing program and use of integrated data to target and arrest offenders. Moreover, New York's existing technological advances in the form of DAS enabled SST to succeed. Mike Will (2017) explains:

> The success factor for NYC is that NYPD is one of the most technologically cutting-edge agencies we've dealt with—the way they use SST is different from other cities in that here it's a much more integrated tool, as part of an overall solution to what they provide. They have the ability to add our gunshot data to all the other data that they have access to in their Domain Awareness System. We are enhancing what they have access to already and SST is just one of those things.

Strengths	Weaknesses
Several feedback loops and institutionalized sharing of best practices between all stakeholders	Inability to attribute gun recoveries or arrests directly to presence of SST casts a shadow over the benefits of SST. For instance, would the gun recovery have occurred if SST was not installed in a certain area? Would someone have made a 911 call for that incident? There is no true baseline scenario to compare against.
Buy-in from leadership and officers (technology users)	
Technology works and supports organization policy goals	
Data is integrated with other crime data, offering a more comprehensive picture of crime in a geographic area	Potential vandalism of SST hardware
Policies are in place that support the use of the technology and data	

Opportunities	Threats
Moving SST sensors to different areas as crime in some regions decrease	Potential officer pushback against new organizational structure, roles, and training programs
Sharing best practices with other police departments	Maintaining the cost-effectiveness of the SST program
Adding data from SST to CompStat reports to show efficacy of technology	Verifying and improving accuracy in locations that are more topographically diverse
	Not optimizing resource allocation

FIGURE 10.6 SST SWOT analysis.

Moving forward, several of the success factors of the SST implementation will continue to be the strengths of the program. Likewise, many of the challenges may become weaknesses. The strength, weakness, opportunity, and threat (SWOT) analysis is presented in figure 10.6.

Conclusion

The implementation of ShotSpotter was part of a larger NYPD shift to "precision-based policing." It was an addition to a growing toolbox of technologies, coupled with human interactions, to collect information to help officers do their jobs. Information, which may be gleaned from technological sources and human interactions, is most essential to officers in testing or verifying hypotheses in deterring and solving crimes. Much of the success of SST's implementation came from the human interactions that contextualized the gathered data: within NYPD, in coordinating the planning and implementation between different work groups, prioritizing its use by executive leadership, and sharing best practices among commanding officers; in the field, in how the data were being used in interactions with the community; and between the NYPD and SST Inc., in continuing to improve the technology. SST is just one technological tool that NYPD has adopted, but its implementation shows the amount of work, coordination, and support that is needed for a successful project.

Note

1. Note that data are from the National Gunfire Index, which is owned, compiled, and published by ShotSpotter Inc.

References

Cuestas, Gianluca, Rocco Parascandola, and Tina Moore. 2015. "NYPD Reveals Increase in Homicides and Gun Violence Across NYC Compared to Last Year, with Half as Many Stop-and-Frisks." *New York Daily News*, June 2. http://www.nydailynews.com/new-york/nyc-crime/cops-seek-sweatsuit-clad-man-shot-bystander-brooklyn-article-1.2242439.

Firestone, David. 1996. "News Analysis: Giuliani Credits Strategy for the City's Safer Streets." *New York Times*, January 27. http://www.nytimes.com/1996/01/27/nyregion/news-analysis-giuliani-credits-strategy-for-the-city-s-safer-streets.html.

Freer, Joseph. 2016a. Personal interview by Tami Lin, February 25, 2016.

——. 2016b. Personal interview by Tami Lin, June 21, 2016.

——. 2017a. Personal interview by Małgorzata Rejniak, March 31, 2017.

——. 2017b. Personal interview by Małgorzata Rejniak, May 1, 2017.

Gagliardi, Pete. 2016. *IBIS–GunOps–ShotSpotter: The Spears of the Trident*. Triple Barrel Strategies, LLC. Accessed May 3, 2017. http://shotcallerglobalinc.com/wp-content/uploads/2016/09/IBIS-GunOps-ShotSpotter-The-Spears-of-the-Trident.pdf.

Goldman, Henry. 2015. "Tisch Scion Forsakes Family Business for New York's War on Crime." *Bloomberg News*, June 12. Accessed May 18, 2017. https://www.bloomberg.com/politics/articles/2015-06-12/tisch-scion-forsakes-family-business-for-new-york-s-war-on-crime.

Goldstein, Joseph. 2013. "Judge Rejects New York's Stop-and-Frisk Policy." *New York Times*, August 12. http://www.nytimes.com/2013/08/13/nyregion/stop-and-frisk-practice-violated-rights-judge-rules.html.

Grawert, Ames, and James Cullen. 2016. "Fact Sheet: Stop and Frisk's Effect on Crime in New York City." Brennan Center for Justice, October 7. Accessed May 18, 2017. https://www.brennancenter.org/analysis/fact-sheet-stop-and-frisks-effect-crime-new-york-city.

Iglesias, Miguel. 2016. Personal interview by Tami Lin, March 26.

——. 2017. Personal interview by Małgorzata Rejniak, May 1.

Naspretto, Ernie. 2012. "The Real History of Stop-and-Frisk." *New York Daily News*, June 3. Web. Accessed May 18, 2017. http://www.nydailynews.com/opinion/real-history-stop-and-frisk-article-1.1088494.

National Institute of Justice. 2017. "Gun Violence." March 27. Accessed May 18, 2017. https://nij.gov/topics/crime/gun-violence/Pages/welcome.aspx.

New York Civil Liberties Union. 2017. "Stop-and-Frisk Data." May 23. Accessed November 12, 2017. https://www.nyclu.org/en/stop-and-frisk-data.

New York State Division of Criminal Justice Services. 2017. *New York State Gun Involved Violence Elimination (GIVE) Initiative: Crime, Arrest, and Firearm Activity Report Data.* Data reported through March 31, 2017. Issued May 16, 2017. Accessed May 18, 2017. http://www.criminaljustice.ny.gov/crimnet/ojsa/greenbook.pdf.

NYPD. 2017. *CompStat* 24, no. 18 (5/1/2017–5/7/2017). Accessed May 18, 2017. http://www.nyc.gov/html/nypd/downloads/pdf/crime_statistics/cs-en-us-city.pdf.

Parascandola, Rocco. 2017. "NYPD ShotSpotter Gunfire Sensors Improve Rate of 911 Calls, Arrests." *New York Daily News*, March 28. http://www.nydailynews.com/new-york/nypd-shotspotter-gunshot-detection-rate-improves-article-1.3010990.

"Stop-and-Frisk Data." New York Civil Liberties Union, Updated May 23, 2017. Web. Accessed November 12, 2017. https://www.nyclu.org/en/stop-and-frisk-data.

Weiser, Benjamin. 2013. "Judges Decline to Reverse Stop-and-Frisk Ruling, All but Ending Mayor's Fight." *New York Times*, November 22. http://www.nytimes.com/2013/11/23/nyregion/appeals-court-refuses-for-now-to-overturn-stop-and-frisk-ruling.html.

Will, Mike. 2017. Personal interview by Małgorzata Rejniak, May 3.

CHAPTER 11

VISION ZERO NYC

Toward Ending Fatalities on the Road

ARNAUD SAHUGUET, *Cornell Tech*

Executive Summary

The primary mission of government is to protect the public. Each year, on average, 4,000 New Yorkers are seriously injured and more than 250 are killed in traffic crashes.

Initiated in January 2014, New York City's Vision Zero lays the foundations for the city's efforts to end traffic deaths and injuries on the streets. Starting from police crash reports and citizen input, the city identified and prioritized dangerous zones and intersections; it designed and deployed practical solutions and measured and reported their impact. Under Vision Zero, New York City managed to deploy effective and impactful solutions in a short time frame and within budget, using three approaches: combining efforts across education, enforcement, infrastructure, and policies; encouraging collaboration across agencies and with the private sector; and involving local communities and their elected representatives beforehand. The Vision Zero NYC case study will show that traffic casualties can be avoided and that the approach can be replicated—effectively and affordably—in other urban environments.

Key Takeaways

1. Safety is a public service. Similar to other public services, such as providing clean water or picking up the trash, a key responsibility of a city is making

its people feel safe in the streets. Pedestrian casualties can be prevented and must be looked at in a systematic way as a public health issue.

2. Vision Zero NYC is a data-driven, collaborative and participatory effort: use of data to rank areas of intervention, to identify target audience for education, to measure impact; involvement from a dozen city agencies, the nonprofit sector, the private sector and elected officials; and participation of citizens and key local actors.

   Vision Zero NYC embraces a four-pronged approach with infrastructure, enforcement, engagement, and legislative components. Legislative aspects may require strong political will, but some, like speed limits or speed cameras, can be real game changers.

3. You can start "cheap" with "paint and plastic," on budget and on schedule. Emerging technologies already show some real promise in making Vision Zero–aligned efforts even more effective.

4. Human tragedies often create a tipping point that moves the project forward.

5. Impact can be hard to measure, and picking the right metrics is key.

6. Even if seen by some as a moonshot, Vision Zero NYC provides an objective take on pedestrian casualties, driven less by public opinion and more by data.

Theoretical Background, Contextual Environment, and Problem Definition

New York City has 8.5 million residents and welcomes more than 56 million tourists annually. Less than 44% of New York City households own a car ("List of U.S. Cities" 2017). With more than 6,000 miles of streets, this is the most walkable city in the United States (Golson 2015). From 2000 to 2013, the city had an average of 300 vehicle fatalities and 5,000 killed-or-severely-injured per year (Vision Zero 2016). But New York City is not the only one.

In the 1990s, facing a similar issue, Sweden came up with the concept of Vision Zero, which stands for "zero casualty." Originated in Sweden in 1994, it was adopted in 1997 by the Swedish parliament as its official road policy.

Founded on the belief that loss of life is not an acceptable price to pay for mobility, Vision Zero takes a systems approach to enhancing safety. Rather than exclusively faulting drivers and other users of the transportation system, Vision Zero places the core responsibility for accidents on the overall system design, addressing infrastructure design, vehicle technology, and enforcement. (Center for Active Design 2014)

Vision Zero design principles can be summarized as follows: (1) blame road system design rather than road users; and (2) design a system that can handle

TABLE 11.1 Road Fatalities

Country	Fatalities per 100,000 population (2014)
Sweden	3
European Union	5.5
United States	11.4
Dominican Republic	40

Source: "The Economist Explains" 2014.

human errors. These designs try to address holistically the main causes of accidents (Whitelegg and Haq 2006):

- Speed
- Impairment (e.g., alcohol, drug, fatigue)
- Lack of body protection (e.g., seat belts, helmets)
- Poor road infrastructure (e.g., sign design, street furniture)
- Noncompliance from users
- Visibility
- Vehicle engineering

Since the implementation of Vision Zero, Sweden's rate of traffic fatalities has dropped by half (Morris 2016) and is now one of the lowest in the world (table 11.1).

Naturally, some U.S. mayors started to pay attention. In January 2014, freshly elected Mayor Bill de Blasio announced the adoption of New York City's Vision Zero (NYC Office of the Mayor 2014), fulfilling one of his campaign promises (Bill de Blasio for Mayor 2013).

Design, Piloting, Development, and Implementation

In January 2014, less than two weeks after being sworn in as mayor, Bill de Blasio announced the creation of the Vision Zero Task Force (NYC Office of the Mayor 2014), a "top-to-bottom" interagency task force including the New York Police Department (NYPD), the Department of Transportation (DOT), the Taxi and Limousine Commission (TLC), and the Department of Citywide

Administrative Services (DCAS), among others. According to Mayor Bill de Blasio, the day Vision Zero was announced, "Our top responsibility is protecting the health and safety of our people. From tougher enforcement to more safely-designed streets and stronger laws, we'll confront this problem from every side—and it starts today."

The mayoral initiative served as a catalyst with a very aggressive timeline (see figure 11.1) and an unconditional commitment from the mayor himself and the partners involved. Key elements were already in place that laid the groundwork for Vision Zero NYC.

First, the concept of Vision Zero had already been created and successfully implemented in Sweden in 1994 and Norway in 1999 ("Vision Zero" 2017). Second, New York City had already transformed its transport infrastructure with the addition of numerous bike lanes circa 2007–2008 and the launch of CitiBike in May 2013. The city had also benefited from the support of nonprofit organizations, such as Transportation Alternatives, advocating for greener and safer transportation, with some concrete and actionable proposals on the table. Third, road and street safety was already a key priority for city agencies, such as NYPD with its Collision Investigation Squad (CIS) and DCAS with the focus on safety and sustainability of its fleet.

It All Starts with the Data

A key component of the Vision Zero NYC project is its data-driven nature. Using crash-report data maintained by DOT and its NYPD partners, DOT managed to identify the most dangerous locations, the time of day, the most likely victims, and the most likely offenders.

> Fatality crash data is obtained from the New York City Department of Transportation (DOT) fatality database, which is populated by New York City Police Department (NYPD) data and maintained by DOT. Injury crash data is obtained from the Finest Online Record Management System (FORMS), which is maintained by the NYPD. (NYC Department of Transportation 2016b)

This information was complemented by crowdsourcing efforts, with New Yorkers reporting instances of streets that felt unsafe (e.g., not enough time to cross the street, cars running red lights, speeding, double parking) on the Vision Zero Map Public Input site, using the Shareabouts open source crowdsourcing platform developed by OpenPlans (McDermott 2014).

The results of this data-gathering were combined into Pedestrian Safety Action Plans (one per borough), which identified priority intersections, priority corridors, and priority areas, based on the data. For the borough of

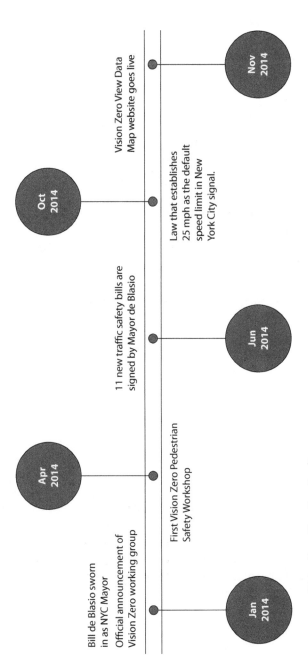

FIGURE 11.1 Vision Zero Year One timeline.

Manhattan Borough Profile

- Pedestrian fatalities in Manhattan have fallen by 60% in the past three decades.
- Manhattan's pedestrian fatality rate is 2.1 fatalities per 100,000 residents, the highest of the five boroughs, but just 1.1 fatalities per 100,000, the lowest of the five boroughs, when taking into account the higher daytime population.
- Where: Manhattan's pedestrian fatalities and severe injuries are most heavily concentrated below Fifty-Ninth Street.
- When: Nighttime (9 PM to midnight) pedestrian fatalities account for a greater share in Manhattan (21%) than in all New York City (15%).
- Who: In Manhattan, seniors account for only 14% of the borough's population but 41% of its pedestrian fatalities.
- What: Trucks are involved in pedestrian fatalities in Manhattan at a far higher rate (25%) than in any other borough (12% for all New York City).
- How: Dangerous driver choices and dangerous pedestrian choices contributed equally to Manhattan's pedestrian fatalities (43% and 43%).

Source: NYC Department of Transportation 2015.

Manhattan, where the author lives, the findings are highlighted in the text box and in table 11.2.

A Participatory Process

As emphasized in the kickoff announcement, Vision Zero NYC was designed as a "top-to-bottom" process with active participation from all stakeholders. The crowdsourcing of safety issues via the Vision Zero Public Input Map received more than 10,000 comments between June and July 2014.

Local communities were frequently consulted and informed through physical workshops and town halls held by community leaders and elected officials. Findings were regularly communicated on the Vision Zero website through publicly available reports, infographics, and open data sets.

A Collaborative Process

From its inception, Vision Zero has been collaborative in nature and by design. The top-to-bottom approach involved the following entities (see figure 11.2):

TABLE 11.2 Priority Corridors, Intersections, and Areas

	Share of borough	Borough	Percent of borough	Share of pedestrian KSI*	Total pedestrian KSI	Percent of total pedestrian KSI	Percent of total pedestrian fatalities
Priority corridors	17 corridors (56 miles)	490 miles	11%	815	1,615	50	51
Priority intersections	66 intersections	3,728 intersections	2%	224	1,615	15	12
Priority areas	6.1 square miles	23 square miles	26%	807	1,615	70	41
Combined total				1,129		70	67

*Pedestrian killed or seriously injured.

Source: NYC Department of Transportation 2015.

LEADERSHIP STRUCTURE

Mayor's office
Commits the city to Vision Zero and plays a key role in managing the process to achieve it

In New York City, the Mayor's Office of Operations created and continues to convene the Vision Zero Task Force.

When Vision Zero first launched in San Francisco, the Mayor dedicated a full-time staff member to Vision Zero.

Vision Zero Task Force / Steering Committee

Key city agencies — including transportation, police, health and the mayor's office — appointed by the mayor to lead the strategy and implementation of Vision Zero

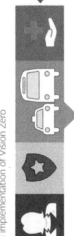

The NYC Vision Zero Task Force includes the Police Dept, Dept of Transportation, Taxi & Limousine Commission, Dept of Health & Mental Hygiene, Dept of Citywide Administrative Services, Law Dept and Office of Management & Budget.

In LA, the Mayor appointed the General Manager of the Dept of Transportation and the Chief of Police (or their designees) as co-chairs of the Vision Zero Executive Steering Committee.

In D.C., the Mayor tapped the Department of Transportation as the lead agency on the Vision Zero Task Force.

Many cities engage community stakeholders in their Task Forces in some way, too

Vision Zero Working Groups / Subcommittees

Often interdisciplinary groups focused on specific aspects of achieving Vision Zero, like engineering or marketing

San Francisco has standing committees on Engineering, Enforcement, Education, Policy, Evaluation, and Budget.

In Los Angeles, subcommittees include Engineering, Enforcement, Education, and Evaluation.

New York City convenes Marketing and Data Working groups.

FIGURE 11.2 Leadership structure.

Source: Vision Zero Network, 2016.

(a) the Mayor's Office, in charge of the vision and the process; (b) the Vision Zero Task Force, including key city agencies, in charge of leading strategy and implementation; and (c) Vision Zero working groups, in charge of achieving the vision along with the various dimensions mentioned above. Rather than a new "entity," Vision Zero NYC was conceived as a unified effort and brand to which relevant stakeholders could contribute. In each agency, people involved with Vision Zero did not get a title changed to "Vision Zero Champion." Because their area of responsibility was relevant for Vision Zero, they were de facto part of the effort.

Agencies involved in the process included the Department of Transportation (DOT), the New York Police Department (NYPD), the Taxi and Limo Commission (TLC), the Department of Health and Mental Hygiene (DOHMH), the Department of Citywide Administrative Services (DCAS), the Office of Management and Budget (OMB), and the Department of Education (DOE). Collaboration involved regular meetings and very transparent communication within the teams and the public. According to Health Commissioner Dr. Thomas Farley, on the day Vision Zero was announced, "Traffic crashes rank among the city's leading causes of injury-related deaths and hospitalizations, but they are preventable. We are committed to working with other city agencies to improve traffic safety and reduce pedestrian fatalities in New York City." Collaboration also involved local nonprofits (e.g., Families for Safe Streets, Transportation Alternatives), elected officials, the private sector, and the media.

The various stakeholders and their contributions are summarized in table 11.3.

Closing the Loop with Data

Data were not only essential for prioritizing actions but were also used for reporting on progress and showing impact. Each new initiative involved an owner, an actionable description, and a set of success metrics. Initiatives are combined into a scorecard that is featured in every Vision Zero report. The city also publishes very thorough annual reports that inform the public about progress toward the vision. Individual agencies also provide their own dashboards—e.g., NYPD with daily and weekly data.

A key aspect of Vision Zero NYC is the definition of meaningful metrics to measure progress and impact. For instance, a focus only on casualties as an indicator often does not provide the big picture. Vision Zero takes a broader view by looking at killed-or-severely-injured (KSI), sliced by location, time of day, and mode of transportation. Metrics also look at the side effects (positive or negative) on the transportation infrastructure—e.g., average speed or average throughput.

TABLE 11.3 Stakeholder Table

Stakeholders	Role played	Interest in the program	Incentives
Mayor's Office	In charge of vision and process		Vision Zero was part of the campaign program
DOT	Design and implementation of infrastructure changes	Part of DOT core mission	Funding
NYPD	Enforcement and education	Part of NYPD core mission	Focus on Vision Zero–related infractions
TLC, MTA, DCAS	Enforcement and education of their driver fleet	Drivers as "traffic pacers" to show good behavior	Financial incentive for good behavior
New York State	Legislative support		Vision Zero is a popular program
Elected officials	Explaining the program to constituents; making sure all parties have a say	Vision Zero improves the quality of life of New Yorkers and saves lives	Vision Zero is a popular program
Nonprofits	Community engagement, design of solutions, education	Part of their mission	Part of their mission
The public	Crowdsourcing of issues; participation in design workshops; activism to convince elected officials to pass legislation	Better quality of life	Vision Zero is a popular program

The data are used not only as a report mechanism but also as a tool to optimize current deployments, based on the reality of the situation—e.g., timing of traffic lights or marking adjustment.

Building upon preexisting knowledge and expertise, Vision Zero NYC acted as a catalyst to address the issue of traffic casualties in New York City on a very aggressive time scale. It leveraged data to identify priority actions and measure progress and impact, and relied on collaboration to enable a true top-to-bottom approach. Additionally, the initiative encouraged broad participation by all stakeholders and provided various and frequent feedback mechanisms.

* * *

The Vision Zero program in New York City is articulated around four pillars: infrastructure, enforcement, education, and legislation.

Pillar I: Infrastructure

The first pillar in the NYC Vision Zero model focuses on equipping street infrastructure—all the elements of the city's infrastructure that have an impact on street safety—to be capable of handling human errors. As incoming DOT Commissioner Polly Trottenberg explained, the day Vision Zero was announced, "We are going to build on what's working, fix what's broken, and make sure that nothing is held back as we make our streets safer."

A Vision Zero infrastructure project is first motivated by the data. A project will belong to a *priority intersection*, a *priority corridor*, or a *priority area*. The life of a project usually consists of the following stages: (1) problem

---

Infrastructure Arsenal

- Simplified complex intersection
- Narrower lanes
- Speed bumps
- Bike paths
- Better visibility for cyclists and pedestrians
- Traffic light timing and synchronicity
- Truck side guards (see Epstein et al. 2014; U.S. Department of Transportation Volpe Center 2017)

identification and definition; (2) solution proposal and stakeholder discussion; (3) project design; (4) design implementation; (5) monitoring and evaluation; and (6) impact measurement and reporting. Some ingredients of an infrastructure solution are suggested in the text box.

New York City has the luxury of having in-house teams inside the DOT to design and implement infrastructure projects. But not all solutions require a huge investment. "Plastic and paint are often an excellent first step," says Rob Viola, Director of Safety Policy Research at DOT. And some safety solutions even contribute to the bottom line. "The cost of a truck is $300,000. The cost of a side guard is $2,000. And a sideguard provides better aerodynamics for your truck and can save you money," says Mahanth Joishy of DCAS.

Pillar II: Enforcement

The second pillar is enforcement. As Police Commissioner Bill Bratton put it, the day Vision Zero was announced, "Our job is to save lives. We will be just as aggressive in preventing a deadly crash on our streets as we are in preventing a deadly shooting."

Before Vision Zero, NYPD was already enforcing safety rules. With Vision Zero, the focus on Vision Zero–related summonses—speed, failure to yield, and texting—was increased (see table 11.4). In order to more effectively capture Vision Zero–related infractions, NYPD and DOT deployed new technologies for automated enforcement, such as speed cameras, red-light cameras, and speed lasers. "Traffic safety always was a key mission. With Vision Zero, we got a focal point which leads to more coordination, a shared mission and sharing of data," says Shawn Aslop of NYPD.

A peculiar aspect of New York City is that it regulates large fleets of vehicles and drivers. DCAS oversees more than 29,000 city vehicles. The Metropolitan Transportation Authority (MTA) oversees more than 4,451 buses in New York City (MTA 2016). TLC licenses and regulates more than 150,000 vehicles, including taxis, "black cars," and transportation network companies (TNC) like Uber and Lyft. For fleets regulated by TLC, a carrot-and-stick approach was used: on the one hand, the TLC Honor Roll program, rewarding good drivers; on the other hand, the ability to suspend and revoke the licenses of drivers who have lost too many points because of infractions. For the city fleets (DCAS and MTA), a similar Good Operator Awards program was established. DCAS also equipped city vehicles with CANceivers, a device used to track driving patterns (e.g., speed, seat belt, hard braking, hard acceleration). Based on the collected data, DCAS generates a per-vehicle report that is addressed to each agency, which chooses whether or not to act upon it. The technology was deployed first in the Fire, Sanitation, and Transportation departments (Harshbarger 2014).

TABLE 11.4 Moving Summonses Before and After Vision Zero

Moving summonses	2011–2013 average	2014	2015	2015 compared to 2011–2013 average
Speeding	77,000	117,768	134,426	+75%
Failure to yield	12,345	33,577	39,852	+233%
Fail to stop on signal	40,214	53,445	55,197	+37%
Improper turns	58,181	73,237	76,047	+31%
Cell phone	143,552	106,503	84,630	+41%
Texting	10,693	32,601	41,205	+285%
Disobey sign	131,842	152,623	165,377	+25%

Source: Vision Zero 2016, 11.

Pillar III: Education and Engagement

In Vision Zero, education was not seen as an isolated activity; both enforcement and education were integrated when it made sense. For instance, the writing of a summons is a good opportunity to educate about the dangers of driving. A joint effort between NYPD and DOT led to "Vision Zero Street teams," which organized a week of education for drivers, cyclists, and pedestrians at intersections, transit hubs, churches, senior centers, and other venues, followed by a week of enforcement. In 2015, more than 820,000 flyers were distributed. Public events also included a pedestrian safety workshop across the five boroughs, as well as a focused day of public awareness (October 30, 2014) with more than 350,000 postcards distributed.

In Situ Education

The existence of fleets of professional drivers also created significant opportunities to scale up education. The TLC organized a "behind the wheel" training course (September 2015) and a twenty-four-hour pre-licensure course and also made a driver awareness campaign video titled *Drive Like Your Family Lives Here* (https://www.youtube.com/watch?v=OAnSw3nzjoU). For city fleet drivers, DCAS publishes clear guidelines (City of New York 2016) and organizes a defensive-driving training class, a state-certified class taken every three years that includes a full hour dedicated to Vision Zero. TLC Chief Operating Officer Conan Freud, on the day Vision Zero was announced, said, "Public safety must always be at the forefront of what we do. Whether it's our drivers and passengers, or the people who share the streets with them, we want to do our part to protect every New Yorker."

DOT also provided the Department of Education (DOE) with educational services and personnel at more than 620 elementary, middle, and high schools. Both agencies are working together to incorporate a Vision Zero curriculum "Cross This Way" for fourth to sixth graders (NYC Department of Transportation 2016a).

Education Through the Media

Media campaigns are a key component of any education or engagement effort. The Vision Zero NYC team used the full palette at its disposal to reach the right people in the right way (Vision Zero Network 2016b). The media channels used included (a) earned media (buy-in from City Hall is crucial here because the mayor always makes news); (b) owned media (through public display and city-owned fleet); (c) social media (e.g., website, twitter, YouTube); (d) paid media (e.g., outdoor billboards as in figure 11.3, TV, online, and radio); (e) public engagement; and (f) direct outreach. For each type and each campaign, best efforts were made to measure the impact.

Pillar IV: Legislation

Legislation can be a very powerful tool. In the context of Vision Zero NYC, its use was limited, though, as a result of some New York State prerogatives.

> Laws and regulations that effectively protect everyone on the street are instrumental to driving traffic crashes down in New York City. While the City Council has some authority to enact safety legislation, many of the laws that determine the safety of our streets are controlled in New York State law and regulations. New York City will work closely with the Governor's office and the state legislature to improve laws and regulations that affect the safety of New York City streets. (Vision Zero 2014)

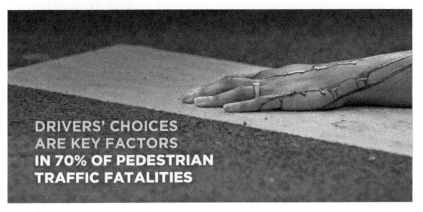

FIGURE 11.3 Public service announcement regarding traffic fatalities at intersections.

Source: YourChoicesMatter.nyc.

The city issued many proposals along these lines, but not all of them were translated into law.

Changes Proposed by New York City for New York State Laws and Regulations Regarding Vision Zero

- Grant New York City local control over its speed camera and red-light camera enforcement programs.
- Allow New York City to lower its citywide speed limit to 25 mph
- Reduce severity of truck crashes.

- Strengthen laws that punish drivers who carelessly harm pedestrians or bicyclists.
- Increase penalties for driving with a suspended license.
- Increase penalties for leaving the scene of a crash.
- Protect workers in work zones from reckless driving.
- Improve state driver education to improve interactions with pedestrians and bicyclists.
- Reform the DMV "point" system.
- Increase penalties for those who flee TLC inspectors.
- Increase sanctions for dangerous TLC driver behavior.
- Combine critical driver (DMV) and persistent violator (TLC) points.
- Require additional driver education and pilot new technologies.
- Allow TLC to use speed cameras to sanction lawbreaking drivers.
- Require rear-wheel and side guards for trucks operating in New York City.

Source: Vision Zero 2014.

Impact and Results

As of this writing, Vision Zero NYC is barely more than three years old. It is therefore premature to draw any definitive conclusion. According to Ydanis Rodriguez, Manhattan councilman and chair of the Transportation Committee, "Vision Zero is not about a statistic; it's about real people and real stories of individual tragedies of innocent victims and of loved ones left behind" (Goldwyn 2014).

Actions That Have Been Taken

Each year, the Vision Zero NYC team provides a scorecard detailing the initiatives and their completion status. Some key numbers summarizing the actions that have been taken across the infrastructure, enforcement, and education dimensions are presented in table 11.5.

Saving Lives: Killed and Severely Injured (KSI) Metrics

The trend shows a steady decline in terms of the number of KSI overall, even without taking into account the growing population (8,008,278 people living in New York City in 2000 versus 8,175,133 in 2010, per the U.S. Census).

TABLE 11.5 Actions Taken

By the numbers	2014	2015
Schools received street safety education	620	578
Speed bumps installed	400	340
Safety projects at priority intersections and corridors	57	80
Speed cameras activated*	40	100
Leading pedestrian intervals installed	55	417
CANceivers installed	15,306	5,287
City drivers completed defensive driving training	20,000	12,000
Truck sideguards installed	107	250
Failure-to-yield summonses	33,577	39,852
Speeding summonses	117,768	134,426
LIDAR guns	226	204

* There is a quota on the number of locations where speed cameras can be installed.
Source: Vision Zero 2016.

Taking these two numbers and doing a very naïve linear regression, KSI per 100,000 would give an even more satisfactory graph. Pedestrian casualties are going down. Bicycle fatalities seem to have remained flat in absolute numbers, despite the constant increase of biking in the city, including personal bicycles, shared bikes, and bike deliveries.

Changing Minds

A key element of Vision Zero is convincing people that the vision can be achieved. Various surveys have indicated that education works. The impact of the "Your Choices Matter" campaign, as measured by survey, can be seen from the following numbers (Vision Zero Network 2016b):

- 72% of drivers recall having seen the ads.
- 79% of drivers identify driver behavior as a cause in fatal crashes.
- 86% of drivers report the ads convinced them to pay more attention to pedestrians and cyclists while driving.
- 75% of nondrivers said the ads made them more careful as pedestrians.

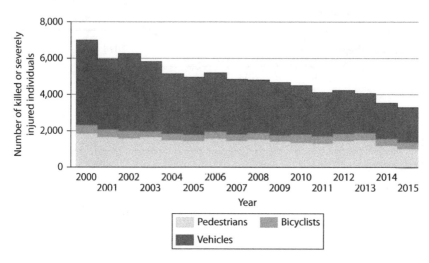

FIGURE 11.4 Number of people killed or severely injured in New York City, 2000–2015.

Source: Vision Zero 2016.

Challenges and Lessons Learned

Deploying a project like Vision Zero NYC requires overcoming several key challenges.

The Message Challenge

The beauty of the Vision Zero vision is its simplicity. Unfortunately, it can sometimes be perceived as naive and unattainable (like a moonshot), as reported for previous initiatives in Sweden and the UK (Whitelegg and Haq 2006). As Vincent Peale said, "Shoot for the moon. Even if you miss, you'll land among the stars."

The Metrics Challenge

Identifying and measuring the right metrics is not obvious. Deaths do not capture the full story. Critical injuries must be added to the mix. We should also keep in mind that injuries and their outcomes evolve over time, and this needs to be accounted for when computing statistics.

When looking at the impact of Vision Zero, it is also crucial to look at the side effects on the functioning of the city, such as average speed, traffic throughput, economic impact, and the like. Although these metrics can be easy to define, in reality they are very difficult to measure. In his analysis, Eric Richardson (2015) goes through the exercise of quantifying every possible impact of a Vision Zero–like policy.

Because Vision Zero is mainly about changing perceptions about safety, one metric that would make sense is people's perception of the issue itself. But this is very difficult to capture accurately.

The Coordination Challenge

Vision Zero is a very ambitious effort that spans multiple city agencies and involves public and private partnerships. Moreover, it has a very direct impact on New Yorkers. Effective collaboration, turf war, credit sharing, communication misalignment, and lack of transparency with the public are all serious issues that could have derailed the project.

Most of these pitfalls were avoided because of (a) the unconditional commitment and leadership of City Hall; (b) the structure of the project, with the Vision Zero Task Force and Vision Zero Working Groups; and (c) the branding of all effort as "Vision Zero."

The Legislative Challenge

Speed reduction and speed cameras are two proven solutions in the Vision Zero arsenal: lower speed leads to reduced impact and higher chances of surviving a crash, and speed cameras are an effective and scalable way of nudging drivers to respect speed limits. Unfortunately, both are legislated at the state level (the New York State government in Albany), not the city level.

New York City is an anomaly in the New York State policy landscape, with legislators in Albany concerned about statewide speed legislation being applied to solve a very specific use case. Regarding speed cameras, some towns have used them as a way of taking money from drivers, and New York State has put in place some rigid laws regarding their deployment to protect its residents. Any "revenue raising" device must be approved at the state level. Speaking candidly, we should not ignore that political turf wars and rivalry between New York City and Albany are most likely at the center of these "policy misalignments."

As for speed limit, the De Blasio administration had to work hard to reach a consensus with Albany to pass legislation reducing the speed limit to 25 mph inside the city (NYC Office of the Mayor 2017). For speed cameras, the city is still in heavy bargaining with Albany, with a small quota of cameras to be deployed exclusively near schools.[1]

The Data Collection Challenge

On the data side, collecting crash data in a timely fashion remains a challenge because of antiquated paper-and-pencil collection and an overcomplicated process. It often takes the city more than twelve months to access the crash database. The data usually migrate from NYPD to the Department of Motor Vehicle (DMV) to Albany and back. Additionally, for a given crash report, the unique identifiers used by NYPD (the city) and Albany (the state) are different, creating another set of challenges. Linking with hospital records is also a challenge.

Crash reports are often subjective and written after the fact, on forms that do not provide enough options to accurately describe the circumstances of the crash based on eyewitnesses. These reports do not always capture what happened, making finding effective solutions more difficult. There is also often a bias against pedestrians (Stanley 2015; Kaufman 2017).

As mentioned before, the data in a crash report are limited and only represent one point in time. For instance, the condition of an injured pedestrian might evolve for the worse, but this would not be reflected in the data from the crash report. Measuring the impact of Vision Zero on the infrastructure itself (e.g., average speed, traffic throughput) is also hard. Erin Akred of Data-Kind has three wishes for better data: (a) a new digital record-keeping system for crash reports with a unique identifier for each collision, (b) a better traffic volume count via Internet of Things solutions, and (c) a reduced delay for crash reports.

The Infrastructure Challenge

At the infrastructure level, a key challenge is implementing changes without disrupting the entire city and coordinating among numerous entities—water, gas, electricity, telephone, cable, etc.—that interact with the city infrastructure. In New York City, it is not rare for a given street section to be "worked out" once per year. Uncoordinated street construction combined with severe weather conditions (cold winter, snow, plowing, hot summer, flooding, etc.) does not play well with infrastructure. "It is hard for things to look good beyond six months. A big challenge is maintenance," notes Rob Viola, Director of Safety Policy Research at DOT.

Another infrastructure challenge is scale. More interventions require more personnel to manage projects, interface with the local communities, and execute effectively on the ground. Even if DOT expands or decides to outsource a project, a knowledge transfer will need to happen, at scale. Today, this is the main limitation to growth beyond eighty projects per year.

✳ ✳ ✳

We now look at how the New York City Vision Zero "model" can be replicated in a different setting. We first present a SWOT—strengths, weaknesses, opportunities, threat—analysis for Vision Zero in New York City (figure 11.5) and then consider the advantages and disadvantages encountered during its deployment. We encourage the reader to also look at the SWOT analysis that

Strengths	Weaknesses
Previous solid and successful track record for Vision Zero deployments at city, state, and country levels. Popular opinion that deaths and injuries are not acceptable in the streets of New York. Existing players (agencies, police, nonprofits) already working toward the goal and a very strong Department of Transportation capable of planning and executing on the mission. A mayor fully behind the initiative.	Vision Zero perceived as an unrealistic and unattainable goal. Need to educate the public on what will be done. Need to educate the public and key stakeholders about how impact will be measured.
Opportunities	**Threats**
Saving lives and offering better quality of life for New Yorkers Saving money Other positive side effects, including reduced noise, reduced air pollution, etc.	New York City vs. New York State politics Disappointing numbers, unforeseeable circumstances Competing interests, e.g. tourism, business, etc.

FIGURE 11.5   Vision Zero SWOT analysis.

was done for Vision Zero in the UK (Whitelegg and Haq 2006, 96) and the policy analysis by Richardson (2015).

Advantages Specific to New York City

Elements that facilitated the deployment of Vision Zero and contributed to its success include:

- A committed police force with existing dedicated teams addressing Vision Zero–related issues
- Nonprofits and advocacy groups—e.g., Transportation Alternatives, Family for Safe Streets
- A strong Department of Transportation capable of designing and implementing infrastructure changes
- A strong mayoral leadership, capable of bringing a sense of urgency, rallying resources and earning media attention, and facilitating cross-agency collaboration
- Large fleets of vehicles regulated by the city that can be used as role models and pacers
- Wide access to media and distribution through owned media and city fleet
- The CitiBike program, which brings more cyclists to the streets

Disadvantages Specific to New York City

Elements that hindered the deployment of Vision Zero and limited its success include:

- A very large city with five radically different boroughs
- A very heterogeneous road driver population that is hard to regulate
- Lots of tourists and commuters who are not necessarily familiar with the city
- A multilingual and multicultural environment where messages must be targeted in one's own language and sensibility
- A city that never sleeps, where changes must be made in real time with limited disruption
- Legislative misalignments because of city versus state prerogatives
- The CitiBike program, which brings more cyclists to the streets
- A city where space is at a premium, which heavily constrains road space, sidewalks, and bike lanes

* * *

We conclude this section by looking at future trends that are relevant for efforts like Vision Zero. As early town planner Patrick Geddes said, "A city is more than a place in space; it is a drama in time."

Vision Zero cannot be reduced to a set of rigid initiatives. It needs to adapt to new trends, new technologies, and new habits. As of this writing, popular smartphone applications such as Pokémon Go are entertaining a lot of pedestrians, drivers, and bikers. It is also probably putting them at risk of being distracted. In this section, we look at improvements that could make the city even safer. Figure 11.6 offers a blueprint of traffic safety strategies and their relationships. We explore some of this design space with a 2017 lens.

Better Data: Richer, Broader, Faster, Integrated

More data can make a big difference, both in terms of project prioritization and impact measurement. Computer vision systems hooked up to CCTV cameras can provide speed and density data about vehicle and pedestrian traffic. They can also provide more objective reports about crashes (Stanley 2015). Some systems even claim they can compute the dangerous nature of an intersection based on pedestrian trajectories and near collisions (Kaufman 2017). Embedded systems for fleet or individual drivers (e.g., CANceivers, ZenDrive) can provide personal information as well as aggregated stats. Access to data sets from large Internet companies like Google, Uber, and Lyft would also provide valuable insights.

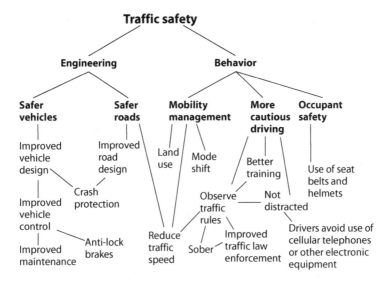

FIGURE 11.6 Traffic safety strategies.

Source: Victoria Transport Policy Institute 2017.

A more far-fetched set of data Vision Zero actors would like to get is what happens in people's heads and whether they have fully absorbed the key Vision Zero messages. As of this writing, such technology does not yet exist.

Smarter Vehicles

Connected vehicles (i.e., vehicles talking to each other) and self-driving vehicles (cars, trucks, buses) have started to appear in urban environments. The Navya Arma (http://navya.tech) deployed in Lyon, France, is 100% autonomous, fully electric, and reaches a peak speed of 25 km/h which is safe for passengers and pedestrians. Such vehicles promise to remove the human-error element from the picture but also to leverage the network intelligence. In New York City, DOT is running the Connected Vehicle Deployment Program funded by the U.S. Department of Transportation (2016) with a focus on vehicle-to-vehicle (V2V) and vehicle-to-infrastructure (V2I) (see chapter 13).

Smarter Infrastructure

Smarter infrastructure is another very big opportunity. Some systems are already helping distracted pedestrians cross the street more safely. In Seoul, South Korea, new traffic signs are being introduced to remind people of the dangers of using their mobile phones while walking. New designs can also inform better and safer intersections (Chant 2016). CCTV technologies, infrastructure-to-car connectivity, and connected urban furniture are other promising avenues.

Smarter Legislation

We have already mentioned that some legislative "misalignment" prevented a broader deployment of proven solutions such as speed limits and speed cameras. Some reforms at the state level would help a lot. Some examples from interviews conducted for this case study are mandatory truck safeguards, inclusion of Vision Zero education by the DMV, a better point system for driving infractions related to Vision Zero such as texting, and accounting for a driver's ticket history when granting the right to drive.

Smarter People

People are the core of Vision Zero. They need to be educated and reminded of their responsibilities as drivers, bikers, and pedestrians. Devices can play a role in this—for example, ZenDrive, which provides quantified-self-like reports for drivers. The use of behavioral economics is also something that can be leveraged to provide incentives, whether carrots or sticks.

Alternate Modes of Transportation

Finally, alternate modes of transportation can also play a key role. An obvious way of reducing crashes is to replace on-wheel transportation with more options such as subways and ferries. Going even further, if the motivation for most rides is commuting to work, then remote work options can also be a good way to reduce traffic casualties.

Conclusion

A key mission of government is to provide safety for its population. Street casualties that kill or severely injure 4,000 people in New York City every year can be prevented and must be looked at and handled as a public health issue.

Rather than reinvent the wheel, New York City chose to piggyback on a proven model pioneered by Sweden to achieve the lofty goal of zero street casualty. Leveraging its natural strengths and aware of its challenges, New York City has embraced a data-driven, collaborative, and participatory approach to deploy Vision Zero. With a fully committed leadership at City Hall and a set of agencies and local partners working together, Vision Zero NYC has unfolded based on four pillars: infrastructure, enforcement, education, and legislation.

Even though it is too early to draw any definitive conclusion, early numbers show some steady trends in terms of KSI reduction, especially when prorated to account for an ever-increasing population of residents and the growth of walking and biking as main means of transportation. New technologies are also showing promising advances in terms of both crash reduction and prevention.

Most of the measures implemented in New York City can be replicated beyond the five boroughs, effectively and affordably. The starting ingredient is the political will to make it happen.

Notes

The author wishes to thank the following contributors who were kind enough to answer questions and provide feedback on early versions of this case study: Juan Martinez (DOT), Cordell Schachter (DOT), Rob Viola (DOT Director of Safety Policy Research), Erin Akred (DataKind), Shawn Alsop (NYPD), Dennis Fulton (NYPD), Council Member Ben Kallos, Mahanth Joishy (DCAS), Geraldine Sweeney (City Operations), Kim Wiley-Schwartz (DOT), Madeline Labadie (TLC), and the *Smart(er) NYC*itywide Research team. The author would also like to thank Lauren Yu and David Sangokoya for comments on early versions of this document. The author is also the founder of TORBI LLC.

1. As of this writing, there are 140 speed camera deployments. These cameras must be located within a quarter mile of a school entrance and be operated only during school hours.

References

Bill de Blasio for Mayor. 2013. "De Blasio Calls for Visionary Street Safety Goal: No Fatalities or Serious Injuries on New York City Streets." Accessed September 2017. https:// web.archive.org/save/_embed/http://dnwssx4l7gl7s.cloudfront.net/deblasio/default /page/-/Visionary%20Street%20Safety%20Goal%20-%20No%20Fatalities%20or %20Serious%20Injuries%20on%20NewYork%20City%20Streets.pdf.

Center for Active Design. 2014. "Vision Zero: Learning from Sweden's Successes." Accessed September 2017. https://centerforactivedesign.org/visionzero.

Chant, Tim de. 2016. "16 Ways to Design a Better Intersection—And Better Cities." *Wired*, October 28. https://www.wired.com/2016/10/how-to-design-better-cities/.

City of New York. 2016. *City Vehicle Driver Handbook*. May 2016. Accessed September 2017. http://www.nyc.gov/html/dcas/downloads/pdf/fleet/city_vehicle_driver_handbook .pdf.

Epstein, Alexander K., Sean Peirce, Andrew Breck, Coralie Cooper, and Eran Segev. 2014. *Truck Sideguards for Vision Zero*. NYC Department of Citywide Administrative Services. Accessed September 2017. https://rosap.ntl.bts.gov/view/dot/12164.

Goldwyn, Eric. 2014. "Can New York City Achieve Vision Zero?" *New Yorker*, June 4. http:// www.newyorker.com/tech/elements/can-new-york-city-achieve-vision-zero.

Golson, Jordan. 2015. "The 10 Most Walkable Cities in America." *Wired*, April 16. http://www
.wired.com/2015/04/10-walkable-cities-america/.

Harshbarger, Rebecca. 2014. "New Tracking Devices for City Vehicles to Save Money,
Boost Safety: Backers." *New York Post*, March 3. http://nypost.com/2014/03/03/new
-tracking-devices-for-city-vehicles-to-save-money-boost-safety-backers/.

Kaufman, Rachel. 2017. "Cameras Can Speed Cities to Improving Pedestrian Safety." *Next
City*, February 3. Accessed September 2017. https://nextcity.org/daily/entry/cities-study
-pedestrian-safety-cameras-data.

"List of U.S. Cities with Most Households Without a Car." 2017. *Wikipedia*. Accessed
September 2017. https://en.wikipedia.org/w/index.php?title=List_of_U.S._cities_with_most
_households_without_a_car.

McDermott, Ellen. 2014. "Using Shareabouts for Vision Zero in New York City." *OpenPlans*,
June 17. Accessed September 2017. http://blog.openplans.org/2014/06/shareabouts-for-vision
-zero-identifying-street-safety-issues/.

Morris, David Z. 2016. "'Zero Traffic Deaths' Movement Gaining Speed in Major U.S. Cities."
Fortune, April 26. http://fortune.com/2016/04/26/vision-zero-eliminate-traffic-deaths/.

MTA. 2016. "The MTA Network." http://web.mta.info/mta/network.htm.

NYC Department of Transportation. 2015. *Vision Zero: Pedestrian Safety Action Plan:
Manhattan*. Accessed September 2017. http://www.nyc.gov/html/dot/downloads/pdf
/ped-safety-action-plan-manhattan.pdf.

——. 2016a. "Press Release: Vision Zero." September 14, 2016. http://www.nyc.gov/html/dot
/html/pr2016/pr16-091.shtml.

——. 2016b. "Vision Zero Metadata." Accessed September 2017. http://www.nyc.gov/html
/dot/downloads/pdf/vision-zero-view-metadata.pdf.

NYC Office of the Mayor. 2014. "Mayor de Blasio Launches Interagency Working Group
to Implement 'Vision Zero,' Prevent Pedestrian Fatalities." January 15. Accessed
September 2017. http://www1.nyc.gov/office-of-the-mayor/news/023-14/mayor-de-blasio
-launches-interagency-working-group-implement-vision-zero-prevent-pedestrian#/0.

——. 2017. "Mayor de Blasio Signs New Law Lowering New York City's Default Speed Limit
to 25 MPH." October 27, 2014. http://www1.nyc.gov/office-of-the-mayor/news/493-14
/mayor-de-blasio-signs-new-law-lowering-new-york-city-s-default-speed-limit-25
-mph#/0.

Richardson, Eric M. 2015. *Vision Zero: Combating Pedestrian Casualties Due to Traffic in New
York City*. Institute for Public Policy Studies, University of Denver. https://www.du.edu
/korbel/media/documents/ipps/richardsonpm.pdf.

Seoul Metropolitan Government. 2016. "New Traffic Signs for Smartphone Users." June 21.
http://english.seoul.go.kr/new-traffic-signs-smartphone-users/.

Stanley, Jenn. 2015. "Better Police Reports on Bike Accidents Might Save Lives." *Next City*,
April 6. Accessed September 2017. https://nextcity.org/daily/entry/study-police-reports
-bike-accidents-save-lives.

"The Economist Explains: Why Sweden Has So Few Road Deaths." 2014. *Economist*,
February 26. Accessed September 2017. http://www.economist.com/blogs/economist
-explains/2014/02/economist-explains-16.

U.S. Department of Transportation. 2016. "Connected Vehicle Pilot Deployment Program."
https://www.its.dot.gov/pilots/pilots_nycdot.htm.

U.S. Department of Transportation Volpe Center. 2017. "Truck Side Guards Resource
Page." Accessed September 2017. https://www.volpe.dot.gov/our-work/truck-side-guards
-resource-page.

Victoria Transport Policy Institute. 2017. "Traffic Safety Strategies." *TDM Encyclopedia.* Accessed September 2017. http://www.vtpi.org/tdm/tdm86.htm.

Vision Zero. 2014. "Legislation." http://www.nyc.gov/html/visionzero/pages/legislation /legislation.html.

——. 2016. *Vision Zero Year Two: Year End Review.* Accessed September 2017. http://www.nyc .gov/html/visionzero/assets/vz-year-end-report.pdf.

"Vision Zero." 2017. *Wikipedia.* Accessed September 2017. https://en.wikipedia.org/wiki /Vision_Zero.

Vision Zero Network. 2015. "9 Components of a Strong Vision Zero Commitment." Accessed September 2017. http://visionzeronetwork.org/wp-content/uploads/2015/12 /VZ-Components-Fact-Sheet.pdf.

——. 2016a. "Collaborating Across Departments to Achieve Vision Zero." Accessed September 2017. http://visionzeronetwork.org/wp-content/uploads/2016/05/Cross-dept -collaboration.pdf.

——. 2016b. "Communications Strategies to Advance Vision Zero." Accessed September 2017. http://visionzeronetwork.org/communications-strategies-to-advance-vision-zero/.

——. 2016c. "How Can We Engage, Educate & Enforce Taxi and For-Hire Drivers to Help Achieve Vision Zero?" Accessed September 2017. http://visionzeronetwork.org/wp-content /uploads/2016/04/VZN-TLC-case-study.pdf.

——. 2016d. "How Does Vision Zero Differ from the Traditional Traffic Safety Approach in U.S. Communities?" Accessed September 2017. http://visionzeronetwork.org/wp-content /uploads/2016/03/VZN-Case-Study-1-What-makes-VZ-different.pdf.

Whitelegg, John, and Gary Haq. 2006. *Vision Zero: Adopting a Target of Zero for Road Traffic Fatalities and Serious Injuries.* Stockholm Environment Institute. https://www .sei-international.org/mediamanager/documents/Publications/Future/vision_zero _FinalReportMarch06.pdf.

CHAPTER 12

MIDTOWN IN MOTION

Real-Time Solutions to Traffic Congestion

LAWRENCE LENNON, *The Cooper Union*

GERARD SOFFIAN, *New York University*

Executive Summary

This Midtown in Motion (MIM) case study demonstrates how a small group of professionals from industry and government can work together, in a remarkably short time frame, to successfully assemble, test, and operationalize a large-scale traffic management system to effectively address what are all too often considered to be intractable urban problems. Their work, while performed at a rapid pace, was the culmination of advancements and experience gained over many years of collaboration and innovation in traffic management at the New York City Department of Transportation (NYCDOT). While MIM has not solved the problem of traffic congestion in Midtown Manhattan, it has provided NYCDOT with effective tools to manage traffic operations comprehensively, in real time, and to prevent emerging traffic problems from deteriorating to "gridlock" conditions.

MIM is a large-scale traffic management system that employs state-of-the-art traffic sensors, advanced communications networks, and complex computer algorithms to detect and respond to changing traffic conditions. Its implementation was accomplished in several phases over a period of five years, between 2011 and 2016. The current project area encompasses all Manhattan streets and avenues between Fourteenth and Seventy-Second Streets, virtually river to river. Controls are based on real-time travel time and vehicle-congestion data collected and transmitted wirelessly to NYCDOT's Traffic Management Center (TMC) in Long Island City, Queens. Traffic signal operations (i.e., traffic lights) are adjusted to manage traffic flow to and through Manhattan's Midtown core area while addressing localized congestion within the core. The program has been credited with improving travel times in Midtown Manhattan by 10% and supporting the goals of the city's Vision Zero initiative by promoting predictable and orderly travel (see chapter 11).

Key Takeaways

- MIM is a large-scale traffic management system that employs state-of-the-art traffic sensors, advanced communications networks, and complex computer algorithms to detect and respond to changing traffic conditions.
- MIM is a proven system with the potential to improve traffic operations in central business districts globally.
- The rapid development and deployment of advanced traffic management and vehicle navigation systems, and the introduction of connected and autonomous vehicles, must be considered as cities investigate the potential implementation of MIM or a similar system.
- New technology holds the potential to greatly improve MIM as more comprehensive data become available.
- Connected and autonomous vehicles may reduce the utility of a central traffic control system like MIM.

Theoretical Background, Contextual Environment, and Problem Definition

Theoretical Background

The term "gridlock" and Manhattan traffic are virtually synonymous. Addressing traffic congestion in Midtown Manhattan has been a paramount concern of city officials since the mid-twentieth century, although acute congestion in Lower Manhattan dates back many more decades to the pre-automobile nineteenth century. An article published in the *Scientific American* on February 8, 1890, describes the formidable dangers faced by city residents because of traffic congestion.

This concern with Midtown traffic conditions has led over the years to the implementation of ever more sophisticated traffic management measures, including the systematic upgrading of Midtown's traffic signal control system. The year 1920 saw the first installation of tall box-type towers on Fifth Avenue. A police officer stood in the tower and manually changed the traffic signal (Gray 2014). (Figure 12.1 shows one of the earliest traffic signals in New York City, circa 1922.) The enhancements to traffic signals culminated in 2011 with

FIGURE 12.1 Traffic Tower at Fifth Avenue and Forty-Second Street, looking north.

implementation of the first phase of Midtown in Motion (MIM), a large-scale travel-time-based active traffic management system that detects and responds to changing traffic conditions. Currently the project area, as expanded, consists of Manhattan streets and avenues between Fourteenth and Seventy-Second streets, virtually river to river (figure 12.2). Controls are based on real-time per-trip travel time, traffic volume, and vehicle-congestion data. The system provides controls on the arterials approaching Midtown and also addresses localized congestion within Midtown.

Similar to the implementation of the LinkNYC system (see chapter 3), which strategically repurposed existing infrastructure (e.g., old payphones, street cabling), MIM integrates several Intelligent Transportation Systems (ITS) technologies made available through preexisting and emerging infrastructure assembled primarily by the NYCDOT. The technologies utilized include advanced solid-state traffic controllers (ASTCs) and sensors (video, microwave radar, electronic toll collection tag readers), New York City Wireless Network (NYCWiN) developed by the New York City Department of Information Technology and Telecommunications (NYCDOITT), and a fiber optic video network.

The project was conceptualized, designed, and implemented under the direction of NYCDOT Commissioner Janette Sadik-Khan and the NYCDOT

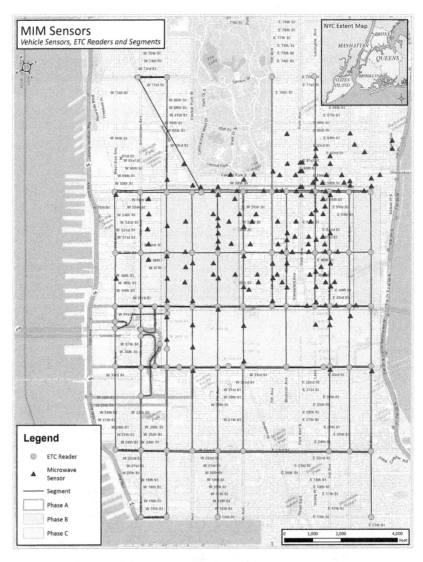

FIGURE 12.2 MIM project area, including Phases A, B, and C.

Division of Traffic Operations. It proceeded under an aggressive timetable in order to address worsening traffic congestion in Midtown Manhattan. Biweekly progress meetings were chaired by NYCDOT Deputy Commissioner of Traffic Operations Gerard Soffian to coordinate the expeditious identification and resolution of issues. The speed of implementation benefited greatly from the prior execution of engineering service agreements (on-call contracts) with the firms involved and partial funding provided by the Federal Highway Administration (FHWA).

The first phase, formally initiated in 2010, was completed in approximately six months after a decision was made by NYCDOT to proceed. The design, testing, and installation were accomplished with close technical consultation between NYCDOT staff and several transportation consulting firms under contract to NYCDOT. These firms included JHK Engineering, P.C., in association with TransCore ITS LLP, which shared procurement with NYCDOT of the traffic sensors, including electronic toll collection (ETC) tag readers (E-ZPass) (figure 12.3) and microwave sensors (figure 12.4); and KLD Engineering, P.C.,

FIGURE 12.3 E-ZPass ETC tag reader.

FIGURE 12.4 Microwave sensors measure traffic volume and queues at midblock locations.

which developed traffic management programs and algorithms. These firms had previously provided ongoing support for the operation of the NYCDOT Traffic Management Center (TMC).

Contextual Environment

Midtown Manhattan is an exceptional piece of real estate that is the commercial center of New York City, an area considered by many to be the premier business district in the nation. It is the home to more than fifty Fortune 500 companies, the Broadway Theatre District, notable public spaces such as Times Square and Herald Square, Rockefeller Center, Madison Square Garden, the United Nations Headquarters, Jacob K. Javits Convention Center, the Garment District, prestigious hotels, world-class signature restaurants, flagship retail stores, teaching hospitals, and now the home of President Donald J. Trump.

It is well served by public transportation, including subway, commuter railroad, buses, and ferries, with many commuters utilizing such notable transportation facilities as Grand Central Terminal, Penn Station, and the Port Authority Bus Terminal. In addition, motorists access Midtown directly via the Lincoln and Queens Midtown Tunnels, Ed Koch Queensboro Bridge, FDR Drive, Route 9A/Henry Hudson Parkway, and numerous avenues. On a typical weekday, 700,000 workers and visitors travel to and within Midtown. Moreover, special events such as the weeklong opening of the UN General Assembly and Fashion Week, place acute burdens on traffic operations.

Midtown Manhattan's extreme concentration and diversity of activities results in substantial traffic demands. Lacking in direct rail freight access, Midtown is dependent on trucks to deliver essential goods for offices and food services. Moreover, circulating on the streets are livery services, including medallion taxis and transportation network companies (e.g., Lyft, Uber, Via). The roadways are also well populated with bicycles, both privately owned and those rented from CitiBike, the city's bike-sharing program.

Vehicular traffic is characterized by a mixture of those traveling to a single destination, such as an off-street parking facility, and a large number of circulating vehicles, many making numerous stops for deliveries and pickups and drop-offs of passengers. These activities do not always occur off-street or within a curbside parking lane but too often take place illegally in a designated travel lane. Curb lanes are also occupied by many food-vending vans and trucks. Adding to the "friction" exerted on traffic flow by this vehicle activity is the presence of extraordinarily large pedestrian volumes throughout the day, as well as a large number of construction sites that occupy sidewalk and street space.

To protect the safety of pedestrians, vehicle "green time" is limited at traffic signals to provide adequate time for pedestrians to safely cross an intersection, and turning vehicles must yield to pedestrians in crosswalks. In addition, there is a citywide prohibition on vehicles turning right on red signals. These signalization strategies were strong building blocks of the city's Vision Zero safety program, as demonstrated in chapter 11. The proliferation of exclusive bus lanes, bicycle lanes, CitiBike stations, and pedestrian plazas has reduced roadway capacity for private vehicles while increasing the network's overall person-carrying capacity, primarily through the introduction of expanded travel choices and priority treatment for transit.

Problem Definition

The street grid of Manhattan, particularly Midtown, owes its origins to the 1811 Commissioner's Plan that established a grid of widely spaced north-south avenues crossed by much more closely spaced east-west streets. This was a masterful template for property development, creating large lots for development, but also creating closely spaced intersections along the avenues that were not very helpful to traffic flow. The congruence of intense commercial activity with excessive demands for motor-vehicle access has resulted in near gridlock conditions, a term conceived by observing traffic operations in Midtown. As noted in a 1973 NYCDOT report, "Since 1946, when it was described as 'unbearable' and 'impenetrable' by *Fortune* magazine, the Manhattan traffic situation has been the subject to a long series of corrective measures—one-way avenues, road widenings, parking restrictions, traffic signal modifications, rush hour lane reversals on bridges and tunnels—yet . . . speeds have declined. Midtown is still impenetrable' " (Ameruso 1983).

Since the 1950s, the city has implemented significant measures to relieve traffic congestion in Midtown. Of particular note was NYCDOT's overriding policy that any measures to improve traffic operations not be accomplished in a manner that would compromise safety for either motorists or pedestrians. Thus, the movement of vehicles could not take precedence over the safety of the traveling public. (The only exception of note would be selected roadway widening in Midtown done in the early twentieth century with the corresponding narrowing of sidewalks.)

A measure determined to be most effective for promoting traffic flow was the conversion of traffic signals to a "progressive" signal-timing system. The 1949 Report of the New York City Traffic Commission presented a plan that "provides for two-way progressive signal timing on major crosstown streets and for progressive signal timing in one direction on alternating north and south avenues." The efficacy of this plan was somewhat limited since at that time the avenues had not yet been converted from two-way to one-way operation.

This plan was to replace "simultaneous" timing, in which signals at each intersection along an avenue change in unison. With progressive timing, the signals up- and downstream are "offset," so that a platoon of vehicles could be greeted at each downstream intersection with a fresh green signal, provided that the vehicles are proceeding at an appropriate speed. Conversion from two-way to one-way operation of the north-south avenues, which would later greatly enhance the effectiveness of a progressive signal system, was initiated in the 1950s. This was accomplished initially on First, Second, Ninth, and Tenth Avenues, and concluded with Fifth and Madison Avenues in 1966. Any remaining simultaneous traffic signal systems on these avenues were retimed to progressive movement. One-way operation not only allowed for more advantageous signal timing but also simplified complex, multilegged intersections such as Times Square. One-way operation allows vehicles to make left turns without conflicts with traffic traveling in the opposite direction. It also simplifies pedestrian crossing of the avenue, reducing the risk of collisions with motor vehicles.

As noted in the 1949 Report, "The ability of a street system to move large volumes of traffic expeditiously is critically affected by the capacity of the intersections. The capacity of an intersection is not a fixed quantity, but is affected by a number of factors, the most important of which is the traffic signal system" (New York City Traffic Commission 1949). In the 1950s, T. T. Wiley, executive director of the Department of Traffic Engineering, initiated a long and steady upgrading of the capabilities and performance of the city's traffic signals. In 1956, multiple-cycle signal controllers were installed, allowing for prearranged timing changes such as adjusting the "split" of time assigned for each movement and providing more green time for the predominant direction during rush-hour peak periods. This preset timing also allowed for setting either a balanced pattern, in which all signals along a roadway would turn red or green simultaneously, or a signal progression pattern, depending on travel demand characteristics.

Beginning in the 1960s, the signal system in Midtown began a major upgrade through its connection via telephone lines to a computer in the NYCDOT Traffic Management Center (TMC) located in Long Island City, Queens. In August 1965, a $5.4 million contract was awarded to the Sperry Rand Corporation to provide for a master electronic signal system that would include interconnecting wired cable installed by New York Telephone. The system initially served 2,693 signalized intersections.

As traffic volumes and consequently congestion continued to grow, traffic management theory and technology attempted to keep pace with these new demands. A major advance in traffic control was the introduction of wire inductive loops embedded in the pavement to detect the presence of a vehicle. This allowed for signal timing to be adjusted remotely as conditions warranted, based on observations made by operators at the TMC utilizing inductive loop sensors and cameras. The system, known as the Vehicle Traffic Control System (VTCS), became operational in 1969. However, VTCS effectiveness was limited by its continued reliance, through the previous-generation electromechanical signal controllers, on time-of-day signal patterns, which constrained its ability to respond to incidents, special events, fluctuating traffic demand, and "oversaturated" traffic conditions. This also reflected the limitations resulting from unreliable loops and limited data management and communications.

As traffic congestion in Midtown persisted, NYCDOT investigated new traffic management concepts utilizing traffic signals, most notably a concept known as "metering" of traffic. Metering is intended to keep traffic in a specific area from exceeding the volume that can be handled by the roadway network.

In many cases, even a small number of additional vehicles can disproportionately degrade traffic operations. "When traffic on any road approaches saturation, each additional vehicle causes an exponential decrease in speed and mobility. The current levels of traffic now approach saturation . . . on the streets below 60th Street during peak hours. Additional vehicles threaten gridlock because their impact will impose much greater stress on the system than their numbers would suggest" (Sandler 1986).

Metering traffic entering the Midtown core could be accomplished by using traffic signals and city streets to effectively store vehicles in managed queues along avenues and then forward the traffic downstream at acceptable flow rates that can be more readily accommodated in the target area (the Midtown core). This application has the secondary benefit of limiting upstream congestion to the north and south of Midtown that can result from the spillover of congestion from within the target area.

As part of the city's continuing efforts to improve traffic operations, it was noted in 1983, "the Department proposes to . . . use the traffic signal system to 'meter' the rate at which vehicles are allowed to enter the most congested areas of the CBD [Central Business District]" (Ameruso 1983). And as noted in a 1979 report, "Other cities have traffic controls that regulate the amount of traffic entering an area. A computer varies traffic signal timings to delay vehicles approaching the subject area until congestion subsides. . . . The key to such a program is a computerized traffic signal network" (Jurow, Tompkins, and Goldstein 1979). A simple, limited version of this metering concept had been applied successfully in other cities, including Zurich (Switzerland), Bordeaux (France), and London (England).

Design, Piloting, Development, and Implementation

Early Efforts

While the concept of metering the flow of traffic into Midtown Manhattan appeared promising for many years, the technology necessary to collect and analyze massive amounts of data in real time, quickly identify appropriate signal plan modifications, and remotely adjust traffic signals from a traffic management center was not available until the early 2000s.

At the time, NYCDOT was operating the traffic signal system on a preplanned schedule with no feedback from the roadway network because the in-roadway inductive loops installed under the VTCS were no longer able to provide reliable data. The loops were often damaged by repeated street pavement cuts and failures of the telephone communication cables. As a result, NYCDOT had begun to deploy alternative vehicle detectors and upgrade

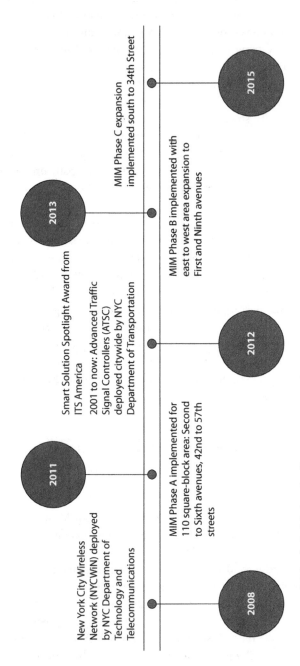

FIGURE 12.5 Midtown in Motion timeline.

New York City Wireless Network (NYCWiN) deployed by NYC Department of Technology and Telecommunications

Smart Solution Spotlight Award from ITS America

2001 to now: Advanced Traffic Signal Controllers (ATSC) deployed citywide by NYC Department of Transportation

MIM Phase C expansion implemented south to 34th Street

MIM Phase A implemented for 110 square-block area: Second to Sixth avenues, 42nd to 57th streets

MIM Phase B implemented with east to west area expansion to First and Ninth avenues

2008

2011

2012

2013

2015

communications, with the goal of ultimately making the system more adaptive to prevailing traffic conditions.

Using NYCDOT engineering service agreements (on-call contracts without specific scopes of services for consulting services on an as-needed basis) for Intelligent Transportation Systems (ITS), NYCDOT began working with KLD Engineering (KLD) on the application of advanced traffic signal control technologies, and with JHK and Associates, P.C., in association with TransCore ITS, LLP, on development of the next version of the city's traffic control system. Key participants included William McShane, president of KLD, and Raymundo Martinez, president at JHK. This work relied on the long-standing technical and financial support provided by Arthur T. O'Connor at the Federal Highway Administration's New York City Metropolitan Office. This support from FHWA directly supported the establishment of the current TMC operated by NYCDOT.

An exceptional opportunity presented itself in 2008 with the ITS World Congress sponsored by ITS America and hosted by NYCDOT at the Jacob K. Javits Convention Center. A goal of the congress was to demonstrate innovative technologies. At the congress, Steve Galgano, an assistant commissioner at NYCDOT, presented a state-of-the-art Active Traffic Management (ATM) system, which was then demonstrated along the Thirty-Fourth Street corridor in Midtown utilizing ETC tag readers mounted at three key intersections. The tag readers were used to measure vehicle travel times between readers and thus obtain travel speed. The data were used to adjust the traffic signals via the TMC to improve traffic flow. The successful use of the equipment to accurately measure travel time provided encouragement for NYCDOT to expand the application to a larger area—Midtown Manhattan. While some at NYCDOT believed that the next test should be a limited installation on Lower Broadway in Manhattan, others at NYCDOT pushed for a more ambitious adaptive-control program in Midtown Manhattan.

Following the demonstration at the World Congress, NYCDOT and KLD next applied the principles of active traffic management to a system on Victory Boulevard at the College of Staten Island in 2009. At the college, traffic demand fluctuated greatly during the day because of the varied schedules of students and staff. This uneven demand necessitated the introduction of "smarter" traffic signals with the ability to respond to frequently changing conditions. This test was supported by Staten Island Borough President James Molinaro, who encouraged NYCDOT to employ state-of-the-art traffic signals in the borough. At the end of the test, NYCDOT evaluations indicated that traffic delays were effectively reduced, and this convinced them that the system could significantly improve traffic operations.

In 2010, Mohamad Talas, NYCDOT deputy director of system engineering and MIM project manager, completed his doctoral thesis, *Pragmatic Use of Advanced Detector Technology in Urban CBD Environments*. His thesis addressed the use of data from existing microwave detectors to assess CBD congestion and identify ATM plans to respond to varying congestion levels. By pursuing his doctorate evenings and weekends while working at NYCDOT, Talas was able to accelerate the adoption of advanced technologies at NYC-DOT. He subsequently became MIM's advocate at NYCDOT, with support from John Tipaldo, NYCDOT assistant commissioner for systems engineering. As Mohamad Talas refined the overall concept utilizing microwave sensors to measure roadway occupancy, John Tipaldo focused on the need to collect and assess travel time rather than traffic volume data, and then on emerging control and operational issues. Building on his experience at the ITS World Congress, Tipaldo had started using ETC tag readers to measure travel speeds. His work was supported by experienced consultants Raymundo Martinez, William McShane, and Satya Muthuswamy.

MIM Phase A

Beginning in 2011, the first phase of MIM was implemented. Phase A consisted of a 110-square-block core area from Second to Sixth Avenues and from Forty-Second to Fifty-Seventh Streets (see figure 12.2 for project map). The program included one hundred microwave sensors, thirty-two traffic video cameras, and ETC tag readers at twenty-three intersections to measure traffic speeds with TransCore's TransSuite® traffic management software, which replaced VTCS, running at the TMC.

The objective of the Phase A deployment was to keep traffic moving by limiting the number of vehicles circulating in the core area. This required metering the flow of vehicles on the avenues approaching the core area, or "box," and effectively storing traffic on the streets and avenues outside the core, as needed. While this slowed traffic somewhat on the approaches to Midtown, it provided for a more even flow and prevented gridlock that would have slowed traffic everywhere. The system deployed was not intended to manage every street and avenue, but rather focused on keeping the north-south avenues moving. Secondarily, the system would keep streets moving at a limited number of key intersections within the core.

The project required a significant amount of systems analysis and integration. Video cameras, microwave radar sensors, and ETC tag readers from several vendors were used to measure real-time individual travel time and traffic volume and vehicle congestion data. These data were then transmitted via NYCWiN and fiber optic/coaxial cable video to the TMC, a control center managed by highly trained staff from NYCDOT. Computers at the TMC analyzed the data to identify potential problems based on travel-time anomalies.

FIGURE 12.6 Video camera on traffic signal mast arm.

TMC operators used video cameras (figure 12.6) for problem confirmation and assessment. Over time, as the MIM algorithms were refined, TMC staff became more confident in their recommendations. The MIM incremental investment was less than $2 million (Talas et al. 2012).

In the design phase, multiple traffic signal timing plans were developed so that the system could propose the best plan for each situation, utilizing an algorithm. The traffic signal timing plans are designed to manage areawide traffic operations through metering on avenues approaching Midtown, or by addressing localized congestion. While the system recommends traffic signal plans, the system operator has the final authority to implement the proposed signal-timing changes, which are then transmitted to local traffic signal controllers.

Determining the appropriate mix of system components and their locations and limitations was challenging, and travel-time detector location proved to be critical to collecting adequate sample sizes. Although the use of "mean" travel-time measurements on a corridor were first thought to be an appropriate metric, this did not work well in practice because the detector network was not complete, so vehicles traveling the roadways were sometimes "lost" for extended periods of time, resulting in some very high travel-time estimates. Eliminating outliers and estimating "median" travel times better replicated actual conditions for the principal platoon of vehicles. Ultimately, the number of stops an average vehicle made during a trip was determined to be the best measure of the quality of traffic operations, and the number of observed stops could be used to make traffic signal changes.

Another consideration was the effect of slowing the traffic progression into, and effectively storing vehicles outside of, Midtown. NYCDOT staff judged that it was critical to manage congestion within the core. Without metering into the core, traffic congestion within Midtown would build and spill outside the core area, causing worse congestion than the tactics used to meter traffic flow into the Midtown core. Similar issues were raised on the decision not to initially meter the cross streets, but it was believed that the general availability of vehicle storage space on the crosstown streets made them less critical from an operational point of view.

Over the course of the first year of MIM operation, engineers in the TMC used the technology to quickly identify congestion issues as they occurred and used networked ASTCs to remotely adjust Midtown traffic signal patterns, unplug bottlenecks, and smooth the flow of traffic. At the close of Phase A, NYCDOT studies indicated that MIM resulted in travel-time savings up to 10% when compared to pre-MIM conditions.

MIM Phases B and C

Phase B was announced in June 2012. The first challenge associated with MIM's geographic expansion for Phase B was identification of the appropriate boundaries in the north-south and east-west directions. Traffic operation in the vicinity of the Ed Koch Queensboro Bridge and Third Avenue would be difficult, with multiple through lanes and turn lanes onto the bridge. On the west side, vehicle storage in the vicinity of the Lincoln Tunnel also would be challenging.

As planning for Phase B progressed, NYCDOT continued deployment of new traffic signal controllers and a more robust network of detectors, and expanded the wireless network. Ultimately, the Phase B expanded service area would cover more than 270 square blocks and include an additional 110 microwave sensors, twenty-four traffic video cameras, and thirty-six ETC tag readers and would be fully operational by September 2012, allowing engineers to respond to congestion throughout the heart of Midtown.

The cost of this Midtown in Motion expansion was stated to be $2.9 million, with $580,000 of that contributed by the city and the remainder by New York State. A further $2 million was invested in 200 new ASTCs, $1.6 million of that from FHWA and the remainder from the city.

While Phase A was initiated and tested with low public visibility, subsequent expansion and refinement phases were developed and implemented with the mayor's endorsement and thus were a heightened priority for Commissioner Sadik-Khan. There was also a need for greater understanding of the operational impacts associated with the systems and programs being deployed. This resulted in higher stress levels for staff.

MIM development and implementation benefited from NYCDOT's continued efforts to test and install traffic signal and management system upgrades. The VTCS was upgraded, replacing the wired communication with a dedicated carrier-free mobile broadband NYCWiN. The in-roadway inductive loops were replaced with wireless sensors, including roadside ETC tag readers, ASTCs, and microwave readers (Xin et al. 2013). Currently, MIM controls more than 300 signalized intersections and utilizes fifty-six cameras, sixty-seven ETC tag readers, and 210 microwave sensors. MIM was expanded in January 2015 under Phase C, which expanded coverage south from Forty-Second to Thirty-Fourth Street (see table 12.1).

TABLE 12.1 Chronology of Events Associated with MIM

Date	Event
1920	Traffic signal towers installed in New York City
1949	New York City Traffic Commission created
1950	New York City Department of Traffic created
1950s–1966	Midtown avenues converted to one-way operation
1964	Solid-state electronic signal controllers introduced
1966	Vehicle Traffic Control System (VTCS) introduced
1967	Super-agency New York City Transportation Administration created
1977	New York City Department of Transportation created
2008	ITS World Congress held in New York City
2009	Victory Boulevard "smart signals" tested at the College of Staten Island
July 2011	MIM Phase A implemented
June 2012	MIM Phase B implemented
January 2015	MIM Phase C implemented

Key Roles, Coordination, and Interactions

The development and implementation of MIM was accomplished through the successful collaboration of approximately a dozen dedicated professionals with complementary levels of expertise in traffic operations and management. These professionals represented organizations with deep experience in traffic signal coordination for arterials and networks operating under saturated conditions such as those experienced in Midtown Manhattan.

MIM's public/private partnership included JHK Engineering, P.C., in association with TransCore ITS, LLC, and KLD Engineering, PC. JHK was responsible for obtaining and testing hardware, primarily ETC readers and microwave sensors. TransCore provided the traffic control system, while KLD was responsible for software and systems engineering to analyze traffic data and adjust traffic signal timing accordingly. NYCDOT engaged with these firms through on-call contracts that supported the rapid execution of new task orders to address MIM development needs. NYCDOT was responsible for completing the upgrade of the traffic signal controllers, installing the sensors in the field, and ensuring reliable communications with the TMC. NYCDOT reviewed and tested the signal timing plans developed by the consultants.

The project team accepted the demanding timetable established by senior management at NYCDOT to install, test, and operate the initial phase of MIM within one year. This schedule created a sense of purpose and urgency that carried its way through project development. Working on an ambitious, but doable, timetable was a key to the successful deployment of MIM.

Biweekly progress meetings were chaired by the DOT deputy commissioner of traffic operations to coordinate the expeditious identification and resolution of issues. These collaborative meetings with concrete action items created a "can-do" spirit, with each team member prepared to report on what had been accomplished since the previous meeting. Key stakeholder roles are summarized in table 12.2.

MIM utilizes two levels of control. Level 1 is area focused, employing a library of signal-timing plans, each characterized by a different set of signal offsets and splits for intersections upstream from the target control core area. "The offsets and splits represent a set of steady control state measures to exert a tapering and rebalancing effect on the traffic before delivering it to the target control area" (Xin et al. 2013).

Unlike Level 1, Level 2 is site specific, addressing critical intersections within the target control area. It adjusts the splits to balance queue/storage ratios to rebalance operations at competing approaches to prevent spillback or possible gridlock. MIM employs a congestion metric called the Severity Index, which relates vehicle roadway occupancy and traffic volume to discrete control

TABLE 12.2 Key Stakeholders

Stakeholder	Role played	Interest in the program	Positive/ negative effect on the program	Incentives needed to engage
NYCDOT	System conceptualization, development, testing, and operations	Responsible for the safe and efficient movement of goods and people in New York City	*Positive*: NYCDOT conceptualized, championed, implemented, tested, and operated MIM	Conforms to department's mission to improve transportation system
Consultants	Technology specification, system integration, and software development	Intelligent transportation system (ITS) consultants under contract to NYCDOT	*Positive*: acted as partners to NYCDOT	Opportunity to extend expertise and to apply skills and services worldwide
New York City residents, businesses, and visitors	Users of the street network and transportation systems	Need to travel safely and efficiently	*Positive*: MIM was supported by users	Improve quality of life through management of traffic
Funding agencies	Financial support for development, implementation, and operations	Responsible for funding projects to ensure the safe and efficient movement of goods and people	*Positive*: city, state, and federal funds were used to develop and implement MIM	Needed to understand the potential costs and benefits of MIM

regimes. The Queue Storage Ratio (QSR) is computed as queue length divided by relevant link length.

Travel-time data are collected using ETC tag readers that are generally deployed on overhead traffic signal poles. Individual per-trip travel time is determined by matching the tag ID at the two ends of the trip. Each travel-time record includes a discrete tag ID number (scrambled to ensure privacy of the vehicle owner), a time stamp, starting and ending points of the trip, and duration of the trip. Travel-time data are processed over fifteen-minute periods. The number of stops per trip provides the basis for selecting different demand-regulating strategies under Level 1 controls.

Level 1 control provides for an even distribution of traffic entering the control area. It works to allow an appropriate rate of vehicle entries based on traffic conditions, evolving bottlenecks, incidents, and unusual roadway conditions. The signal patterns generally consist of simultaneous patterns approaching the target area and progression within the Midtown core. The system assesses the prevailing traffic conditions every fifteen minutes. Once a new strategy is implemented, a fifteen-minute "pattern-hold" period becomes active, during which the system dwells on the new strategy for at least fifteen minutes. This avoids possible adverse impacts associated with transitioning to a new strategy. Signal-timing changes always protect the time needed for pedestrians to safely cross an intersection at the relatively low walking speed of three feet per second.

Level 2 controls use data from microwave sensors, usually placed midblock in advance of an intersection, to obtain data regarding vehicular volume and occupancy in the primary travel lanes. Level 2 controls manage the length of queues to limit the occurrence of spillback of vehicles in the intersection immediately upstream from the microwave sensor by adjusting the traffic signal at the next downstream intersection. Level 2 also receives feedback from Level 1 on avenue performance for an integrated control approach. Signal adjustments typically affect the "split," or the distribution of green time between the roadways approaching the intersection. Level 2 controls provide intersection-specific automated control within the control area that changes signal splits in real time.

Rather than implementing a fully automatic system, MIM was designed to keep the TMC operator in the loop—the operator must accept the system's recommendation before it is implemented. As the operator's level of confidence increased over time, the system has been changed to automatically implement the recommended signal plan unless the operator rejects it. Other system enhancements include improved graphics, such as travel-time maps, and an enhanced operator interface.

Impact and Results

Mayor Michael A. Bloomberg announced MIM implementation on July 18, 2011 (Falcocchio, Prassas, and Xu 2013). It was presented to the media as a new, state-of-the-art traffic management system that would give city engineers the ability to manage Midtown Manhattan traffic to reduce congestion and prevent gridlock. With MIM, engineers sitting in a windowless control room at the TMC in Long Island City would be able to adjust traffic signals to better move cars through the city.

"We are now using the most sophisticated system of its kind in the nation to improve traffic flow on the City's most congested streets—Midtown Manhattan," said Mayor Bloomberg. "The technology will allow traffic engineers to

FIGURE 12.7 Front page of the *New York Post*, July 19, 2011.

immediately identify congestion choke points as they occur and remotely alter traffic signal patterns to begin to clear up Midtown jams at the touch of a button" (Fermino 2011; figure 12.7).

A critical metric utilized to assess the effectiveness of MIM is the number of stops a vehicle makes during its travel through the target area. An analysis of travel times indicated that number of stops was the measure most affecting the quality of travel for motorists, rather than average speed, which is relatively low (below 10 mph) in Midtown; a change in speed on such congested roadways generally would not be a matter of concern or perception to motorists. NYCDOT reports that MIM is currently achieving up to 10% travel-time improvement on most avenues in the core area (Replogle 2017).

On June 5, 2012, NYCDOT Commissioner Janette Sadik-Khan, Federal Highway Administrator Victor Mendez, and Scott Belcher, president and CEO of ITS America, held a press conference to announce the success of MIM Phase A and introduce its Phase B expansion to encompass a larger part of Midtown Manhattan. Also announced was its receipt of a Smart Solution Spotlight Award from ITS America. The commissioner stated that the service area would more than double in size to include Midtown from First to Ninth Avenue and from Forty-Second to Fifty-Seventh Street.

"From cameras to microwave sensors and EZ-pass readers to Advanced Solid State Traffic Controllers, Midtown in Motion is a showcase of the most sophisticated intelligent transportation solutions available to public agencies," said Scott Belcher. "Innovative systems like Midtown in Motion help keep America moving," added Victor Mendez. "This technology improves safety and reduces traffic congestion for drivers, bicyclists and pedestrians, which makes a big difference as they go about their day to day activities" (NYCDOT 2012). Real-time MIM traffic information is available on the DOT's website, on smartphones and tablets, and is accessible to app developers.

Challenges and Lessons Learned

The transportation system serving Midtown Manhattan must satisfy the myriad needs of a variety of users, including pedestrians, bicyclists, motorists, bus riders, goods delivery companies, emergency services, taxis, transportation network company vehicles, food-vending vehicles, service vehicles, and others, while accommodating special events, new development and construction, roadway repairs, and other street uses, all under the overarching mandate to ensure the safety of all travelers. The challenges in satisfying these competing needs are compounded by nonuniversal compliance with traffic rules and controls, which exacerbates chronic roadway congestion.

MIM provides NYCDOT and its TMC with invaluable information on traffic conditions, without which managing the area's roadways would not be possible. A more robust system of sensors could enhance the extent of traffic-data collection and further improve the responsiveness of MIM. Although congestion persists in Midtown, MIM fulfills a vital role in traffic management through the timely recognition of problems causing delays and congestion and the application of an extensive traffic signal system and other resources to expeditiously address traffic problems.

The technology utilized by MIM, while advanced at the time of its adoption, will likely be considered passé as new technology emerges in the automotive and digital worlds. The current and next generation of motor vehicles will be equipped with an extensive array of sensor and communications devices (e.g., cameras, radar, dedicated short-range communications) to monitor the movement of nearby vehicles and pedestrians for potential hazards, and will be programmed to travel on routes and at speeds compatible with ongoing traffic conditions. Newer vehicles are expected to continuously share safety and mobility information with other vehicles, traffic control devices, and pedestrians via two-way short- to medium-range wireless communication, Bluetooth, and other means. The TMC could utilize such forms of communication and, if determined to be reliable, information compiled by third-party data providers (e.g., Google/WAZE, HERE, INRIX, TomTom) to replace ETC tag readers or microwave sensors to monitor and manage traffic.

NYCDOT continues to be an early adopter of new technologies, as evidenced by its current state-of-the-art connected vehicle pilot deployment program (U.S. Department of Transportation 2016)—the nation's largest to date. The U.S. Department of Transportation's Connected Vehicle Pilot Deployment Program encourages partnerships of stakeholders to deploy applications utilizing data captured from multiple sources (e.g., vehicles, mobile devices, and infrastructure) to support improved system performance and enhanced performance-based management. The NYCDOT pilot aims to improve safety of motorists and pedestrians through vehicle-to-vehicle (V2V) and vehicle-to-infrastructure (V2I) "connected vehicle" technologies. It supports the city's Vision Zero initiative to reduce the number of fatalities and injuries resulting from traffic crashes.

NYCDOT's planned deployment provides an opportunity to evaluate connected vehicle technology and applications in the tightly spaced intersections typical of a dense urban transportation system such as Midtown Manhattan. The project area contains four Midtown avenues as well as other areas of the city. Vehicle participation includes approximately 5,800 taxicabs, 1,250 MTA buses, 400 commercial fleet delivery trucks, and 500 city vehicles. The vehicles are being equipped with connected vehicle technology to communicate with other connected vehicles to warn of potential conflicts. Also being deployed will be dedicated short-range communications (DSRC) at approximately 310 signalized intersections for communication between vehicles and traffic signals. The project will focus on reducing vehicle/pedestrian conflicts through in-vehicle pedestrian warnings and an additional V2I/I2V project component to equip approximately one hundred pedestrians with personal devices to assist them in more safely navigating city streets.

Conclusion

The Midtown in Motion program has been recognized by industry leaders as a significant advancement in the application of active traffic management

Strengths	Weaknesses
MIM uses proven, readily available technology. Traffic delays are reduced and gridlock prevented. MIM is scalable in scope and geographic coverage, and permits detailed focus on critical sub-areas. The system can evolve as traffic control system and vehicle technologies advance.	There are limits to MIM's ability to accommodate growth in traffic volumes, particularly with the popularity of the services offered by transportation network companies such as Lyft, Uber, and Via. MIM's limited ability to improve overall traffic flow given the growing need to better accommodate transit, bicycles, pedestrians, and goods movement. MIM's central control strategy may be less appropriate as vehicle and navigation systems advance (e.g., autonomous and connected vehicles). NYCDOT's overriding emphasis on ensuring the safety of the traveling public (e.g., Vision Zero) further constrains the unimpeded movement of motor vehicles.
Opportunities	**Threats**
Traffic congestion is common in many of the world's central business districts, and the techniques employed are universally applicable. Advancements in traffic system and vehicle technologies may be used to enhance MIM capabilities. Increasing population and employment in Manhattan will result in greater traffic demands increasing MIM's benefits.	Traffic congestion may continue to grow as traffic volumes increase and capacity is constrained. New control system and vehicle technologies may reduce the utility of a central control system like MIM. The adoption of automated vehicle technologies may result in more travel by private automobile and less by transit.

FIGURE 12.8 Midtown in Motion SWOT analysis.

principles. This recognition has been confirmed by numerous awards, including the Smart Solution Spotlight Award from ITS America in 2012, an International Road Federation (IRF) Global Road Achievement Award in 2013, and a Diamond Award for Engineering Excellence from the American Council of Engineering Companies of New York.

As summarized in figure 12.8, MIM is a proven system with the potential to improve traffic operations in other central business districts. However, the rapid development and deployment of advanced traffic management and vehicle navigation systems and the introduction of connected and autonomous vehicles must be considered as cities investigate the potential implementation of MIM or a similar system. New technology holds the potential to greatly improve MIM as more comprehensive data become available to feed the TMC. Alternatively, connected and autonomous vehicles may reduce the utility of a central traffic control system like MIM. The only certainty is that technology will continue to improve, and NYCDOT will continue to adopt cutting-edge systems.

This case study reveals that NYCDOT's expeditious development and implementation of the successful MIM traffic management program was directly related to the following factors:

- Leadership (and a commitment to innovation) at NYCDOT, coupled with a management team empowered to champion innovative new programs
- NYCDOT's ability to form teams of skilled and experienced professionals within its organization, assisted by experts from the private sector through preexisting on-call contracts
- NYCDOT's long history of innovation in traffic control and traffic management through many years of ITS deployment and equipment upgrades, which provided the building blocks necessary to quickly implement the MIM system

This combination of leadership, talent, tradition, and technology is the product of a long-standing commitment to incrementally address chronic traffic congestion problems and the constant search for opportunities to improve traffic operations.

Note

The authors dedicate this case study to the memory of Steve Galgano for his lasting contribution to the safety and mobility of all New Yorkers. The authors also wish to thank the following contributors who played a critical role in preparation of this report: Raymundo Martinez, William McShane, Satya Muthuswamy, Arthur O'Connor, Mohamad Talas, and John Tipaldo.

References

Ameruso, Anthony. 1983. *City Streets: A Report on Policies and Programs*. New York City Department of Transportation.

Falcocchio, John, Elena Prassas, and Zeng Xu. 2013. *Development of Traffic Performance Metrics Using Real-Time Traffic Data*, Final Report. Polytechnic Institute of NYU. University Transportation Research Center–Region 2. Accessed November 9, 2017. http://www.utrc2.org/sites/default/files/pubs/Final-Traffic-Performance-Metrics_0.pdf.

Fermino, Jennifer. 2011. "Bloomberg Unveils System That Aims to Tame Midtown Traffic." *New York Post*, July 19. https://nypost.com/2011/07/18/bloomberg-unveils-system-that-aims-to-tame-midtown-traffic/.

Gray, Christopher. 2014. "A History of New York Traffic Lights." *New York Times*, May 16. Accessed November 9, 2017. https://www.nytimes.com/2014/05/18/realestate/a-history-of-new-york-traffic-lights.html.

Jurow, Steven, Marcia E. Tompkins, and Eric Goldstein. 1979. *Innovations in Transportation Solutions to New York City's Mobility Problems*. Natural Resources Defense Council.

New York City Traffic Commission. 1949. *Report*. December 31, 1949.

NYCDOT. 2012. "NYC DOT Announces Expansion of Midtown Congestion Management System, Receives National Transportation Award." June 5, 2012. http://www.nyc.gov/html/dot/html/pr2012/pr12_25.shtml.

Replogle, Michael. 2017. Deputy Commissioner for Policy, New York City Department of Transportation, Smart Traffic Data Analytics Symposium/Hackathon, NYU Tandon School of Engineering. January 13, 2017.

Sandler, Ross. 1986. *An Approach to Reducing Vehicle Congestion in New York City: A Report to Mayor Edward I. Koch*, rev. 9/10/86. New York City Department of Transportation.

Scientific American 62, no. 6 (February 8, 1890): 81.

Talas, Mohamad, William R. McShane, Wuping Xin, and John Tipaldo. 2012. *New York City Midtown in Motion: ITS Deployment Project and Operation for NYC Active Traffic Management*. Nineteenth ITS World Congress, October 22–26, 2012.

U.S. Department of Transportation. 2016. "Connected Vehicle Pilot Deployment Program." Accessed November 9, 2017. http://www.its.dot.gov/pilots/pilots_overview.htm.

Xin, Wuping, Jinil Chang, Satya Muthuswamy, and Mohamad Talas. 2013. *"Midtown in Motion": A New Active Traffic Management Methodology and Its Implementation in New York City*. Transportation Research Board 2013 Annual Meeting. http://docs.trb.org/prp/13-4145.pdf.

PART IV

**BECOMING
A SMARTER CITY**

CONCLUSION

Becoming a Smarter City

ANDRÉ CORRÊA D'ALMEIDA, *Columbia University*

KENDAL STEWART, *Columbia University*

Innovation is often presented as being in the exclusive domain of the private sector. Yet despite the widespread perceptions of public-sector inefficiency, government agencies have much to teach us about how advances occur. Improving governance on the municipal level is crucial to the future of the twenty-first century city, from environmental sustainability to economic development and equality, social inclusion, public health, and beyond. In this age of acceleration and massive migration of people into cities around the world, this book demonstrates how innovation from within city administration makes urban systems smarter and shapes life in New York City.

We often equate innovation with technological advancement and data analytics, but it is far broader. Moreover, because of their limited resources and fiscal stress, idealized tech-centered futures are unrealistic for the vast majority of cities around the world. To challenge the notion of a tech- and data-centric view of urban innovation, we need to look at cities and local governments more holistically. This book brings together economists, engineers, computer scientists, sociologists, business managers, lawyers, environmentalists, planners, health scientists, public officials, technologists, design thinkers, and private consultants to offer a multidisciplinary and integrated perspective of what it means to become a smarter city. Using a series of twelve case studies, this book describes the forces and constraints behind urban innovations in New York City. This book helps imagine new possibilities from within city administration. It offers roadmaps and practical lessons on municipal innovation for city officials, urban planners, policymakers, civil society, and potential private-sector partners in New York City, the United States, and around the world.

In analyzing the twelve case studies, we have identified thirteen critical issues that anchor a city on its quest to become smarter.

1. **Data access**. Democratize access to data within city agencies and improve cross-agency data-sharing, while ensuring adequate security and privacy protocols are in place.

2. **Performance-enhancing technology**. Adopt technology incrementally to enhance decision-making, operations, and performance.

3. **People empowerment**. Build adaptable, resilient, and connected units within city agencies, staffed with motivated, talented, curious, and trained practitioners, and empower them to incubate innovation by giving them the autonomy to experiment.

4. **Leveraging context**. Leverage the institutional context when possible and strive to make it increasingly innovation-enabling.

5. **Control and delegation**. Encourage and empower strong leadership at all levels of city administration. Big ideas and citywide goals can be set centrally, but the authority and resources to discover, design, and implement new solutions should be delegated through networked systems and public entrepreneurship.

6. **Community building**. Foster silo-breaking interagency partnerships, as well as open dialogues with the private sector and civil society.

7. **Shared purpose**. Cultivate a citywide culture of innovation incubation, while focusing on purpose and keeping the end user, residents, and global impact at the forefront.

8. **Strategic planning**. Balance the interplay of innovation drivers and strategically leverage them to move from an idea to action.

9. **Transformational incrementalism**. Adopt innovation as an agile process, build incrementally on what exists, one success at a time, and achieve transformational outcomes to mitigate the fear of trying.

10. **Institutionalized learning**. Institutionalize evidence-based decision-making at all levels of city administration, monitor results, promote transparency, and incentivize intra- and interagency learning.

11. **Citywide clusters**. Develop citywide innovation clusters to accelerate results through connectivity and synergies.

12. **Diversified funding**. Diversify funding for innovation, from fully public to fully private and variations that combine sources.

13. **Complexity**. Embrace complexity and nonlinearity, because innovation is packed with hesitation and fears about how to address key decision points and critical junctures. Solutions must be found locally, but the New York City case helps us ask smarter questions.

A "smarter city" is one that (i) understands how these critical issues emerge locally from the interplay of innovation drivers throughout innovation processes and (ii) continuously tries to incorporate them into innovation efforts. This chapter describes and explains in detail how these thirteen critical issues emerge and operate within the Becoming Smarter Framework (BSF) and what our definition of "smarter city" means in practical terms.

The Becoming Smarter Framework (BSF): A Framework for City Innovation

As illustrated by our case studies, the many relevant variables, the large number of combinations between them, the different contexts where they operate, and the diverse languages used by a variety of technical and scientific fields involved make understanding urban innovation a very complex task. Discussions on innovation must occur at multiple levels and within specific spatial and temporal scales. As such, no discipline owns a monopoly of theoretical concepts driving the "becoming smarter" function. There is no single optimal way to innovate and become smarter that can be used for all programmatic purposes and circumstances. Feedback loops constantly change existing conditions and assumptions, making urban systems and program outcomes too dynamic and complex to be reduced to deterministic cause-and-effect theories or models.

The introduction to this book promised that our twelve case studies would produce practical knowledge about how New York City agencies innovate—how they are becoming smarter—with the goal of explaining what "smarter city" means and offering roadmaps for replicability in other cities around the world. We developed the Becoming Smarter Framework for city innovation and applied it to the twelve case studies. The BSF is a conceptual and practical tool that helps explain and accelerate innovation in urban systems and make cities smarter. It considers a wide range of internal and external variables and integrates the language of multiple disciplines to promote change and improve life in the city.

This is the key contribution of this chapter: to present the BSF holistically and demonstrate how this new framework can be applied to the total urban system based on New York City's experience. As explained in detail in the book's introduction (see figure 0.2), the BSF considers two dynamic and interdependent axes simultaneously:

- *Innovation is a process*—from problem identification, to program design, implementation, and evaluation.

    Along this "process" axis, the BSF can map critical elements necessary to answer questions such as the following:
    - What motivates and/or triggers innovation?
    - How can we describe the innovation process? What accelerates it or slows it down?
    - How is innovation funded?

- *Seven multidimensional forces, both internal and external, drive success in innovation*—data, technology, organizational structure, institutional context, leadership and decision-making, networks and collaboration, and results and impact.

  Along this "driving forces" axis, the BSF can map critical elements necessary to answer questions such as the following:
  - How do innovation drivers operate? How do city agencies use, in practical terms, these drivers to improve the urban systems that affect people's lives?
  - What exactly do these drivers mean within the context and experience of specific cities?
  - Who benefits from innovation? At what risk? What incentives are needed for engagement?

The innovation drivers are in constant interaction with each other throughout the innovation process. Taken as a whole, the BSF can help explain what characterizes a smarter city administration and what is the applicability of lessons learned to other cities.

Becoming a Smarter City: Opening Thoughts

While individual chapters provide innovation- or agency-specific lessons and actionable insights, this conclusion explores trends and common themes found citywide. The goal of this meta-analysis is to understand what it means to become smarter for cities as a whole. The above questions this book addresses apply in varying degrees to all urban systems, and the quest for answers should matter to all those interested in accelerating urban innovation and improving life in cities.

Table C.1 provides the first entry point in our meta-analysis to an integrated understanding of the practical meaning of becoming smarter at a citywide administration level. We highlight the primary outcome and lesson learned from each innovation studied, offering a first citywide overview of how critical it is to have a balanced (nontechnocentric) understanding of how innovation drivers interplay. While the role of institutions is highlighted in the cases of organic-waste collection and green infrastructure, it is the organizational structure that lies at the center of lessons learned for the NYPD ShotSpotter and MODA. Networks and collaboration are at the core of the Neighborhood Innovation Labs and energy demand response program, whereas technology and data drive the Business Atlas and Vision Zero. Leadership plays a particular role in the syndromic surveillance system and Midtown in Motion. Results and impact are paramount for OneNYC and LinkNYC.

TABLE C.1 Becoming Smarter: Primary Outcome and Lesson Learned

Innovation	Becoming Smarter: Primary outcome	Becoming Smarter: Primary lesson learned
OneNYC and SDGs	The establishment of a holistic, multisectoral vision for the city's development, with actionable targets and precise measurement indicators, that will enable the city to develop integrated programs that respond to the pressing challenges of environmental and economic development, while also shining a light on how to tackle the pernicious challenge of inequity.	The challenges associated with sustainable development require new forms of planning that engage a wide variety of stakeholders and cross sectoral boundaries. Although conceptually broad, such plans can be made very actionable through concrete, quantitative targets and indicators.
MODA	An institutional innovation in city government: leading data strategy and offering advanced analytics as a shared service to city agencies to improve how civil servants make decisions using data and analytical tools.	A center of excellence for advanced analytics in a large governmental organization enables tactical delivery of public value through limited project engagements while also building analytical capacity across other service areas through data governance and open data functions.
LinkNYC	A strategically redesigned franchise and bidding model that utilizes the city's creative sector and public/private partnerships, transforms the city's public communications infrastructure, and lays a foundation to give every resident access to free high-speed public broadband by 2023 with minimal use of taxpayer money.	Design enables the use of technology intentionally to engage and enliven the city fabric by leveraging the creative economy for better resident services, urban growth, and cultural enrichment.

(continued)

TABLE C.1 Becoming Smarter: Primary Outcome and Lesson Learned (*Cont.*)

Innovation	Becoming Smarter: Primary outcome	Becoming Smarter: Primary lesson learned
Business Atlas	A demonstration of how open data, cross-government collaboration, and cross-sector engagement create new economic opportunity—including for industries and businesses that are neither data- nor technology-driven.	"If you build it, they will come" is not an optimal strategy for open data initiatives. The innovation's pivot toward clearer problem definition and more targeted engagement with partners places it on a stronger path toward meaningful positive impact on small businesses.
Energy demand response	The reduction of electricity use when demand peaks, known as demand response, which is a form of responsive energy management that benefits both electricity suppliers and end users who cooperate to mitigate power failures in the city's grid.	The successful implementation of a demand response program requires a collaborative effort by the principal agency and its private-sector partner to understand agency needs and incentives and tailor the program accordingly as it is rolled out.
Green infrastructure	The institutionalization of a program for stormwater management that provides opportunities for continued use of green infrastructure for enhanced water quality and its future use for building resilience to the effects of climate change.	Green infrastructure can be utilized as a cost-effective approach to resilient stormwater management—even in older, dense cities—while providing a variety of additional co-benefits for urban residents.
Organic-waste collection	A successful organics diversion program, demonstrating that very large, complex sanitation systems can adapt their infrastructure and human assets to be innovative drivers of sustainability in cities.	Ambitious policies, key private-sector partnerships, and a phased piloting approach can be leveraged to implement a large organics diversion program.

TABLE C.1 *(Continued)*

Innovation	Becoming Smarter: Primary outcome	Becoming Smarter: Primary lesson learned
Syndromic surveillance	An electronic data platform that collects and analyzes administrative data from across the city and provides the Department of Health and Mental Hygiene with actionable insights into the daily health patterns of residents.	Even seemingly simple routine data can generate powerful public policy insights when collected and analyzed by knowledgeable, talented, and, above all, curious staff.
Neighborhood Innovation Labs	A scalable model for testing and deploying urban data and civic technologies, while leveraging data analytics to support community empowerment, neighborhood planning, urban research, and technology evaluation in real-world experimental environments.	Prerequisites to its success lie in the ability of local residents to formulate shared collective needs within a given neighborhood; city agencies to respond to the new knowledge created through increased data collection, evaluation, and analysis; and initiative leadership to address privacy, data management, and ROI concerns.
NYPD ShotSpotter	A more effective response to gun violence.	Technological tools are most effective if used as part of a larger policy shift.
Vision Zero	A citywide public safety program aiming at zero fatalities or serious injuries involving road traffic.	You can start "cheap" with "paint and plastic," on budget and on schedule.
Midtown in Motion	A large-scale traffic management system, which employs state-of-the-art traffic sensors, advanced communications networks, and complex computer algorithms to detect and respond to changing traffic conditions, thus improving traffic operations in the central business district.	Public-sector leadership and a commitment to innovation, in partnership with experts from the private sector, can provide the building blocks necessary to quickly implement a successful state-of-the-art traffic management system.

A smarter perspective of urban innovation requires an understanding of how outcomes and lessons from individual innovations depend on a smarter combination of innovation drivers and furthermore how they are affected by other innovations developed citywide (see figure C.1). A smarter perspective of urban innovation requires both these inward and outward understandings. Jeff Merritt, coauthor of chapter 9 in this volume, now with the World Economic Forum, argued at the 2017 NYC Smart Districts Summit that "a sum of smart projects does not make for a smart city." What is happening in New York City is that the degree of connectivity and interdependency between new programs is making the city administration look like much more than just a sum of smart projects. Figure C.1 shows how the city administration looks more like an innovation cluster in itself—an interdependent and evolving web of design, implementation, and outcomes woven together by synergies and complementarities that are making the city smarter. While some innovations, such as OneNYC (chapter 1), play a more central role in the planning and functioning of the cluster, others focus on more specialized, not necessarily peripheral, domains of life in the city, such as energy consumption (chapter 5), public safety (chapter 10), and traffic mobility (chapter 12).

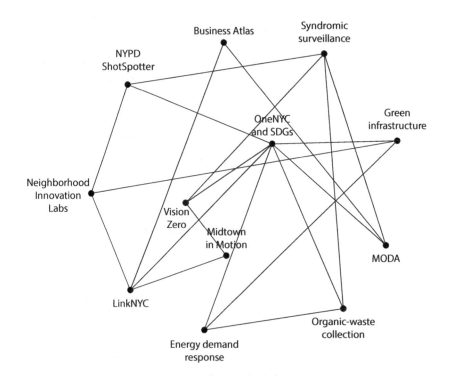

FIGURE C.1 City innovation cluster—a schematic representation.

The links connecting these nodes represent a sample of interdependencies or synergies shared between innovations, as described in each case study. Using the terminology of the BSF, each link represents one or more innovation drivers shared between agencies or programs, such as a data set or task force. (See in-depth discussion in the next sections about innovation drivers and process.) Innovation drivers need to be understood within the internal dynamics of each innovation or agency as well as externally, for they materialize the connectivity, fluidity, and exchanges of which innovation clusters are built.

Before going deeper into the citywide BSF, we used NVivo—a qualitative data analysis computer software—to explore innovation patterns hidden in the text of all cases combined. The main goal was to discover features of innovation citywide that may not be identifiable from the analysis of individual cases. Since the purpose of each case study was to document and analyze separately how certain innovations unfolded in approximately 7,500 words, the content analysis of almost 100,000 words together uncovered features of innovation emerging across the city and helped answer the questions raised in this book.

First, the aggregated text of the twelve case studies was coded according to problem identification, program design, implementation, and evaluation to create four text bundles—one for each innovation phase. Second, each innovation driver was coded according to a set of words most associated with its concept (see the appendix at the end of this conclusion). Third, we calculated a series of metrics related to the number of times each of these "grouped words" was mentioned in each phase of the innovation process.

Figure C.2 looks at the comparative interplay of drivers throughout the innovation process to highlight how the role of each driver varies across phases. For example, looking at the role leadership plays, it stands out that this driver is particularly critical for problem identification when the innovation agenda is set. The relevance of the institutional context during implementation, compared with the intensity of this driver in other phases (see spike in figure C.2c), highlights how critical external variables are for agencies and their innovation efforts.

While innovation requires an ongoing coordination of drivers, their mix throughout the process varies, which requires flexible, agile organizational and governance structures. Problem definition, goal-setting, and the identification of new opportunities can be triggered by conditions that typically already exist in any type or size of city, such as leadership with access to data or some technology capability. Once the problem has been identified and the agenda set, networks and collaboration kick in very consistently throughout the innovation process, as illustrated in figure C.1 with the formation of citywide clusters. Organizational structures also play a consistent role throughout the process, but their role kicks in earlier—right from problem identification, which points

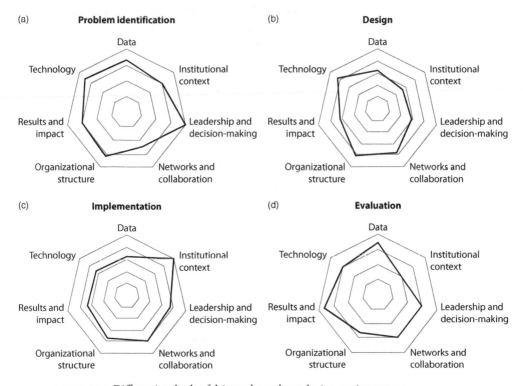

FIGURE C.2 Differentiated role of drivers throughout the innovation process.

once again to agencies as the epicenter and cradle of innovation. While it would be expected for data and results to be particularly critical in the evaluation phase of the innovation process, as figure C.2d shows, their roles are central in problem identification and agenda-setting as well (see figure C.2a).

Becoming a Smarter City: The Innovation Drivers

Our twelve case studies collectively reveal how the seven multidimensional innovation drivers operate in New York City and how city agencies are leveraging them to improve service delivery. We begin the discussion of each driver with a synthesis (in text boxes): the overarching critical issue that characterizes the opportunity for the city, followed by a more detailed list of smarter takeaways that city practitioners and "public entrepreneurs" can apply. Afterward, we illustrate the meaning of each smarter takeaway with examples extracted from the case studies and show how they can be applied to innovation efforts in practical ways.

Data: Shared but Secure

Craig Campbell and Stephen Goldsmith define data analytics as "the rough art of making sense of a morass of information to improve how decisions are made," further noting the complexity of this process within the context of public administration (chapter 2). In several of our case studies, big data is at the heart of the innovation. Both Midtown in Motion (chapter 12) and the syndromic surveillance system (chapter 8) process data points from numerous sources, in order to manage traffic and detect potential health epidemics early, respectively. However, this is only part of the data story. Across the twelve case studies, we have seen how New York City agencies have approached this "art:" how they have leveraged the volumes of data that are generated within the five boroughs across the innovation process, what value they have found, and what ongoing challenges they face.

Critical Issue for City Agendas

Democratize access to data within city agencies and improve cross-agency data-sharing, while ensuring adequate security and privacy protocols are in place.

Smarter Takeaways

- Data analytics should support the complete project cycle, from problem identification to evaluation.
- Data democratization helps city staff optimize their decision-making and motivates on-the-job performance.
- The city must strategize how to overcome challenges in collecting, sharing, and using data, including the protection of personal privacy.
- Data-sharing is a powerful strategy for agencies to gain credibility, autonomy, and a bigger voice at the city's policy table.

Using Data Across the Innovation Process

The Mayor's Office of Data Analytics (MODA) recognizes the importance of using data to "support the full span of a project, rather than isolating the 'analytics' phase as a particular step in the process" (chapter 2). Beginning with the problem-identification phase, data provide evidence of the existence and magnitude of a problem, whether the number of traffic-related fatalities or quantity of carbon emissions due to waste. In knowing the current status of a problem, the city can set ambitious goals with indicators, as we have seen with Vision Zero (chapter 11) and OneNYC (chapter 1). OneNYC in particular was grounded in "deep research, modeling, and analysis of the current population, economic, social, and environmental conditions in the city, along with a review of existing and proposed infrastructure."

Data can help guide program design, particularly with respect to prioritizing the target population that is anticipated to yield the best results. For example, the New York City Department of Sanitation (DSNY) selected low- to medium-density neighborhoods with high historic recycling rates for the organic-waste collection pilot areas, based on research on composting programs in other cities and assumptions about human behavior (chapter 7). The New York City Department of Environmental Protection (NYCDEP) selected green infrastructure sites based on an analysis of geospatial tax-lot and land-use data as well as factors like combined sewer overflow (CSO) volume, frequency, and water-quality conditions (chapter 6). City agencies also collect data on the status of their programs in order to monitor progress, evaluate results, and continuously make improvements.

Data Democratization

The City of New York has embraced "data democratization," which refers to expanding direct access to data in a way that a broader internal and external audience can easily understand and use. Several of our case studies demonstrate how increased access to data—particularly in real time—can be a tool for city staff to optimize their decision-making, motivate on-the-job performance, and connect leadership's vision with staff operations. With the energy demand response program (chapter 5), building managers work with an enthusiastic and empowered sense of mission once provided access to real-time energy-consumption metering and customized web-based dashboards. The same motivation-boosting effect is observed with the New York Police Department (NYPD) street patrols who receive real-time gunshot notification alerts (chapter 10). These examples reflect the importance of—as the City of New York's former Chief Analytics Officer, Amen Ra Mashariki, articulates—"lead[ing] with people and not data. It's all about whom you engage, how you engage them, and what tools you give them with which to respond" (chapter 4).

Beyond using data analytics to improve service delivery, the City of New York furthermore values data transparency and data democratization with the public. At the agency level, the Department of Health and Mental Hygiene

(DOHMH) shares the data it collects not only with other relevant agencies but also with the public by making the data publicly available online (chapter 8). MODA argues that the next stage of open data projects should go beyond publishing raw data (as on the Open Data portal) to provide user-centered added value (chapter 4). The Neighborhood Innovation Labs (chapter 9) present a progressive vision of the community's having access to and ownership of data collected within the project. LinkNYC (chapter 3) could also be viewed as the first city-led initiative to democratize access to digital information via broadband twenty-first-century communications infrastructure.

Twenty-First-Century Data Opportunities in Twentieth-Century Organizational Cultures

Although big data is driving innovation in these aforementioned ways, city agencies continue to face—and strategize how to overcome—challenges in collecting, sharing, and using data because they are often building upon antiquated systems. Vision Zero (chapter 11) shares the most extreme example. Accessing the crash database can take longer than a year, since crashes are reported on paper that travels from the NYPD to the Department of Motor Vehicles (DMV) in Albany and back, with two unique identifiers per crash generated along the journey.

Given the existence of massive amounts of data and the expensive venture of collecting new data, city agencies generally seek to acquire what is already available, as in the case of the syndromic surveillance system (chapter 8). High-level buy-in across city agencies and senior officials advances data-sharing and collaboration in a typically highly segmented and bureaucratic city government. However, moving beyond individual email data requests to a standardized process in sharing data across agencies takes time and can often be deterred by misaligned incentives and independent agency budgets. MODA has therefore been pioneering the creation of a "Citywide Intelligence Hub," a platform that allows citywide data-sharing in which the data remain with the source agency to enhance fidelity (chapter 2).

Once the data sets have been acquired, city agencies face challenges related to cleaning and analyzing them. Data sets from different sources are often formatted differently, presenting the same information with varying metrics. Tackling this problem through legislation, the New York City Council passed Local Law 108 of 2015, requiring geospatial standards for all data sets on the Open Data portal that include street addresses (chapter 2). At the program level, when faced with diverse file formats and transmission protocols, the DOHMH provided direct technical assistance to hospitals in order to implement certain standardizations for the syndromic surveillance system (chapter 8). This case furthermore notes the importance of integrating feedback mechanisms to continually improve the data quality. Public interest in open data also drives better use of data internally in city agencies.

Contrary to what might be expected, city data analysts—as the MODA case demonstrates—do not need to be at the cutting edge of data-science techniques. However, they should ask the right questions—such as "What goes with what? How much?" (chapter 2)—and carefully consider how data were collected and where they came from when using data in a way for which they were not originally intended.

Privacy and Security

While smart devices offer great promise for collecting information, the potential infringement on personal privacy is a serious issue. Midtown in Motion (chapter 12) and Business Atlas (chapter 4) responded to this challenge by anonymizing personally identifiable information. Neighborhood Innovation Labs (chapter 9) are sharing data with the community in an aggregated, anonymized manner as well, but will provide more granular data to city agencies and researchers who follow specific protocols designed to ensure the protection of privacy. As the authors of this chapter state, "This is an ongoing debate—on legal, technical, and moral grounds—and a discussion that needs to be handled in an open, transparent dialogue among city representatives, technology and data providers, data analysts, and the community."

Technology: Modularity and Human Behavior

City agencies report that technology companies often approach them, promising solutions to all their urban problems. As expressed in the LinkNYC case (chapter 3), "Technology is a tool. . . . The power of creative cities is their ability to intentionally design community using technology as a facilitator, not as the end goal." Midtown in Motion provides a clear example (chapter 12). The *idea* of metering the flow of traffic had existed for many years, but it became feasible only in the early 2000s when the necessary technology became available and affordable.

Value of Smart Sensors

The foundational role of technology in typical "smart cities" frameworks is to facilitate data collection, storage, and sharing, such that the city can—as

Critical Issue for City Agendas

Adopt technology incrementally to enhance decision-making, operations, and performance.

Smarter Takeaways

- City agencies improve operations and service delivery by deploying sensors that channel real-time information through the Internet of Things (IoT), though they should follow a citywide policy to ensure a coordinated and responsible practice.
- New technology should be tested first to see if it produces the anticipated results before piloted and then deployed at scale.
- New technology should be integrated with existing technology and infrastructure, in a way that carefully considers how staff will interact with it.
- Technology can enable decision-making, but staff should still make all key decisions based on their expertise, critical reasoning, and ethics.
- Given the swift evolution of technology, city agencies should continue to follow technology trends, upgrading the technology periodically using modular design when deemed cost-effective.

articulated in the previous section—improve decision-making and ultimately service delivery. Though our case studies intentionally do not detail all of the technologies that enable this transformation, many feature the application of sensors that channel real-time information back to the agency through the Internet of Things. For example, the DSNY tracks its fleet's movements through GPS (chapter 7), and the NYPD detects outdoor gunfire using a network of sensors attached to buildings (chapter 10). The New York City Department of Transportation (NYCDOT) relies on multiple types of sensors to gauge where congestion may cause a problem (chapter 12), and the NYCDEP identifies leaks in the municipal distribution system through automated water meters (chapter 6). Given these diverse uses of sensors, the Mayor's Office of Technology and Innovation (MOTI) crafted the NYC Guidelines for the Internet of Things in order to provide a framework for city agencies and their partners to "responsibly deploy connected devices and IoT technologies in a coordinated and consistent manner" (City of New York 2017).

Value of Testing

Our case studies demonstrate the importance of carefully selecting any new technology and testing it first to see if it produces the anticipated results before piloting and then deploying it at scale. The Neighborhood Innovations Labs (chapter 9) were conceived for community residents to test new technologies in real-world settings. The ShotSpotter (chapter 10) case provides a concrete example of the value of methodical research and testing. The NYPD had previously abandoned another gunshot-detection technology when it generated too many false alerts during a trial. When exploring this technology a second time, the NYPD engaged both officers who patrol the streets and those in the information and technology section to evaluate gunshot-detection hardware and software from multiple companies. Before selecting and piloting ShotSpotter, they visited police departments in other cities that had installed the technology in order to understand the benefits and weaknesses.

Integration of New Tech with the Existing System

When designing an innovation, city agencies should consider the relationship between existing, new, and emerging technologies and infrastructure. This could mean integrating the technology with an existing digital information platform (as the NYPD integrated ShotSpotter into its Domain Awareness System in chapter 10), seamlessly merging a new platform with existing ones (as DSNY integrated SMART with other citywide systems like human resources and fleet management in chapter 7), or developing a new platform based on existing technologies (as NYCDOT leveraged various sensors and networks in chapter 12). Modular design offers the ability to grow and encompass new technologies over time.

The promise of an innovation should furthermore neglect neither the consideration of current practices nor the limitations of an innovation. For example, the Green Infrastructure (GI) Plan (chapter 6) replaced planned gray infrastructure projects with GI only in cases where the latter would prove more cost-effective and efficient. The NYPD continues traditional policing strategies in violent areas that are too small for ShotSpotter to add sufficient value (chapter 10).

Our case studies also underscore the importance of integrating new technologies with human systems. Sometimes human behavior will not change to accommodate a new technology, as we see in the organic-waste collection program (chapter 7). As noted in the roundtable, DSNY piloted the installation of radio-frequency identification tags on bins to track participation but found that sanitation workers were lifting the bags out of the bins and hauling them to the trucks, so that the tags were often not registered. At other times, technology can encourage employee performance in unexpected ways, as previously referenced in chapters 5 and 10.

Tech as Enabler, Not Key Decision-Maker

Technology can accelerate routine decision-making, but—regardless of how sophisticated the data science may be—people must provide the judgment required to derive insight and determine action. In Midtown in Motion (chapter 12), traffic engineers monitor the data flowing in and can override automated solutions that the traffic management system proposes. Similarly, the syndromic surveillance system's SaTScan software analyzes spatial, temporal, and space/time data, but epidemiologists must assess this analysis and determine whether to confirm or refute it. As the case articulates, "Advanced data-analysis techniques are powerful tools, but professional expertise, contextual knowledge, and critical reasoning are what make such tools effective" (chapter 8). MODA agrees with this philosophy, ensuring that people—not algorithms—will make any key ethical decisions (chapter 2).

Tech Challenge/Opportunity

One challenge—and opportunity—for city agencies with respect to technology is that it evolves swiftly. As the NYCDOT recognizes with Midtown in Motion (chapter 12), the technologies used at the time the program was launched "will likely be considered passé as new technology emerges in the automotive and digital worlds." City agencies should continue to follow technology trends, upgrading the technology periodically when deemed cost-effective. Indeed, NYCDOT continues to be an early adopter of new technologies. However, as chapter 9 argues, city agencies often face challenges in gaining exposure to cutting-edge solutions and evaluating them rapidly in ways that consider policy-relevant impacts. The Neighborhood Innovation Labs are presented as a potential model for city agencies to invite universities and industry to direct their research and development toward specific urban problems.

Organizational Structure: Internal Culture Matters

To use the Smart Cities New York motto, this work is "powered by people." How effectively organizations—and in the BSF we are focused on city

Critical Issue for City Agendas

Build adaptable, resilient, and connected units within city agencies, staffed with motivated, talented, curious, and trained practitioners, and empower them to incubate innovation by giving them the autonomy to experiment.

Smarter Takeaways

- City innovation occurs in different types and sizes of city agencies.
- Recruiting and retaining smart human capital is critical for a city to become smarter.
- Professional development, peer-to-peer learning, autonomy, and encouragement are four strategies for securing the buy-in of on-the-ground employees.

government—drive innovation depends on the people who work there. It depends on who they hire and retain, how they are structured vertically and horizontally to allow for staff to interact, and what internal culture they promote.

Organizational Size and Dynamics

City innovation occurs in different types of city agencies and units. Swift change is often associated with small, lean, highly skilled teams, such as MODA (chapter 2) and the DOHMH's syndromic surveillance unit (chapter 8). In 2013, flexibility and agility allowed MODA's new leadership to set up a new vision and course of action when it faced uncertainty with the election of Mayor de Blasio. In the second example, a small team of scientists and epidemiologists at DOHMH has been pushing administrative and scientific boundaries for two decades to develop improved versions of a syndromic surveillance system that, among other capabilities, reduces the risks of communicable diseases in New York City and around the world. They have benefited from a considerable degree of bureaucratic autonomy.

However, large agencies—often seen just as slow-moving bureaucracies—can pioneer innovations as well. Indeed, the NYCDOT (chapter 12) and DSNY (chapter 7) pride themselves on their history of implementing cutting-edge work. The Department of Citywide Administrative Services (DCAS) furthermore demonstrated how to engage multiple city agencies efficiently by setting up a citywide networked system (chapter 5). Dozens of agencies participate in an energy demand response program that could only survive with widespread engagement and ownership across city agencies. One thing is to develop bilateral or trilateral agency-to-agency partnerships for a certain program (as will be discussed later); another much more complex approach is to set up the entire operation of a program in a networked system with decentralized communication protocols, autonomous roles, feedback loops, and reward mechanisms.

City Talent and Public Entrepreneurs

Regardless of an agency's size, recruiting and retaining smart human capital is critical for a city to become smarter. Though the public sector cannot compete with the private sector on the basis of salary to attract the best and the brightest, not all talented professionals look for salary as their single, or even most important, decision variable when seeking a new job. Ambitious policy goals—like OneNYC—and the autonomy to explore and pilot creative ideas capture the minds of those seeking to have an impact on their city. Chapter 3 recognizes that an agency might already have the requisite talent in-house, as in the case of the point person from the Department of Information Technology and Telecommunications (DoITT) with over a decade of experience overseeing the payphone franchise, or elsewhere in city government, such as the general counsel of the NYC Taxi and Limousine Commission who transitioned to a new role at DoITT. Public entrepreneurs can be identified internally if the agencies' leadership provides staff the training and autonomy to experiment.

Professional Development, Learning, and Staff Buy-In

Securing the buy-in of on-the-ground employees is critical because each innovation likely requires changes to their duties and—as in the case of Midtown in Motion (chapter 12)—could add stress to teams working on highly visible initiatives. Professional development, peer-to-peer learning, autonomy, and encouragement are four key ways to inspire them to support the innovation and the changes that come with it. DCAS sponsored building managers to complete semester-long university certificate programs and furthermore recognizes demand response achievements (chapter 5). When rolling out ShotSpotter (chapter 10), the NYPD created a space for commanding officers to share best practices and ideas for improving the technology at periodic meetings. In the case of the organic-waste collection (chapter 7), the commissioner and program staff personally meet with sanitation workers early in the morning before the collection routes begin to explain the key role they play in the program's success.

Institutional Context: Pros and Cons of External Variables

Organizations do not function in a vacuum. The institutional context within which a city agency operates can propel—or constrain—innovation.

Legislation

Legislation can provide a foundation of support. Chapter 7 presents a table of critical and complementary state and local laws dating back to 1988 that have helped shape the current organic-waste collection program. However, existing

---

Critical Issue for City Agendas

Leverage the institutional context when possible and strive to make it increasingly innovation-enabling.

Smarter Takeaways

- Legislation provides a foundation of support for innovation, but it can also inhibit progress when city, state, and federal priorities are not aligned.
- The commercial availability and affordability of data software, technologies, and other goods and services that cities need are a prerequisite for some urban innovations, as is a strong supply chain.
- The market in general moves at a faster pace than governments do, which is another reason to build flexibility into the implementation process.
- Municipal, national, and global trends provide momentum as well as incentives for innovation.
- The administrative empowerment of neighborhoods channels bottom-up citizen feedback to support city-led innovation.

legislation can also inhibit innovation, when city, state, and federal priorities are not aligned, as a result of political rivalries or other forces. Chapter 11 highlights the challenges that the de Blasio administration faced when negotiating with Albany regarding city-level changes to state-legislated speed limit and speed cameras, which are central components of Vision Zero.

Market Structure

When designing and rolling out innovations, the city government relies on the private sector for procurement (as will be discussed later). The commercial availability and affordability of goods and services are therefore a prerequisite, as is a strong supply chain. For example, the vision of Midtown in Motion (chapter 12) existed long before the necessary technology became available. Chapter 7 discusses the challenges that the DSNY faced when expanding the organic-waste collection, considering the limited number and capacity of both processing and final disposal sites near the city. The "chicken and egg" problem that Kathryn Garcia, the DSNY commissioner, discussed in terms of increasing the supply or demand first could resonate with many other innovations.

Market forces of course move in neither a coordinated nor a linear fashion. The energy demand response case (chapter 5) describes potentially competing interests between the New York Independent System Operator (NYISO), the sole operator of New York's power grid, and the Independent Power Producers of New York (IPPNY), a trade association of power supply companies. To reiterate an earlier point made about the swiftness of technological evolution, the market in general moves at a faster pace than governments do, which is another reason to build flexibility into the implementation process.

Emerging New Trends

Municipal, national, and global trends can provide momentum as well as incentives for innovation. PlaNYC reflected growing concerns about climate change, and OneNYC was developed as a global consensus was reached around sustainable development (chapter 1). The City of New York also stays apprised of what other cities are doing, always seeking to learn from and implement other urban successes like Vision Zero (chapter 11) and ShotSpotter (chapter 10). While often not pioneering the implementation of urban technologies to avoid taking on too much risk, the City of New York does strengthen its brand as a global leader when adopting innovation early.

Administrative Organization of the City

New York City is known for its well-defined neighborhoods. Whether shaped by historical tradition, grassroots activism or urban planning, the identities of these communities vary. Community districts and boards represent the administrative organization that allows neighborhoods to have their voices heard in the political arena. The Neighborhood Innovation Labs (chapter 9) tell the story of how these administrative entities, capable of mobilizing ideas, local stakeholders, and resources, allow the city to test locally and pilot scalable city solutions.

Leadership and Decision-Making: Control and Delegation

Beyond one person, agency, or sector, strong leadership from different fronts is necessary for moving innovation forward. "Smarter city" leaders contribute new ideas and expertise in how to strategically leverage key assets and furthermore overcome obstacles across the innovation process.

Critical Issue for City Agendas

Encourage and empower strong leadership at all levels of city administration. Big ideas and citywide goals can be set centrally ("control"), but the authority and resources to discover, design, and implement new solutions should be decentralized ("delegation") through networked systems and public entrepreneurship.

Smarter Takeaways

- Mayors can champion innovation, but sustaining their initiatives across administrations can be a challenge if the civil service has not been fully engaged.
- The City Council, borough presidents, and agency administrators and managers can also take the lead on innovation.
- Like their counterparts in city government, private-sector leaders and managers are instrumental to the success of public/private partnerships.
- Nonprofit organizations and citizen groups can mobilize and advocate for specific policies; they can be the difference.

City Leadership

Mayors can drive innovation. Beyond launching bold new initiatives in the early days of an administration to follow through on campaign pledges, mayors can also raise the profile of an agency-led innovation in other ways. For example, former Mayor Michael Bloomberg invited businesses to submit proposals for the "Payphone of the Future" in a promotional video (chapter 3). Mayor de Blasio elevated the organic-waste collection pilot through his Zero Waste by 2030 policy goal in OneNYC (chapter 7). Both mayors—through PlaNYC and OneNYC—called for increased participation in the energy demand response program in order to reduce the city's greenhouse gas emissions (chapter 5). Sustaining innovations across administrations is a challenge, particularly when they are closely associated with the outgoing mayor. As MODA's founding director Mike Flowers expressed it, one key element is closely engaging the civil service and getting them "on board as major participants" (chapter 4). Beyond the mayor's leadership, several case studies reference the importance of the City Council in passing key local legislation and the borough leadership in championing projects, such as former Staten Island Borough President James Molinaro, who encouraged NYCDOT to pilot state-of-the-art traffic signals (chapter 12).

Agency and Unit Leadership

Though MOTI spearheads the city's "smart city" strategy, innovation is not just the domain of one agency, as evidenced in this book. Agency administrators and managers play a role in pushing forward innovation too. For example, Marcy Layton, a longtime senior DOHMH official, persuaded city officials and private-sector partners to support and collaborate on the syndromic surveillance system (chapter 8). Mohamad Talas, a senior NYCDOT engineer, leveraged his doctoral research to substantiate the case for NYCDOT to adopt advanced technologies (chapter 12). In a third example, Tami Lin—when senior energy policy adviser at the NYCDEP—took the initiative, alongside colleagues at the Energy Office, to develop demand response protocols that their agency's facility managers could follow (chapter 5). These types of situations are described in all case studies: empowered public entrepreneurs enabling innovation in critical junctures of the process.

Private Sector and Civil Society

Though the book was designed to document city-led innovations, the cases do reference how other actors have played a key role. Like their counterparts in city government, private-sector leaders and managers are instrumental to the success of public/private partnerships. The energy demand response case (chapter 5) describes how NuEnergen president and CEO Kevin Hamilton approached DCAS as "more of a collaborative partnership than a mere business association." In alignment with this philosophy, the company's director of field operations personally visited each city facility in order to customize the energy demand response program to its needs. CityBridge took similar ownership in the planning and implementation of LinkNYC (chapter 3), working closely with many constituent groups in a way that even facilitated DoITT's gaining approval from the Franchise and Concession Review Committee.

On the other hand, civil society can drive innovation by advocating for specific policies. GrowNYC and other organizations that currently partner with DSNY on the organic-waste collection had previously lobbied for a Zero Waste policy (chapter 7), and—in the case of Vision Zero—groups of citizens pressured the administration to lower the maximum speed limit (chapter 11). Similarly, community organizations influenced the NYCDEP to consider green infrastructure, at a time when New York City was assumed to be too densely populated for it (chapter 6). They formed the Stormwater Infrastructure Matters coalition to demonstrate the success of GI projects throughout the city and engage with the NYC Mayor's Office more closely on water-quality initiatives. In a different example, Professor Jeffrey Sachs of Columbia University—special adviser to the UN Secretary General and co-chair of NYC's Sustainability Advisory Board—spearheaded the alignment between OneNYC and the Sustainable Development Goals (chapter 1).

Networks and Collaboration: Silo-breaking, Cross-sectoral and Trust-building

In "disrupting" the status quo for improved results, urban innovation by nature affects a complex ecosystem of many actors. Across our case studies emerged various models of collaboration and trust building that the City of New York employs to engage internal and external stakeholders in the innovation process. Such collaboration galvanizes support for change, avoids conflicting programming, and leverages the expertise and resources of different actors.

Agency-to-Agency Partnerships

Our case studies feature various mechanisms for breaking down silos and achieving agency-to-agency collaboration. Interagency task forces can spearhead planning, particularly if they are created by or have the backing of the

Critical Issue for City Agendas

Foster silo-breaking interagency partnerships as well as open dialogues with the private sector and civil society.

Smarter Takeaways

- Interagency task forces and targeted, bilateral partnerships are two mechanisms for breaking down silos across agencies for improved collaboration. Balanced incentives should be considered, given distinct budgets, objectives, and capacities.
- City agencies have the opportunity to improve their vendor engagement through iteration and learning.
- A strong relationship between the government client and vendor speeds up innovation, particularly if objectives and incentives are aligned.
- Beyond procurement of needed services, public/private partnerships offer city agencies the opportunity to promote inclusive local economic development.
- Partnerships with civil society are particularly relevant in times of limited resources, given the social capital that community-based organizations offer and the data collection and analysis capacities academic institutions can commit.
- Consultation is critical for engaging many stakeholders in the design phase of an innovation and ensuring that diverse perspectives are heard and considered.
- Through education and outreach to residents, city government can inform residents of new initiatives that could affect them and encourage their participation.

mayor. A task force must have representation from all relevant city agencies, in some cases with more senior staff and in others with midlevel managers. Given the comprehensive nature of sustainability planning, the OneNYC planning featured interagency collaboration at both levels: an executive steering committee as well as eight cross-cutting thematic working groups that engaged city officials from more than seventy-one agencies. Both the OneNYC (chapter 1) and LinkNYC (chapter 3) cases reference the importance of creating a space for open discussion and disagreement. Early dialogue can save time in the long run by addressing tensions, streamlining processes, and identifying initiatives requiring cross-agency coordination from the beginning.

Agencies can collaborate in more targeted ways, leveraging the assets and expertise of one another. For example, the NYPD reached out to other agencies to seek advice in deciding which public buildings would be best for installing the ShotSpotter sensors (chapter 10), and the DSNY partnered with the NYC Department of Education (NYCDOE) to increase the participation of schools in organic-waste collection (chapter 7). In longer-term partnerships, agencies should establish clear roles and responsibilities through a written agreement, as NYCDEP has done for various green infrastructure projects (chapter 6).

Regardless of the mechanism, city agencies must devise balanced incentive systems to foster collaboration, which is challenging considering distinct budgets, objectives, and capacities. The energy demand response program was successful in enrolling agencies in great part because DCAS customized its service to account for specific agency needs and designed the enrollment process to make it as burdenless as possible for participating agencies (chapter 5). In another example, MODA recognized the futility of competing with other agencies over the "sexy tech projects" and instead prioritized projects that "no one felt ownership over" and for which data analytics could be used as a force multiplier to improve another agency's existing operation (chapter 2). Chapter 11 notes that interagency turf wars could have derailed Vision Zero, but unified branding helped recognize each agency's contribution as valuable and share credit across government.

Vendor Engagement

Any mention of government procurement often elicits groans, whereas public/private partnership is the buzzword that offers hope for many cities. Our case studies provide a glimpse of how the City of New York is improving both vendor engagement models through iteration and learning. One area of careful consideration is the level of specificity of the city's initial requirements. After reviewing a prior round of contracts, the DSNY conducted research and began stipulating what type of machine should be used to ensure vendors would meet their preprocessing needs (chapter 7). In a different example, DoITT launched a design competition without prescribing rigid criteria, after a traditional Request for Information generated uninspiring proposals (chapter 3). Both the LinkNYC (chapter 3) and the energy demand response (chapter 5) cases highlight the importance of revisiting the contract regularly, given the very iterative nature of the innovation process.

A strong relationship between the government client and vendor can speed up innovation, particularly if objectives and incentives are aligned from the beginning. For example, institutionalized feedback loops help NYPD and ShotSpotter continue to improve the technology and its use (chapter 10). In the case of chapter 5, NuEnergen's profits are based on the city's total demand response revenue.

As the LinkNYC (chapter 3) case authors articulate, "design[ing] the right mix of expertise" is a key to success. This means reflecting on what expertise the city agency already has in-house and being strategic about filling the gaps. In some cases, as LinkNYC and Midtown in Motion (chapter 12) reflect, the best private partner will be a bigger firm that has decades of experience and the necessary financing. There is also value in engaging smaller firms that historically do not seek government contracts because of a lack of awareness of these opportunities or inexperience in cutting through the red tape, as evidenced by the imaginative designs submitted to the Reinvent Payphones Design Challenge from the likes of urban designers and technologists (chapter 3). However, the city should use open-minded diligence when engaging early-stage companies. They may propose the most compelling solution, as many new disruptive companies do, but they might not be stable enough to deliver at scale nor affordable to the vast majority of cities around the world.

Beyond procurement of needed services, public/private partnerships offer city agencies the opportunity to promote local economic development. Chapter 9 makes the case for lowering barriers to entry for startup tech companies in order to level the playing field for them to compete with large vendors. By easing permitting processes (among other features), Neighborhood Innovation Labs seek to create space for local entrepreneurs to pilot their prototypes and validate their proof-of-concept ideas. Inclusive hiring practices are another key component of local economic development. Chapter 3 showcases the benefit of hiring project staff from underrepresented communities, as the design and media firm Intersection did for LinkNYC.

Partnership with Civil Society

Whereas the private sector has financial resources and the capacity to take on risk, civil society can offer other relevant resources and expertise. First, community-based organizations often have great social capital because of their understanding of the neighborhoods where they work. Indeed, Brownsville was selected as the first Neighborhood Innovation Lab (NIL) in part because of the presence of strong local organizations like the Brownsville Community Justice Center (BCJC). BCJC serves within the NIL governance structure as the primary community partner and participates alongside other local civic leaders on an advisory board, which identifies priority areas that new urban technology could address (chapter 9). In another example, chapter 6 documents how the NYCDEP was able to expand its green infrastructure siting on public spaces by joining an existing partnership between the nonprofit Trust for Public Land, the NYC Department of Education, and the NYC School Construction Authority. The NYCDEP provides the funding for the green infrastructure components, and the Trust for Public Land liaises with school staff and students in the design and training.

Second, academic institutions—as also evidenced in the Neighborhood Innovation Labs case (chapter 9)—can contribute their research and data-analysis capacities, while benefiting from access to community-based experimental test beds. Partnerships with local academic institutions are particularly relevant for city agencies in times of limited resources and increasing responsibility to demonstrate quantitative impact. One key lesson that chapter 9 articulates is the challenging and time-consuming process of establishing legal agreements among such diverse stakeholders, given the different "languages" they speak and the complexity of defining how funding is channeled and expenses are covered.

Consultation with Stakeholders

Consultation is critical for engaging many stakeholders in the design phase of an innovation and ensuring that diverse perspectives are heard and considered. During the OneNYC planning process, the Mayor's Office of Sustainability (MOS) employed multiple consultative tools in order to reach different target audiences (chapter 1). A Sustainability Advisory Board was formed with members from the private, nonprofit, and public sectors to advise the city's high-level Steering Committee. New York City staff consulted City Council members and the borough presidents and also collected feedback on a draft of the plan from all fifty-nine community boards. MOS also reached out directly to residents through surveys in order to "sense-check" the framework.

Though the OneNYC consultation process was necessarily the most complex, given its comprehensive nature, various other cases highlight the value of consultation in the design phase. Chapter 3 shares how DoITT and CityBridge collaborated closely with community-based organizations to craft a common vision for expanding broadband access to low-income communities and subsequently to test prototypes with residents. In another example, NYCDOT developed the Vision Zero Public Input Map to crowdsource safety issues to help prioritize dangerous zones and intersections (chapter 11).

Education and Outreach to Residents

In an ideal world, the city could engage all residents directly in the innovation process through partnerships and consultation. However, such a goal would be impractical because of capacity, time, and funding limitations. Education and outreach are therefore still important ways city governments can inform residents of new initiatives that could affect them and encourage their participation. Chapter 6 documents how the NYCDEP's community construction liaisons share maps of planned projects with community boards, distribute printed materials to property owners before construction begins, and continue to update communities during construction. This case highlights the importance of developing an outreach model from the beginning of the project, as the NYCDEP was able to increase education in communities that unexpectedly voiced concerns about GI projects.

Door-to-door outreach, public demonstrations, and marketing methods (including traditional and social media) can furthermore be effective tools for influencing human behavior, as employed in the organic-waste collection program (chapter 7) and Vision Zero (chapter 11). The DSNY found in the pilot phase that educational campaigns were associated with a tenfold increase in tonnage collected and a 70% participation rate. A total of 85% of drivers surveyed said that the Vision Zero media campaign influenced them to pay more attention to pedestrians and cyclists while driving. Such work can be time-consuming, particularly in a multicultural and multilingual environment like New York City, but the DSNY and the NYCDOT were able to scale their outreach by partnering with natural allies—community organizations and the NYPD, respectively—who already had a strong on-the-street presence.

Results and Impact: The Strength of Purpose

Impact will likely be generated at various levels. As table C.2 presents, many of the twelve innovations featured in this book reduced the cost of operations, and most improved operations and increased the speed and/or quality of decision-making. All but energy demand response directly enhanced the quality of life for residents, though the case could be made that it does so indirectly. At the end of the day, all urban innovation should ultimately contribute to enhancing the quality of life for residents, which is the overarching mission of city government.

As the age-old adage goes, success breeds success. Pilots that produce positive results can more easily mobilize the resources and support needed for implementation. Chapter 10 provides a good example. The NYPD decided to expand the coverage area of ShotSpotter after the pilot resulted in eight arrests and thirteen gun recoveries. Commanding officers who had been skeptical at first witnessed the benefits of this technology and rallied behind it. Scaled programs that generate positive results can more easily be renewed and even

Critical Issue for City Agendas

Cultivate a citywide culture of innovation incubation, while focusing on purpose and keeping the end user, residents, and global impact at the forefront.

Smarter Takeaways

- Pilots that produce positive results more easily galvanize hierarchies, mobilize resources, and build the alliances needed to support implementation. Scaled programs that generate positive results can more easily be renewed and even expanded.
- Successful, impactful innovation drives further innovation, locally as well as nationally and even globally.
- Purpose matters, and new programs must be developed with a results framework that considers local communities and residents first, as well as global impact.

expanded. As ShotSpotter is being implemented, the NYPD continues to evaluate its effectiveness in terms of factors like firearm and ballistic recoveries and will make an evidence-based decision about the future of this program upon completion of the five-year contract.

The impact of an innovation can often be reported in many ways that extend beyond any monitoring and evaluation (M&E) framework (to be discussed later). The NYPD has noted that ShotSpotter has enhanced its responsiveness to public needs, enabling the broader policy shift toward "people and geography" and a closer engagement with communities (chapter 10). To turn to a different example, Midtown in Motion (chapter 12) has garnered national attention for improving travel time by 10% on most avenues in the core area. Industry leaders have recognized the active traffic management system with various awards, such as the Smart Solution Spotlight Award from ITS America in 2012 and the International Road Federation Global Road Achievement Award in 2013. Such previous acclaim likely helped the NYCDOT secure participation in the U.S. Department of Transportation's Connected Vehicle Pilot Deployment Program. OneNYC (chapter 1) is seen as a model for localizing the Sustainable Development Goals, with San Jose and Baltimore contextualizing this innovative approach in their own cities. Innovations that produce positive results can drive further innovation, locally as well as nationally and even globally.

TABLE C.2 Direct Benefits Generated by the Innovations

Innovation	Improved operations	Reduced cost of operations	Increased speed of decision-making	Increased quality of decision-making	Enhanced quality of life for residents
OneNYC and SDGs	X		X	X	X
MODA	X	X	X	X	X
LinkNYC				X	X
Business Atlas	X		X	X	X
Energy demand response	X	X	X	X	
Green infrastructure	X	X			X
Organic-waste collection	X				X
Syndromic surveillance	X		X	X	X
Neighborhood Innovation Labs	X	X	X	X	X
NYPD ShotSpotter	X		X	X	X
Vision Zero		X		X	X
Midtown in Motion	X	X	X	X	X

Becoming a Smarter City: The Innovation Process

Though the City of New York does not have a standardized step-by-step methodology for developing innovation, the twelve case studies do suggest a pattern that we articulate in the BSF. The aforementioned drivers operate in various ways and intensities across an innovation process—from problem identification to design, implementation, and evaluation. Monitoring and learning cut across all phases. As in the previous section, the discussion of each phase begins with a synthesis: the overarching critical issue, followed by a more detailed list of smarter takeaways.

Problem Identification and Innovation Opportunity

The first step in an innovation process is to identify both the problem and the opportunity to address it. The problems that the twelve innovations

Critical Issue for City Agendas

Balance the interplay of innovation drivers and strategically leverage them to move from an idea to action.

Smarter Takeaways

- Multiple drivers often interact synergistically, whether at once or over a longer period of time, to give impetus to innovation.
- Leadership and institutional context are key drivers for creating a space for innovation by laying out and rallying support for bold visions.
- A visioning process with all relevant internal and external stakeholders can articulate ambitious, citywide goals, which should then be grounded in practical considerations such as funding, feasibility, and external dependencies.
- A comprehensive city strategy provides a framework for city agencies to innovate, particularly when they are given autonomy to chart a path for reaching ambitious goals.
- The city government should diversify funding for innovation: from fully public to fully private and variations that combine sources.

address—from traffic to organic waste and crime—were previously known, but drivers were instrumental in moving from an idea to bold action at a given time. Multiple drivers often interact synergistically, whether at once—as in the case of Mayor de Blasio's equity agenda and the city's mandate for a four-year sustainability plan (chapter 1)—or over a longer period of time, as the green infrastructure case (chapter 6) articulates. Leadership and institutional context in particular played key roles in pushing forward many of the innovations documented in this book.

Leadership

Leadership at different levels can catalyze innovation. Two cases—ShotSpotter (chapter 10) and Vision Zero (chapter 11)—illustrate how mayoral initiatives can jump-start innovation, providing focus and momentum at the start of a new administration. Soon after his inauguration in January 2014, Mayor de Blasio tasked NYPD Commissioner William Bratton with shifting from "stop-and-frisk" to "precision-based policing" in order to target the worst offenders. At the same time, he launched the Vision Zero Action Plan, thereby making "a commitment to decisively confront the epidemic of traffic fatalities and injuries on our streets" (chapter 11). The LinkNYC case (chapter 3) demonstrates how city agency leadership can leverage the expiration of a contract to sunset outdated infrastructure and introduce needed services to the public.

Institutional Context

Legislation can spark—or even mandate—innovation. Under New York City's Charter, the city must craft a long-term sustainability plan every four years. Rather than simply updating PlaNYC, Mayor de Blasio took advantage of this opportunity to localize the UN Sustainable Development Goals and feature social inclusion in OneNYC (chapter 1). In the case of MODA (chapter 2), Local Law 11 of 2012 requires that all public data be made available on a single web portal by the end of 2018, and in the case of organic-waste collection (chapter 7), Local Law 77 of 2013 mandated that the DSNY pilot a curbside residential organic-waste collection program.

Emerging new trends and events—whether planned or not—can also galvanize action. The smart-city movement is one example. MOTI, the NYC Economic Development Corporation and New York University's Center for Urban Science and Progress responded to President Obama's smart city initiative to support community-led solutions by partnering to develop Neighborhood Innovation Labs across all five city boroughs (chapter 9). NYCDOT began to design Midtown in Motion (chapter 12) after successfully demonstrating a state-of-the-art traffic management system during the 2008 Intelligent Transportation Systems World Congress in New York City. Emergency response is a radically different example, propelling MODA to develop new processes and technology in 2011 after five people died in fires and in 2015 with the outbreak of Legionnaires' disease (chapter 2).

Ambitious Yet Practically Grounded Goal-Setting

Once city agencies have the impetus to innovate, they can articulate ambitious, albeit feasible, goals. Chapter 1 presents a compelling case for developing a comprehensive strategy with a shared citywide vision and long-term goals through an intentional, multistakeholder process. In the words of Colin O'Donnell, chief innovation officer at Intersection (one of the LinkNYC partners), "Be passionate about goal and flexible how you get there. Getting people behind a common vision and moving everyone forward is the hardest part of the work" (chapter 3). Indeed, one strength of OneNYC—as with PlaNYC— is that it provides city agencies with "authority, space, and time" to develop specific plans that align with an overarching, citywide framework (chapter 1). Beyond a silo-breaking organizational innovation in and of itself, OneNYC (and its predecessor) subsequently spurred innovations featured in many of our cases, as illustrated earlier in figure C.1 of the New York City innovation cluster.

Not just visionary, the OneNYC process grounded the goals in practical, evidence-based considerations. After identifying key priority issues based on data, cross-agency working groups determined which ones should be included in the strategy through a backcasting approach and by assessing "feasibility, ambition, scalability, funding, and external dependencies" (chapter 1). MODA's project cycle similarly starts by ensuring that the client agency is clear about the project goals, the "potential for operational impact," and that sufficient resources are available (chapter 2). This type of careful, data-driven analysis sets the innovation up for success.

Diversified Funding

As just noted, identifying the innovation opportunity entails identifying a way to pay for it from the start. The massive migration to cities, the urgency of improved public services, and the fiscal stress of cities require new ways of thinking how to fund innovation. Table C.3 summarizes the methods of financing employed for each of the innovations studied, thereby revealing smarter insights at the city level. Only five of the twelve innovations are funded by the

TABLE C.3 Innovation Financing

Innovation	Reallocation of existing funds	New funding provided by city	Funding from state or national government	Public/private partnership	Private financing	Consumer purchases
OneNYC and SDGs	Yes	Yes	Yes	Yes	Yes	
MODA	Yes	Yes			Yes	
LinkNYC				Yes	Yes	Yes
Business Atlas		Yes				
Energy demand response				Yes		
Green infrastructure	Yes	Yes				
Organic-waste collection		Yes				
Syndromic surveillance	Yes		Yes			
Neighborhood Innovation Labs		Yes		Yes		
NYPD ShotSpotter		Yes				
Vision Zero	Yes	Yes		Yes		
Midtown in Motion	Yes	Yes	Yes			

city alone. More than half (7) are co-funded either by state/federal or private funds. The private sector co-funds as many innovations as the city alone, two of which without taxpayer money. The City of New York has been diversifying its portfolio of funding sources, from fully public to fully private and variations that combine sources. Of course, fundraising for urban innovation requires an increasingly specialized set of skills and knowledge capable, for example, of designing procurement configurations adjusted to each innovation type. However, even when resources are scarce, our cases demonstrate that city agencies can start "cheap" with "paint and plastic" on budget and on schedule (chapter 11), by building incrementally based on what assets and resources they currently have.

From Design to Implementation

Once the overarching goal is clear, city agencies tend to design the program, pilot it, evaluate results, make adjustments, and expand high-potential innovations to additional targeted areas.

Value-Infused Design

The design phase articulates the specific strategies and plans for reaching the goal, which should be based on stakeholder input and relevant data (as previously discussed). Citywide values—such as those at the heart of OneNYC (growth, sustainability, resiliency, and equity)—can be designed into the innovation (chapter 1). Chapters 3 and 9, in particular, detail how diversity and inclusion can be built into the DNA of a project. Both LinkNYC and the Neighborhood Innovation Labs take a community-first approach that is not only about making residents feel good, heard, or included, but that views residents as co-designers of innovation and entrepreneurs in the transformation of their living spaces.

Multistakeholder collaboration is therefore just as important in the design phase as in the problem identification phase. Chapter 3 emphasizes the importance of "design[ing] engagement with other city agencies early," primarily to ensure operational success. By forming a planning team with other relevant city agencies before launching the design competition, DoITT was able to collaborate with them to address potential cross-agency friction before the pilot and furthermore develop a strong interagency working relationship that would prove beneficial during implementation.

The end user—often a city resident—should also be included in the design process to ensure that the product or service will actually provide value.

Critical Issue for City Agendas

Adopt innovation as an agile process, build incrementally on what exists, one success at a time, and achieve transformational outcomes to mitigate the fear of trying.

Smarter Takeaways

- Good design is evidence-based and engages relevant stakeholders, both city agencies to ensure operational success and end users to ensure that the final product or service will provide value and remain focused on purpose.
- Not just for social entrepreneurs, human-centered design is a powerful methodology for the public sector.
- When adopting an urban innovation originating from another city, city agencies should take great care to contextualize it during the design phase.
- Given that governments avoid risks of failure and perceived misuse of public money, city agencies can first test the cost/benefit of an innovation before investing in it at scale.
- City agencies should overestimate the complexity of scaling up the innovation, customize it for different target populations or geographies, and expand in phases.
- Given the pressures of political or legal timelines, there is no need to perfect the strategy before rolling out an initiative. Instead, embed flexibility and reflective practice into the process, allowing the space for shifting strategy if necessary.

Chapter 3 highlights the important role that human-centered design played in LinkNYC. User ethnography, prototyping, and testing were done before the Links were actually built, uncovering important insights such as the need for an easier Wi-Fi log-in process. Chapter 4 notes the value of this design methodology as well, but suggests that adopting it adequately requires sufficient expertise and commitment. MODA sought to design the Business Atlas from a human-centered perspective from the beginning, partnering with the NYC Department of Small Business Services to conduct interviews with small-business owners to understand what information was most relevant for them. However, the end result of this first iteration still reflected an ineffective "if you build it, they will come" approach.

These lessons are still relevant for innovations that originate in other geographies. The City of New York adopted the general design principles of Vision Zero (chapter 11) that had been developed in Sweden. However, much effort was made to contextualize the design to the five boroughs through data-driven, multistakeholder engagement.

Concept Validation Through a Pilot

Before scaling up, city agencies test and validate the concept. NYCDOT first tested an active traffic management system in Staten Island, finding that traffic delays were reduced (chapter 11). Similarly, NYPD installed ShotSpotter sensors in fifteen square miles in the Bronx and Brooklyn before expanding another nine square miles the following year and committing to a total of sixty square miles in all five boroughs (chapter 10). Given that city governments avoid risks of failure and perceived misuse of public money, this piloting model allows an agency to test the cost/benefit of an innovation before investing in it at scale. Small wins can furthermore produce a contagious effect and galvanize the entire team, as seen with ShotSpotter when initial skepticism by some commanding officers was overcome.

Pilot programs across multiple neighborhoods enable comparative testing and identification of optimal scalable solutions, as seen in chapters 9 and 6. Designed for that exact purpose, the Neighborhood Innovation Labs serve as a platform for piloting technologies at the community level that could potentially be scaled citywide if successful. In the case of implementing the Green Infrastructure (GI) Plan, the NYCDEP evaluated twenty-five pilot projects using different technologies in different types of sites, determining that GI effectively retained stormwater. Beyond water flow, the evaluation also considered ecological, community, and operational factors, thereby acknowledging—as does Neighborhood Innovation Labs—that context matters.

Complexity of Implementation

A proven concept, however, does not guarantee successful implementation. Several of our case studies articulate the challenges of scaling up infrastructure projects, while avoiding disruption in a city that never sleeps. Installing one Link versus fifty Links weekly is quite different, given factors like seasonal changes, city street-paving schedules, and bureaucratic permitting processes (chapter 3). A massive scale-up also implies a knowledge transfer, as more staff must be trained to manage and execute projects. Indeed, this challenge is currently a limitation for Vision Zero to complete more than eighty projects annually (chapter 11). The importance of overestimating the complexity of the scale-up from the initial design is a lesson that could apply to many innovation programs.

There is not one formula for determining how city agencies should prioritize where and how to scale in order to reach their end goals. When rolling out the energy demand response program (chapter 5), DCAS first targeted agencies whose energy use exceeded 500 kW, based on a threshold that Con Edison had established for equipping buildings with interval meters. In this way, DCAS could reach out to the biggest electricity consumers first, while benefiting from new technology. The DSNY took a different approach, backcasting (as OneNYC did in chapter 1) from the long-term quantitative goal of citywide access to organic-waste collection services in order to establish incremental steps in the short and medium term (chapter 7). However, in both cases, the agencies piloted and expanded their work in phases, making adjustments along the way.

Given that cities are composed of diverse neighborhoods with different types of buildings, public spaces, and infrastructure, scaling an urban innovation often requires adjustments and customization for different target populations or geographies, as already illustrated with the green infrastructure case (chapter 6). The organic-waste collection program is another example (chapter 7). DSNY developed multiple strategies, depending on the population density of neighborhoods and types of residential buildings, which range in New York City from single-family homes to high-rise condominiums. Such customization adds a layer of complexity to the implementation. Learning from past unsuccessful organic-waste collection pilots, DSNY has embedded flexibility and reflective practice into the program, allowing space for shifting strategy if necessary.

However, not all agencies have the benefit of moving at a "reasonable" pace, given the realities of political or legal timelines. When developing OneNYC, the city had to complete the next sustainability plan in less than five months. Chapter 1, therefore, brings to light another related theme; city agencies often cannot wait to perfect the strategy before rolling out an initiative.

Organizational Serendipity and Iteration

Not all innovation is conceived in a methodical, visioning process that proceeds as an intentional, planned pilot and a structured implementation. Rather, chapters 2 and 8 illustrate organizational innovations that developed over time in an ongoing improvement process. For example, MODA originated as a financial-fraud detection program. Though the team built a strong data analytics model, the results were not ultimately actionable, leading

Mike Flowers to approach city agencies in the future as clients. Syndromic surveillance began as a bioterrorism defense system, proving itself with the early detection of major flu outbreaks. The DOHMH then built on this success, integrating new data streams and adopting more advanced analytical tools in order to address communicable diseases and subsequently noncommunicable diseases. In both cases, the city recognized the value of a proven method and sought to leverage it—with adaptations along the way—to address additional urban challenges.

Incremental Progress

Our case studies reveal a commitment to ongoing improvement with a forward-thinking perspective. During the roundtable, Don Weiss, the director of surveillance at the Bureau of Communicable Diseases, commented that he and his team are considering the integration of artificial intelligence for the syndromic surveillance system (chapter 8). The CityBridge team is examining how Links can "further expand economic growth, deepen inclusion, and amplify cultural participation across New York City" (chapter 3). NYCDOT already has plans to deploy connected vehicle technologies within Midtown and is exploring other cutting-edge technologies that could at some point replace ETC tag readers or microwave sensors that are currently central to Midtown in Motion (chapter 12).

Given that the innovations selected for this book are recent by design, we do not yet know how they will progress and evolve. However, we can look at how they originated and unfolded in order to gain insights about how city agencies might continue them. The underlying message that emerges is that—rather than creating a "smart city" from scratch—city agencies are experimenting through trial and error and building upon previous work to become smarter. Perhaps this is most evident with OneNYC (chapter 1), which expanded upon PlaNYC's focus on environmental sustainability and economic growth to shine a spotlight on poverty reduction and social inclusion.

Innovations today often have their roots in city initiatives that were implemented many decades earlier. The DSNY has been improving its waste-management systems since it was founded in 1881, with organic-waste collection first piloted in the 1990s (chapter 7). The NYCDOT has been modifying traffic signals to relieve Manhattan's traffic congestion since the 1950s (chapter 12), and energy demand response programs have been around in New York City since the 1990s (chapter 5). These lessons speak both to the City of New York's incremental approach to innovation and also to the cyclical nature of the process, as transformational innovation drives future innovation.

Monitoring, Evaluation, and Learning

There is a growing recognition of the importance of evidence-based public policy, including within city administrations. As the OneNYC case highlights, "if it cannot be measured, it cannot be done" (chapter 1). However, putting into practice a rigorous evaluation framework is easier said than done. Our case studies collectively describe how the City of New York has been approaching M&E as well as learning.

Designing M&E Frameworks

Given the large potential gap between theory and practice, establishing and implementing a clear M&E framework for any public innovation is fundamental. Chapter 4 illustrates how MODA learned this lesson the hard way. When MODA realized the challenge in capturing the real-world impact of the

---

Critical Issue for City Agendas

Institutionalize evidence-based decision-making at all levels of city administration, monitor results, promote transparency, and incentivize intra- and interagency learning.

Smarter Takeaways

- Given the large potential gap between theory and practice, establishing and implementing a rigorous monitoring and evaluation (M&E) framework are fundamental.
- Where possible, city agencies should move to focus their metrics on outcomes, not just outputs.
- Real-time metering, artificial intelligence, and machine learning offer unprecedented opportunities for improved M&E, but—where not currently feasible—city agencies can use the best available data to minimize delay.
- More than a tool for governmental accountability, M&E supports an institution's learning culture in an ongoing effort to make evidence-based improvements to service delivery and prepare for an uncertain future in the face of so many global threats.

Business Atlas, the team began to shift toward a metrics-focused approach, as evidenced now with the Time-To-Open measuring stick that can evaluate the impact of new small-business-focused interventions by how long new restaurants take to open.

The City of New York does not employ a standard M&E framework for all projects and innovations, though goals with indicators should be measured at a bare minimum. Chapter 1 describes how a citywide M&E system was designed based on a detailed clear set of comprehensive performance indicators to track and report annual OneNYC progress. The indicators are primarily quantitative and specify long-term target achievement dates, with agencies responsible for developing short- and medium-term milestones and for reporting monthly progress to City Hall. Vision Zero (chapter 11) similarly publishes annual reports, sharing progress made on defined metrics via a scorecard. Chapter 9 describes the Neighborhood Innovation Labs' community-level M&E framework, which includes a baseline analysis for understanding neighborhood conditions, clear goals and timelines for each technology deployed, and regular community feedback.

Metrics of Success

Identifying and measuring the right measures of success are not easy, particularly in the public sector compared to the private sector (chapter 2). In the case of Midtown in Motion (chapter 12), NYCDOT experimented with various metrics—from mean and median travel time to the number of observed stops an average vehicle makes—until finding this last one to be the most accurate in practice. In another example, chapter 11 recognizes the complexity of measuring the number of critical injuries and deaths, because injuries evolve over time.

Many of the city agencies featured in this book have started to integrate M&E practices; however, their metrics are still very much focused on outputs rather than outcomes, given the resource-intensive nature of measuring impact. For example, chapter 5 notes that while DCAS exceeded its goal in terms of megawatts enrolled and revenue generated by the energy demand response program, it has not been able to quantify any associated greenhouse gas reductions. Similarly, the success of LinkNYC has been measured in terms of public perception and adoption rates, but not yet in terms of the impact on reducing the digital divide (chapter 3). The authors of chapters 9 and 11 furthermore recognize the importance of considering the economic, environmental, and social impacts of innovations beyond their specific goals, given unintended side effects (whether positive or negative), the unique role of place, and the complexity of urban systems.

Leveraging Data and Tech for M&E

In the past, data had to be specifically collected for monitoring and evaluation. A smarter city can extract data for M&E directly from the innovation itself, as in the energy demand response program (chapter 5). Real-time metering, artificial intelligence, and machine learning offer unprecedented opportunities for timely, actionable, and informative data that can help the city better monitor, track, and improve design and implementation, particularly as the cost of such technology has been decreasing. However, that vision is still a somewhat idealized future and, regardless, a sensor is not a one-size-fits-all solution. In cases such as OneNYC (chapter 1), where baseline data did not exist, city agencies developed programs using the best available data and analysis to minimize delay.

Learning from M&E

More than a tool for governmental accountability, M&E can support an institution's learning culture in an ongoing effort to make evidence-based improvements to service delivery. As previously explained, the DSNY continues to make adjustments as the organic-waste collection program is expanded. Louise Bruce, senior program manager for NYC Organics, commented, "This is an incremental program in which learning occurs at every step" (chapter 7). The NYPD similarly integrated a "[constant] feedback loop of learning" from the beginning of ShotSpotter: coordinating with other cities, sharing results with the vendor, and encouraging peer-to-peer learning among commanding officers (chapter 10). The NYCDEP has furthermore institutionalized learning by adopting an adaptive management strategy (chapter 6). It tracks the success of thousands of GI projects and makes adjustments where necessary to ensure the greatest possible CSO volume reduction. By taking an adaptive, learning approach to innovation, city government can build resilience in the face of future uncertainty, like changes in climate and demographics.

The Becoming Smarter Framework (BSF) Visualized

Data visualization accelerates learning and understanding of a particular concept or data set. The BSF visualized consists of thirteen innovation arenas (see figure C.3), one for each critical issue discussed in this chapter (see page 332). Each arena is defined by the two perpendicular axes discussed at length in this book:

- the horizontal x-axis, which refers to progression over time through the four innovation phases (from problem identification to evaluation), and

- the vertical y-axis, which refers to the seven innovation drivers that are con-stantly at play with one another during these phases.

While in reality, and as illustrated in our case studies, multiple innovation driv-ers are in constant interaction (y-axis) through the innovation process (x-axis), each one of the following thirteen visual signatures represents a snapshot (i.e., one possible configuration of the more complex interactions underlying each critical issue). None of the visual signatures are intended to be prescriptive or determin-istic. We have already established that "there is no single optimal way to innovate and become smarter that can be used for all programmatic purposes and circum-stances." These visual signatures are illustrative of how the BSF operates and how it can be used to explain the emergence and development of innovation in local government. Ultimately, the BSF visualized is an additional learning tool, and each arena is an invitation to strategize, experiment, shape, and innovate (see figure C.3).

Deconstructing an Example with the Critical Issue "Data Access"

Agencies need to develop communication protocols and an organizational cul-ture (O) that promotes the democratization of data access (D) using strategic partnerships and supporting networks (N). This is particularly relevant in the design phase of an innovation when a variety of different stakeholders' perspec-tives, as well as a multitude of variables, trade-offs, and alternative strategies, need to be considered. The institutional context (I) shapes the incentive systems driving these stakeholders' interests and will affect outcomes and results (R) (see the "Data Access" visualization in figure C.3).

FIGURE C.3 The BSF visualized—drivers' mix throughout the innovation process.

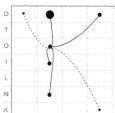

1. Data access

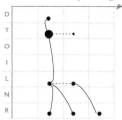

2. Performance-enhancing technology

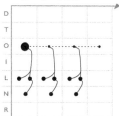

3. People empowerment

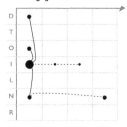

4. Leveraging context

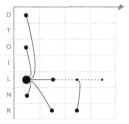

5. Control and delegation

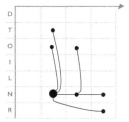

6. Community building

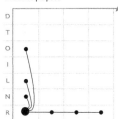

7. Shared purpose

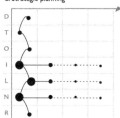

8. Strategic planning

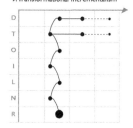

9. Transformational incrementalism

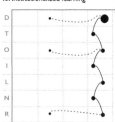

10. Institutionalized learning

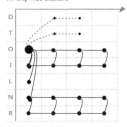

11. Citywide clusters

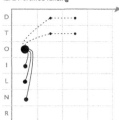

12. Diversified funding

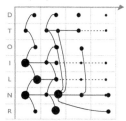

13. Complexity

FIGURE C.3 (*Continued*)

Closing Thoughts and What Comes Next

Urbanization is happening faster than at any given time in history. In 2050, two-thirds of the world's population will live in cities, 80% of the world's GDP will be produced in cities, and cities will be responsible for three-quarters of the energy consumption, 50% of greenhouse emissions, with one billion vehicles on the streets (assuming autonomous vehicles and shared-ownership systems are not adopted) (The Economist 2016). The demand for public services, the pressure on urban systems, and the environmental impact have already reached unprecedented levels and will continue to grow. If we want to have a positive impact on the planet, starting with cities is a safe bet.

Cities need to become smarter in order to accelerate how urban problems are addressed, new solutions implemented, and current systems improved. Life in cities around the world will not be sustainable if city administrations do not create new ways to enhance the performance of public systems and make them more efficient, resilient, and inclusive. Though this book focuses on how city agencies incubate innovation from within, we also articulate the key role that the private sector, civil society, and individual residents play in this urban transformation through collaboration and networks. In Batty's words (2017, 3), "if we accept the argument that cities are largely built from the bottom up, then the degree to which they might become 'smarter'—as we tend to anthropomorphise their collective behaviour—depends on each and all of us acting intelligently."

McKinsey & Company (2017) estimates that over $3.5 trillion of improved government outcomes (or the equivalent reduction in expenditures) could be realized by using best practices. This book uses case study methodology to document and disseminate best practices on how city government agencies can improve service delivery by using a mix of innovation drivers beyond data/technocentric models. We have focused on the practical knowledge and intel necessary to understand how city agencies function and innovate. We cannot improve systems without first understanding how they operate, how they are connected with other systems, how they were built (for what, by whom), and what their strengths and weaknesses are. While we cannot be part of the solution without first understanding the problem, we are also more likely to pursue a solution if we know others have already achieved positive results. Equipped with this new knowledge, we are now in a better position not only to make New York City even smarter but also to make cities around the world smarter as well. Solutions must be found locally, but the New York City case helps us identify the critical issues needed to become a smarter city and to design smarter city innovation processes.

The innovation roadmaps that the twelve case studies offer for specific agencies and programs, plus the Becoming Smarter Framework (BSF) for citywide innovation, are practical tools that can be used to accelerate innovation worldwide. The BSF is a key contribution of this book and can be applied to both single agencies and citywide administration. City agencies around the world vary in size, mandate, and degree of autonomy from the mayoral office, among others. However, they all operate with some degree of connectivity, under the rule of a certain authority and the influence of the drivers discussed in this book. The lessons and practical knowledge this book offers are organized around thirteen critical issues and 46 smarter takeaways for city agendas. These innovation tools are built to help mitigate the fear of change and fear of failure, encourage investment in curiosity, support trial and error, and offer a methodology for program design, piloting, and scaling up.

The epilogue that follows will help contextualize the case of New York City within a global perspective—how the twenty-first century will lead to fundamentally new designs for our cities through the continued evolution of government operations and urban life.

Appendix

Coding of Words for NVivo Analysis

(*: any words that include that prefix)

- *Data*: data* OR inform* OR fact* OR stat* OR signal* OR assumption OR quant* OR analy* OR metering OR trends OR bytes NOT state NOT staten NOT states NOT factories NOT stated NOT station NOT stations NOT statutory
- *Institutional context*: institu* OR context* OR legisla* OR law* OR protocol* OR incentive* OR reward* OR statutory OR rule OR directive OR regul* NOT institute NOT institutes NOT regular NOT regularly
- *Leadership and decision-making*: leade* OR manag* OR decision* OR entrepreneur* OR inclusive* OR responsive* OR behav* OR human
- *Networks and collaboration*: trust* OR partner* OR collaborat* OR communic* OR shar* OR agree* OR net* OR inter* OR connect* OR coordinat* OR agencies OR stakeholders OR engage* OR learn* OR exchang* NOT intervals NOT interval NOT sharp NOT internet NOT internal NOT internally NOT shari NOT interesting NOT intervention NOT interestingly NOT connecticut NOT intermediate NOT interests NOT interim NOT interventions OR people* OR commun* OR neighbor* OR citizen* OR person* OR group*

- *Organizational structure*: org* OR bureau* OR team* OR talent* OR hierarch* OR manag* OR system* OR function* OR operat* OR structu* OR decentral* OR central* OR creat* OR role* OR silo OR operation OR operations OR unit OR agency OR agencies NOT creating NOT systematic NOT systematically
- *Technology*: tech* OR infrastructure OR know* OR machi* OR equip* OR internet OR portal OR wi-fi OR broadband
- *Results and impact*: result* OR metric* OR impact* OR assess* OR evaluat* OR change* OR service* OR deliver* OR improve* OR monitor* OR outcome* OR measure*

References

Batty, Michael. 2017. "The Age of the Smart City." *Spatial Complexity Working Paper*. Accessed August 30, 2017. http://www.spatialcomplexity.info/files/2017/06/BATTY-Working-Paper -The-Age-of-the-Smart-City.pdf.

City of New York. 2017. "Guidelines for the Internet of Things." Accessed December 4, 2017. https://iot.cityofnewyork.us.

McKinsey&Company. 2017. "Government Productivity: Unlocking the $3.5 Trillion Opportunity." *McKinsey Center for Government*. Accessed March 18, 2018. https://www.mckinsey .com/industries/public-sector/our-insights/the-opportunity-in-government-productivity.

The Economist. 2016. "Empowering Cities: The Real Story on How Citizens and Businesses Are Driving Smart Cities." *Intelligence Unit*. Accessed July 30, 2017. http://empoweringcities .eiu.com.

EPILOGUE

Future Possibilities: Now, Next, and Next After Next

JERRY MACARTHUR HULTIN, *Global Futures Group*

It must be considered that there is nothing more difficult to carry out, nor more doubtful of success, nor more dangerous to handle, than to initiate a new order of things. For the reformer has enemies in all those who profit by the old order, and only lukewarm defenders in all those who would profit by the new order, this lukewarmness arriving partly from fear of their adversaries, who have the laws in the favor; and partly from the incredulity of mankind, who do not truly believe in anything new until they have had an actual experience of it.

—Machiavelli [1513] 1989

We are on the cusp of one of the fastest, deepest, most consequential disruptions of transportation in history. By 2030, within 10 years of regulatory approval of autonomous vehicles, 95% of U.S. passenger miles traveled will be served by on-demand autonomous electric vehicles owned by fleets, not individuals, in a new business model we call "transport-as-a-service" (TaaS). The TaaS disruption will have enormous implications across the transportation and oil industries, decimating entire portions of their value chains, causing oil demand and prices to plummet, and destroying trillions of dollars in investor value—but also creating trillions of dollars in new business opportunities, consumer surplus and GDP growth.

—Arbib and Seba 2017

I will explore the recent evolution of technology and change in cities, as characterized by the twelve case studies in this book. As these cases demonstrate, during the past several years there have been a number of experiments and pilot projects to improve the operation of our cities. Much of this change has been incremental, and it has only tapped the surface of the power of twenty-first-century technology—faster and cheaper computing, smartphones, GPS, high-tech sensors, inexpensive data storage, artificial intelligence and automation, 5G communications, and ubiquitous connectivity—to transform cities. I will call this phase of urban innovation Smarter Cities 1.0, or "Now," and I will explore ways to increase the rate of urban innovation and change and to improve the outcomes and benefits for urban citizens.

Then I will take a look at the major trends shaping urban growth and explore how twenty-first-century technology in the hands of developers, urban planners, city officials, and citizens will lead to fundamentally new designs for our cities. We can call this phase Smarter Cities 2.0, or "Next," for during it we will see the next evolution of government operations and urban life. Finally, I will briefly consider the even deeper shift in the organization of cities that is likely as incipient technologies mature and become even more powerful forces in our cities. These technologies and applications, especially artificial intelligence, automation, and smart machines, are already shaping Smarter Cities 2.0, but as they mature they are likely to dominate production and perform almost all the repetitive tasks and jobs that provide work and income for billions of people. As this happens, cities will be called upon to support a shift as dramatic as that when society transitioned from agriculture to industry. This era will be called Smarter Cities 3.0, or "Next After Next" (see table E.1).

Smarter Cities 1.0: Now

These twelve cases represent successful examples for urban leaders around the world to put twenty-first-century technology to use in improving their cities' operations and to deliver better services at lower costs to their citizens. Because more than thirty agencies were part of our study, these cases offer students and researchers, agency leaders, mayors, and citizens a detailed and comprehensive set of examples, ideas, and lessons for improving urban government and enhancing the quality of life of cities, no matter where in the world we live. For example, Vision Zero (chapter 11) is making use of big data to better understand traffic accidents and pedestrian flow and thus reduce injuries and fatalities in New York City. LinkNYC (chapter 3) is employing a creative private/public partnership model to finance the construction and operations of nearly 7,000 new, innovative Wi-Fi kiosks which are today providing free connectivity to citizens across the city. The Mayor's Office of

TABLE E.1 Smarter City Timeline

Era	Smarter city phase	Characteristics	Time frame
SC1.0	Techno-efficiency	• Improve core systems • Top-down design and implementation • Efficiencies	25 years (1995–2020)
SC1.5	Powered by people	• Citizen input • Bottom-up participation in decisions • Increased emphasis on quality of life	10 years (2010–2020)
SC2.0	Quality of life	• Fundamentally new urban designs • Quality of life is dramatically improved • Core systems are transformed	Next 10 years (2020–2030)
SC3.0	Production and creativity	• Automated production replaces most human labor • Priority is given to education and creativity of humans • Emphasis is on uniquely human skills	Next After Next (2030–2050, but may begin sooner)

Technology and Innovation has set in motion a series of Neighborhood Innovation Labs (chapter 9) to speed up innovation, to engage residents in the design of new innovation, and to create tangible examples of smarter-city programs and benefits. To reduce peak demand in the city's energy usage, DCAS (chapter 5) collaborated with city agencies and private-sector consultants to collect real-time data and earn the city more than $6 million of savings rebates while reducing power consumption. In developing New York's strategic plan, OneNYC (chapter 1), Mayor Bill de Blasio directed each city agency to collect citizen input so the people's perceptions and aspirations were taken into consideration in setting the city's goals. In addition, to assure that citizens' needs and desires were fully reflected in the plan's priorities, the Mayor's Office adopted the globally recognized Sustainable Development Goals (SDGs) as a framework for OneNYC. Indeed, each of the twelve cases that we studied made use, in some fashion, of twenty-first-century technology to achieve these reforms.

There are, however, opportunities to accelerate and improve the outcomes of such reforms, broaden the areas of urban life that are improved by smarter-city technology, and strengthen the capacity of leaders and managers to design, develop, and implement similar change here in the United States and in cities throughout the world. So one can ask, "What does it take to increase innovation in our cities?" While there are many factors that influence innovation and change in cities, here are a few that merit additional attention. These include smarter-city rankings, a smarter-city wiki, better budgeting, increased access to skills and training, and more smarter-city research and development.

Measuring and Ranking Smarter Cities

An authoritative smarter-city index can be an effective force for change. With the rising ease of global travel and mobility, a number of ranking systems have been published that identify cities' positions relative to one another. These rankings cover a wide variety of urban qualities, including livability, tourist appeal, cost of living, suitability for retirement, competitiveness, innovativeness, and more. As the idea of a "smarter city" spreads around the world, a number of smarter-city indexes have been created, and more are on the drawing boards.

Such indexes not only have public appeal but also motivate urban leaders to improve government operations and the quality of life in their cities. As urban leaders follow the rise or fall of their city's ranking in these indexes, they study the factors leading to a more favorable ranking and often initiate programs and projects designed to improve their city's ranking.

The risk of unintended consequences is real, however, so choosing the criteria for these rankings is critical. If the qualities being measured are biased or skewed, they will often be gamed by urban leaders, thus resulting in the false appearance of progress without true improvement.

One solution to this risk is to design such ranking systems with the advice of a reputable and independent cross-section of urban leaders and experts. As an index gains influence, its shortcomings and biases receive increasing attention by mayors and other urban leaders who feel handicapped by biases imbedded within the index. Indeed, if the scrutiny applied to the university and college ranking systems is a guide, the more influential a smart-city index becomes, the more intense will be the review of its biases.

In addition, other methods of ranking can produce a more nuanced view of the smarter-city qualities of a city. One example is the information-technology industry's "readiness/maturity assessments," such as those developed by Carnegie-Mellon and CMMI Institute. These ratings use a scale from immature to mature to rate a number of factors that cut across all aspects of an organization's operations. For instance, a factor such as data collection and usage is rated from immature (data are seldom used to make policy or program decisions) to moderately mature (data are collected and used case-by-case to inform policy and program decisions) to mature (data are collected and analyzed on a continuous basis to inform policy and program decisions). Such maturity assessments, when applied to the smarter-city attributes of a city, avoid reliance on too few factors, provide a more comprehensive picture of the city's "smarter-city readiness," and generate a more orderly roadmap for a city to design, implement, and improve its smarter-city policies and programs.

Information on Advances in Government Operations

With the increasing role of twenty-first-century technologies in government operations, the publication of information about urban government operations has grown. This growth includes Government Technology, Smart Cities Council, the Atlantic's CityLab, and Government Executive's Route 50, plus major reports and analyses by consulting firms such as McKinsey, Boston Consulting Group, Accenture, Deloitte, KPMG, and others. These varied sources of smarter-city information provide a growing reservoir of solutions and opportunities for improvement that leaders and managers can use in their own city. In addition to reporting on solutions, a number of platforms and networks now exist, with others on the drawing boards, that allow city leaders and managers, plus urban-system inventors and entrepreneurs, to self-report on their smarter-city programs and policies.

This growing abundance of information may not be as helpful as hoped because there is little consensus on methodology to determine which of these programs and policies work well and achieve beneficial outcomes, although the twelve cases presented in this book represent an important step forward in understanding what works best to improve city government. The creation of a "wiki" of smarter-city solutions would provide an even more comprehensive, open source of peer-generated analysis of urban projects. Such a wiki, combined with an authoritative set of criteria for ranking smarter-city solutions (discussed below), could add value and context to the implementation and benefits of the growing body of smarter-city policies and programs (McKinsey & Company 2017).

Smarter City Standards and Protocols

The question is often asked, "Which city in the world is the model of a smart city?" Currently there is no broadly accepted definition of what makes a city "smart" and no single city that exemplifies all the attributes of a smart city, even though cities such as Singapore, Dubai, Copenhagen, Shanghai, and New York are becoming smarter and each aspires to and often claims such prominence. However, each of these high-profile cities would concede that, while they each have elements that are smart, "smartness" does not pervade all aspects of their city.

Although the real-world template for "smart city" is still to be codified, a number of smart-city standards have been promulgated. These include the ISO 37120 (urban data; International Organization for Standardization 2014a), ISO/TR 37150 (2014b), and ISO/TS 37151 (urban infrastructure; 2015); the British Standards Institute (2017) and Future Cities Catapult PAS 180, PAS 181, PAS 182, PD 8100, and PD 8101, which cover leadership guides, terminology, frameworks, and data-concept models for smart cities; the City Protocol smart-city framework initiative that originated in Barcelona (CISCO 2012); and the NIST Smart City Framework, which is in development (National Institute of Standards and Technology 2016).

A problem arises with standards because they often incorporate a bias against innovation and change, especially when standards are based on current state-of-the-art technology or are built on a theoretical or ideal view of the smart city. As smarter-city policies and programs become ubiquitous, a consensus is likely to grow for a core set of standards that facilitates progress and encourages innovation.

Supporting Innovation by Urban Governments

Is there one best way to promote innovation in urban government? The challenges facing cities and the capacity of twenty-first-century technologies to improve government operations have spawned numerous ways to encourage and support the design, development, and operation of smarter-city government systems.

For instance, in the twelve cases documented in this book, the new program was often designed and led by a single person or small team within the operational unit, in some cases supplemented by the mandate of OneNYC and encouraged by top management such as, more recently, the Mayor's Office of Technology and Innovation.

In many cities, there is a team, distinct from the operational departments, that identifies, develops, and implements innovation. Especially in the past thirty years, this innovation function was most often centered in the information technology (IT) department because, as the new kid on the block, IT was able to use new technology as the catalyst for reengineering government processes. Today the locus of innovation is shifting to a new class of public innovation leaders: chief innovation, chief technology, or chief data officers and their staff, who are chartered with identifying and directing innovation in government. These CIOs, CTOs, and CDOs do not "own" the processes of city government, but use their knowledge of twenty-first-century technology and their skills at change management to encourage and support the owners of city government processes to innovate and change. In the future, as smarter-city solutions are better understood and become more routine, leadership for such innovation is more likely to shift from being a staff function supported by IT or a CIO to a more organic process in which the government process operators themselves—not the IT department or the innovation chief—will design, develop, deploy, and operate their own smarter-city solutions. This is especially exemplified by two of our cases, the Business Atlas (MODA; chapter 4) and syndromic surveillance (DOHMH; chapter 8).

In other cases, there are innovative programs that are external to the government, such as the UK's Future Cities Catapult, MIT's Senseable City Lab, NYU's GovLab and Center for Urban Science and Progress (CUSP), Bloomberg Associates, the U.S. Department of Transportation's Smart City Challenge, and Global Futures Group's nonprofit network of urban innovation hubs known as CIV:LAB. In our twelve cases, the Neighborhood Innovation Labs (chapter 9) created an environment in which citizens have the opportunity and incentives to generate urban innovation.

In some cases, an external team joins forces with internal change agents to greatly increase the rate of innovation. When Bloomberg Associates served as external advisers on smart-city innovation for the government of Prime Minister Modi in India, the Bloomberg team suggested to the prime minister that he abandon the traditional top-down, prescriptive regulations of the Indian civil service and substitute a bottom-up "smart city" competition that engaged India's nearly 500 large cities. The prize of the competition was funding and recognition as one of India's top-100 smart cities. Three major benefits were realized from this approach: first, in a country where the civil service is very powerful and prone to prescriptive edicts, India avoided using a one-size-fits-all approach to designing its smart cities; second, the competition resulted in urban leaders across India's 500 major cities—whether they eventually won or not—giving serious thought and direction to their own city's "smart city strategy" as they prepared their city's submission; and, third, leaders of the top-100 winning cities were enticed into a "race to the top" as each winner wanted to show that its approach was the better than all the others (Government of India 2017; Bloomberg Philanthropies 2015).

In another instance, the U.S. Department of Transportation teamed up with a private-sector philanthropist, Paul Allen, to organize a similar competition in which the federal government pledged $40 million and the philanthropist provided an additional $10 million for a total prize of $50 million. More than seventy-seven cities competed for the prize, with Columbus, Ohio, winning. What gave Columbus an edge in this competition was the private-sector's pledge of more than $90 million to augment the original $50 million prize. Since the date when Columbus was announced as the winner, the private sector of Columbus has made pledges exceeding $370 million.

A major advantage of competitions is the multiplying effect generated by the competition, whose benefits extend well beyond those received by the winner. President Obama's Secretary of Transportation Anthony Foxx explained (Marshall 2016):

> Columbus isn't the only winner here. The six losing finalists can pursue their own plans, with technical and financial assistance from the DOT and its private sector partners, including Alphabet, Mobileye, Autodesk, NXP Semiconductors, and Vulcan. Even those who didn't make it to the final round now hold detailed plans that could lead to their own equitable transportation futures. Columbus is just the first guy on the dance floor.

Two examples of externally generated innovation exist in our case studies. The first is New York City's newly minted Neighborhood Innovation Labs (chapter 9), a project of the Mayor's Office of Technology and Innovation in coordination with the New York City Economic Development Corporation, NYU's Center for Urban Science and Progress (CUSP), and neighborhood organizations. The second is NYCLink (chapter 3), where proposals were solicited from the private sector to replace New York's obsolete payphone booths with something new, but at no additional cost to the city government. The resulting competition produced a privately financed plan that will produce, when complete, more than 7,000 Wi-Fi towers or kiosks throughout the city.

The Restraint of Culture

Peter Drucker is credited with the insight that "culture eats strategy for breakfast" (Anders 2016). Regardless of who is assigned to lead innovation, culture is a powerful force in urban governments, sometimes promoting but more often restraining innovation. Culture is influenced by many factors—responsibility and authority, promotion and recognition, skills and training, funding of experiments and pilots, opportunities for new assignments, tolerance of failure, budget policies and practices, and the values exemplified by leaders—and these factors are clearly in play in the twelve cases presented in this book.

Unless managers and employees believe that innovation will lead to better opportunities, culture will almost always impede innovation, as most managers and employees believe that "size matters" and will seek to preserve and expand their turf and jobs. Without addressing culture, the risk is high that culture will act as a roadblock to change.

Access to Skills and Training

A ready and easily accessible means of giving employees new skills and training is always a powerful force for innovation and acts as a "security blanket" against job obsolescence and loss. For instance, New York University's CUSP—one of the winners of Mayor Bloomberg's Applied Sciences NYC competition—provides a master's degree program that each year graduates more than seventy-five computer science, engineering, urban planning, and public administration students, including a number of New York City employees, with the skills and training to effectively employ twenty-first-century technology in city government processes. Queens College, Hunter College, Brooklyn College, and Baruch College each have four-year degrees in urban studies or public administration. The City of New York, through its Citywide Learning and Development program, offers training courses, scholarships, fellowships, and prizes to encourage and assist city government employees to learn new skills, use twenty-first-century technology, and lead innovation. At the community college level, CUNY's Guttman Community College offers an associate degree in urban studies.

Creating Innovation Resource Centers

Even if the leadership for innovation projects is imbedded in operational units, there is almost always a need for well-informed, creative, and trustworthy expertise and experience with innovation to help leaders design, develop, and implement successful innovation projects. In the case of large urban governments, this may include organizing a separate office with sufficient funding to invent, design, and implement major advancements. Medium and smaller cities need less expensive options, such as organizing a consortium of cities to create and share funding for a university or college "smarter city center of excellence," or creating a central repository of innovative ideas with the support of organizations like the U.S. Conference of Mayors, the U.S. League of Cities, or the National Association of Counties.

Budgeting Practices

Budgeting practices, as discussed earlier, often lead to negative incentives for innovation and change. Even if managers and employees see the benefits of change, budgeting practices often penalize individual departments by taking away the savings that their innovative reforms produced. Faced with such a Catch-22, culture wins and resistance to change sets in.

Understanding the appropriate mix of negative and positive budgeting incentives is critical—and unintended consequences abound. Does a mandate to reduce costs lead to innovation or an arbitrary elimination of services? Does one increase innovation by allowing a department to retain some or all of its savings? If a department is allowed to retain its savings, should it be required to expand its services? And since the loss sustained by one department may be the gain of another, what looks like progress to one manager may seem like a loss to another.

Research and Development

The combination of three forces—the benefits to be gained from twenty-first-century technology, the mounting financial pressures on urban governments, and the increasing demand for services—presents a major opportunity for universities and colleges, think tanks and consulting firms, and business incubators and entrepreneurs to invent, develop, and implement new solutions and skills for more effectively delivering urban services. Research organizations such as NYU's CUSP and GovLab, MIT's Senseable Cities, NYC's Media Lab, and our NYCitywide Research Group (the authors of the case studies in this book) offer proof that academia recognizes the value of solving urban problems. In addition, urban incubators are becoming ubiquitous as city leaders around the world encourage entrepreneurs to use twenty-first-century technologies, combined with new business and operating practices, to invent and develop transformative solutions for cities. Many of these incubators have strong academic support, like NYU's Urban Futures Lab, while others have city government support, such as The Hub @ Grand Central Tech and New Lab in the Brooklyn Navy Yard.

Smarter Cities 2.0: Next

The successful investor Jeremy Grantham calculated a few years ago that if, in 2050, all 10 billion of the earth's inhabitants lived as we live in America now, it would take six Earths to meet the resource demands and dispose of the waste that these 10 billion people will produce. In other words, we may need six Earths to survive, yet we have only one (Grantham 2008). Stephen Emmott (2013), Microsoft's head of computational research at Cambridge University, contends our problems are so desperate that there is little hope: "Every which way you look at it, a planet of ten billion looks like a nightmare."

What follows from Grantham's and Emmott's analyses is that something dramatic is needed to increase the efficiency with which we "operate" our cities. While helpful and important for guiding government leaders and managers who are assigned responsibility for making change in urban government operations, the scale of the improvements and gains documented in these twelve cases is insufficient to meet the challenges of the coming decade, when over 2.5 billion more people are expected to migrate from rural to urban life.

Yet cities do appear to be the best place to focus our attention. Cities are where people work, goods are produced, food is delivered, waste is disposed of, families live, health care is dispensed, and students are taught. Since cities are where the action is, cities can be the anvil upon which we hammer out new forms of urban life. Even more fortunately, people around the world seem to agree that cities are one of the world's best hopes.

- The United Nations created the Sustainable Development Goals, including Goal 11 specifically directed toward smarter cities (United Nations 2015).
- Habitat III (2016) convened in Quito, Ecuador, in October 2016 and agreed on a new agenda for cities.
- Smart Dubai (2017) has set an audacious goal of building a city so smart that it has the world's happiest citizens.
- In India, as discussed earlier, Prime Minister Modi and former New York City mayor Michael Bloomberg teamed up to organize a bottom-up competition that generated a hundred different proposals for smart cities (Government of India 2017; Bloomberg Philanthropies 2015).
- In China, we see a "race to quality" as mayors across the country seek to make their cities competitive by inventing smart-city solutions. They know that to attract and retain talent—which is essential to economic growth and political survival—they must design and build cities with less congestion, cleaner air, better housing, more vibrant culture, and an innovative ecosystem (Bagehot 2017).
- In the United States, mayors are now seen as "America's best hope" for improving the quality of urban life (Bagehot 2017).
- In Britain, the *Economist* reports, politician aspirants would rather run for mayor than for Parliament (Bagehot 2017).
- The Trump administration has promised one trillion dollars of infrastructure for the United States, with much of this new infrastructure spending headed for America's cities (Kelly 2017).

- *U.S. News & World Report* has created a Maker-City Index to rank the capacity of cities to use Industry 4.0 to transform design, prototyping, and production of everything that businesses in cities do (Kelly 2017).
- Steve Ballmer (2017), former CEO of Microsoft, has organized USAFacts (2017) to help citizens see what each government earned, spent, and accomplished—a 10-K for governments. This will give citizens and entrepreneurs the data they need to innovate, to create new solutions, and to hold their leaders accountable.
- Michael Bloomberg, former mayor of New York City, announced his American Cities Initiative and pledged $200 million in June 2017 to back innovative policies at the city level, including making government more effective (Bloomberg Philanthropies 2017).
- Tim Cook, CEO of Apple, said in August 2017, "The reality is that government, for a long period of time, has for whatever set of reasons become less functional and isn't working at the speed that it once was. And so it does fall, I think, not just on business but on all other areas of society to step up" (Sorkin 2017).

We are about to enter a new era for cities, which I call Smarter Cities 2.0. It will be a more transformative era, in which design, architecture, infrastructure, and the core government functions of cities will be more fully shaped by twenty-first-century technology. For instance, the automation of business processes that has proven so effective in the private sector will lead to new ways of running urban governments (Hultin et al. 2017). As awareness of the benefits of artificial intelligence and automation grows, urban government leaders will come under pressure to adopt similar solutions not only for business processes within city government—finance and accounting, human resources, procurement, information technology, logistics, and facilities—but also for more complex urban systems such as mobility, environment and resources, security and safety, health and wellness, and education and training.

Around the world we have already seen projects like Masdar City in Abu Dhabi, Hudson Yards in New York City, and Water Street Tampa in Florida, and whole cities like Singapore, where the design and layout of urban space are heavily influenced by new technology. But more transformative change is coming as driverless vehicles, new approaches to mass transit, delivery by drones, wearable technology, and the circular and shared economies offer architects, urban planners, developers, city leaders, and citizens the opportunity to fundamentally transform the physical layout of cities. In these new and redesigned cities, a fresh balance will be struck in which the virtual will be the equal of the physical.

Major transformation will be located in the developing world where, even though capital is harder to obtain, cities are less constrained by existing infrastructure and thus truly transformative designs are possible. Cities such as Singapore and Dubai feel as though they are in the developed world, but each started as smaller cities or settlements in the developing world; now both are on a march to be the world's smartest city.

Cities in the developed world must contend with existing infrastructure, thus making change more difficult and solutions less dramatic. Change in the developed world seems more likely to be incremental.

However, it is not out of the question that even in the developed world we will see abrupt and calamitous change when one or more cities become dysfunctional and collapse under the burden of obsolete infrastructure and the pressures of massive population growth. We know that cities in ancient times flourished and then died and disappeared. So perhaps an urban "Pearl Harbor" is in our future, with urban change as dramatic and abrupt as the transition from battleships to aircraft carriers at the opening of World War II.

Smarter Cities 3.0: Next After Next

In the coming decade, and most certainly by 2030, the world faces an even more pervasive force for change in our cities. Inherent in the new technologies and innovations of the twenty-first century is the power of artificial intelligence and smarter machines to match or exceed human performance in many areas of life and take over the production of most goods and services. Often called Industry 4.0, this "smarter" automation of work will provide enormous efficiencies to businesses and governments but in doing so will eliminate millions, many say billions, of tasks and jobs around the globe.

Leaders in governments around the world are now beginning to ask how our cities will work if its citizens no longer need to work. In this SC3.0 world, new roles for cities are needed that go well beyond the mission and mandate of urban leaders today. Yet increasingly during the next twenty years, as Smarter Cities 3.0 comes into being, our urban leaders will be called upon to help citizens acquire new skills, create new services, generate new jobs, and design a new ecosystem that supports and augments human creativity while machines do most of the repetitive work that has defined many of our lives for the past 200 years. The disruption of society and our cities will match or exceed the change that occurred as the world transitioned from an agricultural to an urban industrial economy.

In the long run, if history is a guide, Smarter Cities 3.0 will be a beneficial time for human society, even if many of the details are faint and fuzzy. With machines producing most of our goods and services, many humans will be freed from most repetitive tasks and jobs and will have the luxury of engaging in the higher-order pursuits for which we are uniquely qualified. But early in this transition, as tasks and jobs are performed by smarter and smarter machines, the pain of the individual worker whose job is gone and whose way of life is uprooted will be brutal and devastating. Cities should be a source of relief from such pain by providing new skills and creating new opportunities for all citizens to thrive.

Conclusion: It's a Hurricane, Not a Summer Storm

In the past decade, a new way of leading, managing, and funding innovation and outcomes in cities has begun to take shape. This period, Smarter Cities 1.0, is filled with tangible, exciting, and productive ways of using technology and information to more effectively and efficiently operate our cities. The twelve cases presented in this book and the stories generated by the thirty agencies we studied give a firsthand picture of what makes Smarter Cities 1.0 work. In each of these twelve cases, we documented how these advances were designed and implemented and we verified the gains and benefits achieved. The results are promising. But the challenges of Smarter Cities 2.0 and 3.0 are more like a hurricane than a summer storm.

The advent of Smarter Cities 2.0, with the rise in the world's population and a massive migration to cities, will put enormous pressure on cities to improve the way resources are created, goods and services are consumed, and waste is handled. Soon cities will constitute 70% of the world's population and 80% of the world's gross production, making cities one of the best places to invent and design the powerful new solutions that are needed to meet the impending hurricane of urban population growth and demand for urban services. If the leaders and citizens of cities rise to this challenge, we should see a dramatic improvement in the quality of life for people in cities around the world. If leaders and citizens fail to meet the challenge, the collapse of society as we know it seems likely. This is the challenge of Smarter Cities 2.0, "Next."

However, the emergence of Smarter Cities 3.0, with the ascent of smarter machines and the automated production of goods and services, will introduce a new round of even greater pressure on cities to accommodate and adjust to automated production while they simultaneously offer new ways for humans to live in harmony with smarter machines. This is the challenge of Smarter Cities 3.0, "Next After Next."

Whether we are capable of adjusting to the two transformations posed by SC2.0 and SC3.0 is the fundamental question of our century. It is good that we have the benefits produced by these thirty agencies and that we can learn from the lessons identified in our twelve case studies, but much more will be required if our cities are to fully meet the challenges and reap the benefits implicit in Smarter Cities 2.0 and 3.0. The lessons learned in these twelve cases are a beginning, but to meet the challenges ahead of us, we will need massive urban change that uses what we have learned in these twelve cases—and much more—to create change that has a far more fundamental and profound impact on our cities.

References

Anders, George. 2016. *Quora*, March 27. Accessed November 23, 2017. https://www.quora .com/Did-Peter-Drucker-actually-say-culture-eats-strategy-for-breakfast-and-if-so -where-when.

Arbib, James, and Tony Seba. 2017. *Rethinking Transportation 2020–2030*. A RethinkX Sector Disruption Report. https://static1.squarespace.com/static/585c3439be65942f022bbf9b/t /591a2e4be6f2e1c13df930c5/1494888038959/RethinkX+Report_051517.pdf.

Bagehot. 2017. "Bring on the Mayors." *The Economist*, April 27. Accessed November 23, 2017. https://www.economist.com/news/britain/21721377-cohort-powerful-new-mayors-will -do-more-change-country-most-mps-elected.

Ballmer, Steve. 2017. "5 Facts About the U.S. Government That Blew My Mind." *Time*, July 12. Accessed November 23, 2017. http://time.com/4853270/steve-ballmer-usa-facts/.

Bloomberg Philanthropies. 2015. "Bloomberg Philanthropies Partners with the Government of India to Encourage Smarter Urban Development that Improves People's Lives." Accessed November 23, 2017. https://www.bloomberg.org/press/releases/bloomberg-philanthropies- partners-with-the-government-on-india-to-encourage-smarter-urban-development-that -improves-peoples-lives/.

——. 2017. "Michael R. Bloomberg Announces $200 Million American Cities Initiative to Help U.S. Cities Innovate, Solve Problems, and Work Together in New Ways." Accessed November 23, 2017. https://www.bloomberg.org/press/releases/michael-r-bloomberg -announces-200-million-american-cities-initiative-help-u-s-cities-innovate-solve -problems-work-together-new-ways/.

British Standards Institute. 2017. "Smart City Standards and Publications." Accessed November 23, 2017. https://www.bsigroup.com/en-GB/smart-cities/Smart-Cities-Standards -and-Publication/.

CISCO. 2012. "Barcelona, GDF SUEZ and Cisco Announce the Launch of the City Protocol." *The Network*, August 27. Accessed November 23, 2017. https://newsroom.cisco.com /press-release-content?articleId=998539.

Emmott, Stephen. 2013. *Ten Billion*. New York: Vintage Books.

Government of India. 2017. "What Is Smart City." Smart Cities Mission, Ministry of Hous- ing and Urban Affairs. Accessed November 23, 2017. http://smartcities.gov.in/content /innerpage/what-is-smart-city.php.

Grantham, Jeremy. 2008. "Career Risk and Bubbles Breaking: That's All That Matters." Eleventh Annual Lynford Lecture at Polytechnic Institute of NYU. Author's recollection.

Habitat III: The United Nations Conference on Housing and Sustainable Urban Develop- ment. 2016. "The New Urban Agenda." Accessed November 23, 2017. http://habitat3.org /the-new-urban-agenda/.

Hultin, Jerry, Cynthia Trudell, Atul Vashistha, and Taylor Glover. 2017. "Implications of Technology on the Future Workforce." Defense Business Board. Accessed November 23, 2017. http://dbb.defense.gov/Portals/35/Documents/Meetings/2017/August%202017/Implications %20of%20Technology%20on%20Future%20Workforce%20-%20Aug%202%202017%2 0presentation%20-%20Public%20Release%20Approved.pdf?ver=2017-08-21-164258-027.

International Organization for Standardization. 2014a. "ISO 37120: 2014: Sustainable Development of Communities—Indicators for City Services and Quality of Life." Accessed November 23, 2017. https://www.iso.org/standard/62436.html.

——. 2014b. "ISO/TR 37150: 2014: Smart Community Infrastructures—Review of Existing Activities Relevant to Metrics." Accessed November 23, 2017. https://www.iso.org/standard/62564.html.

——. 2015. "ISO/TS 37151: 2015: Smart Community Infrastructures—Principles and Requirements for Performance Metrics." Accessed November 23, 2017. https://www.iso.org/standard/61057.html.

Kelly, Brian. 2017. "Moving Makers to the Top of the Conversation." *US News & World Report*. Accessed November 23, 2017. https://www.usnews.com/news/maker-cities/articles/2017-05-23/maker-cities-moving makers-to-the-top-of-the-conversation.

Machiavelli, Niccolo. [1513] 1989. *The Prince*. Long Grove, IL.: Waveland Press.

Marshall, Aarian. 2016. "Columbus Just Won $50 Million to Become the City of the Future." *Wired*, June 23. Accessed November 23, 2017. https://www.wired.com/2016/06/columbus-wins-50-million-become-city-future/.

McKinsey & Company. 2017. "Government Productivity: Unlocking the $3.5 trillion opportunity." Accessed March 23, 2018. https://www.mckinsey.com/industries/public-sector/our-insights/the-opportunity-in-government-productivity.

National Institute of Standards and Technology. 2016. "International Technical Working Group on IoT-Enabled Smart City Framework." U.S. Department of Commerce. Accessed November 23, 2017. https://pages.nist.gov/smartcitiesarchitecture/.

Smart Dubai. 2017. "Our Vision Is to make Dubai the Happiest City on Earth." Accessed November 23, 2017. http://smartdubai.ae/about.php.

Sorkin, Andrew Ross. 2017. "Apple's Tim Cook Barnstorms for 'Moral Responsibility.'" *New York Times*, August 28. https://www.nytimes.com/2017/08/28/business/dealbook/tim-cook-apple-moral-responsibility.html.

United Nations. 2015. "Sustainable Development Goals: 17 Goals to Transform the World." Accessed November 23, 2017. http://www.un.org/sustainabledevelopment/sustainable-development-goals/.

USAFacts. 2017. "Our Nation, in Numbers." Accessed November 23, 2017. https://usafacts.org/.

CONTRIBUTORS

Ana Isabel Baptista is assistant professor of professional practice and chair of the Environmental Policy and Sustainability Management graduate program at The New School. She also serves as the associate director for the Tishman Environment and Design Center. Prior to working at The New School, Ana was director of environmental justice and community development for the Ironbound Community Corporation in Newark, New Jersey, where she oversaw advocacy for revitalization projects. Ana holds a BA in evolutionary biology from Dartmouth College, an MA in environmental studies from Brown University, and a PhD in urban planning from Rutgers University.

Craig Campbell is a special adviser at the NYC Mayor's Office of Data Analytics, where he works on strategic communications and policy development for the NYC Open Data and NYC Analytics programs. Prior to working in local government, Craig researched urban governance and government technology at the Harvard Kennedy School, where he supported a variety of research programs and urban policy networks at the Ash Center for Democratic Governance and Innovation. Craig holds a bachelor's degree in mathematics and architecture from Amherst College.

André Corrêa d'Almeida is adjunct associate professor of International and Public Affairs at Columbia University, where he is also assistant director of the Master of Public Administration in Development Practice program (MPA-DP) at the School of International and Public Affairs and the Earth Institute. At the MPA-DP he created and leads the Development Practice Lab for high-potential development practitioners. He is the founder of ARCx–Applied Research for Change, where he created and coordinates a network of collaborators from ten universities and twenty-two research centers to work on cities, innovation, and development. Data marketplaces for cities is one of his main areas of focus currently. In Portugal he is principal investigator at the Catholic University, where he created the Smarter LisbonX program. A former senior adviser to the United Nations Development Program, André has more than twenty years of entrepreneurial, consultancy, academic, and leadership experience in the United States, Europe, Central Asia, Africa, the Middle East, and China. He holds a PhD from the University of Colorado, Denver (United States), an MSc from the University of Saint Joseph (China), and a Licenciatura from the New University of Lisbon (Portugal).

Sander Dolder is a director and associate vice president at the New York City Economic Development Corporation, where he leads the efforts to support the Smart Cities and Cleantech ecosystem (Urbantech NYC), in addition to fostering sector innovation, advocating industry and sustainability policy, and developing local and international partnerships. He previously worked in management consulting at Ernst & Young and Capgemini in their organizational design and digital strategy practices, respectively. Sander holds a BS in finance and marketing from Indiana University and an MBA and MS in sustainable systems from the University of Michigan.

Jessica Espey is a senior adviser to the United Nations Sustainable Development Solutions Network (SDSN), based in Cambridge, Massachusetts. Before moving to Cambridge she was associate director and head of SDSN's New York Office. She previously served as special adviser within the Office of the President of Liberia. She has also worked as a senior researcher at Save the Children, the Overseas Development Institute, and the British Institute in Eastern Africa. Jessica holds a BA Hons in modern history from the University of Oxford and an MSc in political economy from SOAS, University of London.

Balazs Fekete is an assistant professor in the Department of Civil Engineering, at City College of New York. Before his faculty appointment, he worked as project director of the Environmental Sciences Initiative of the CUNY Advanced Science Research Center, where he is still an affiliate faculty. Prior to his move to New York, he worked as a research scientist at the University of New Hampshire.

Stephen Goldsmith is the Daniel Paul Professor of the Practice of Government and the director of the Innovations in American Government Program at Harvard's Kennedy School of Government. He previously served as deputy mayor of New York and mayor of Indianapolis, where he earned a reputation as one of the country's leaders in public/private partnerships, competition, and privatization. Stephen was also the chief domestic policy adviser to the George W. Bush campaign in 2000, the chair of the Corporation for National and Community Service, and the district attorney for Marion County, Indiana, from 1979 to 1990. He has written *The Power of Social Innovation*, *Governing by Network: The New Shape of the Public Sector*, *Putting Faith in Neighborhoods: Making Cities Work Through Grassroots Citizenship*, *The Twenty-First Century City:*

Resurrecting Urban America, and *The Responsive City: Engaging Communities Through Data-Smart Governance.*

Megan Horton is an assistant professor in the Department of Environmental Medicine and Public Health at Icahn School of Medicine at Mount Sinai. Megan is an environmental epidemiologist and her research focuses on understanding how exposure to chemical and non-chemical environmental stressors impact human cognition and behavior at critical life stages. She holds a PhD in environmental health science, a MPH from Columbia University, and an MS in biology from the University of Nebraska at Omaha.

Jerry MacArthur Hultin is cofounder and CEO of Global Futures Group, LLC, and president emeritus of Polytechnic Institute of New York University (now NYU Tandon School of Engineering). Jerry is the leader of the Global Futures Group, a consulting, media, and financial advisory firm that supports the use of twenty-first-century technology to create smart communities and improve the quality of life of urban citizens around the world. He leads Smart Cities NY, one of the world's largest smart cities expositions, held each May in New York City. He has worked with leaders and young people around the world to create more innovative and entrepreneurial economic growth. This includes communities as diverse as New York City, Vancouver, London, Stockholm, Shanghai, Nanjing, Kyoto, Kuala Lumpur, Singapore, New Delhi, Abu Dhabi, Tel Aviv, Bogota, and Barcelona.

Constantine E. Kontokosta is an assistant professor of Urban Informatics jointly at the NYU Department of Civil and Urban Engineering and the Center for Urban Science and Progress (CUSP); director of the Urban Intelligence Lab at NYU; CUSP Deputy Director for Academics; and a visiting professor of Computer Science at the University of Warwick. He is the founding principal investigator and head of the CUSP Quantified Community research initiative. Constantine's research is funded by the MacArthur Foundation, the Sloan Foundation, the National Science Foundation (NSF), and the U.S. Department of Housing and Urban Development, among others, and he has received several honors, including the NSF CAREER Award, the IBM Faculty Award, the Google IoT Research Award, and NYU's Award for Teaching Excellence. He holds a PhD, MPhil, and MS from Columbia University, an MS from New York University, and a BSE from the University of Pennsylvania.

Lawrence Lennon is deputy chief planning officer at the Metropolitan Transportation Authority in New York City, and an adjunct professor of transportation planning at the Cooper Union. His prior experience includes senior management positions at several global planning and engineering consultancies, and time as director of the Transportation Division of the New York City Department of City Planning. He is a seasoned project and program manager with more than thirty years of experience directing multidisciplinary teams on complex transportation assignments. A licensed professional engineer and certified planner, he holds a BE in civil engineering from the Cooper Union, an MS in transportation planning and engineering from NYU's Tandon School of Engineering, and an MBA in strategic planning from NYU's Stern School of Business.

Christopher Lewis graduated from Columbia University in 2016 with an MPA in development practice from the School of International and Public Affairs. He is interested in pragmatic and innovative approaches to solving urban governance, growth, and sustainability problems in East Africa. He lives with his wife in Nairobi, Kenya.

Tami Lin has nearly a decade of experience in the management of infrastructure projects (water, wastewater, energy, public spaces) and municipal government operations. She currently advises federal, state, and local governments on infrastructure finance and delivery as an associate at a global consulting and advisory firm in Washington, D.C. She is passionate about innovation and efficiency in government operations. Tami previously served as the deputy director of the Office of Energy at the New York City Department of Environmental Protection and worked for the New York City Department of Transportation. She holds a master of public administration degree from Columbia University and a BA degree in geography and political science from the University of California, Los Angeles (UCLA).

Maren Maier is an adjunct associate professor in the Graduate Program of Design Management at the Pratt Institute School of Art. She also serves as editorial director for Catalyst (catalystreview.net), the program platform for shaping global conversations on creative enterprise leadership and leading as if life matters. Maren is currently a partner at CoCreative Consulting, a consulting group specializing in the design of multistakeholder collaborations to address complex system challenges across sectors, industries, and our shared world. She recently founded Creative States, a platform producing creative research, events, and conversations to help clients and the public develop new ways of thinking imaginatively, legibly, and critically about the future we want to live in. She holds a BA from Columbia University and an MPS from Pratt Institute.

Mary McBride is chair and professor for Creative Enterprise Leadership international graduate programs in Arts and Cultural Management and Design Management at the Pratt Institute School of Art. She is also a partner at Strategies for Planned Change, an international consulting group specializing in strategic leadership of creative industries. Pratt's educational mission has a societal focus: "To educate artists and creative professionals to be responsible contributors to society." The programs in Creative Enterprise Leadership share this focus and educate emerging leaders in the creative and cultural industries to lead as if life matters using the arts of enterprise. The program platform for creating global conversations is Catalyst (catalystreview.net). Catalyst also hosts learning journeys throughout the world for its alums, participants, and invited others.

Paul McConnell is an adjunct associate professor in the Graduate Program of Design Management at the Pratt Institute. Paul is the head of design at Intersection, an urban innovation company that integrates technology to create better customer experiences for cities, citizens, and brands. His award-winning work, including LinkNYC, has been deployed around the globe. He serves on the Board of Directors for the Society for Experiential Graphic Designs (SEGD) and helped to create Urban Assembly Maker Academy, the first public high school in New York City with a design and technology centric curriculum. Paul is the author of the O'Reilly Media report "Designing for Cities: Technology and the Urban Experience," and his work has been featured in publications such as *Wired*, Communication Arts, Fast Company, and City Limits. Paul holds an MPS from Pratt Institute.

Jeff Merritt is an internationally recognized government leader and innovator with more than fifteen years of experience in the United States and abroad. In 2014, he was named New York City's first Director of Innovation and led efforts resulting in New York's being named "Best Smart City." Additional highlights include helping organize the first entirely online public election in U.S. history; laying the groundwork for the world's largest, fastest municipal Wi-Fi network; and leading the creation of guidelines for the responsible expansion of the Internet of Things.

Nilda Mesa is the director of Columbia University's Urban Sustainability and Equity Planning Program at the Earth Institute, and adjunct professor with the School of International and Public Affairs. She has an extensive career in environment, energy, sustainability, and urban issues from the national to the local level. She was the first director of New York City's Mayor's Office of Sustainability under Mayor de Blasio. In that role, she headed the innovative OneNYC long-term sustainability plan for the city, and led the climate, energy, transportation, waste, air, and environmental justice initiatives in the Mayor's office. She also founded Columbia's sustainability office, instituting an award-winning program. Other roles she has taken on include associate director at the White House Council on Environmental Quality, counsel to the NAFTA Task Force at U.S. EPA, negotiating the environmental side agreements' implementation, and assistant deputy at the U.S. Air Force overseeing environmental review and lands issues. She is a graduate of Harvard Law School and Northwestern University.

Mihir Prakash is an urban planner with a Masters in Public Administration—Development Practice degree from Columbia University's School of International and Public Affairs. Most recently, Mihir has been working with the United Nations Statistics Division and the Sustainable Development Solutions Network (SDSN) in New York on issues of urban sustainability and data for the SDGs, including leading SDSN's technical work on the first ever U.S. Cities SDG Index. In the past, he has also worked on several urban and regional development projects with the World Bank, the government of India, and various municipal governments in the United States and abroad.

Małgorzata Rejniak is an MPA candidate at Columbia's School of International and Public Affairs (SIPA), studying urban and social policy. Prior to SIPA, Małgorzata worked as a strategy consultant serving clients in the technology, media, and telecommunications industries. Her projects on smart cities and the Internet of Things (IoT) sparked her passion for urban innovation. She wants to devote her career to integrating technology and data analytics into the urban fabric to make cities safer, more functional, and more energy efficient. Małgorzata holds a bachelor's degree from Yale University, where she majored in economics.

Bernice Rosenzweig is a research associate with the Environmental Sciences Initiative of the Advanced Science Research Center at the Graduate Center of the City University of New York. Her research focuses on urban green infrastructure and resilience to extreme meteorological events. Bernice holds a BS in environmental geology from Rutgers University and a PhD in environmental engineering from Princeton University.

Joseph Ross works at ICAP at Columbia University supporting the global operations of an extensive portfolio of public health research and service awards. He also works as an independent consultant supporting the strategy development of urban initiatives centered on making cities healthier and more livable. Previously he worked as a health system strengthening analyst and program manager supporting projects in Africa, South Asia, and South America for a major public health consulting company. Joseph holds a BA in international relations, economics, and human neuropsychology from Bucknell University, and an MPA in development practice from Columbia University's School of International and Public Affairs.

Sandra M. Ruckstuhl, PhD, is a governance and human development specialist who provides applied research, capacity building, and advisory support to sustainable development policy and investment operations worldwide. For more than seventeen years, Sandra has worked for the World Bank, the United Nations, the U.S. government, and their field partners to improve socially inclusive and equitable outcomes of development programs in the Middle East and North Africa, sub-Saharan Africa, Asia, and the United States. At present, she is working with the UN Sustainable Development Solutions Network (SDSN) on city-level implementation of the Sustainable Development Goals (SDGs). She is the program manager for SDSN's USA Sustainable Cities Initiative, a project that supports SDG achievement strategies in three pilot cities: Baltimore, San Jose, and New York.

Arnaud Sahuguet is currently the director of The Foundry at Cornell Tech, which transforms research and ideas into products. Prior to that, he was CTO of the Governance Lab at NYU. Arnaud spent eight years at Google as a product manager for speech recognition and Google Maps; he founded and launched the OneToday mobile fundraising platform for Google; he also worked on child protection and civic innovation. Before Google, he spent five years at Bell Labs research as a member of the technical staff working on standardization and identity management. Arnaud holds a PhD in computer science from the University of Pennsylvania, an MSc from École Nationale des Ponts et Chaussées, and a BSc from École Polytechnique in France.

Gerard Soffian is a licensed professional engineer working on challenging projects involving transportation safety, adaptive traffic signals, accessible traffic signals for low-vision pedestrians, traffic management centers, and better travel for bicyclists. Gerard serves as an adjunct professor at NYU's Tandon School of Engineering, Department of Civil and Urban Engineering, and as a senior engineer at Sam Schwartz Transportation Consultants. He is retired from a productive career at the New York City Department of Transportation, where he served as deputy commissioner for traffic operations, and is a lifelong resident of New York City.

Kendal Stewart is the practice manager for the Master of Public Administration in Development Practice program (MPA-DP) at the School of International and Public Affairs (SIPA) and the Earth Institute at Columbia University, where she oversees applied learning programs and manages partnerships with international development organizations. She previously worked and consulted for more than eight years in affordable housing, community development, and strategic urban planning for Habitat for Humanity El Salvador, the Quelimane Municipal Government (Mozambique), and the UN Sustainable Development Solutions Network's Sustainable Cities Initiative. She holds a BA in Interdisciplinary Studies—International Development from Davidson College and an MPA-DP with a focus on sustainable urban development from SIPA. She serves on the board of directors of the nonprofit organization Seeds of Learning.

Stefaan Verhulst is cofounder and chief research and development officer of the Governance Laboratory at New York University (GovLab) where he is responsible for building a research foundation on how to transform governance using advances in science and technology. Verhulst's latest scholarship centers on how technology can improve people's lives and the creation of more effective and collaborative forms of governance. Specifically, he is interested in the perils and promise of collaborative technologies and how to harness the unprecedented volume of information to advance the public good.

Andrew Young is the knowledge director at the Governance Laboratory at New York University, where he leads research efforts focusing on the impact of technology on public institutions. Among the grant-funded projects he has directed are a global assessment of the impact of open government data; comparative benchmarking of government innovation efforts against those of other countries; a methodology for leveraging corporate data to benefit the public good; and crafting the experimental design for testing the adoption of technology innovations in federal agencies.

INDEX

Page numbers in italics indicate figures or tables.